WHICH SUBJECT?
WHICH CAREER?

ALAN JAMIESON

Acknowledgements

The editor and publishers would like to thank the many individuals and organisations who have taken the trouble to respond to requests for information and pointed out changes that have recently happened or are about to happen to the entry specifications for courses and careers. Appreciation is also extended to the contributors who drafted the specialist chapters and the entries in the A to Z of careers.

Which? Books are commissioned and researched by The Association for Consumer Research and published by Consumers' Association, 2 Marylebone Road, London NW1 4DF, and Hodder & Stoughton, 47 Bedford Square, London WC1B 3DP

CONTENTS

INTRODUCTION

The purpose of this book is to provide information and advice to enable young people (and their parents) to make informed and sensible decisions at key points during their school careers. These decision points are:

- at 13/14, when choosing courses and subjects which lead to public examinations at 16
- at 15/16, when decisions have to made about A-levels (H-grades in Scotland), leading to public examinations a year or two later, or the alternative, a two-year further education course at 16+ leading to a BTEC national diploma or a City and Guilds award
- at 17/18, when choosing a degree, higher national diploma or diploma course at university, polytechnic or college.

At each of these stages there are important career implications. This book suggests what these are, pointing to the possibilities and dangers if this or that subject is taken or dropped, or if this or that course is taken. Throughout the book, the emphasis is on providing sufficient information for young people and for parents who would like to become involved in and assist the decision-making process. All too often parents are excluded because they don't know enough, are uncertain about the new developments in education (after all, it may have been 20 years or so ago since their schooldays), or are dismissed by their children as ignorant fuddy-duddies. *Which Subject? Which Career?* is designed to put that right.

As well as pointing out the important aspects of each decision point, it examines recent educational innovations including:

- the National Curriculum and its impact on courses and careers
- CPVE – changes to the Certificate of Pre-Vocational Education course
- TVEI – the Technical and Vocational Education Initiative, which provides a technological introduction to careers and jobs
- BTEC – the awards of the Business and Technician Education Council, and the courses in colleges and polytechnics that prepare students for BTEC (SCOTVEC in Scotland) examinations

- GCSE – the General Certificate of Secondary Education which replaced CSE and O-level in 1988 and the educational merit of which is now fully recognised
- the National Certificate – Scotland's system of secondary and further education awards
- YT – Youth Training.

Part 1 looks at some of these recent developments in secondary and further education, and also deals with the major critical factors in choosing GCSE subjects, A-levels and degree courses, particularly in relation to jobs and careers.

Part 2 of the book deals with the move, at the age of 16, from secondary education into work, training, or a further education college, or staying on for A-levels. After that, the entry requirements for higher education are explained, and the sequence of events in applying for a place at university, polytechnic or college is described. Additionally, in this edition of the book, opportunities for sponsorship are examined. At each stage the career implications are identified. What parents invariably ask at parents' evenings or other teach-in events are:

- what use are particular GCSE subjects and grades for jobs?
- what careers do A-levels (H-grades in Scotland) lead to?
- what are the most useful degree and diploma courses for certain careers?

Part 3 of the book gives short descriptions of over 200 careers from accountancy to zoology. For each career the following factors are picked out:

- the subject
- the career prospects
- the courses and qualifications needed for entry
- essential or useful GCSEs and A-levels (H-grades)
- where to get further information.

Now in its fourth edition, *Which Subject? Which Career?* is recognised as a valuable guide for parents and pupils. This edition discusses the consequences of changes to the pattern of youth training, with YTS replaced by a new scheme, augmented by training credits. It also looks at the implications for careers and jobs arising out of recent government proposals for a Parent's Charter, a new Diploma in Vocational Education, and the anticipated re-naming of polytechnics and universities.

GLOSSARY

Find your way around the acronyms

Like every other professional group, the educationalists love their jargon, abbreviations and acronyms.

This check-list should help you to interpret the abbreviations; undertstanding them requires a little more reading and research.

ADAR   Art and Design Admissions Registry

A-level   Advanced level, GCE

BTEC   Business and Technician Education Council: validates awards at national diploma, higher national diploma and other levels

CCETSW   Central Council for Education and Training in Social Work

COIC   Careers and Occupation Information Centre, Sheffield

CPVE   Certificate of Pre-Vocational Education

CQSW   Certificate of Qualification in Social Work

CSYS   Certificate of Sixth-Year Studies in Scotland

CNAA   Council for National Academic Awards

ET   Employment Training

FE   Further Education

GCE   General Certificate of Education (formerly O-level and A-level, now A-level only)

GCSE   General Certificate of Secondary Education (which replaced O-levels)

H-grade   Higher Grade examinations and awards set in Scotland

HNC   Higher National Certificate ⎫
HND   Higher National Diploma ⎬ Awards given by BTEC
HD   Higher Diploma ⎭

LEC   Local Enterprise Companies (in Scotland)

NCVQ   National Council for Vocational Qualifications

NVQ   National Vocational Qualification

O-grade	Ordinary Grade examinations and awards in Scotland; slowly being replaced by Standard Grade
O-level	Ordinary level, GCE: replaced by GCSE
PCAS	Polytechnics Central Admissions System
RSA	Royal Society of Arts
SCE	Scottish Certificate of Education: at O-grade, S-grade, H-grade and CSYS
SCE	Scottish Education Department
SCOTVEC	the Scottish Vocational Education Council which awards diplomas and HNDs in Scotland
TEC	Training Enterprise Councils: 82 in England and Wales to stimulate and assist training and business
TEED	Training, Enterprise and Education Directorate
TVEI	Technical and Vocational Education Initiative
UCCA	Universities Central Council on Admissions
YT	Youth Training: the scheme from 1990
YTS	Youth Training Scheme: operated until 1990

PART 1

School courses

CHAPTER 1

CHOICES AND DECISIONS AT 13/14

AFTER the foundation course of three years (two years in Scotland) from the ages of 11 or 12 to 14, secondary school pupils have to make their first major subject or course choices. The reason is that at this point, usually at the end of the third year, pupils start courses that lead to the General Certificate of Secondary Education (GCSE) which in 1988 replaced O-level and CSE.

The decisions taken at 13/14 are vitally important because they influence the course taken later – A-level (Higher grade in Scotland), and subsequent degree or diploma courses. For example, if a pupil drops chemistry at 14, he or she might bitterly regret it later when it becomes clear that entry to many science careers and courses is impossible without a qualification in that subject.

In the past, until the age of 13/14, pupils followed a general course, learning the basics of the different subjects. Then came the decisions. Which subjects should be taken? What did the school advise? What combination of subjects would be best? Why choose anyway? If these questions were puzzling to pupils, they were often incomprehensible to parents. This traditionally was the pattern of choice. However, the first stage of a new educational reform, the National Curriculum, was introduced in autumn 1989. Radical changes have already resulted from it and over the next ten years its implications will revolutionise schools, with consequences for the curriculum and for students' choice of courses.

What is the choice?

Until the National Curriculum is fully implemented, which is not expected to happen until 1997, there will continue to be a lot of choice. But is it a choice? The teachers will already have made their judgements about pupils. The staff will have decided whether a certain pupil is able to cope with a full set of subjects (up to nine in some schools) or fewer subjects, leading to the GCSE exams. The GCSE is subject-based like the former examinations (O-level and CSE), but performance is assessed differently. There is more information about the GCSE in Chapter 6, but here we are considering *choice of course*. Most schools put most pupils on GCSE courses (now 70 to 80 per cent of a year group), although there are also other courses on offer, at a lower standard, leading perhaps to a county certificate or a school award.

It could therefore be asked, 'Is there any choice at all?'. There certainly is not a completely free choice because the main courses are likely to be plotted out. But parents can still have their say. Most schools have a parents' evening when course and subject options are discussed by teachers, pupils and their parents. That is the time to find out about the courses and the subjects, and to ask the teachers' advice about how the National Curriculum will affect pupils' chances.

Subject choice

For most pupils the real question is not about the courses but about the *subjects*. Teachers want to offer pupils the best deal they can within the resources of the school. The resources are the teachers. For example, the school might have only one qualified physics teacher, so it cannot offer physics to every pupil. A pupil may be desperate to study electronics only to find it is not among the subjects offered because no teacher is qualified or available to teach electronics, and, in any case, it would be impossible to fit the subject into the timetable.

A school draws up its option-choice system according to the available resources of staff, accommodation, equipment and time. Some examples from different types of school are provided later in this chapter. They illustrate the elaborate systems of choice offered in comprehensive and private schools. These systems show that pupils do have choices, built into carefully designed groupings of subjects that reflect the school's resources.

Why is there not a free choice?

The National Curriculum forms an important part of the Education Reform Act that became law in 1988. It prescribes a number of school subjects, so freedom of choice for pupils is now severely curtailed.

All pupils are required to cover programmes of study in *ten* subjects. There are three *core foundation subjects* and seven *foundation subjects*. All ten subjects must be taught throughout the compulsory years of school. A modern language is the one exception: it is only compulsory at the secondary level of 11+. Schools are also required to teach religious education although it is not one of the subjects in the National Curriculum.

Core foundation subjects
English★
Mathematics
Science
★(In Wales, Welsh is also taught as a core foundation subject where Welsh is the language of instruction in the school. In other Welsh schools it is a foundation subject.)

Foundation subjects
Art
Geography
History
A modern language
Music
Physical education
Technology

There is, therefore, not a great deal of choice. Other subjects have to be fitted in around these ten subjects. If a secondary school wants to offer, for example, economics or computing, or social studies, it (or they) have to be additions to the National Curriculum subjects.

The National Curriculum is not yet implemented in secondary schools; the final date for completion is 1997. However, during the next few years, schools will be adapting their curriculum to match the needs of the National Curriculum, and it will directly affect subject choice and therefore career choice.

Subject choices and careers

At 13 or 14 (Year 8 and Year 9 in the National Curriculum) it is unrealistic to expect children to have much idea of the kind of work they want to do after their full-time education is finished. On the other hand, parents take a longer view, and think ahead to career possibilities for their children. The wise thing to do is for pupils *not* to make up their minds too early about a career. That is why schools use the word 'flexibility' to describe their option-choice system. They encourage pupils to keep their options open for later courses and careers by choosing a wide range of subjects for courses from 14 to 16 (Years 10 and 11). Until the secondary school stages of the National Curriculum are implemented (from 1992 onwards) students will continue to choose from alternative groupings.

When the National Curriculum is fully implemented in secondary schools there will be fewer options. Until then, schools will still offer combinations of subjects.

Teachers encourage pupils to choose subjects selected from groups, and these are generally the sciences, humanities, arts, practical subjects and, in some schools, business studies. This avoids a narrow concentration on, say, sciences or humanities, which would limit careers or higher education courses later. As mentioned above, under the National Curriculum there is no choice over English language, mathematics and a science subject, but in any case without a good grounding in these subjects pupils would encounter great difficulties in finding any kind of job.

Once a choice has been made, is that it?

Once a subject and course choice has been made, the next two years of a pupil's career are fairly well fixed. However, if a mistake has been made and a pupil wants to remedy it, a subject can be changed at the beginning of the fourth year, now Year 10.

Most schools have another way of counteracting any mistake. If, at 16, for example, a pupil realises too late that he or she should have taken German to GSCE level, the school might be able to offer German as an extra subject in the sixth form, so the pupil could take the subject alongside A-levels. However, within the limitations of staffing and timetabling, it may *not* be possible to offer a GCSE class in one subject.

The remedy then is to look at the local further education or technical college: it is possible that the local college has a GCSE class in the subject, and the school can make arrangements for the pupil to attend the classes.

GCSE, RSA and City and Guilds

The first courses for GCSE officially started in September 1986 with the first set of exams in May 1988.

Some schools also provide courses that lead to qualifications provided by the Royal Society of Arts (RSA) and by the City and Guilds of London Institute. These courses will continue; there is no intention of phasing them out.

Up to September 1986 pupils studied for CSEs and O-levels; since then it has been the GCSE. In addition, they may be taking parallel courses leading to RSA, City and Guilds and other qualifications.

School courses

During the 1990s, secondary schools will gradually implement the National Curriculum. Until this happens, they are likely to offer a traditional curriculum, so the following examples still apply.

Every school has its own system of option-choices which are gradually being influenced by the National Curriculum. The following three examples can be taken as representative of most schools. The schools are a country comprehensive, a comprehensive in a city and a school in a town.

1 Country comprehensive

This option-choice system is for a country co-educational school of 900 pupils. The school offers a limited choice of subjects because its resources (staffing, accommodation and timetabling) impose their own constraints. The school prepares pupils for GCSE examinations. Many students take public examinations in eight subjects at the end of the fifth year. Everyone does physical education. Some students take courses leading to the Royal Society of Arts (RSA) examination in typing. Others take a course leading to a certificate awarded by the Local Education Authority. About 90 per cent of the 14 to 16 age-group take courses including one or more GCSE subjects.

1 OPTION PATTERNS

The fourth and fifth year course of studies is made up of two sections.

Foundation or common core subjects
All children are required to follow a course of study in *each* of these subjects:
1 English
2 Mathematics
3 A science subject (physics, chemistry, biology or general science)
4 Social education
5 Physical education

Option subjects
All children are required to study *one* subject from each group.

Option A		Option B	
Geography	❏	Home economics	❏
History	❏	Craft, design and technology	
Religious education	❏	(metalwork and woodwork)	❏
		Drama	❏
		★Vehicle maintenance	❏
		★Electronics	❏

Option C		Option D	
Biology	❏	Typewriting	❏
Art	❏	Technical drawing	❏
Computer studies	❏	Environmental studies	❏
Child development	❏	French	❏
Physics	❏	Chemistry	❏

★Indicates courses to be run at the local college of further education
Please think of a second choice if your first choice is likely to be typewriting, vehicle maintenance or computer studies.

Further education college
The further education college offers a one day per week, five-term course leading to two examinations in building crafts and building trades. Students interested in these courses must be prepared to travel to the college at their own expense.

Foundation or common core subjects

This school formerly provided mathematics courses leading to O- level, CSE and a county certificate for pupils who did not take the O-level or CSE examinations. However, like all schools, this comprehensive has adapted its option-choice system to the needs of the GCSE. The examples given here illustrate a system of choices that will change in the 1990s as the National Curriculum is gradually implemented.

As in all schools, English language is regarded at this comprehensive as a subject of major importance. Radical changes are taking place which will alter the ways in which English language skills are measured. The option sheet reveals the kind of assistance that a good school gives to parents and to pupils who are thinking about the course.

1 ENGLISH: FOUNDATION CORE SUBJECT

Fourth-year pupils are being prepared for the GCSE examination in English language and literature. Successful candidates are awarded grades ranging from A to G, with grades A to C equivalent to the old O-level pass grades. As this is a two-year course, it means that the school will no longer be able to follow the practice of entering some candidates for an external examination in the fourth year.

Local award
About 10 per cent of pupils do not study for the GCSE syllabus. For them we offer a course in social and transactional English by which they acquire, through constant practice, the skills in the kind of spoken and written English that they need in adult and working life.

There is no formal examination. The candidate submits ten pieces of work showing skills in handwriting, letter-writing, note-taking, spelling, punctuation, form-filling, and creative personal writing. The course ends with an assessment session when, in company with candidates from other schools, they are interviewed and demonstrate their ability to take messages and retrieve information from timetables, directories, catalogues and maps. If successful, they gain a School Achievement Award which shows the level of skill they have attained in these tasks.

Pupils staying at school for a one-year sixth-form course now follow a CPVE course. This course aims to develop the communication and vocational skills which will be necessary in the outside world. Pupils staying at school for a two-year course will be prepared and entered for A-level or AS-level English.

2 MATHEMATICS: FOUNDATION CORE SUBJECT

Mathematics is a compulsory subject for all pupils in the fourth and fifth years. The aim is to develop the pupils' mathematical abilities and their understanding of mathematical principles, to explore the practical applications of mathematics, to continue practising basic arithmetical skills and to improve their knowledge of standard processes. The mathematical syllabus is gradually being amended to fit the requirements for attainment targets set for the National Curriculum.

The courses provided lead to:
(a) GCSE mathematics
This aspect of the course forms a basis for those who wish to continue to study the subject at A-level in the sixth form
or
(b) The School Mathematics Achievement Award
The course provides for those pupils who are unlikely to be entered for GCSE. At the end of the course a certificate is awarded to pupils who have achieved the appropriate standard in calculations and general mathematics.

3 SCIENCES: FOUNDATION CORE SUBJECTS

(a) PHYSICS

Pupils are entered for the GCSE examination.

The syllabus includes:
1 Forces
2 Linear motion
3 Energy
4 General physics
5 Molecules
6 Electric charge and current
7 Electrical circuits
8 Electromagnetism
9 Nuclear physics
10 Waves
11 Optics

There is a considerable amount of mathematics in the course and therefore pupils should consider their mathematical ability before making a firm choice.

(b) CHEMISTRY

The importance of chemistry for society and its power to contribute to the changing pattern of society in the future is now so great that the need for its inclusion as part of a general education has had an important influence on the character of the syllabus, which stresses the unifying concepts and principles of chemistry.

The syllabus consists of four main parts:
1 Introductory investigations
2 Chemistry of the elements
3 Principles of chemistry
4 Chemistry in society

The examination consists of a written paper, as well as coursework which counts for 50 per cent of the total assessment.

Chemistry offers a challenging option for any student and is especially suitable for those studying another science and for those intending to study biology and home economics to A-level or AS-level.

(c) BIOLOGY

The aims of the GCSE syllabus are:
1 To develop an understanding of essential biological principles, based upon knowledge of living organisms and their environment.
2 To encourage a respect for all living organisms and their environments.
3 To stimulate an attitude of curiosity and scientific enquiry.
4 To develop an appreciation of scientific approaches and methods.
5 To recognise the inter-relationships between various areas of biology.
6 To appreciate how biology affects people and the environment.

The syllabus content is:
1 Ecology – the study of living organisms within our environment
2 The functioning of living organisms
   (a) Cell structure
   (b) Plant nutrition and transport
   (c) Animal nutrition and transport
   (d) Respiration
   (e) Excretion
   (f) Reproduction
   (g) Genetics
   (h) Nervous system and the co-ordination of the above functions.

This syllabus emphasises the importance of making and recording accurate observations and designing, carrying out and assessing simple investigations. These skills play a vital role in a student's understanding of the subject and are part of the coursework which is an important element of the GCSE course.

Assessment takes the form of written papers, a practical element and coursework which includes several assignments.

(d) GENERAL SCIENCE

Among the science options as part of the common core, the school offers general science. It has traditionally been taken by pupils who found the specialist sciences (physics, chemistry, biology) difficult. General science is now offered as part of the GCSE options and also for the local certificate award.

The syllabus contains these topics:
1 Fuels and energy
2 Forensic science
3 Food science
4 Pollution
5 Heating and lighting in the home
6 Cosmetic science
7 Fibres and fabrics
8 Building science
9 Health and hygiene
10 Paints and dyes
11 Flight

4 SOCIAL EDUCATION

The main aim of the social education programme is to help prepare students to take their place in a changing, complex society. To achieve this, pupils are given opportunities to develop their own personal, social and moral values.

The course is divided into a series of blocks of work, many of which involve discussion and create situations in which the students are asked to make decisions. The programme includes careers, work experience and community service.

The last two topics involve all the pupils in being out of school at some time during the fourth and fifth years. In addition to this, other areas of study include (in outline form only):

1 *Health education*
   The social problems of smoking, drugs and alcohol; diet, fitness and personal hygiene; sex education; leisure time in today's world.

2 *Relationships*
   Relationships with family, friends and the opposite sex; marriage; the role and responsibilities of parenthood; a study of how we care for people in need of help.

3 *Self-assessment*
   This section includes topics on personal behaviour, beliefs and standards, areas of prejudice, personal interests, communication skills, and the use of leisure time.

4 *The world of work*
   Life after school, including subjects such as working life, the first wage packet, trade unions, the law, hire-purchase and insurance.

5 *Today's world*
   The work in this section looks beyond Britain to the world at large and in particular topics such as world poverty, nuclear arms, the European Community, United Nations, the environment, and a day-to-day look at current affairs.

4 GERMAN

Fourth- and fifth-year pupils work towards the GCSE examination. By the end of the fourth year the majority of grammatical structures have been introduced and the fifth year concentrates on revising and extending structures and vocabulary. The four skills of language are practical speaking, writing, reading and listening. A high percentage of the final mark in the examination depends on oral ability, so there is continued emphasis on the skills of conversation, storytelling and coping with real-life situations such as shopping and eating out. The foreign-language assistants give the pupils extra practice.

Pupils are encouraged to take part in the German visits and in 'German days' organised by the school and county advisers.

5 PHYSICAL EDUCATION

The school has a very good record in physical education, providing a wide range of recreational and sporting activities. The aim is to promote pupils' interests in sports or games which will continue to give them enjoyment long after they have left school.

Fourth year
The year is divided into two groups. The pupils have two double lessons of physical education or games a week.

   The fourth year is a transitional period in which the pupils have a wide choice. Minority sports are introduced while pupils are encouraged to develop their main interests to higher levels.

For girls the activities include:
hockey, netball, basketball, trampolining, badminton, table-tennis, golf, bowling, keep-fit, rounders, tennis, athletics. Horse-riding, squash, archery and swimming have also been options, but these depend very much on the interest shown by the pupils and the availability of facilities.

For boys the activities include:
circuit training, rugby, cross-country running, soccer, hockey, basketball, athletics and cricket, while in other periods they have a chance to try badminton, squash, handball, table-tennis, volleyball, swimming, tennis, weight training and golf.

The range of activities offered depends solely on interest and the number of staff available.

Fifth year
In the fifth year an even wider range of activities is offered. In one double lesson, a similar single-sex programme to the fourth year is followed, while in the other double period the pupils work in mixed sex groups and the activities are geared towards the recreational sports mainly followed in adult life.

Some major subjects and courses have been singled out here for special attention. A good school such as this one describes every subject in much the same terms – objectives, syllabus content and methods of assessment. Parents should look for this kind of information from every school.

2 City comprehensive

The city school is another comprehensive. This school is mixed, with 1,200 pupils from 11 to 18. The school provides a booklet describing its option-choice system called *Your Choice* from which the following extracts are taken.

QUESTIONS AND ANSWERS

What is this booklet about?

It is about choosing the subjects that are going to be studied in the fourth and fifth years. These choices are called **options**.

Until the third year your courses have been chosen for you. Now you are about to begin two of the most important years in your school life, leading to the final examinations before you leave school. This booklet will help you make the best possible start by choosing your examination courses carefully.

Are any subjects compulsory?	Yes! Every pupil is required to study English, mathematics, physical education and personal and social education.
Why choose some subjects?	We offer a choice of 20 subjects. There are only 40 lesson periods in the week, so there just would not be enough time to study them all.
Why do we have to choose this year?	GCSE examination courses are two years in length and final examinations usually take place just after Easter in the fifth year. Even with homework, it is sometimes hard to fit in all the work.
How do we know which subjects to choose?	Your subject teachers will talk to you about your work. Other senior staff will also help and advise you. Your examination results will help you and the school to decide whether you are better in some subjects than others. Of course you know the subjects you enjoy and often these are the ones you are best at. There will also be an evening for your parents to come to school to discuss your courses with us.
Why do I have to choose a science, humanities and practical or creative subject?	It is important that you have a broad education until you are 16, and don't choose too many subjects that are all similar, as this may limit your career choices later. If you are good at a language, for example, you should also think seriously about continuing with it.
Can I change my options in the autumn term if I don't like them?	Only with *very good reason* in *exceptional cases*. You will have a lot of discussion in school before making your choices. The school timetable is worked out in the summer term. It is important for everyone that you make a good start in September. The further you study a course the more difficult it becomes to change it.
Are all subjects open to boys and girls?	Yes.
How will I know which subjects I need for a career?	The Head of Careers and someone from the Careers Service will talk to you and your parents and answer your questions. Don't worry too much. Most employers want to know that you can achieve a good standard of English and mathematics and have a good balanced general education. Of course, there are some careers where

	certain subjects are more important: art is important if you want to be a designer, home economics is important if you want to be a chef.
Are all subjects as difficult as each other?	No. Some are more difficult or the type of work needed may not suit you. Your teacher will advise you about this.
Can I be sure that I will have all my option choices?	No. We have only a certain number of places in each group, and some groups have to be limited in size to ensure safety, as in the science laboratories. If the number of students choosing a subject is very small we may sometimes have to take it out, or if the number is too large there may be problems. We will do our best to give you your choices.
Remember	Choose the subject you like, not the teacher you like; you may not get the same teacher as last year. Do not choose subjects just because your friends have chosen them; you will choose different jobs when you leave school.
What happens at the end of the fifth year?	You can leave school and find a job, go to a college of further education, join one of the training schemes, or stay on at this school to take A-levels.

3 Town school

Parents should be properly briefed about options. This is normally done at a parents' evening. Some schools encourage pupils to attend these evenings, and some do not, so that the discussions are confidential. Finally, the pupils make their choice of course and subjects. They generally do this by completing a form. The third example of a school's consultations with pupils and parents is reproduced below. In this school the core subjects of English language, mathematics, social education and physical education are not shown on the option sheet because they are not options. They are compulsory subjects which everyone takes. You may also notice that none of these three schools offers Latin. If we had picked an option sheet for an independent school, it would have contained Latin and possibly other subjects not offered by these three schools.

For parents

THE SUBJECT OPTION FORMS

The option form will be the basis upon which students' fourth- and fifth-year courses will be arranged and, therefore, it must be completed with care.

Before completing the form, it is essential that *you*, as parents, obtain as much help and advice as possible. This can come mainly from two sources:

1 your children, with whom you should discuss the subjects that interest them, those at which they display ability and those that are relevant for prospective careers;
2 their teachers, who will give you their experienced opinion as to whether your child is capable in their particular subjects and whether their subject, together with the others chosen, provide a suitable pattern for the sort of career your child wishes to pursue. They will also be able to give information about courses in the sixth form, e.g. which subjects may be considered at A-level. For this reason a third-year parents' evening has been arranged.

Following that consultation evening, we will require the option form to be returned to school. Changes in the initial selection may be made since it is important for us to ensure that the finally agreed choice is both educationally sound and takes into account the individual differences and needs of students.

You are asked to complete the option form by choosing one subject from Pool A, B and C and writing it in the space provided. You must choose two subjects from Pool D and again indicate these in the two spaces. If you choose commerce from Pool D, then since it is a double subject you should write it in each of the two Pool D boxes.

1 All five boxes must indicate a subject from the respective pools.
2 You must not select the same subject twice – except commerce in Pool D.

It should be noted that only a limited number of pupils will be permitted to take control technology and commerce.

SUBJECT OPTION FORM

Choices at 14 leading to GCSE
Surname
Christian name
Form

Pool A	Geography
Biology	Religious studies
Physics	Spanish
Chemistry	Classical studies
Science studies	*Pool C*
	Art
Pool B	Craft, design & technology
French	Fashion & clothing
German	Home economics
History	Control technology

Pool D	
Commerce (double)	Geography
French	Art
Biology	Design communication
Chemistry	Computer studies
History	Music
	Control technology

Your choice – to be completed by parents and students	*Finally agreed choice* – for school use only
Pool A————————————	Pool A————————————
Pool B————————————	Pool B————————————
Pool C————————————	Pool C————————————
Pool D————————————	Pool D————————————

Making the option choice

Having studied the three examples of option-choice systems, it is now possible to see how each pupil can make his or her own choices and build up a study course.

Compulsory subjects are maths, English language, physical education and social education (called 'personal and social education' in the city school). That makes *four* subjects. Some compulsory subjects may not necessarily be for public examinations (physical education certainly is not). Science is compulsory for the country school, and since pupils in the city and town schools *have* to choose a science subject, science is compulsory in them too. That's *five* subjects. These three schools are therefore implementing the core foundation proposals set out in the National Curriculum, that is to make English, mathematics and a science subject compulsory; they have all added physical education to the core.

In the country school, pupils have to choose another four subjects, one from each group, making nine subjects. In the town school all pupils have to add another five subjects, one from Pools A, B and C, and two from Pool D, making a total of ten subjects. Notice that the subjects are spread across groups:

- humanities (geography, history, religious studies, foreign languages)
- sciences (biology, physics, chemistry, general science)
- crafts or practical (art, CDT – craft, design and technology – metalcraft, woodcraft, needlecraft)

- commerce subjects (typing, home economics, and other schools offer business studies)

The total package therefore is nine or ten subjects but made up from different groups or types of subjects. As you can see, the option-choice system is complicated, and is based on GCSE courses which can be confusing to parents accustomed to the former CSE and O-level system. Parents, more than ever, require a thorough briefing by the school, no matter whether it is in the comprehensive or the independent sector.

This briefing will become more important than ever as the ten subjects of the National Curriculum are introduced.

CHAPTER 2

NEW AND TRADITIONAL SUBJECTS

New subjects

Parents may be unfamiliar with some of the subjects now being taught in schools and which may be offered as option-choices. This chapter deals with some of these subjects.

Personal and social education

This is concerned with the growth and development of individuals based on personal needs, responsibilities, opportunities, beliefs and values. The course is quite likely to include the following topics:

- religious education
- outdoor pursuits – canoeing, survival skills in the countryside, life-saving, camping crafts, archery, squash, rock climbing, hill walking, horse-riding
- politics – understanding local and central government, citizens' rights, duties and responsibilities, current affairs
- social studies – the health service, childcare, hygiene, the care of the sick and the old, community services
- vocational guidance – careers guidance and advice
- health education – the care of the body and mind; likely to include sex education
- community service – could involve working in a nursery or primary school or with elderly people.

Personal and social education is not a GCSE subject, nor is it a core or foundation subject within the National Curriculum. Nevertheless, schools will continue to provide personal and social education, as it is very useful for all kinds of jobs, including the social services, health care, local and central government and many more.

Human and social biology

The course deals with the structure and function of various parts of the human body, and includes health education. The major areas are:

- cells and cell structure
- food and digestion
- respiration and breathing
- blood and its circulation
- temperature control
- skeleton, muscles and movement
- the nervous system, sense organs and reproduction
- inheritance
- personal hygiene, disease and environmental health.

For examination purposes there are two subjects: human biology and social biology, and students can take examinations in them at GCSE and A-level (H-grade). Either subject is useful for pupils who want to work with children or with people in general. However, with the increasing interest in health and well-being, human and social biology can offer something of interest and importance to most pupils.

Computer studies

Computer studies is a very useful preparation for working life and for careers in every kind of area. Computing, and knowledge of it, is essential for all kinds of jobs and courses. The old gap or split between 'arts' and 'sciences' has disappeared: arts teachers/lecturers/designers use computers for information storage, for word processing, and for design.

The courses at GCSE are interesting, but it is not a necessity to take this subject. Many schools allow pupils and students some recreational time on the schools' computers, and good schools encourage everyone to become 'computer aware'. Pupils who are hoping to go into any secretarial and office jobs certainly need to know about computing.

Among the topics included in GCSE courses are:

- 'hands-on' experience of using programs – about 40 per cent of the time

- the history of computing
- how a mainframe and a micro work – the major components of the machine
- flowcharts
- logic circuits
- computer languages
- the uses of computers in industry and everyday life.

Computer studies is clearly a very useful preparation for careers in many areas of work. The course will not, however, lead to a job as a programmer; that kind of training takes much longer. If pupils want to become programmers they can take courses after 16 or 18. It is *not* essential to take computer studies to GCSE standard to get on to a course at 16 or 18: people can start at any time.

Commerce and business studies

This group of subjects, which can be taken to GCSE (O-grade) and in some cases to A-level (H-grade) (business studies, accounting and economics), gives a very useful introduction to jobs in a business and commercial environment.

The various courses include:

- business studies – how companies work, the structure of businesses, simple accounting
- commerce – a similar subject but including world trade, all kinds of industrial companies, office practice in small and large firms
- typing – keyboarding skills that should now include some aspects of computing and certainly word processing
- accounts – a simple introduction to accounting practices
- economics – closely linked to commerce, but more theoretically based and dealing with money, trade and financial processes.

Craft, design and technology

There are several courses or subjects in this group, and the areas of study often overlap. Sometimes the subject is called CDT – craft, design and technology – or communication design. The courses can be for GCSE (O-grade) and can lead into engineering science and other subjects at A-level (H-grade).

The courses usually cover:

- design – this could relate to any kind of technological design, as in transport, urban planning, microelectronics, architecture and interior design
- craft – the skills taught are usually metalwork and woodwork, but schools may also have ceramics and pottery. The course includes the study of shape, form, space, materials, and there is practical work in workshops and studios
- technology – this part of the course deals with applied science: designing a chair, a lever kit, a gate, and so on.

This course is very popular, for it includes interesting craft work skills allied to theoretical studies of technology. In terms of courses and careers later on, it leads into engineering work at all levels, and after A-levels (H-grades) it could lead to degree courses at polytechnics and universities in technological and engineering subjects. It is *not* a course just for the boys: more and more girls are being attracted to it.

Alongside CDT, or instead of it, a school may have craft skill courses such as metalwork, woodwork, ceramics, and so on.

The introduction of technology into the primary and secondary stages is one of the major changes of the National Curriculum; so this subject will continue to grow in importance.

Performing arts

The performing arts are divided into three areas: dance, theatre studies (or drama) and music. Any of these subjects studied seriously could lead to a career in that particular field, or to working more generally in the media.

Dance

This is a two-year course leading to a GCSE award. The subject is designed to encourage personal expression through movement. Students learn the aesthetic aspects of dance by creating and performing individual and team dances. Then there is theoretical work and a considerable amount of written work and private study.

Theatre studies/drama

This course, which can lead to GCSE, deals with the history of the theatre and also with today's theatre. Pupils complete written work on these themes, as well as learning the various aspects of theatre work, such as acting, stage management, costume, make-up and design.

Music
Offered at all levels, music involves theoretical work and performance. It is possible to take the subject *without* being a practised performer, but obviously it helps if the pupil can play the piano or other instrument. Bugles, banjos and the mouth organ all qualify!

Art and design

Under this heading are all kinds of courses in design. Art is generally on most school option lists; there may also be design studies which cover furniture, dress and fashion, textiles, ceramics, jewellery, different kinds of interior decoration, and so on.

Design work, which is derived from careful observation, can be developed into pictorial composition, textile design, fashion design, printing, embroidery and many other subjects and topics. When pupils take this course for the GCSE, they are required to keep a portfolio of their work which is assessed as part of the course. This includes all the classwork and homework, drawing, painting and design work, perhaps with the teacher's comments or assessments. For some GCSE examination courses each candidate is required to mount a display of his or her work which is then assessed by the school staff and by an external examiner. As well as the obvious areas of art and design work, studies in this field could lead to work in the media or the various technical communications industries.

Home economics

Subjects for GCSE and non-certificate courses include:

- home economics
- fabrics and fashion
- dress design
- fabric study and care
- textile studies
- hairdressing, grooming and health
- food and nutrition.

These courses may lead into jobs at 16 or into further education courses at the same age. Fabrics, furnishing, clothing, cookery, nutrition and needlework can be the components of a course, or can be separate courses in themselves.

Secretarial studies

As well as typing, the course borrows from the business studies syllabus and includes office practice and organisation. Career opportunities are obvious. At the end of courses such as these, pupils can gain qualifications which give them entry to commercial and secretarial courses at further education or technical colleges or qualify them for junior positions in the commercial and industrial world.

Traditional subjects

In the National Curriculum and on offer at GCSE (O-grade) and A-level (H-grade) are subjects whose titles are unchanging: English language, mathematics, physics, chemistry, and so on. However, the content and the approach within these subjects have changed vastly over the last few years.

Mathematics

This is a core foundation subject. Besides being important in its own right, it is also a 'service' subject, necessary for technical drawing, geography, computer studies, physics, and so on.

Mathematics at GCSE level aims to increase pupils' confidence. The emphasis is still on number work but, with calculators and other aids, maths is no longer a subject only for people who can do quick mental calculations. The new courses involve problem-solving and apply maths to everyday situations – shopping, at work, in the home. The relationship between maths, science and technology is constantly emphasised, and pupils use graphs, tables and diagrams to show the patterns in maths.

Sciences

General science
General science courses were designed for pupils who had difficulty

with the various science disciplines (chemistry, physics, biology). These courses, which can lead to GCSE, can include topics such as:

- fuels and energy
- food science
- pollution
- heating and lighting in the home
- cosmetic science
- fibres and fabrics
- building science
- paints and dyes.

Chemistry
GCSE syllabuses stress the importance of chemistry for society as well as dealing with the principles of chemistry and the chemical elements. There is also a considerable amount of practical work in the laboratory.

Physics
Courses for GCSE contain such topics as:

- mechanics − how and why things move
- energy − the study of different sources and types of energy
- electricity − the use of electrical appliances and how they are powered
- light and sound − how sound waves travel, colour, reflection, mirrors, lenses
- nuclear physics − an introduction to radiation, nuclear power, safety.

Again, as with chemistry, much of the work is of a practical nature in workshops and laboratories.

Biology
Biology is concerned with the study of life and living organisms. The major areas studied, for both plants and animals, are:

- cell structure
- reproduction
- respiration
- plant growth
- excretion
- nutrition

- nervous control and sense organs
- genetics and evolution.

The sciences are indispensable for so many careers that to drop all of them too early would be a major error. The range of possibilities within the category of science is wide enough to provide a subject to interest most pupils. Furthermore, by 1997 there will be no choice, for science is a compulsory core foundation subject in the National Curriculum.

Mathematics, as well as being a necessity for many careers, services other subjects too. Physics and chemistry at this level are clearly important, too. Entry to engineering jobs is usually conditional on some kind of qualification in physics. And for most industrial jobs chemistry and physics are extremely useful.

Biology is a useful subject for people wanting to work with plants, animals, children or with people generally, in all kinds of jobs. Obvious examples include agriculture, horticulture, biotechnology (a new industry), medicine, dentistry, nursing, the food industry and catering.

Environmental studies

With the great interest in our environment, this has become a popular subject. For GCSE, pupils study:

- the Earth
- energy and natural resources (water, coal, iron), soil, weather, plant and animal communities
- the influence of man on the environment from the Stone Age to the Nuclear Age
- population growth and its consequences
- conservation.

English

English is an essential subject. The reasons are obvious, for no job or course can be tackled without the skills of communication. Nowadays, these skills are closely analysed and progress in them assessed. A pupil is expected to show ability and progress in:

- listening skills – this might seem obvious but it is amazing how bad people are at listening carefully and following instructions

- reading skills – not just reading books, but reading work documents, newspapers, instructions, exam papers, skills that may need practice
- verbal skills – pupils need help and practice to express themselves effectively. For example, much attention is paid to interviewing, how to make the best of yourself and win through at an interview
- visual skills – learning how to express ideas and information by visual means, drawings, photographs, graphs, and so on.

The humanities

The 'humanities' is a title used to describe a group of traditional subjects that includes history, geography, religious education, social studies, economics, foreign languages, classical languages and classical civilisation.

History

The teaching of history has changed considerably over the last few years. Emphasis is placed on weighing evidence, assessing causes and consequences, looking at local history, and examining the physical remains of the past. Nevertheless, history is still an academic and bookish subject, and whatever course or period is studied it involves a great deal of reading. Increasingly, twentieth-century history is becoming one of the more popular options, but other periods of history, from classical times to the nineteenth century, also feature in school syllabuses and public examinations.

Geography

Geography is another subject in which the approach and syllabus have changed over the last few years. The emphasis is placed on examining and assessing the interaction between peoples and their environment. Courses for GCSE are designed to help students to understand some of the aspects of the physical world. Topics and subjects that arise in the classroom and appear as examination options include:

- population studies
- the local environment
- the movement of peoples
- pollution, conservation and the control of the environment

- the use of skills such as fact-finding, observation, using maps and books, taking and using photographs as evidence.

Religious studies

The origins and history of Christianity are studied, together with studies of other religions and religious observances. Examination syllabuses take an equally wide view of religion.

Social studies

Social studies or courses of a similar type and title explore how people live, work and relate to each other within contemporary society both in Britain and in other parts of the world. This course involves reading, discussion and perhaps visiting social services departments to see the work that goes on in caring for the sick, handicapped and elderly. Pupils also study various aspects of modern society including crime, punishment, politics, central and local government, the economy and other topics.

Economics

Economics is also concerned with politics, but the major aspect of the study of this subject is to look at various methods of organising the economy both on a governmental scale and on a personal basis. Banking, insurance, economic theories, money and other subjects are included in the syllabus.

Modern languages

Schools like to offer as many different language courses as they can, but often have to concede to lack of pupil interest, resources or teachers. French is likely to be on the curriculum of every school. Spanish, German and Italian may be other GCSE options, and a very small number of schools offer Russian. Most schools advise pupils to take a maximum of two foreign languages in any course from 14 to 16. Therefore, for pupils who choose, say, French and German for GCSE, and are also very keen to take Spanish or Italian, or both, it may be possible to take one or both of these subjects as extras in the sixth form.

For pupils who have no ability with foreign languages, some schools have a course called European studies which deals with the history, geography and culture of Europe or of some European countries.

Classics

As other subjects have increased in popularity, so the study of Latin and Greek language and literature has steadily declined until only a few (mostly independent) schools now offer it. Some other schools arrange courses in classical studies or classical civilisation which are a mixture of language, history and the culture of the ancient civilisations.

The place of subjects within the National Curriculum

In this chapter, subjects have been described in relation to the content of study for GCSE courses. However, these same subjects feature in the National Curriculum and by 1997 GCSE subject content will have to match National Curriculum requirements. This book now considers the details of the National Curriculum.

CHAPTER 3

THE NATIONAL CURRICULUM

A MAJOR change which, when completed, will have dramatic effects on all primary and secondary schools, is the National Curriculum. Its introduction caused great controversy, and changes have already been made to the original plans; even so, it is one of the most significant educational reforms of the twentieth century.

Aims

The National Curriculum forms part of the Education Reform Act 1988. The aims are:

- to prescribe the school subjects which are to be taught
- to define the knowledge, skills and understanding that pupils of different abilities and maturities are expected to have
- to make arrangements for assessing pupils in these subjects and across the total curriculum.

Core and other foundation subjects

All pupils are required to study programmes in *ten* subjects. Three of the subjects are called the *core foundation subjects*; seven are other *foundation subjects*. These subjects have been included in schools for many years; what is different now is that pupils must study them throughout their school career and not drop them at any stage.

The core foundation is made up of English, mathematics and science. The other seven subjects in the foundation are art, geography, history, a modern language, music, physical education and technology. In

Wales, Welsh is taught as a core foundation subject where the medium of instruction in the school is Welsh.

All ten subjects must be taught through the compulsory years of schooling, that is up to 16, except for a modern language which is only compulsory at the secondary-level stage, that is 11+ onwards.

Religious education is also compulsory, although it is not part of the ten core subjects.

Attainment

As well as requiring schools to include the ten subjects in the curriculum, the Education Reform Act also demands that the content and attainment levels should be defined by the Education Department. Four terms are used to explain what is needed. These are

- Attainment targets
- Levels of attainment
- Statements of attainment
- Profiles.

Each subject is defined by its *attainment* targets. In science, for instance, there are 17. These are:

1 The exploration of science
2 The variety of life
3 Processes of life
4 Genetics and evolution
5 Human influences on the Earth
6 Materials – their types and uses
7 The making of new materials
8 Explaining how materials behave
9 Earth and atmosphere
10 Forces
11 Electricity and magnetism
12 Information technology and microelectronics
13 Energy
14 Sound and music
15 Light
16 The Earth in space
17 The nature of science

Attainment targets

Each of the attainment targets is divided again, this time into ten *levels of attainment*. Level 1 is the attainment that children in their first year of school (that is 5 to 6 years of age) might be expected to achieve. Level 10 would define their anticipated achievement ten years on, that is at about 16. For example, taking the 'processes of life', children of 6 would be expected to know that there is a life cycle for humans and animals, and by Level 10 they would understand human and animal reproduction and the processes of growing, ageing and decay.

Levels of attainment

For each subject, the expected levels of attainment have been defined. In discussing and defining them, there has been a lot of argument and disagreement between the experts, but eventually the levels have been worked out, although the job is by no means finished.

As you can imagine, the job is immense because there could be, say, ten different levels for each of the 17 attainment targets, that is 170 different statements for history, geography, English, and the other subjects. This kind of work will keep teachers and educational experts busy for years.

Programmes of study

The ways that attainment targets and statements of attainment are to be taught are set out in *programmes of study*. Teachers and pupils must follow them. They define content and methods of teaching and learning.

Profile components

The fourth term used in the 4-part National Curriculum is *profile component*. What this means is the record of the level achieved by each pupil set against each attainment target. Parents have a right to know about these results, but in the report the scores will be clustered together in a group to form a *profile component*. In science, there are two of these components and, when the National Curriculum is fully implemented, parents will receive information about the levels achieved in each component.

This is part of the Government's commitment to providing information for parents: all schools (under the terms of what will be a Parent's Charter) must give parents information about their children's achievements on the different attainment targets, leading up to a score for the profile component.

Most parents will already be cross-eyed with puzzlement, but there's more to come yet.

Key stages

The law says that what should be taught at each stage should be defined. Four key stages in the 17 attainment target pattern have been fixed. They are:

Key Stage 1:   5-to-7 year olds
Key Stage 2:   9-to-11 "   "
Key Stage 3:   11-to-14 "   "
Key Stage 4:   14-to-16 "   "

In order to ensure that all schools follow the key stage pattern, and relate it correctly to year groups, the National Curriculum has changed the way that teachers talk about year groups. Many schools have already switched to the new system which looks like this:

Age of pupils at the end of the school year	Key Stage	Year group description
5		R (Reception)
6	1	Y1
7		Y2
8	2	Y3
9		Y4
10		Y5
11		Y6
12	3	Y7
13		Y8
14		Y9
15	4	Y10
16		Y11
17		Y12
18		Y13

Note that the National Curriculum applies to 5 to 16 year olds, so R, the reception year, and Y12 and Y13 (the sixth-form years) are technically *outside* the National Curriculum and are not directly affected by the reforms.

Progress so far

The programmes, targets and statements of attainment were designed by working parties set up in 1989 by the Secretary of State for Education. They produced reports. These were then the subject of a great deal of consultation and discussion – and in some cases, as with history, fundamental disagreements on the content of the subject that should be taught.

Controlling and presiding over these discussions, which went on throughout 1989-91, and are by no means finished, was the National Curriculum Council. But final decisions on the National Curriculum and on its content, methods of teaching and attainment targets are, in the final report, within the authority and the power of the Minister who will rely on Parliament to support these decisions.

Time and motion

Parents might like to know that the Education Reform Act does not say for how long or for what percentage of the week each subject will be studied. Following the Act, DES Regulations will put it into effect, but so far all they say is that 'a reasonable amount of time' should be spent on National Curriculum subjects.

There has been a lot of debate about time allocations. Since the National Curriculum is at primary school stage of development, with secondary school implementation not really effective until 1994, the debate will continue for some time yet.

The responsibility for time allocation to the ten subjects (plus religious education) is left to each school. So, parents need to read carefully any information sent out by the school. Furthermore, it is possible that between now and 1994 some of the requirements may be dropped, such as that all ten subjects are compulsory and none dropped. There could therefore be changes to the scheme outlined in this chapter.

Subjects – or not?

You have to realise, too, that some schools do not teach in terms of 'subjects'. Will they have to change? Another unknown: very few primary schools divide the week up into ten or eleven subjects. At present, they have to implement Key Stage 1, but the testing of the attainments has been much changed already.

Many secondary schools at present combine subjects, such as history, geography and social studies into 'humanities'.

There is no reason why schools should stop doing this. Provided that (and it's a big 'provided') attention is given, and time is allocated to the teaching of the content of the ten subjects so that the attainment targets can be met.

What may happen to subject teaching? By the time the National Curriculum is implemented in secondary schools, it is more than possible (that is probable) that separate subjects will have returned to the secondary school curriculum. This means that history and geography are likely to be taught separately and equally, and that dance and drama, highly important though they are, will give way to or strongly reflect the content, attainment targets and programmes of study of art and music.

Non-National Curriculum subjects and cross-curricular themes

Ever since the first publication of proposals for the National Curriculum, in 1987, there has been agitated discussion on the place of non-National Curriculum subjects.

Where, people ask, will subjects that are seen to be vital to pupils' development be fitted in? These subjects include:

- personal and social education
- careers education
- health education
- economic and industrial understanding and social studies
- environmental education.

Each one of these areas has its advocates, its champions, and in some way or another they feature in the school's curriculum now. This is the area of *cross-curricular themes,* for this was the Government's answer to the critics of the National Curriculum.

The National Curriculum Council did not abandon these subjects. They have recommended that they be banded into cross-curricular themes and are timetabled as well as the National Curriculum subjects.

It is important to appreciate that the National Curriculum does not cover the whole of the school curriculum. Children will study subjects and take part in activities which are *additional* to the National Curriculum subjects. What the Government *does* say, however is that schools should have a *prospectus* that sets out the variety, and range of subjects for all years, so that parents can see and understand where the subjects fit into the total curriculum.

For further information, *A Guide to the National Curriculum* by Bob Moon, published by Oxford University Press, is strongly recommended. The NCC also provides helpful literature, including some specialised leaflets for parents. The addresses are:

- National Curriculum Council, Albion Wharf, Sheldergate, York YO1 2XL

- Curriculum Council for Wales, Suite 2, Castle Buildings, Womanby Street, Cardiff CF1 9SX

- National Curriculum Council for Scotland, New St Andrew's House, St James Centre, Edinburgh EH1 3TB

CHAPTER **4**

SUBJECT AND CAREER CHOICES, 14 TO 16

Subjects for study at GCSE

The choice of subjects for a course from 14 to 16 can, theoretically, be made from a vast list of possibilities. There are over 170 subjects on offer for GCSE. The list is continually changing and being updated, but the subjects on the following list are currently available. The syllabus for each of the subjects and specimen examination papers can be obtained from the appropriate Examining Group, whose addresses are given at the end of Chapter Five. A small charge is made for the exam papers and for the syllabus.

The major subjects are as follows:

Accounting	CDT: Design and communication
Agricultural science	CDT: Design and realisation
Applied science	CDT: Technology
Arabic	Chemistry
Archaeology	Chemistry (Nuffield)
Arithmetic	Chemistry (Salters)
Art and design	Chinese
Astronomy	Citizenship
	Classical civilisation (SCP)
Bengali	Classical civilisation (Greek and Roman)
Biology	Commerce
Biology (human)	Communication
Biology (human and social)	Computer studies
Biology (Nuffield)	Control technology
British government and politics	Craft (metal)
British industrial society	Craft (wood)
Building studies	Craft and design (engineering)
Business and information studies	Craft and design (metal)
Business studies	Craft and design (metalwork)
	Craft and design (wood)
Catering	Craft and design (woodwork)

Creative arts

Dance
Design
Drama
Drama and theatre arts

Economics
Electronics
Engineering science
Engineering workshop theory and
   practice
English
English as a second language
English literature
Environment
Environmental science
Environmental studies
European studies

Food and the community
Food and nutrition
Food studies
France: language and culture
French

General maritime knowledge
Geography
Geography (Avery Hill)
Geography (Bristol Project)
Geology
German
Germany: language and culture
Government, politics and law
Graphic communication
Greek
Greek civilisation
Greek and Greek civilisation
Gujerati

History
History (Britain, Europe and the
   world 1848–1980)
History (British and European)
History (British 1485–1714)
History (British 1815–1983)
History (British social and economic)
History (modern world)
History (Schools History Project)
History and appreciation of art and
   design

History of appreciation of music
History of art
History of medicine and
   nursing in western society
Home economics: child development
Home economics: family, home and
   food
Home economics: food
Home economics: home and food
Home economics: home studies
Home economics: textiles
Humanities

Industry and society
Information technology
Integrated humanities
Irish
Italian

Keyboard applications
Keyboard communication
Keyboarding

Land surveying
Latin
Latin (SCP)
Latin and Roman civilisation
Latin with classical civilisation (SCP)
Law
Law in society (rights and duties)
Local history

Marine navigation
Manufacturing technology
Mathematics
Mathematics (SMP)
Mathematics (SMP) 11–16 (Inter-Group
   National Curriculum Project)
Mathematics (additional)
Media studies
Metalwork
Meteorology
Meteorology and oceanography
Modern Hebrew
Motor vehicle engineering
Motor vehicle studies
Music

Nautical studies

Office skills

Office studies
Office studies and information
   processing

Photography
Physical education
Physical science
Physics
Physics (Nuffield)
Polish
Political studies
Politics and government
Psychology
Punjabi

Religious studies
Roman civilisation
Rural science
Russian

Science
Science (biology, chemistry,
   physics)
Science (combined science)
Science (integrated)
Science (modular)
Science, technology and society
Seamanship

Social science
Social studies
Sociology
Spanish
Statistics
Surveying
Systems electronics

Technical communication
Technical design and graphic
   communication
Technology
Textile studies
Typewriting
Typewriting and keyboard skills

Ukrainian
Understanding industrial society
Urdu

Vehicle design and engineering

Welfare and society
Welsh first language: language
Welsh first language: literature
Welsh second language: extended
Welsh second language: foundation
Woodwork

Subjects and possible careers

A question that pupils and parents often ask is 'What do these subjects
lead to?' meaning where do the subjects lead in terms of A-levels and
higher education courses later, and also in terms of possible careers and
jobs.

One way of attempting to answer this difficult question is to group
the eighty or so subjects listed for the GCSE examination. In the space
of this analysis it is impossible to cover the whole vast range of jobs, but
the exercise shows the types of career to which the subjects could lead.

GROUPS	SUBJECTS	SUBJECTS
Business	Accounting	Law
	Business studies	Typewriting
	Commerce	Understanding
	Economics	industrial society

IMPORTANT FOR THESE JOBS	OF DIRECT USE IN THESE JOBS	USEFUL FOR THESE JOBS
Accountant	Banking	Clerk
Any kind of business job	Building society work	Secretary
Civil service	Financial services	All types of jobs in business, commerce, government
Local government jobs	Jobs in education	

GROUPS	SUBJECTS	SUBJECTS
Maths and sciences	Applied science	Geography
	Arithmetic	Geology
	Biology	Information technology
	Chemistry	Mathematics
	Computer studies	Physics
	Control technology	Statistics
	Electronics	Surveying
	Engineering practice	. . . and many more
	Environmental science	

IMPORTANT FOR THESE JOBS	OF DIRECT USE IN THESE JOBS	USEFUL FOR THESE JOBS
Biochemist	Agricultural work	Air transport
Biologist	Dentist	Cosmetics industry
Chemist	Doctor	Horticulture
Computer programmer	Energy industries	Manufacturing industry
All types of computer work	Hospital work	Museum work
Electrician	Medicine	Printing, papermaking, packaging industries
All types of engineering	Nursing	Research work
Food manufacturing	Transport industry	Soap and other chemical industries
Geologist	All jobs in industry	Textile industries
Pharmacist		
Physicist		
Statistician		
Surveyor		

GROUPS	SUBJECTS	SUBJECTS
Humanities and languages	Classical civilisation Communication English European studies French German	History Italian Photography Social studies Spanish
IMPORTANT FOR THESE JOBS	OF DIRECT USE IN THESE JOBS	USEFUL FOR THESE JOBS

Civil service
Journalism
Librarian
Local government
Any overseas job
Social work
	English is necessary
	  for most jobs
	Other humanities
	  subjects are
	  important too
		Archaeologist
		Archivist
		Museum work
		Teaching
		Travel work and
		  holiday industry
		Work involving
		  children, the old,
		  the handicapped

GROUPS	SUBJECTS	SUBJECTS

Creative and practical	Art and design
	Craft
	Craft and design
	Drama and theatre
	  arts
	Food and nutrition
	Home economics
	Keyboard
	  applications
		Media studies
		Metalwork
		Music
		PE
		Technical
		  communication
		Textile studies
		Woodwork

IMPORTANT FOR THESE JOBS	OF DIRECT USE IN THESE JOBS	USEFUL FOR THESE JOBS

Advertising
Commercial art
Craft skills
Exhibitions
Fashion, furniture and
  other design
Fashion industry
Musician
Office work
Shops
Teaching
TV, film, theatre
	In all kinds of
	  businesses from
	  design studios to
	  manufacturing
	  companies,
	  workshops,
	  studios
		Caring for people
		Craft trades
		Hotel work
		Industry as a whole
		Publishing
		Shops and the retail
		  industry
		Tourism

The really important thing about choosing a course from 14 to 16 years is that no career possibilities should be excluded.

This will not occur if the pupil takes a broad course, which includes

English language, science, maths, humanities, creative and business subjects.

'Required' or 'essential' subjects

To gain entry to some higher and further education courses and to some careers, employers and colleges stipulate that students should have studied certain subjects to GCSE standard. A subject may be 'preferred' or 'required' for entry to some courses and some jobs. Most employers or admissions tutors at colleges regard English language and mathematics, often to GCSE pass standard, as essential. This is why the National Curriculum has mathematics and English language as compulsory subjects. Take English language as an example. Employers and colleges look for a GCSE pass in English for entry to a wide range of careers, from accountancy to zoology and including virtually all subjects in between. To put the point another way, a pupil who was allowed to drop English language as a subject would find it virtually impossible to find a job that requires any passes at GCSE level.

Schools try to make mathematics (or arithmetic or a variety of maths) another compulsory subject for everyone in the 14 to 16 age-group. The reason is that some kind of qualification in maths (generally GCSE) is needed for almost all courses and jobs that ask for any qualifications. Similarly, science is an important subject because it leads into many careers and job opportunities. Schools therefore generally insist on pupils taking at least mathematics, and often insist also on their taking another science subject as well. If a pupil drops maths, he or she will find that a wide range of opportunities is closed.

The National Curriculum, when fully implemented, will require attainment targets to be at 14 to 16, and by then GCSE syllabuses will be integrated into the new system.

Sciences

Some of the career opportunities for which good GCSE results in sciences are generally essential are given in Part 3 of this book, An A to Z of Careers. The importance of science cannot be underestimated; nor can the danger if science subjects are dropped or neglected.

Other subjects

Other subjects are often not *directly* linked to career opportunities. History, for example, is 'required' or 'preferred' for very few careers. A degree in history or a related subject is obviously needed if someone wants to become an archaeologist, a museum curator or a history teacher, and this means selecting history as a GCSE (O-grade) and A-level (H-grade) option during his or her school career. But apart from these three jobs there are few others that need a history qualification (and in fact it is possible to become an archaeologist, museum curator or history teacher *without* a degree in history, for there are other routes into these jobs). On the other hand, employers think a history qualification at any level (GCSE, O-grade, A-level, H-grade, or degree) is a very useful accomplishment because it shows that the student is able to handle facts, assess evidence and express ideas and information on paper.

Similarly, to become an interpreter, translator or overseas exporter, a good knowledge of modern languages is essential. But there are very few jobs as translator or interpreter, and these are seized by the very best language graduates. Modern languages, as a subject, does not lead directly into jobs, but, like history, some kind of qualification and knowledge of languages is highly rated by employers as a skill and as evidence of the candidate's abilities.

A qualification in geography, to take a third example, can lead towards courses in cartography, landscape architecture, environmental planning, town and country planning, geology, oceanography and similar high-level courses. But, as with history and languages, geography is not a subject directly linked to many careers, and yet it, too, is well thought of by employers.

The conclusion from this analysis is that most employers who recruit 16- or 18-year-olds look for a sound, all-round education. Although they attach importance to passes at any level in English language, mathematics and a science subject, they look closely at other subjects studied at school as evidence of a pupil's all-round ability. In the future they are going to look at a student's achievements in all the subjects of the National Curriculum.

Jobs without qualifications

Employers who are recruiting young people for jobs look for a broadly based education. If a job requires GCSE passes, the employer will expect passes in English language and mathematics or a science subject to be among them. The employer will also look for other factors – the personal qualities or potential that will help the recruit make a success of the job. Among the qualities that employers rate highly are: reliability, loyalty, honesty, willingness to learn, the ability to get on with people and to accept responsibility. These factors can be just as important as passes in examination subjects, for employers know that some people who are not good at passing exams are capable of being excellent employees in all kinds of jobs.

There are many jobs for which exam passes are not essential. For a full list of them read *Careers and Jobs Without O-levels*, published by Hobsons. Some groups of jobs that require no formal GCSE qualifications include:

Clerical work

Includes typing, word processing, clerical work, receptionist, office work, operating office machines. These jobs can be in estate agents, local and central government offices, insurance and building society offices, and in company offices. For these jobs, useful school subjects studied include: English language, maths, social studies and typing.

Outdoor work

Includes farm work and other outdoor jobs, including gardening, market gardening, parks, stables, kennels. Most of these jobs are in the countryside, and in towns there are jobs within councils such as parks and gardens, road repairs, maintenance work, house building. Useful school subjects are woodwork, metalwork and other craft subjects, biology, rural science or general science, and maths.

Social and 'caring' work

Among these is work in hospitals, residential homes and council care services for the old, sick and the young. In addition, there's hairdressing, canteen work, work as a shop assistant, in hotels and in social services. Useful school subjects are home economics, cookery, English and craft subjects.

Creative and practical work

There are jobs linked to dancing, drama, art and design, dressmaking, window dressing, music, and as shop assistants in different kinds of businesses. As with the other groups of jobs, there is unskilled work and highly skilled work. For the latter, people have to train and perhaps take higher qualifications. Among useful school subjects are English and the 'creative' subjects of music, cookery, needlework, craft subjects, art and design.

Industrial

The kind of jobs that occur in this group are unskilled ones in industry, although there are fewer of them now than there used to be. However, there is a substantial need for drivers, transport staff, cleaners and factory workers, although most of these people acquire their skills through training. In the building trade there are plasterers, bricklayers, plumbers: people don't need exam passes to get into these jobs, but they certainly need to take training courses to do them properly. Useful school subjects are any of the sciences and the craft subjects.

CHAPTER 5

THE EXAMINATION JUNGLE

IN THE past the universities dominated the examination system. Traditionally, the universities laid down the qualifications needed, both at O-level (O-grade) and at A-level (H-grade), by applicants for degree courses. This influenced what schools taught. To ensure that pupils had the chance to take, say, a science degree course in biology, chemistry or physics, schools had to provide A-level (H-grade) courses in those subjects. But in order to do the A-levels (H-grades), pupils had first to take O-levels in the same subjects. So the sciences went into the 14 to 16 courses. The universities went further. They expected schools to give pupils a good grounding in the basic elements of a subject, and therefore the universities' expectations also dominated what was actually taught in classes, i.e. the curriculum or content of studies.

Furthermore, five of the six Examination Boards that set O-level and A-level examinations were university-based: Oxford, Oxford and Cambridge, Cambridge, the Northern Universities Joint Board and London. The exception was the Associated Examining Board. Thus the universities' control of syllabuses was a very real one.

Changes to the system

Questions about the universities' power arose from several quarters. Pressure for change came from politicians, industry and commerce and the educational world. In the first place it was felt that a more sophisticated system of assessment could be introduced which would describe what a pupil or student could do, rather than define achievements simply in terms of pass or fail grades. Secondly, it was felt that CSE, O-level and other 16-plus qualifications could be merged into one examination, avoiding the need for students to choose between two or more routes to a qualification at 16. Thirdly, it was agreed that any new system should be for the great majority of pupils in the 14 to 16 age-group rather than for a selection of them. For these reasons the government decided to reform the examination system. This change was announced in 1984 'in order to improve examination courses and to raise the standard of performance of all candidates'. GCSE courses were to begin in September 1986 and the first examinations would be taken in 1988.

GCSE, GCE and CSE

GCSE

In 1983 the Government set up the Secondary Examinations Council (SEC) with the responsibility for monitoring examinations. This indicated to teachers and the universities that the Government intended to take a much greater interest in the form and the standards of future examinations. Meanwhile, the CSE and GCE Examination Boards were developing the criteria on which assessment for a new single system of examining at 16-plus would be based. This new system, called the General Certificate of Secondary Education (GCSE), which replaced CSE and O-level, is administered by five regional Examining Groups, formed from the amalgamation of CSE and GCE Boards.

GCE

The General Certificate of Education (GCE) was introduced in 1951. For the 14 to 16 age-group the appropriate level of work was towards the Ordinary level examination. For 16-plus students the examination is at Advanced level (A-level), with Scholarship level (S-level) suitable for candidates who wish to take A-level a stage further. GCE applied to England, Wales and Northern Ireland. Scotland has its own system of Ordinary Grade, Higher Grade and a Certificate of Sixth-Year Studies: details of the Scottish system are given in Chapter 14.

Traditionally, pupils took O-levels at the end of the fifth year of a secondary school when they were about 16 years of age. It was possible to take O-levels at an older age, and indeed there were adult education classes in colleges of further education which provided O-level courses for mature students.

At O-level, school pupils took all kinds of subjects from traditional ones, such as mathematics, chemistry and history, to new ones such as textiles, environmental science and human biology. Achievement grades were A, B, C, D and E, with the first three recognised as pass grades.

O-levels were the currency of school-leaving qualifications at 16 since they were first introduced. Every employer knew what O-level meant and was able to base entry requirements on it as a guaranteed level of student achievement. The last candidates for O-level took the examination in 1987. From 1988, GCSE replaced O-level and pupils who were 14 in 1986 were entered for the new examination. However, for some years to come, applicants for jobs will offer O-levels, and in a few cases a mixture of O-levels and GCSEs.

CSE

The Certificate of Secondary Education (CSE) was first introduced in 1965 as a national examination for students mostly in the 14 to 16 age-group but also for older students. The examination was designed for the top 60 per cent of all 16-plus pupils in a very wide range of subjects. (O-level had been taken by the top 30 per cent of 16-year-olds.) However, as CSE developed, more pupils were entered for it, until by the mid-1980s about 95 per cent of the age-group took one or more CSE subjects. In 1980, for example, there were over three million subject entries for over half a million candidates, and over 90 per cent of 16-plus pupils obtained one or more CSEs or O-levels.

CSE candidates received a certificate, as did GCE candidates, with one of four grades awarded for each subject. Grade 1 was equivalent to grades A, B or C at O-level; grade 2 was equivalent to a D, and grade 3 to an E. Grade 4 was the standard achievement for a candidate of average ability.

CSE, like GCE, was recognised nationally as an examination with guaranteed standards. For instance, CSE was accepted by universities, colleges, professional organisations and employers.

The control of CSE was in the hands of fourteen CSE Boards throughout England, Wales and Northern Ireland (Scotland has never had a CSE system). The CSE Boards, like the GCE Boards, published syllabuses, set the standards and carried out the examinations. CSE, like GCE, has been replaced by GCSE; however, as with O-levels, people who qualified at school before 1988 will show CSE qualifications and employers need to know what they mean.

Other courses and qualifications

City and Guilds, BTEC and SCOTVEC

For many years the City and Guilds of London Institute (CGLI) has approved courses leading to the awards of the Institute. These courses lead to commercial and industrial qualifications and are highly thought of by employers as a firm basis for work skills. The Business and Technician Education Council (BTEC), which was formed in 1983 from the amalgamation of the Business Education Council (BEC) and the Technician Education Council (TEC), also approves courses and gives awards in vocational subjects. These two bodies have a very powerful influence on what is taught in 16-plus courses offered at colleges of further education, polytechnics, art colleges and other institutions. In Scotland, the Scottish Vocational Education Council (SCOTVEC) exercises much the same effective influence over 16-plus courses there.

Traditionally there was a fairly firm dividing line between O-level/CSE courses in schools and CGLI and BTEC or SCOTVEC courses in further education. This division, however, is now being eroded. In the past it was possible for students to take O-levels and A-levels at colleges of further education: nowadays the colleges offer courses for GCSE, A-level, BTEC and City and Guilds.

CPVE

The Certificate of Pre-Vocational Education (CPVE), described in Chapter 7, is a joint school/college course, often arranged by a consortium of schools and a local college. City and Guilds certificates can be taken in schools. Furthermore, City and Guilds and BTEC intend to develop other pre-vocational and vocational courses for the 14 to 18 age-group. These schemes have the support of industry and commerce, for many employers believe that the school examination system, with its traditional emphasis on theoretical and subject-based knowledge, has diverted many able students away from industrial careers, and has also left those pupils who cannot perform well in academic subjects with an unmerited sense of failure. From 1988 many students have combined some GCSE subjects with CPVE.

TVEI

The confusion over courses for the 14 to 18 age-group was further complicated not only by the CPVE course for 16-plus students but also by another important educational development for 14 to 18s, the Technical and Vocational Education Initiative (TVEI) (see Chapter 8). These schemes cut across GCSE subject boundaries; they are work-linked, practical courses, attractive to students who have attended them, and highly thought of by employers because of the industrial and commercial connections within the courses.

The market-place

If GCSE, BTEC, CPVE and TVEI are confusing to parents and pupils, they are also a jungle for employers. Employers tend to offer fairly simple answers to questions about courses and the young people emerging from them. They point to the needs of the market-place, stressing that employers look for practical skills, understanding of the business world, and a readiness to train and re-train for a job market that is constantly changing.

When pressed about GCSE (when they know about it), they always mention English and mathematics. They know about City and Guilds and BTEC courses because many staff already in employment have taken these courses, leading to craft, technician, supervisory and managerial qualifications. They are aware of the courses directly related to their industry, such as building, catering, retailing, engineering, computing, and in some cases – if they are training officers or personnel staff – they are likely to sit on committees set up by the examination boards or awarding bodies. They are generally in favour of City and Guilds and BTEC qualifications and they approve of TVEI and Youth Training (see Chapter 12) schemes because the trainees gain experience of work environments as part of the learning and training course.

Parents' views

Generalising about employers' attitudes is dangerous because the sample of employers consulted may not be a satisfactory cross-section of views. Similarly, generalising about parental opinion can be just as dangerous. However, the evidence from schools, careers officers and parents themselves is that, in general, parents tend to be more conservative than any of the other groups involved in educational reform – the government, employers, teachers, or pupils. The evidence suggests that in the recent past parents preferred their children to take traditional examination courses with subjects in closed compartments, taught by firm, didactic methods. The major reason for this view of the educational process is because parents see education as a means of getting 'a good job' – or any job – and they tend to suspect alternative methods of teaching and new, unproven courses.

The government, employers and the teaching profession have been much keener on change than parents. They acknowledge that there are other routes to jobs than by taking GCSEs, O-grades and A-levels (H-grades). And there is a growing realisation among parents as well as educationalists that examinations are poor predictors of future performance, particularly in the market-place. This is not altogether surprising, since examinations rarely measure creativity, oral abilities, practical skills, determination, perseverance and the other qualities required for finding out and applying knowledge and for carrying out the needs of a job to an employer's expectations.

So far, parents have been satisfied to accept the opinion of educationalists that GCSE is a significant reform. They will have to be convinced too that the National Curriculum and the new assessment methods associated with it will also benefit schools, and in particular their own children.

CHAPTER 6

THE GENERAL CERTIFICATE OF SECONDARY EDUCATION (GCSE)

IN JUNE 1984, after years of discussion, the Government announced a major educational reform. There was to be a single system of examinations at 16-plus, the General Certificate of Secondary Education (GCSE), which would replace O-level, CSE and other 16-plus examinations in England and Wales with effect from the summer of 1988.

To prepare for this substantial educational change, the regional Examination Boards, Local Education Authorities and teachers' organisations began the formidable task of preparing teachers and students for the new examination.

Aims

The underlying objective of the Government in proposing the GCSE was to improve the quality of education and to raise standards of attainment. It was felt that the whole ability range of the 14 to 16 age-group had potential that could be realised through a common examination system. In general terms the objective was to bring 80 to 90 per cent of the 14 to 16 age-group to an educational level approximate to the old CSE grade 4. Improving standards was one aim; others were to set clear targets for teachers and pupils, to provide stimulating courses, and to assess all work done in the two-year period, including coursework, assignments and other forms of students' work.

The main features of GCSE

These are:

● All syllabuses and assessment and grading procedures are based on 'national criteria', set out in documents published by the Department of Education and Science (DES).

- Assessment techniques have been introduced so that candidates can demonstrate effectively what they know, understand and can do.
- Grades are awarded on a seven-point scale, A to G.
- Standards set for GCSE are no lower than those set for CSE and O-level examinations prior to 1988.
- The GCSE is administered by six Examining Groups, made up from the Boards that previously administered CSE and GCE O-level, and monitored by the Secondary Examinations Council. In addition, there is a separate Board for Northern Ireland. In Scotland, where GCSE was not introduced, the Scottish Examination Board administers a different set of awards, at Ordinary, Standard and Higher Grades.

The GCSE – questions and answers

Have standards fallen or risen?

Standards are as high as those for O-level and CSE. There have been some criticisms that GCSE does not challenge higher ability skills, but evidence presented by the Examining Boards has indicated that pupils of all abilities have improved their performance in most subjects.

Do employers accept GCSE as they did O-level and CSE?

Yes. Employers need to know what GCSE aims to do and what the grades A to G mean, but they fully accept that the new examination is a proper test of a 16-year-old's achievements.

What does GCSE test?

The GCSE has been designed to test knowledge, the orderly presentation of facts, a student's understanding of what he or she has learned, and give students the full opportunity to learn and display practical skills over the full period of the course.

Does coursework over the two years of the course count?

Yes. Some syllabuses and assessment schemes (as in some English courses) require the whole assessment (100 per cent) to be based on coursework. For other subjects, coursework is a percentage of the total. Early in 1992, the Government announced its intention to alter assessment criteria so that coursework will be a figure between 20 and 50 per cent. In *all* subjects, a student's work over the two years is taken into consideration in making the award. Furthermore, the criteria for assessing coursework have been strengthened, with pupils being required to collect and present for assessment a full portfolio of their work.

What are the 'national criteria'?

All GCSE courses follow nationally agreed criteria. These describe the objectives, content and methods of assessment of a particular subject, such as history. Syllabuses devised for all subject courses offered by the Examining Groups have had to conform with these criteria. During the 1990s the criteria will be re-examined alongside the attainment targets set for the National Curriculum subjects.

How is GCSE graded?

Successful candidates (those who 'pass') are graded on a seven-point scale. Grades A, B and C are equivalent to the old O-level grades of A, B and C and CSE grade 1. Grades D to G are equivalent to the old CSE grades 2 to 5. The equivalent grades are therefore as follows:

GCSE	O-level	CSE
A	A	1
B	B	1
C	C	1
D	D	2
E	E	3
F		4
G		5

Unsuccessful or 'failed' candidates are ungraded.

Have teachers been retrained for GCSE?

Each Local Education Authority had the responsibility for training teachers to use the new exams, and there were meetings, seminars, trial exams and teach-ins on how to mark coursework, projects and written papers. The Secondary Examinations Council and the Open University produced teachers' guides for 20 subjects, and these have been distributed, discussed and acted on.

However, despite all these preparations, there was considerable discussion about teachers' anxieties over the GCSE. It was said (and confirmed by many teachers) that insufficient time was given to switching to the new examinations. Perhaps the emphasis placed on coursework has caused most of the problems. To assess students' work over the two years of the course is an admirable objective, so avoiding the once-and-for-all set-piece exam. But it has proved difficult to persuade all pupils to complete every piece of coursework (and in many cases it has become a real burden). It has been difficult to get all coursework marked to a set of complex instructions in order to finish by tight deadlines. As a consequence, teacher training and guidelines provided by the GCSE examination boards have concentrated on setting coursework, its completion and assessment.

How many subjects can students take?
Each school has the right to make its own decisions on the maximum and minimum number of subjects studied by each student. There are few differences between the range of subjects formerly offered for CSE/O-level and now for GCSE. For example, some pupils are entered for only one, two or three GCSE subjects, while others might take nine or ten. Some students combine CPVE and/or TVEI with GCSE; others simply take GCSE exams.

What about failures? Is it possible to re-take?
Yes. Pupils can re-sit the examinations the following year. They also have to complete all the coursework. It may be that because they did insufficient coursework, they were not entered for the exam or failed it; this can be put right by doing all the work and sitting or re-sitting the written papers later. They can keep going until they obtain a grade (A to G) or give up. And they can re-take to improve their grade (from, say, E to A, B or C).

Does the new system affect A-levels?
No. A-levels are, for the moment, continuing as before. However, it is likely that by the mid-1990s A-level courses may be changed, and that AS-levels will become more popular.

What can parents do?
They should attend the 'briefing' meetings put on for parents by school staff for different year groups. Parents who haven't heard of a briefing

or information meeting should ask the school when and where it's going to be held. Good schools organise regular teach-ins on GCSE and other educational topics.

What about Scotland?

The GCSE was devised for England, Wales and Northern Ireland. Scotland has its own examination system, described in Chapter 14.

Who can take GCSE?

Anyone. Courses and examinations are offered in state (LEA) schools, private (independent) schools, further education colleges and private colleges.

Who benefits most – the bright children or the less bright?

Both. For the bright, the GCSE brings a guarantee that knowledge and the abilities to use that knowledge are taught and tested. Employers are continually asking for evidence of this. Bright children can obtain grades A to C at GCSE and are well prepared for A-levels, or for work at 16. The less bright are assessed within grades A to G, and therefore can obtain a record of real achievement which shows they did a course over two years and reached a certain standard. But how teachers and the Examining Groups are to distinguish between grades A to G is a different question, and assessment therefore needs to be explained.

GCSE: the future

GCSE results released by the Examining Boards in 1991 have confirmed these statements. This was that pupils of all abilities improved their general performance, and this was in most subjects.

Reports from the Boards showed that the proportion of pupils awarded grades A to C (the old O-level pass grades) rose to 47.2 per cent in 1991 from 42.5 per cent in 1988. The proportion of passes at A grade has increased from 8.61 per cent to 10.5 per cent. These results were better than O-level equivalents in the pre-1988 period.

What does this show? It could indicate rising standards of achievement, particularly at the A grade. On the other hand, some critics have said that the figures show that GCSE is not at the standard set by O-level grades A to C, i.e. indicating that standards have fallen. But how do we judge? It would probably be fair to say that the GCSE examination boards' figures show a genuine improvement in levels of attainment.

After three years of experience, the burden of coursework does not seem so oppressive, although there are still numerous complaints from pupils, parents and teachers about the amount of work set, which in turn has to be marked and assessed towards a final grade and, as indicated earlier, the proportion of course work may change in the future.

The verdict, after the first three years, strongly favours GCSE on the grounds that it genuinely attempts to develop and measure students' skills rather than factual knowledge, although there is a vociferous lobby in the educational world that insists that knowledge is paramount.

Examples of syllabuses

Here are some examples of syllabuses, assessment methods and course-work from printed syllabuses, reproduced with the permission of the Groups.

History

(The Modern World, 1914–The Present Day)

AIMS

---

1 To stimulate interest in and enthusiasm for the study of the past.
2 To promote the acquisition of knowledge and understanding of human activity in the past, linking it, as appropriate, with the present.
3 To ensure that candidates' knowledge is rooted in an understanding of the nature and use of historical evidence.
4 To help pupils, particularly in courses on British history, towards an understanding of the development over time of social and cultural values.
5 To promote an understanding of the nature of cause and consequence, continuity and change, similarity and difference.
6 To develop essential study skills such as the ability to locate and extract information from primary and secondary sources; to analyse and organise this information and to construct a logical argument (usually through the medium of writing).
7 To provide a sound basis for further study and the pursuit of personal interest.

It should be noted that not all these aims can be translated readily into assessment objectives.

ASSESSMENT OBJECTIVES

Candidates should be able:

1 to recall, select and deploy relevant knowledge and communicate in a clear and coherent form;
2 to demonstrate understanding of historical terminology and concepts (cause and consequence, change and continuity, similarity and difference);

3 to reveal empathy with individuals and societies in their historical setting;
4 to interpret and evaluate a wide range of historical sources and their use as
   evidence, viz.
   (a) to comprehend;
   (b) to locate and extract relevant information;
   (c) to distinguish between fact, opinion and judgement;
   (d) to indicate deficiencies, such as gaps and inconsistencies;
   (e) to detect bias;
   (f) to compare and contrast a range of sources and to reach conclusions based
        upon their use as evidence.

Sources used should include both primary and secondary material, statistical and
visual material, artefacts and orally transmitted information.

Note: All the types of source in assessment objective 4 should be used in the school
course. The ability to discuss the value of the full range of types of source will be
looked for in the course assessment, mainly in Paper 2 and in coursework. Even
where artefact material is in pictorial form, candidates will be expected to appreciate
the value of artefacts to historians. Orally transmitted information can include story
and legend, hearsay evidence and interviews, written down some time after the
events described.

The relationship between Assessment Objectives and the components of the
Scheme of Assessment is shown in the following grid.

	Paper 1		Paper 2 (30%)	Coursework (30%)
	Section A (15%)	Section B (25%)		
Objective 1	★	★	★	★ ★
Objective 2		★	★	★
Objective 3				★
Objective 4			★ ★	★

. The number of stars shown gives an approximate indication of the relative
weighting *within each component* of the objectives to be assessed.

Reproduced by permission of the Midland Examining Group

Economics

INTRODUCTION

The educational purpose of this syllabus is:

1 To provide students with that economics knowledge and those economics skills
   which will enable them to understand better the world in which they live.
2 To develop an initial and yet critical understanding of important economic forces
   and institutions with which they will come into contact and of the interdepend-
   ence of economic actions.

3 To prepare students to participate more fully in decision-making processes as consumers, producers and citizens.
4 To develop the ability to communicate accurately and effectively in using knowledge and ideas in verbal, numerical, written, diagrammatic and graphical ways.

AIMS

1 To understand the basic economic problem of allocating scarce resources and ways in which it may be resolved.
2 To develop a knowledge and understanding of the main aspects of the UK economy with reference to individuals, groups and organisations within the local, national and international community.
3 To develop an awareness of major issues of economic policy within the UK.
4 To develop an understanding of basic economic terminology, the tools of economic analysis and the ability to use and apply them correctly in particular situations.
5 To develop a basic economic numeracy and literacy and the ability to handle simple data.
6 To develop the ability to identify and discriminate among differing sources of information.
7 To acquire and develop the ability to distinguish between facts and value judgements in economic issues.

ASSESSMENT OBJECTIVES

Candidates should be able:

1 to demonstrate recall of knowledge in relation to a specified syllabus content;
2 to demonstrate an ability to use this knowledge in verbal, numerical, diagrammatic, graphical and pictorial form;
3 to demonstrate an ability to explain and apply appropriate terminology, concepts and elementary theories;
4 to select, analyse, interpret and apply data;
5 to distinguish between evidence and opinion, make reasoned judgements and communicate them in an accurate and logical manner.

The relationship between the Assessment Objectives and the components of the Scheme of Assessment is shown in the following grid.

Assessment Objectives (as listed above)	Paper 1	Paper 2 Section A	Section B	Coursework	Weighting of Assessment Objectives
1 and 2	18	6	6	15	30%
3	10	10	20		25%
4	12	24	4		25%
5			10	25	20%
Marks for each component	40	80		40	100%

SCHEME OF ASSESSMENT

	Duration	Weighting
Paper 1	1 hour	25%
Paper 2	2 hours	50%
Coursework	–	25%

Paper 1 (1 hour)
Candidates must answer *all* questions. The paper will consist of 40 multiple-choice items based on the entire syllabus. [40 marks]
   Calculators may be used in the examination room.

Paper 2 (2 hours)
Candidates must answer *all* questions in Section A and *two* questions in Section B.
Section A will consist of an actual situation or situations (for example, a report, a table of data, a graph, a photograph) which tests economic comprehension. [40 marks]
Section B Candidates must answer *two* questions out of five questions set. [40 marks]
   Calculators may be used in the examination room.

Coursework [40 marks]
(a) Candidates must attempt *three* units (topics) chosen from the five topics pre-
      scribed (see below). These topics will be reviewed every three years. Centres
      are invited to submit topics for consideration.
         It should be borne in mind that coursework is 25% of the total assessment,
      and each unit should be capable of being completed within not more than 1000
      words.
(b) (i)   Sources of published information must be stated and a log of visits, surveys
           and interviews should be included in the study, where appropriate.
      (ii) Photographs, newspaper cuttings, diagrams, maps, graphs, tables, tapes,
           videos may be included where they are relevant to the topic.
(c) Each unit (topic) will be marked out of a total of 40 marks (total 120 marks)
      which will be reduced to a final total of 40 marks.
         Teachers must indicate clearly how the total marks for each unit of
      coursework is arrived at using the following sub-totals:

Collection and presentation of relevant data	[15 marks]
Analysis, interpretation and evaluation of data collected	[25 marks]

COURSEWORK

Centres must choose three of the topics marked by ★ for submission of Coursework.
Others are given as a guide to topics which are appropriate for study.

1 ★Using local newspapers, do a survey of second-hand cars. What factors do
   advertisers consider important to stress? What factors do you consider determine the prices of second-hand cars?
2 ★A local study of part of a town, a village or the area around the school classifying
   business functions and types and explaining their presence and importance to
   the community.
3 ★A diary following an economic issue, using cuttings and with comments e.g.
   a wage claim, factory closure.
4 A survey of local house prices. Explanation of the factors which influence
   supply, demand and price.

5 *The local authority budget. Briefly consider how the authority finances and spends its budget and comment on its priorities. Take a sample of people in your neighbourhood (e.g. wage-earner, unemployed worker, pensioner) and evaluate the effects of the budget on individuals.

6 Study of a local firm/industry following a visit and explaining its locational features, importance to the local/national economy. **(Exemplar 1 attached to specimen questions.)**

7 *Shopping basket survey. Take a sample of ten well-known branded items and cost them in a local small shop, a voluntary retail chain and a national supermarket. Record and comment on the results

8 Work out the costs of running a freezer taking all aspects into consideration. **(Exemplar 2 attached to specimen questions.)**

9 Record, present and comment on the movement in prices of some commodity, e.g. livestock, gold, coffee, over a three-month period.

10 Survey the prices of some fruits, vegetables and fish in a local market over the summer term. Account for the variations in price of similar items.

Reproduced by permission of the Midland Examining Group

Physics

INTRODUCTION

This Physics syllabus is designed to provide students with knowledge and awareness of the physical world relevant to those who wish to continue their studies to a higher level, to those who require Physics in a vocational context, and also to those who will not pursue the subject beyond this level. It is intended, therefore, that candidates who have followed this syllabus will have had the opportunity to see Physics within the overall framework of the physical world and as a contribution to life in a modern society. While not neglecting the academic rigour of the subject, the applications of Physics within the context of other Pure and Applied Sciences, of Engineering, and of Craft, Design and Technology together with the social and environmental aspects should be emphasised whenever possible. The need for candidates to be involved in a wide range of experimental work is also essential.

AIMS

A course based on this syllabus should enable the following to be achieved:

1 to stimulate and sustain an interest in, and an enjoyment of, Physics and its applications;

2 to promote awareness and understanding of the social, economic, environmental, and other implications of Physics;

3 to show that Physics is a coherent and developing framework of knowledge, based on fundamental theories of the structure and processes of the physical world;

4 to provide a basic knowledge and understanding of the principles and applications of Physics which contribute to the quality of life in a technologically based society

5 to provide a worthwhile educational experience for all, whether or not they are intending to study Physics beyond GCSE level;

71

6   to provide an appropriate body of knowledge, understanding, and skills for:
    (a) those not intending to study the subject further;
    (b) those who will undertake further studies in Physics;
    (c) those who will study subjects or take up careers for which a Physics
         background is relevant;
7   to develop the skills of observation, experimentation, processing and inter-
    pretation of data, evaluation of evidence, and formulation of generalisations and
    models;
8   to encourage candidates to apply, qualitatively and quantitatively, their knowledge
    and understanding of physical principles to familiar and unfamiliar situations;
9   to ensure that candidates:
    (a) can follow instructions;
    (b) understand the need for, and comply with, safety precautions;
10 to foster relevant communication skills.

ASSESSMENT OBJECTIVES

The examination will assess a candidate's ability to:

1   know and recall: facts, vocabulary, conventions, physical quantities and units in
    which they are measured, requirements for safety, names and uses of common
    measuring instruments;
2   show understanding of:
    (a) definitions and laws;
    (b) concepts, theories, and models;
    (c) information presented in various forms;
    (d) the use, applications, and implications (including social and environmental
         aspects) of physical facts and principles;
    (e) safety procedures;
3   show with reference to familiar and unfamiliar situations that they can:
    (a) use given formulae;
    (b) apply laws and principles;
    (c) explain phenomena in terms of theories and models;
    (d) solve problems by designing, conducting, and interpreting the results or
         simple experiments;
    (e) translate information from one form to another;
    (f) extract and evaluate information from that which is given;
    (g) present information in a precise and logical form;
    (h) recognise mistakes, misconceptions, unreliable data, and assumptions;
    (i) draw conclusions and formulate generalisations.

ASSESSMENT PATTERN

General Level	Candidates are eligible for the award of Grades C to G
Paper 1 Objective Test 45 minutes 28% of the total marks	Forty multiple-choice items, testing the objectives shown below. Responses to be made on the Group's Answer Sheet.

Paper 2 Written Paper 1 hour 15 minutes 42% of the total marks	Approximately twelve short-answer and structured questions with no choice of question, testing the objectives shown below. Answers to be written on the Question Paper.
Paper 3 A teacher assessment of practical work 30% of the total marks	Testing the objectives shown below.

Candidates who enter for the General Level will not be eligible for the award of Grade A or B.

Extended Level	Candidates are eligible for the award of Grades A to G
Paper 1 Objective Test 45 minutes 20% of the total marks	Forty multiple-choice items, testing the objectives shown below. Responses to be made on the Group's Answer Sheet.
Paper 2 Written Paper 1 hour 15 minutes 25% of the total marks	Approximately twelve short-answer and structured questions with no choice of question, testing the objectives shown below. Answers to be written on the Question Paper.
Paper 3 A teacher assessment of practical work 30% of the total marks	Testing the objectives shown below.
Paper 4 1 hour 15 minutes 25% of the total marks	Approximately seven structured and free-response questions with no choice of question, testing the objectives shown below. Answers to be written in a separate Answer Booklet.

In addition to achieving an appropriate standard overall, to be awarded Grade A or Grade B candidates will have to reach the appropriate standards in Paper 4. The grade obtained by a candidate at General Level will not be lowered as a result of a poor performance in Paper 4.

Papers 1, 2 and 3 are identical at both Levels. Papers 1 and 2, however, carry smaller percentages of the total marks at the Extended Level than at the General Level.

A candidate may carry forward the mark obtained on the teacher-assessed component to subsequent examinations.

Relationship between Objectives, Assessment, and Subject Content

	(a) Questions will be set on any part of the Subject Content in any paper except where specific restrictions to

73

Paper 4 are shown in the Subject Content. Papers 1 – 3 overall will therefore aim to provide a complete syllabus coverage.

(b) The objectives may be grouped as follows:

Objective 1	Recall
Objective 2(a) – (e)	Understanding
Objective 3(a) – (i)	Processes

The relationship between the grouped objectives and the components of the assessment is shown in the table below.

General Level

Paper	Recall (%)	Understanding (%)	Processes (%)
1	40	30	30
2	30	30	40
3			100
Overall for Papers 1–3	24	21	55

Extended Level

Paper	Recall (%)	Understanding (%)	Processes (%)
4	10	20	70
Overall for Papers 1–4	17	18	65

Reproduced by permission of the Southern Examining Group

GCSE – a summary

The objectives of any course for 14- to 16-year-olds are to give pupils a good general education suitable for a job, a training scheme, a further education course, A-levels or any other alternative at 16-plus. What is important about GCSE is that pupils who pass one or more subjects can go directly on to one of these courses or into a job, knowing that they have received a good grounding in that subject during the two-year course. In addition, the assessment of their work and progress is likely to be more detailed and helpful for employers and for colleges.

The GCSE examination is still developing. It is a major educational change and it is likely to last for many years. Pupils, parents and employers therefore need to know about its objectives, syllabuses and methods of assessment, and it is the duty of schools as well as of the government and the six Examining Groups to undertake this work. Parents, if they are not fully aware of a school's policies on GCSE, should contact the school and ask for information about how the examination is being implemented.

GCSE Examining Groups

Joint Council for the GCSE
Netherton House, 23-29 Marsh Street, Bristol BS1 4BP

London and East Anglian Group
Stewart House, 32 Russell Square, London WC1B 5DN

Midland Examining Group
Purbeck House, Purbeck Road, Cambridge CB2 2PU

Northern Examining Association
12 Harter Street, Manchester M1 6HL

Southern Examining Group
Stage Hill House, Guildford, Surrey GU2 5XJ

Welsh Joint Education Committee
245 Western Avenue, Cardiff CF5 2YX

CHAPTER 7

THE CERTIFICATE OF PRE-VOCATIONAL EDUCATION (CPVE)

FROM 1985, when it was introduced, the Certificate of Pre-Vocational Education (CPVE) has been available for young people in the 16-plus age-group in England, Wales and Northern Ireland. Other Foundation courses were developed side by side with CPVE. Then, in September 1991, it was announced that CPVE and the Foundation programmes would be incorporated into a new qualification, the Diploma of Vocational Education.

What does this all mean? CPVE was designed as a course that would link school-based academic programmes with the world of work. CPVE, which is administered by a Joint Board of the City and Guilds of London Institute (CGLI) and the Business and Technician Education Council (BTEC), is built around work experience and the skills needed at work. Students learn practical, vocational and social skills, working at their own-pace programmes or arranged and supervised by a tutor.

In its first six years, CPVE provided a basic course. But times change, and so do educational ideas and plans. In the first place, work experience placements are difficult to find: Britain's economic troubles, translated into companies that have cut staffing levels to the bone, have meant that firms cannot provide enough places to meet schools' needs and demands, and cannot offer thorough supervision of the students who are on work-experience placements.

The Diploma in Vocational Education has yet to be implemented. Much planning and discussion has to be done before it can be properly introduced: in the immediate future, therefore, CPVE will continue in many schools as a course for 16- to 17-year-olds who anticipate going into a job at 16 or into a Youth Training programme.

The objectives, content and certification of the award are described clearly in a leaflet published by the Joint Board from which these extracts have been taken.

What is CPVE?

'CPVE is awarded on completion of a one-year programme (or two years if combined with A-levels) which employers helped to design. The programme equips students for adult and working life. Young people have the opportunity to acquire basic skills and experience in a work-related context. They are given help to develop the attitudes, knowledge, personal and social maturity which they need and which employers want. CPVE courses involve activity-based learning, i.e. learning by doing. Each course includes work experience integrated with other learning activities.

'The aim is to encourage young people to develop the skills, knowledge and attitudes that are essential for successful adult life. This is the "core" of the CPVE programme.

'CPVE students learn practical skills such as how to operate a computer keyboard. They learn basic numeracy, how to express themselves clearly and how to work as part of a team. The CPVE programme also provides time for community activities, leisure, recreation and reflection.

'CPVE is available to 16- and 17-year-olds with a positive wish to achieve their full potential. Students normally embark on CPVE immediately after completing compulsory secondary education. Although CPVE is designed to provide a practical approach to education, using young people's interests to encourage learning, it is not solely for those who fail to achieve on traditional academic courses. It can, therefore, be combined with A-levels.

'In addition to the Certificate itself, every student is able to offer an employer a detailed profile which records his or her achievements as they have happened and a summary of experience and activities. Profile statements relating to the "core" or basic skill areas are selected from a "bank" of possible statements, thus ensuring a uniformity of approach and national standards.'

Who is CPVE for?

CPVE is intended for students of 16-plus in England, Wales and

Northern Ireland who have not yet decided which specific career or educational path they intend to follow. The main idea is that for a year the students on a CPVE course can study a range of subjects and topics as a 'pre-entry course' prior to taking a vocational course closely linked to a career or job. CPVE, therefore, is for 16- to 17-year-olds. It is for a wide range of students, and certainly not only for those who fail the traditional academic courses of GCSE. It has been designed for anyone still unsure of the career direction he or she wishes to take.

CPVE is attractive to the non-A-level student. It is based on practical skills so is most suitable for students who do not want to take an academic course leading to A-levels. At 17, after taking the CPVE qualification, students are equipped to go into a job, with or without further education, or they could continue in full-time education, going on to a vocational course leading to a City and Guilds or BTEC qualification or join a Youth Training programme, or take an A-level course.

Where is CPVE offered?

CPVE courses are provided in schools and colleges with 16-plus students, i.e. secondary schools, sixth-form colleges and tertiary colleges (these are colleges that provide the full range of courses for 16- to 18-year-olds, including A-levels, City and Guilds, BTEC and other awards). In addition, CPVE is now part of the work of most colleges of further education. In some cases a group of up to six local schools have formed a consortium with a local college of further education to offer a wide range of suitable courses.

Links with work

CPVE was not designed purely by educationalists – employers played a significant part in drafting CPVE. One advantage of CPVE for an employer is that students are older, more mature and more aware of both their needs and their potential when they leave CPVE and look for a job. Secondly, during CPVE they have a period of work experience which provides a realistic view of what is needed in a job. The methods of assessment for CPVE (which include profiles of a student's achievements) are designed to help an employer by giving evidence of what the student can or cannot do. CPVE can also be taken as the first year of a two-year Youth Training programme which strengthens its work-related relevance.

What is studied within CPVE?

CPVE has three main elements. These are:
- 'core' studies
- vocational studies
- additional studies.

Core studies

In the 'core' element, the following ten areas are studied:

Personal and career development
Thinking and talking about one's personal needs and interests; careers and jobs, and where to find out about them; family life; the rights and responsibilities of citizens.

Industrial, social and environmental studies
The workings of modern industry and society, and an introduction to basic economics, politics and the study of the environment.

Communication
Listening, speaking, reading, and writing skills; communication at work.

Numeracy
The maths needed for jobs and everyday life – numbers, decimals, percentages.

Social skills
Working in groups; working alone; listening and responding; judging and understanding how people behave, act and respond; interview techniques; dealing with customers.

Science and technology
The courses do not repeat school physics and chemistry but are planned to show the applications of science and technology to real problems in practical situations.

Information technology
Students are given 'hands-on', practical experience of computers to show them the many ways by which computers and other forms of information technology affect our everyday lives both at work and in leisure activities.

Creative development
This may include the design implications involved in the manufacture of a car or a domestic appliance; and participation in creative activities such as plays, magazines, news-sheets, music, art and dance.

Practical skills
Using materials, equipment, tools and computers to carry out practical tasks.

Problem-solving
Students are expected to cope with particular situations by a structured approach to problem-solving. The course sets tasks which require students to devise plans to tackle personal problems, set targets, identify what is needed to reach those targets and take the decisions necessary to bring about an acceptable conclusion.

The areas covered by the core are thought by the planners of CPVE to be essential for everyone taking the course. If the core is taught in an enterprising and imaginative way, using materials, equipment, practical activities and workshops, it is very stimulating indeed. But, like any course at school or college, it is the quality of the teaching which determines whether students think it is any good or not.

Vocational studies

Within CPVE courses there are five broad categories of vocational studies:

Business and administrative services
Industrial and commercial organisations and local and central government. Among the subjects are advertising, selling, accounting, and so on, and the roles of people who are concerned with these tasks – managers, sales staff, storekeepers, accounts clerks, civil servants, travel agents, and so on.

Technical services

The functions of technical services, which include designing, planning, giving customer advice, training, using machines, writing, keyboarding. Students also examine the roles of people working in these areas such as engineers, systems analysts, telephonists, typists and computer operators.

Production

Having studied manufacturing as a general topic, students can specialise in one or more of these areas: textiles, plastics, leather, rubber, metals, wood, ceramics, paper, minerals, plant, vehicles, shipping, electrical systems, food, packaging, furniture, consumer goods and other industries. They find out about large- and small-scale manufacturing, and look at the work of people such as toolmakers, dressmakers, designers and many other jobs.

Distribution

Students examine retail and wholesale distribution and the various ways they are organised, such as cash and carry, warehousing, department stores, multiple stores, corner shops and direct selling. As in the other categories, they find out about such jobs as sales, checkout, display, buying, personnel work, stock-keeping, clerical and accounting work.

Services to people

In this, as in the other categories, there is an emphasis on 'activity-learning', and students are expected to conduct local surveys of services, which will include schools, residential homes, medical services, community provision, home helps and work with the disabled. The functions looked at include caring, assisting, minding and supporting young, old and sick people, and the jobs examined would include nurses, mothers' helps, youth workers, dental staff and therapists. Nor is the use of leisure and recreation neglected, for a student's personal study could include team games, clubs, music, camping, sailing, gardening and local entertainment.

Levels of learning

Because CPVE is a pre-vocational, pre-job scheme, students are not restricted to studying only one of the categories. On the other hand, they could not study *all* these activities and jobs within one or two years, and so students specialise, learning about one or two vocational areas.

Students are expected to work at their own pace and the practical projects are expected to help them apply the core skills and knowledge. Many students lose interest in subjects such as physics and chemistry because they are taught in separate compartments, so great emphasis is put on integration. In CPVE courses, the idea is that the industry, the job, and the student's own investigations dictate how subjects such as these are used.

In addition, there are three levels of learning within the vocational studies. These allow the undecided student an opportunity to find out more about various occupations, while those who are more committed have the chance to specialise. The three levels of learning are:

- introductory
- exploratory
- preparatory.

Introductory
Students find out, in the broadest terms, about the way an industry is organised, the various roles within it, legislation relevant to it, and so on. Then, if their interest has been aroused and they wish to pursue the subject area further, they can move on to the exploratory level.

Exploratory
This provides a more detailed insight into the jobs and careers available within the field and also examines in greater detail specific functions such as marketing (from *business and administrative services*) or simple programming (from *technical services*).

Preparatory
This is for those students who have pretty well decided where they want to specialise and are starting to acquire specific competencies – as a prelude to progressing into that career area through employment or Youth Training.

To a large extent, students can work at their own pace. Some do not proceed beyond the introductory level. Others move rapidly through from the introductory to the exploratory level and then on to the preparatory level – at which point they take learning modules which are closely allied to existing City and Guilds and BTEC occupational schemes. The emphasis within this progression is entirely on students negotiating with their teachers to agree on which module (or group of modules) is appropriate as a next step.

Additional studies

Additional studies can take up to 25 per cent of the available time on a CPVE programme. There is no requirement to take additional studies, and the time can be spent on the core programme or on vocational studies.

In some cases the college or school may decide to use the additional studies time for one or two GCSE or A-level subjects. Equally, however, the time could be spent on sports and games, on community activities, or on artistic or recreational projects. Each institution is allowed to make its own arrangements for additional studies.

Work experience

Work experience also has an important part to play in CPVE. A minimum of two weeks' work experience is essential. The student joins a company or organisation for at least two weeks, and sees at first hand how it operates. A major problem with work experience, however, is that there are more students than places, for many schemes (CPVE, City and Guilds, BTEC and sandwich degree-course programmes) are all looking for work-experience placements. Facing up to this problem, some schools and colleges have devised 'simulated' work-experience programmes which in many cases provide well-planned alternatives.

Assessment

There are two kinds of CPVE assessment: formative and summative.

The formative assessment programme is drawn up by the schools and colleges and is approved by the Joint Board for CPVE. Students' work is judged on a regular basis as the course proceeds, and the results are made known to students so that the information can help them with the next step in their programme.

Summative assessment is recorded at the end of the CPVE course. National criteria in the form of a 'bank' of descriptive statements have been drawn up. Students are given a certificate which sums up their achievements during the scheme. The certificate refers to all ten areas of the core, together with work done on the preparatory modules.

Experience so far has shown that summative assessment is particularly useful for students seeking jobs. Employers like to see a statement which gives a broader picture than the dismissive 'pass' or 'fail'.

Furthermore, at the end of the course, a student should have a portfolio of his or her work which can be taken along to job interviews as proof of both academic and vocational achievements.

What is CPVE worth?

Because of its flexibility, CPVE is able both to equip young people with a core of essential transferable skills and to give them a taste of a variety of occupational and industrial experiences. It is an ideal scheme for students who feel the need for a further period of full-time education but who also want to start building bridges to their future careers.

As indicated at the start of this chapter, CPVE is an *introductory* course, which may well lead to jobs and further training. The course tackles practical skills head-on. It also devotes a generous amount of time to maths and to English language skills. The vocational studies part of the course describes how industry works, and also describes some of the jobs within industry and commerce that young people should know about. There are opportunities in most programmes to obtain some training in computing and in other practical skills. There is also the opportunity to look at a college of further education's full course programme, without a firm commitment to any one course. CPVE keeps students' options open a little longer.

Those employers who understand CPVE are impressed by it, but many employers simply do not know about or understand CPVE. However, when combined with Youth Training, they are much more knowledgeable and appreciative of its value. Students appear to like the courses, in particular the links between school and further education, the work experience, the sampling of possible employment opportunities, and the activity and practical-based learning ideas. It has been a useful experiment, a preliminary to the new scheme leading to the Diploma in Vocational Education which is to be developed and instituted in the 1990s.

CHAPTER 8

THE TECHNICAL AND VOCATIONAL EDUCATION INITIATIVE (TVEI) AND VOCATIONAL STUDIES

IN 1982 the Prime Minister invited the Manpower Services Commission (MSC) to launch a major new educational idea, the Technical and Vocational Education Initiative (TVEI). The first projects in England and Wales began in September 1983 and a further group (which included five in Scotland) started in the autumn of 1984. Between 1984 and 1991 many more projects were initiated. Now, all LEAs offer some form of TVEI, with over 60,000 students involved in the scheme.

TVEI is a four-year programme for 14- to 18-year-old students. It is largely organised through projects that involve technical skills – using machines, learning about computers, designing and making things. It is, however, also vocational, which means the projects are related closely to real jobs and are devised to give an insight into technical work, careers and courses.

The background

The school curriculum has been constantly developing, influenced by changes in people's thinking, in industry and in the needs of young people. Now it is to be designed into a National Curriculum. Before the advent of TVEI, the government asked Local Education Authorities and schools to think again about their policies for the curriculum. At the same time there were loud demands from industry and commerce that the school curriculum should be more relevant to the world of work, with more active student-centred styles of learning. *Better Schools*, a government document published in 1985, described the government's aims of reaching an agreement with Local Education Authorities about how changes could be made to the school curriculum.

TVEI started before *Better Schools* was published, but had the same objective: to make the school curriculum more suited to the needs of working life. Another major factor in planning TVEI and later changes to secondary school courses (such as the introduction of GCSE) has been the massive reshaping of British industry. For example, the introduction of sophisticated new electronic technology in most industries has led to a demand for higher levels of skill and knowledge. In the future many more people will be employed in non-manual occupations than in the past. Young people need to know about computer technology and need to have skills that can be added to as they grow older and as their jobs change to suit new industrial developments.

The anxiety about unemployment is another important factor. Manpower analysts point out that the better qualified and trained a person is, the better are his or her employment prospects. There are vacancies and shortages of key staff in technological areas, notably computing, electronics and other science-based industries. TVEI, as with CPVE and Youth Training, puts considerable emphasis on technical and science-based skills related to work experience. It is felt that this kind of 16-plus training is better suited to the market-place.

Another influence on the origins of TVEI was the view held by the government and many economic analysts that Britain's salvation as an industrial and commercial nation is dependent on people showing more enterprise. A readiness for people to strike out on their own, to start up new businesses, to become self-employed and thus to be in control of their own careers and business destinies is regarded as being highly desirable.

These are all very ambitious objectives for TVEI, a scheme that at present caters for about ten per cent of the 14 to 18 age-group. But, nevertheless, TVEI is an influential scheme and, together with other trends in school and in further education, indicates the way in which the education and training of young people is moving.

Direction and control

As an indication of the government's determination to change the pattern of secondary and further education, MSC, now the Training, Enterprise and Education Directorate (TEED), was invited to take the initiative in setting up TVEI by working with Local Education Authorities and consulting the Department of Education and Science, traditionally the voice directing education. TEED is advised by a national steering group which draws its membership from education and industry, and has assessors from the DES, HM Inspectorate, the Welsh Office and the Scottish Office. The national steering group has produced national criteria and guidelines for the scheme, but, as with other aspects of the school curriculum, the precise details were left to the Local Education Authorities.

Although TVEI was first thought of as a means of bringing technical courses back into schools, it has now become a mechanism for broadening the curriculum. TEED is paying for TVEI extension schemes as a method of improving the training of young people.

The content of TVEI

TVEI projects have been devised and managed by the Local Education Authorities. They are all different, testing different approaches to organising and managing technical and vocational education. All the projects, however, must:

- be a two-year course of technical and vocational education starting at 14 years of age
- include work experience
- be for pupils across the whole ability range, i.e. for those who are preparing for GCSE, A-level and other exams as well as those who are not on examination courses
- be for both boys and girls
- lead to nationally recognised qualifications: TVEI projects can lead to GCSE, Royal Society of Arts, BTEC, City and Guilds, A-level and other qualifications
- be organised within existing schools and colleges
- be optional: the participation of young people in the scheme is voluntary
- include careers advice and personal counselling.

Course objectives

The general objective of the scheme is to enrich and widen the curriculum in ways that will help those taking part to prepare for work and adult life. TVEI is designed to assist in the development of individual initiatives related to technical competence. This is an ambitious aim for the scheme and, as yet, it is too early to say whether it is being achieved. However, the reactions of students and teachers involved with TVEI programmes indicate a high level of approval. Of course, new ideas generally lead to initial enthusiasm, so TVEI is no different in this respect from other educational initiatives, but the evidence so far from teachers, employers and pupils is that the projects have introduced new ideas to the curriculum and that the students emerging from the scheme appear to be well prepared for further vocational training or for jobs. It is apparent that the approaches and techniques of TVEI (practical projects, student-centred learning, work experience, vocational training) are influencing the ways in which GCSE, City and Guilds and BTEC courses are being developed.

The curriculum

The majority of TVEI projects require students to take certain 'core' subjects. These are usually English language, mathematics, science, religious education, physical education and some element of humanities such as history, geography or social studies. However, there are a few projects which allow a relatively free choice within a wide band of subjects.

The core subjects can be taken as far as GCSE. The rest of the TVEI programme rests on the voluntary principle since the criteria for the whole scheme require pupils to decide whether they should join a project or not.

However, for those who do opt to join a TVEI project, there are different varieties of structure. A popular method of organisation has been a modular programme. Modules are short units of learning: a student can choose different modules and combinations of modules and build up a personal programme over the first two years of the course to meet his or her particular needs.

Options

Within the idea of a balanced curriculum, the pilot projects have an extensive set of options. All projects offer technology. In most cases this means computing, office technology (typing, word processing, the use of a desk-top computer), and basic electronics, engineering or design technology. Almost all projects also contain craft and design subjects, such as design applied to graphics, fashion and dress, furniture, consumer goods and packaging. And all have a business studies course which describes how companies and organisations are formed, how they function, and how they market and sell their products. Most projects include community care – the care of the young, handicapped, elderly and sick. Most projects also have a local studies option – perhaps agriculture, or local industry, leisure studies for holiday and tourist interests, fishing, and so on.

The following list gives some idea of the varying options available within many of the TVEI projects:

- engineering
- craft technology – metalwork, woodwork, textiles, printing, photography
- fashion design and manufacture
- business studies
- computing, information technology and computer graphics
- rural studies, agriculture, horticulture
- electronics
- languages – especially the commercial uses of foreign languages
- graphics, design, and arts subjects such as music, fine art, dance, theatre arts
- community care
- nautical studies
- leisure and recreation studies
- construction work – building, bricklaying, planning layouts of gardens
- food studies – food science, the preparation of food, the food industry
- home economics
- media studies including photography, video, drama, television studies
- retail trade including all aspects of the work of shops and stores, direct selling, advertising, distribution.

Many of these subjects appear on traditional school and college timetables. The differences between other courses and TVEI projects are that a pupil's studies are linked both to practical projects and to work experience placements. For instance, if a pupil is taking a modular course in retail distribution, a practical project could be to study the methods of attracting customers, selling goods and dealing with all the supporting services in a large store. In addition, the work experience placement is likely to be in a store, to give relevance to the classwork.

Examples

The following examples are from advisory documents about TVEI. Such projects vary widely from one Local Education Authority to another, often according to the area's industries and opportunities.

In the first example, students select several new options, one from each of blocks 1 to 6. All students also take the common core elements of English, mathematics, physical education, moral education and general studies and attend one period of assembly (blocks 7 to 12).

The second example gives details of a new programme shown as blocks 2a to 5a.

All students take English, mathematics, physical education and recreation (blocks 6 to 9). All students take creative and aesthetic studies. For students following the new programme, this forms part of a wider programme which also includes computer studies (block 5a).

Students choosing the new programme follow four 'taster' units (each of twenty weeks' duration) in art, technical studies, home economics and business studies during the first year of the programme. In addition, they select two options, one from block 1 and one from either of blocks 2 or 3. Taster units in home economics and business studies may be selected from option block 2a or 3a according to which option is chosen in block 2 or 3. For example, students wishing to study chemistry (block 2) should select taster units from block 3a. In the second year, students choose a range of modular options providing progression from the taster unit; these are built upon in successive years. Students not following the new programme select options from blocks 1 to 4.

Options 60%	1	Art, light crafts, biology, chemistry, European studies, food studies and catering, music, information technology for business studies	1
	2	Biology, business studies, German, design technology, French, information technology, needlecraft, social studies, typing, office practice	2
	3	Photography, biology, French, geography, physics, science for living	3
	4	Art, physics, chemistry, typing/office practice, control technology, English literature, history, life skills, home economics (3 periods) and PE (1 period)	4
	5	Business studies, design technology, technical drawing, community studies, history, home economics, home management, information technology, Latin, religious education, typing/office practice	5
	6	Art, drama, design technology, French, geography, technical drawing, home management, typing/office practice, information technology for business studies	6
Common core 40%	7	Assembly	7
	8	General studies	8
	9	Moral education	9
	10	Physical education	10
	11	Mathematics	11
	12	English	12

Option 50%	1	History, geography, modern studies, social studies		1	
	2	Chemistry, Italian, art and design, economics, fashion and fabrics, science	Business studies	2a	
			Home economics		
	3	French, technical drawing, accounts, science	Home economics	3a	
			Business studies		
	4	Physics, biology, craft, food and nutrition, secretarial studies	Art	4a	
			Technical studies		
Core 8%	5	Creative and aesthetic studies	Creative and aesthetic including computer studies	5a	
Common core 42%	6	Recreation		6	
	7	Physical education		7	
	8	Mathematics		8	
	9	English		9	

TVEI for 16- to 18-year-olds

The previous examples illustrate the first two years of a TVEI programme. A full four-year programme is now common to all projects.

The problems of designing a suitable programme for 16- to 18-year-olds have been substantial because within the 200 to 300 students on any one project there are the same number of individual needs.

In general, the common core programmes continue into the second phase so that students maintain their studies in English, maths, science and the other components. Students can take A-levels in these or any other subject(s) as part of the TVEI 16 to 18 programme, and/or they can take City and Guilds, BTEC and RSA courses. Because of their earlier studies at 14 to 16 years of age, some students have been able to proceed to A-levels in engineering science, electronics, design technology, theatre studies, surveying, accounting, computer studies, communication studies and other subjects which are not traditional A-level subjects.

Some Local Education Authorities have complex arrangements so that TVEI students can combine GCSEs or A-levels with BTEC and City and Guilds courses. Among the popular options have been City and Guilds courses in engineering, commercial studies, business studies and computing. Among BTEC modular course programmes are engineering studies, motor vehicle studies, construction, automobile engineering, information technology and many other topics. The BTEC courses are based on the unit-programme of BTEC courses, and students either take Level 1 units or their studies give exemption from Level 1. Other courses available and included in some TVEI projects are Royal Society of Arts (RSA) certificate courses in computer literacy, typing, information technology, clerical studies, and so on.

In addition, some projects have incorporated CPVE (Certificate of Pre-Vocational Education) programmes into courses for 16- to 18-year-olds. Finally, some pupils have left school at 16, entering a job or going on to a Youth Training programme.

Records of achievement and profiles

As well as being prepared for nationally recognised qualifications, all students on TVEI projects receive a written record of achievement on completion of their studies. This record describes the qualifications obtained and records other aspects of the student's progress, such as what was done during work experience and other non-examinable work.

Some Local Education Authorities are well advanced with 'profiles'. A profile is a detailed statement of what a student has done and has achieved, not simply a pass/fail record, as in some traditional methods of assessment. Profiles, for instance, record aspects of a student's record in the following:

- physical skills
- personal attitudes – determination, perseverance, patience
- confidence and willingness to tackle new tasks
- co-operation with other people by working in a team
- initiative, especially in showing fresh ideas
- personal relationships – friendly, helpful, and so on
- communication skills such as speaking clearly, listening, telephoning, following instructions, reading and writing

● self-reliance – being able to take decisions and act on one's own.

The chart below shows a profile used on one project. In this case, the assessor ticks the box; in others the assessor writes a sentence or two about each personal quality.

Relationships and attitudes

Co-operation	Very co-operative	❏
	Very helpful	❏
	Reasonably helpful	❏
	Occasionally uncooperative	❏
	Sometimes difficult; can be a source of trouble	❏
Friendship	Capable of friendships	❏
	Quite popular; makes friends easily	❏
	Has an average group of friends	❏
	Has difficulty establishing relationships	❏
	Very shy and nervous; avoids other people	❏
Personality	Very strong personality	❏
	Fairly self-assertive	❏
	Dominant only when occasion demands	❏
	Usually prefers to avoid limelight	❏
	Passive, almost negative	❏
Dependability	Exceptionally reliable	❏
	Usually dependable	❏
	Reasonably dependable	❏
	Some doubt about dependability	❏
	Unreliable	❏
Initiative	Quick to seize opportunities and develop them	❏
	Fairly resourceful; can make own decisions	❏
	Can take initiative but prefers guidance	❏
	Inclined to play safe	❏
	Lets opportunities slip by; little initiative	❏
Resilience	Exceptionally resilient; copes easily under stress	❏
	Usually takes problems in stride	❏
	Manages fairly well under pressure	❏
	Does not cope well under pressure	❏
	May go to pieces under pressure	❏

Profiles also take into account other initiatives such as:

- Duke of Edinburgh Award scheme participation
- swimming and life-saving awards
- music, art, drama or other arts certificates, awards or accomplishments
- athletic and sporting awards or membership of clubs
- Scout and Guide achievements
- first-aid certificates
- any special school commendations, such as appearing in a school play, musical or team event
- club membership of any kind
- records of any special individual achievement.

A profile containing all these elements gives an employer a much more informative and balanced view of a potential employee than the pass/fail or 'fair'/'tries hard' kind of report.

Work experience and employer contacts

An important part of TVEI is its links with business and industrial companies and work experience.

Work experience means that pupils go out to companies to spend time observing adult workers and doing work themselves. When it is not possible to spend several weeks with employers, project organisers arrange visits, work observation or 'simulations'. This means that a special scheme is set up in a training centre or the college and students simulate or copy 'real-life' situations. One successful method of doing this has been through 'mini-enterprises': this is where the group of students works out a plan for a business enterprise – making, selling or distributing something, or providing a service.

Vocational studies

Another aspect of the present Government's reform of vocational education can be seen in the decision to relax the rule that schools cannot offer BTEC courses. From 1992, schools will be able to prepare and enter pupils for BTEC First Diploma awards in vocational subjects. (These courses have traditionally been at further education colleges.) To allow schools to offer the First Diploma alongside or instead of A-levels is evidence of renewed Government efforts to raise the status of vocational studies.

At least one-in-ten schools and colleges initially interested in the pilot courses from the Business and Technician Education Council and the City and Guilds of London Institute backed off after a few months. But, far from being disappointed, the vocational exam bodies are surprised more schools did not drop out, given the number of initiatives still arising out of the Education Reform Act.

New courses were called for in the autumn of 1991 with more vocational skills training. The Certificate of Pre-Vocational Education is to be revamped and sixth-forms will be allowed to offer BTEC First courses and City and Guilds would have sole responsibility for new foundation courses for 14- to 16-year-olds. Schools lacking resources and hi-tech equipment for BTEC First Diplomas have been urged to form consortia with FE colleges. Despite misgivings that moves to give colleges their independence would kill off co-operation, over 17 consortia came forward in the first stage. Predictably, applications for business and finance dominated, though other courses were popular: science, engineering, leisure and caring.

But in many ways the real challenge is for schools where courses for 14- to 16-year-olds must be accredited independently of GCSE and yet fit the National Curriculum. With extra demands including three weeks' work placement for all on the City and Guilds courses and new vocational studies geared to individual needs, it is not surprising that some schools dropped out of the early stages. However, this radical change in vocational education will gather pace, as the Education Reform Act and the National Curriculum are implemented.

CHAPTER 9

THE CITIZEN'S CHARTER AND THE PARENT'S CHARTER

THE TWO 'Charters' are blueprints for future educational policy, given that election promises are usually converted later into Acts of Parliament.

The Citizen's Charter is based on the Government's view that people should be freed from centralised and local bureaucratic control and that they should have 'rights' which ought not to be limited by officialdom.

The theory behind the Citizen's Charter is that market forces cannot always be relied upon to produce the goods, particularly when consumers have to deal with public-sector monopolies such as the National Health Service, British Rail or Local Education Authorities. The 'Charters' offer alternatives to the rigid administration of these monopolies: they are said to protect the citizen's and the parent's rights.

A feature of the Charters is information. Parents will be entitled to an annual report on their child's progress. They will be informed of the relative performance of state schools, including successes at GCSE, A-level and university/polytechnic entry.

The Charters might help parents to decide on the choice of a school. But when children are already in one, what rights do parents and citizens have then? In a way a school has a monopoly of power over its pupils. The only way that parents and children can break the monopoly is to leave school – which generally means only one thing – paying enormously for private education.

The Charters therefore tackle the problem of maintaining standards in these public-sector monopolies. It is said that British Rail may in the future be sued or claimed against if its trains don't run on time; NHS staff can be charged for neglect; inspectors will visit schools annually, inspect them and provide a written report for parents.

The content of the Charters must await more concrete proposals from the Government. In the meantime, while the present Government implements its programme of enhancing the effectiveness of parental choice, the pressure-points of the Charters are already causing changes in schools and colleges.

The Parent's Charter

One of the Government's proposals for the reform of education is to have a *Parent's Charter*. In a way, the Department of Education and Science has been preparing a Charter since the Education Reform Act of 1988. The Act encouraged openness in state schools by giving a great deal more authority to governors and required schools to incorporate parent-governors into the team. Another philosophic foundation of the Charter is to provide freedom of choice in state education, as far as this is possible in a system of neighbourhood schools. An aspect of this freedom is the encouragement given to governors and staff of a state school to opt out of local authority control and to go for grant-maintained status, by which schools are funded directly by the DES and not by the LEA. In introducing the idea of a Parent's Charter, the Education Secretary said it was meant to remedy 'the operation of schools ... which has been a mystery to the vast majority of people'.

These are some of the freedoms associated with the Charter. Critics say that the Government's educational tactics widen the gap between the privileged and the under-privileged, that grant-maintained schools are financially favoured. These schools therefore attract the most ambitious (and usually well-off) parents who approve of academic pressure on achievements in GCSE and A-level examinations. Critics say that these factors widen the gap between the grant-maintained schools and those that remain within LEA control: they argue that the Charter will lock certain schools into a cycle of decline.

All this is political argument – for and against. In this book we are trying to assess the effects of Government proposals on schools and careers guidance in the period 1992-4, that is if the Government stays in power and if it continues with its present educational policies. If these two factors are overturned a different system entirely may prevail.

Freelance inspections

Another feature of the proposed Parent's Charter is freelance school inspection. This is another radical change. At present, schools and FE colleges are inspected by Her Majesty's Inspectors (HMI) who are part of the DES, and by local inspectors employed by LEAs. The Government has proposed to reduce the 480 HMI to about 175; LEAs are free to employ and deploy local inspectors as they wish.

The Government has proposed that private companies will be allowed to compete with local authority inspectors for approval to conduct 6,000 school inspections a year. Inspection teams would include at least one person not working in education and would be expected to seek parents' views when making their report.

Furthermore, school governors would be provided with £70 million of the £135 million given to inspection and advisory services. Reports will be provided every four years and governors will have to give parents a summary of the report and explain the action they intend to take to fulfil the recommendations.

The Government will keep a register of people allowed to lead trained inspection teams and will set inspection standards. Staff on the register will themselves be inspected, and will be removed if they don't match up to requirements.

The terms of the Charter

The Parent's Charter is founded on the principle of opening schools to parent power. It guarantees information on class sizes, teaching methods, examination results, job and college destinations of leavers and other matters. The Charter has yet to be defined in a White Paper, but the main pillars of the Charter are that parents will receive five key documents.

- an annual written report on the progress of their own children
- performance tables providing information on all schools in the area. This will apply to grant-maintained schools, City Technology Colleges and independent schools as well as the local authority schools
- a short, straightforward summary of a recent inspection report from independent inspectors on the strengths and weaknesses of their child's school

- an action plan from governors on how they will tackle problem areas in the light of the inspectors' reports
- an annual report from the school's governors, prepared for discussion at their annual meeting with parents. This document will contain information about exam and National Curriculum test results for the school, truancy, school leavers' destinations, the school budget and procedures for election of parent governors.

Parents will also be able to ask for an expanded prospectus or brochure about the aims of the school and the achievements of its pupils.

The Charter will be distributed to parents in England and Wales and will also be available in main libraries and post offices, national newspapers, and so on. Local radio will carry advertisements telling parents about the Charter and how to obtain copies.

The leaflet is available in English and will shortly be available in five Asian languages as well as in Greek, Turkish and Chinese.

There may well be other implications of the Parent's Charter, not realised when this edition of *Which Subject? Which Career?* was written. The Charter may never be fully implemented; it may disappear, as opponents claim, as another example of 'educational gimmickry', lost during or after a General Election. However, as long as it is an aspect of the present Government's view of education, parent–readers of this book will be interested to see how the idea develops in the next few years.

PART 2

FURTHER AND HIGHER EDUCATION

CHAPTER 10

OPTIONS AT 16

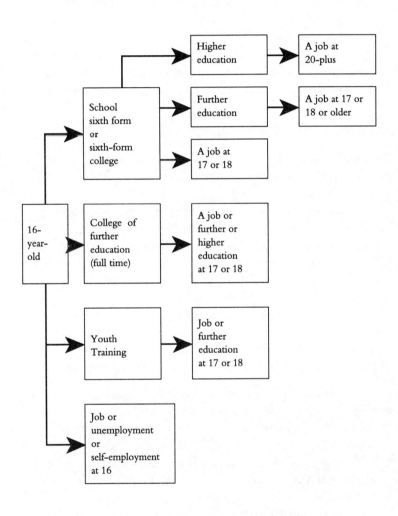

A 16-year-old can take any of the paths shown in this diagram

A 16-year-old who wants to add to his or her qualifications has a number of choices. Depending on the area and the institutions within it, one of these school-based options may be available:

- staying on in the sixth form of the present school, which could be a comprehensive for 11- to 18-year-olds, a school for 14- to 18-year-olds, an independent school or a school of some other type
- leaving school and going to a sixth-form college. There are now over 150 sixth-form colleges in England and Wales, with more opening each year. To provide a wider range of A-level subjects, some Local Education Authorities have merged the sixth forms of several schools into one sixth-form college.

Staying on in the sixth form

A student choosing to go into the sixth form of his or her present school usually stays for one or two years to take subjects leading to GCSE or A-level examinations.

Most students who stay on at school after the age of 16 are aiming for higher qualifications, the main objective being A-levels (H-grades in Scotland). These are needed for entry to courses that start at age 18 or to jobs that require a better qualification than GCSEs

A student's choice of A-levels (H-grades) is vitally important. Although they do not give special training in anything, they add to one's resources when applying for a course or a job. They also show an employer that a student has the ability to learn at a higher level. Choosing A-level subjects is discussed in greater detail in Chapter 13.

The advantages of staying on at the present school include:

- the student is in a familiar place with friends
- there is more time to think and plan for the future
- the teachers are known and know the student's strengths and weaknesses
- plans for higher education are based on the five- or seven-year course in school where there's been continuity of teaching
- there is the chance to take a leading role in the sporting, social or recreational life of the school as a member of a school team or club
- a contribution can be made to school life, for instance by coaching younger pupils, editing a school newspaper or magazine, taking part in plays

- students can take a mixture of courses such as repeating GCSEs failed earlier, or take new subjects, or take a mixture of GCSEs and A-levels, or follow a non-examination course which in some Local Education Authorities leads to the award of a county certificate.

Among the disadvantages of staying on at school are:

- there is no change of surroundings
- the teaching staff are the same
- the stimulus of a fresh start is lacking
- the subjects or courses that the student particularly wants are not available at the school
- the school lacks the adult atmosphere many students now want
- the facilities in school reflect the majority, younger age-groups.

If a student is thinking about staying on at school, going to a sixth-form college, or taking one of the routes to further education, Youth Training or a full-time job, the advantages and disadvantages, along with the reasons for them, must be discussed. Some families find it difficult to sit down and talk about these things, but every effort should be made to do so, for the consequences of any decision taken at the age of 16 are very important indeed and can have a profound effect on the person's future.

Sixth-form college

The advantages of transferring to a sixth-form college include:

- everyone is aged 16 to 19, so there are no younger pupils to distract the students
- there is more competition because students come from several different schools
- there is usually a wider choice of A-level subjects; for instance, a sixth-form college may be able to offer law, engineering science or psychology, which an ordinary school cannot
- there is a freer, more adult attitude
- there may be a range of courses on offer – A-levels, GCSEs, City and Guilds
- no school uniform
- social activities may be good – dances, discos, clubs, sports.

Sixth-form colleges concentrate on academic work. They expect that most people will be taking A-levels and going on to polytechnics, colleges and universities. For other kinds of courses linked directly to jobs, a college of further education may be the best bet.

Of course, this advice is not much use if there is no sixth-form college in the area. But these colleges are becoming more and more numerous. So ask the Local Education Authority office or the careers service if there is one in your area, or if one is planned.

CHAPTER 11

TAKING A FURTHER EDUCATION COURSE

Colleges of further education

The student of 16 or 17 who leaves school but wants to continue his or her education has a number of options, as the diagram on page 103 shows. A college of further education is one option. Colleges have various names. Among them are:

- college of technology
- college of arts and technology
- technical college
- college of art and design or school of art
- college of horticulture, agriculture, building, printing, furniture, music or drama.

Another variation is a tertiary college, which is a college that offers A-levels, GCSE, RSA (Royal Society of Arts) certificates, City and Guilds, and BTEC (Business and Technician Education Council) courses.

The advantage of going to a college of further education is that it offers a second or third chance to repeat school subjects in a different environment. In addition, colleges of further education (sometimes called FE colleges) offer courses not normally available in secondary schools, such as City and Guilds, BTEC and other courses. Another attraction is that a college of further education has a more adult atmosphere because it also caters for adults who attend in order to take part-time craft, recreational or retraining courses. There is therefore a mixture of people, just as at work, and many students flourish in this adult environment.

Attendance at a college can be by various means:

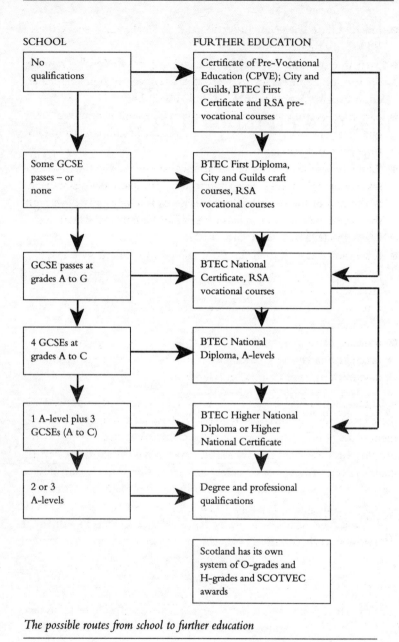

SCHOOL   FURTHER EDUCATION

| No qualifications | Certificate of Pre-Vocational Education (CPVE); City and Guilds, BTEC First Certificate and RSA pre-vocational courses |

| Some GCSE passes – or none | BTEC First Diploma, City and Guilds craft courses, RSA vocational courses |

| GCSE passes at grades A to G | BTEC National Certificate, RSA vocational courses |

| 4 GCSEs at grades A to C | BTEC National Diploma, A-levels |

| 1 A-level plus 3 GCSEs (A to C) | BTEC Higher National Diploma or Higher National Certificate |

| 2 or 3 A-levels | Degree and professional qualifications |

Scotland has its own system of O-grades and H-grades and SCOTVEC awards

The possible routes from school to further education

- full-time attendance in order to take A-levels, City and Guilds, BTEC or other courses
- part-time day attendance ('day release') as part of Youth Training off-the-job training, or as part of apprentice or trainee further education for people who are in full-time jobs
- part-time evening courses for people who need to improve their qualifications but are unable, for one reason or another, to obtain time off during the day
- 'block release' which means that trainees attend college full time for, say, six or eight weeks, returning to their company or organisation at the end of the period. Block release can be over a two-year or three-year period, and in some cases can be combined with day-release courses
- recreational classes in all kinds of subjects including hairdressing, photography, crafts, art, music, drama, languages and so on are arranged in all kinds of ways, from day or half-day attendance over a term, to a regular evening class, or a combination of day and evening attendance
- training courses for industrial and commercial companies are arranged on all kinds of patterns from one-day courses to variations of day, evening, week and term courses.

A large college of further education is likely to provide courses in all these categories, for a wide cross-section of adults, and in this environment many young people are stimulated to work because they mix with people who are already in jobs and are attending college to improve their qualifications and prospects.

Some further education courses

Pre-vocational courses

Pre-vocational courses are designed to help people *before* they make any kind of decision about a career or a vocational course. Most are one-year courses and are being drawn into the Certificate of Pre-Vocational Education (CPVE) which is described in Chapter 7.

In addition, the Royal Society of Arts offers qualifications in 'vocational preparation' and in subjects such as clerical and secretarial studies, retailing and distribution, as well as single-subject examinations including English language, mathematics and foreign languages.

Vocational courses

The next stage comes when students have decided what kind of job or career they want to enter, and attend a college on a part-time or full-time basis to take a vocational course leading to craft, trade, technical or business qualifications. For example, there are one-year, full-time courses in electronics, automobile and other kinds of engineering, office studies and many more subjects which can lead to further City and Guilds and BTEC courses. Alternatively, there are part-time courses on day or block release for students who enter jobs at 16 or 17. Again, these are likely to lead to City and Guilds, RSA or BTEC awards.

A-level and GCSE

Colleges of further education also offer a chance to re-take GCSEs and A-levels. Re-taking these exams in a college rather than a school can have advantages because of the opportunity to learn from new staff in a different environment. On the other hand, the continuity of the relationship with school staff is lost, and the decision to leave school and attend a college of further education or stay at school for re-takes has to be carefully weighed.

Colleges of further education often offer A-level subjects not normally available at school.

Training Agency courses

The Youth Training programme (YT), which is a two-year programme, is another possibility. It is described in detail in Chapter 12. Youth Training provides one or two years of training incorporating off-the-job education which is often (but not always) in a college of further education. Other TEED-sponsored courses are often available at colleges, for example for disadvantaged people, and for adults requiring training or re-training.

City and Guilds

This organisation (together with BTEC) dominates the work of a college of further education because it offers a wide selection of nationally recognised vocational qualifications.

Some 16-year-olds go straight into a job and acquire their craft or trade skills within their firm by attending part-time courses at colleges. Among the industries that take part in City and Guilds of London Institute awards are: electronics; clothing and footwear; motor vehicles and other kinds of engineering and manufacturing industries; furniture; food manufacturing and food supply; farming; design, photography and printing; hairdressing and fashion; office work; building and construction; and transport.

To get on to trade skills courses, GCSE passes may be needed, as the competition is very keen for a job offer that leads to training. But in most cases no specific educational qualifications are needed apart from a good general education. To find out about City and Guilds courses in your area, ask at the careers office or Local Education Authority office or enquire at the local library.

BTEC

BTEC exists to promote work-related education. It offers nationally recognised qualifications in the main occupational areas including agriculture, business, computing and information systems, construction, design, distribution, hotel, catering and leisure services, engineering, public administration and science. There are also more general pre-vocational courses and a range of continuing education studies for adults.

One of the great attractions of the BTEC course programme is that school-leavers with few or no GCSEs can climb the qualification ladder. They can progress from one course and award to the next and go all the way to a degree. Young people can therefore get a second or third chance to obtain valuable business and technical qualifications even if they left school without any.

Courses for BTEC awards are offered in colleges of further education (and in some cases in polytechnics and in schools) throughout England, Wales and Northern Ireland. These courses can be studied by means of the different modes already described, plus correspondence and sandwich courses.

There are four main categories of BTEC awards: First Certificates and Diplomas, National Certificate or National Diploma, Higher National Certificate (HNC) and Higher National Diploma (HND) and awards for specific courses for mature students.

111

First Certificates and Diplomas

These provide an initial vocational qualification for those entering work at 16 years of age, or later, who have already chosen the area of work for which they intend to train. The First Certificate can be taken as a one-year part-time course, while a one-year full-time or two-years' part-time course leads to the First Diploma. No particular examination passes are required although a CPVE portfolio or attendance on a BTEC or City and Guilds preparatory programme or GCSE passes are very useful.

National Certificate or National Diploma

Students should be at least 16 and most courses require four GCSE passes at grades A to C. For some technical courses in engineering, science, construction and technology subjects, students may be admitted with three GCSE passes in science and mathematics subjects and a subject using English. The courses are generally two or three years part time for the National Certificate and two years full time or three years part time for the National Diploma.

Higher National Certificate (HNC) and Higher National Diploma (HND)

Students should normally be at least 18 and hold a BTEC National award or suitable A-level passes in at least one subject.

For the HNC the length of the course is generally three years part time, and for the HND it is two years full time or three years of sandwich study.

Continuing education

Continuing education courses are designed for adults and students who should normally be at least 21 years of age. Entry qualifications vary according to the length of the course and the student's background. Students can be admitted to these courses on the basis of their experience in employment. Among the qualifications offered by this route are the Certificate in Management Studies, the Certificate in Business Administration and the Certificate for Accounting Technicians.

Art and design

BTEC is also responsible for art and design courses. These give a good basis for careers in all kinds of design – fashion, furniture, industrial design, advertising, photography, printing and publishing, television and film and, of course, art.

Students get jobs in studios, companies and all kinds of institutions and organisations that are concerned with newspapers, books, magazines, packaging, exhibitions – anything manufactured that begins with a basic design, which includes virtually everything.

These courses can be taken in the same variety of ways – part-time study, full-time courses or sandwich courses for advanced qualifications. On a sandwich course the student spends, say, six months in industry, six months in college, and six months in industry etc. There are various combinations of the industry/college slices of the sandwich.

Grants

Grants for most further education courses are 'discretionary'. This means that it is up to the Local Education Authority whether or not it gives a grant to a particular student. With the present state of local authority finances, some are refusing applications and are agreeing to pay only those students who have particularly difficult financial problems or home circumstances. The discretionary grants are intended to cover living expenses but not college fees, although students under 18 normally have their fees paid for them by the local authority; those over 18, and all overseas students, are generally required to pay the tuition fees.

For the 16 to 19 age-group, the financial circumstances are little different from staying on at school: parents are expected to help with maintenance, and tuition is generally free. Some students take part-time or holiday jobs if they can get them. Youth Training trainees are different, of course, because they are paid a weekly training allowance.

Students of over 18 on an advanced course (degree, HND and some other courses) can apply for a mandatory grant paid by the Local Education Authority. These grants are 'means-tested'; in other words the awards depend on the parents' income.

What do employers think of these courses ?

The employers who are aware of BTEC, City and Guilds, Youth

Training and other pre-vocational and vocational courses think they are good. But, unfortunately, many employers do not know about them. The reason is that managers may be so involved in their work that they do not have much time – or reason – to understand the nature of these courses. Anyway, they often suspect the educational world for its use of jargon. What they do like, put in crude terms, are young employees who can do a job effectively, are willing to learn, to adapt, to help the company through its good times and its bad times. So, if pressed, they are very keen indeed on courses that provide practical skills, understanding of business and are linked to economic objectives. When BTEC, CPVE and City and Guilds courses are explained to them they are enthusiastic.

On the other hand, there are thousands of managers who understand what BTEC, Youth Training and City and Guilds are and what these schemes are aiming to do. They are usually the training managers, or the personnel or recruitment staff, or managers with a close interest in the links between education and industry.

Very few employers or their representatives dislike what BTEC and other organisations are doing. The real problem is ignorance or misunderstanding of these courses and their objectives.

CHAPTER 12

Youth Training and Training Credits

Youth Training

In May 1990 the Government launched a new programme, Youth Training (YT) which replaced the Youth Training Scheme (YTS); it is available to all young people of 16 years of age and over who are not in full-time education.

The objectives of YT are to provide a basic programme of broadly based vocational education and training arrangements which are designed to give all trainees the opportunity to engage in valuable training activities leading to National Vocational Qualification (NVQ) awards at Level 2.

New organisations were set up to deliver YT (and other) training programmes. These were the Training and Enterprise Councils (TECs): there are now 82 of them, distributed across England and Wales. Scotland has its own group – LECs (Local Enterprise Companies). Northern Ireland also has its own programme.

The way that YT now operates is that each TEC or LEC makes contracts with training providers (further education colleges, local authorities, independent and private training organisations or companies to deliver training for an agreed group of youngsters.

Who qualifies for Youth Training?

YT is *not* for youngsters on full-time courses in school or at an FE college. It therefore *excludes* A-level, BTEC National Diploma and other students of 16 to 18 who are taking full-time courses. It *includes* (and is primarily for) youngsters who leave school at 16 or 17 and who want a job. Trainees are paid a minimum weekly allowance of £29.90 at 16 and £35 at 17 (1991 rates). A major problem, however, in the 1990-2 recession was that many 16- to 18-year-olds could not get a job or find a sponsoring company: the TECs had money washing around in their bank accounts because employers and their managing agents (who are financially assisted in the YT programme) were reluctant to take on any staff, including young trainees.

What does YT provide?

The benefits of YT for young trainees are:

- It provides a structure of employment linked to training which should guarantee that all 16- to 18-year-olds continue with education and training either as full-time students at school or college or as partners in a training compact. The weakness, however, for the trainees is that, because of the national economic situation, they cannot find an employer who provides a job and a base for the skills to be learned and practised.
- The skills learned on Youth Training are intended to fit into the pattern of NVQs. This should enable youngsters who have acquired training skills at, say, Level 2 of an NVQ scheme to transfer these skills and the NVQ guarantee to a new employer during their later working life. In theory, then, this makes the trainee more employable. The weakness of this aspect of YT is that few craft courses linked to training have yet been NVQ-ed. That is, the employers' organisations responsible for applying for NVQ status for their craft training have not yet been successful in persuading the Council for National Vocational Qualifications to approve their proposals. Trainees on YT programmes can study for City and Guilds and/or BTEC awards at a further education college, but as yet there is a big gap and hold-up in matching these to NVQ standards. Perhaps five years on from now all this will have been resolved but in 1991-2, while jobs for 16-year-olds are in short supply, and so few NVQs have been approved, the Youth Training programme has more promises to it than successes.

Training credits

One of the main aspects of the Government's radical shake-up of education came in April 1991 with the introduction of Training Credits.

The purposes of the Training Credit scheme are to:

- encourage school-leavers to regard training as a right and a lifelong process;
- motivate employers (particularly in small firms) to invest in training.

The scheme is for 16- and 17-year-olds who are not in full-time education. The idea is that school-leavers of 16 and 17 would have a 'credit' that is a cash entitlement in the form of a credit card. This enables them to 'buy' vocational training from providers. These could be further education colleges or independent companies and organisations that offer training courses and planned programmes of vocational training side by side with employers.

The concept is that any 16- or 17-year-old can shop around to buy this training. Employers are encouraged to take on these youngsters as employees. If they do, there's something in it for the employers: if they recruit a school-leaver the employer receives up to £4,000 to meet their NVQ training costs.

NVQ again. The Government's intention is that all school-leavers will work towards an NVQ qualification. However, as we will see in the chapter on NVQs (Chapter 15), few NVQs have been approved, although the Government set a target of 900 accredited NVQ qualifications approved by the end of 1992.

YT is included

The new scheme includes Youth Training. Since YT is funded by the new 82 TECs, the Government also put Training Credits into TEC control.

The TECs have taken different approaches to the credits. Some operate the scheme already described, where young employees can buy training with their credit card which is exchanged for free access to college courses. Other TECs are using the financial funding from the Government to assist *all* unemployed people in their area with training.

CHAPTER **13**

A-LEVELS, AS-LEVELS AND CAREERS

CHOOSING A-levels (or Higher grade subjects in Scotland) is one of the key decisions at school or college. This is because students must choose the correct A-levels (H-grades) and the right grouping of them to ensure that they can move on later to degree or diploma courses or a career. Before the final choice of A-levels (H-grades) is made, therefore, students and their parents should do some research. They need to know which subjects are required for a university or polytechnic place, and they should find out what is actually involved in the study of, say, economics at A-level (H-grade) before they embark on what could be a difficult and testing course.

Another good reason for finding out what A-levels (H-grades) are available is that there may be some interesting subjects that a student has never seriously considered. For example, there are A-levels in sociology, engineering science, theatre studies, statistics, computer studies, history of art, photography, psychology, and law to name but a few. Finding out what the school or the local college of further education offer at A-level is well worth the time spent on the enquiry.

A further reason for research into A-levels is that in all subjects there is a world of difference in the syllabus, standard and approach between GCSE and A-level. So a student who enjoyed, say, French or physics at GCSE level may find the requirements for A-level in the subject much less attractive.

Parents and students should start with a book called *Your Choice of A levels*, published by Hobsons. This lists over sixty A-level subjects and describes what is involved in studying them. Each entry (written by an examiner in that subject) explains what the subject is about, the syllabus, the examinations, and the career implications in terms of what the particular subject could lead to.

The next stage of the research is to link the A-level subject with possible degree courses. The book to be consulted here is *University Entrance, The Official Guide* (see Chapter 21) which lists all subjects that may be studied at university, and describes the course requirements in terms of what GCSE subjects and A-levels are needed. For example, if a student is interested in a degree course in bacteriology or microbiology, *University Entrance* lists all the university courses in these subjects and explains the course length, total A-level passes needed, and particular A-levels required. In fact, *University Entrance* is an essential reference book and it can usually be consulted at school or college or in a public library.

A-level subjects and the Examination Boards

There are eight Examination Boards for England and Wales which award A-levels. In Scotland, the Scottish Examination Board runs Scotland's own scheme of Higher Grade and Certificate of Sixth-Year Studies syllabuses and examinations. Northern Ireland has its own Examinations Council.

Not all the Boards offer the same subjects. This can have serious consequences for a student's choice. Any student who wants to study for an A-level in a subject not offered by the Board(s) whose examinations his or her school takes must find out if a local further education college offers the subject at A-level, or else study the subject privately and try to find a centre (a school or college) which arranges examinations for those Boards that do offer the subject.

Although there are more than sixty A-level subjects, no school or college could provide all of them. In practice, therefore, a student is restricted to the ten to twenty subjects offered by the school or college. Some Local Education Authorities allow a student to take one or two A-level subjects at school, and (if the timetable allows it) attend a local college of further education for an A-level in another subject (or more than one).

There are other possibilities which are not always explored by schools, students or parents. For instance, it is possible to study different A-levels from different Boards at the same school. To do so creates problems – the school will have to apply to be an examination centre for more than one Board, and make sure that the examination timetables for these Boards are arranged correctly, for example. But these are administrative problems which can be overcome with a little effort, and parental pressure can help to bring about a solution.

There are no particular advantages in taking courses set by different Boards except the obvious one that it allows for a wider choice of subjects. But few schools have the resources to offer a particularly wide range of subjects in any case, and even if they did the classes in some subjects would be too small to justify offering those A-levels.

The standards of the eight A-level Examination Boards are generally the same, and to ensure this the Boards have meetings in order to compare papers, marking and the grades awarded. So the popular view that one Board's examinations are easier than those of another is incorrect.

A question often asked about A-level is whether a school can choose to take the examinations of any Board. The answer is yes. The same is true of the GCSE examinations; schools have the freedom to choose which Group's syllabuses and examinations will be taken. There are some regional loyalties. For instance, the Joint Matriculation Board's courses are popular in the north of England because the JMB is based in Manchester, although candidates from all over Britain apply to take JMB papers. And Cambridge, Oxford and London are not regionally organised or supported; as with the JMB and Associated Examining Board (AEB), candidates come from all over the country.

A-level subjects

This list shows the subjects offered by the different Boards. The list is subject to change.

KEY

AEB	Associated Examining Board
C	University of Cambridge Local Examinations Syndicate
L	London University School Examinations Council
O/C	Oxford and Cambridge Schools Examination Board
JMB	Joint Matriculation Board
O	University of Oxford Delegacy of Local Examinations
S	Southern Universities' Joint Board for School Examinations
W	Welsh Joint Education Committee

SUBJECTS	BOARDS							
Accounting	AEB				JMB	O		W
Accounts, principles of					JMB			W
Ancient history			L	O/C	JMB	O		W
Ancient history and literature					JMB			
Archaeology	AEB	C						
Art	AEB	C	L	O/C	JMB	O	S	W
Art and crafts	AEB							
Art and design								W
Art, history of	AEB		L	O/C	JMB	O		

SUBJECTS	BOARDS							
Biology	AEB	C	L	O/C	JMB	O	S	W
Botany		C	L	O/C		O		W
British constitution								W
British economic and social history			L					
British government and politics					JMB			
Building construction	AEB							
Business studies	AEB	C						
Ceramics						O		
Chemistry	AEB	C	L	O/C	JMB	O	S	W
Classical civilisation							S	
Classical studies	AEB							
Computer science	AEB	C	L					
Computer studies					JMB	O		
Constitutional law	AEB							
Craft (design and practice)					JMB			
Design and craft (metal)	AEB							W
Design and craft (wood)	AEB							W
Design, communication and application	AEB							
Design/craft/technology			L			O		W
Domestic science					JMB			
Drama (see theatre studies)								
Dress	AEB		L					
Economical and political studies				O/C				
Economic and public affairs		C						
Economic and social history	AEB		L			O	S	W
Economic geography	AEB					O		
Economic history	AEB							
Economics	AEB		L	O/C	JMB	O	S	W
Electronics	AEB	C						
Embroidery	AEB							
Engineering						O		
Engineering design, elements of		C						
Engineering drawing	AEB		L			O	S	W
Engineering science	AEB		L		JMB			
English	AEB	C						W
English literature	AEB		L	O/C	JMB	O	S	
Environmental biology					JMB			
Environmental science					JMB			
Environmental studies	AEB		L					
Fashion and fabrics					JMB			
French	AEB	C	L	O/C	JMB	O	S	W
General studies	AEB	C			JMB	O		
Geography	AEB	C	L	O/C	JMB	O	S	W
Geology	AEB	C	L	O/C	JMB	O		W
Geometrical and building drawing		C						
Geometrical and engineering drawing					JMB			
Geometrical and mechanical drawing		C						
Geometrical drawing (building)	AEB							
German	AEB	C	L	O/C	JMB	O	S	W
Government and politics	AEB		L					
Graphic communication	AEB							
Greek		C	L	O/C	JMB	O	S	W
History	AEB	C	L	O/C	JMB	O	S	W
Home economics		C	L					W
Home economics/dress and fabrics						O		

SUBJECTS	BOARDS							
Home economics/food and nutrition						O		
Home, family and society					JMB			
Horticultural science						O		
Human biology	AEB							
Italian	AEB	C	L	O/C	JMB	O		W
Latin	AEB	C	L	O/C	JMB	O	S	W
Latin with Roman history				O/C				
Law						O		W
Law, English	AEB							
Logic			L					
Mathematics	AEB	C	L	O/C	JMB	O	S	W
Mathematics, applied	AEB	C					S	W
Mathematics, further		C	L	O/C	JMB			
Mathematics, higher			L					
Mathematics, pure	AEB	C	L		JMB	O	S	W
Mathematics, pure and applied	AEB							
Mathematics, pure with computations	AEB							
Mathematics, pure with statistics	AEB		L		JMB		S	
Mechanics, applied				O/C				
Metalwork		C			JMB	O		
Modern European languages (other than French, German, Italian, Russian and Spanish)			L					
Modern languages, other approved					JMB			W
Music	AEB	C	L	O/C	JMB	O	S	W
Needlework and dressmaking		C						
Oriental and African languages			L					
Philosophy	AEB				JMB			
Photography	AEB							
Physical science	AEB	C			JMB			
Physics	AEB	C	L	O/C	JMB	O	S	W
Physics and mathematics						O		
Political studies				O/C		O		
Politics and government		C						
Psychology	AEB				JMB			
Religious studies	AEB	C	L	O/C	JMB	O	S	W
Russian	AEB	C	L	O/C	JMB	O	S	W
Social biology		C						
Sociology	AEB	C	L		JMB	O		
Spanish	AEB	C	L		JMB	O	S	W
Statistics	AEB	C			JMB			
Surveying	AEB							
Textiles and dress			L					
Theatre studies	AEB							
Welsh								W
Woodwork		C			JMB	O	S	
Zoology		C	L	O/C		O		W

Advanced Supplementary level

A new examination – Advanced Supplementary level (AS-level) – was introduced in September 1987. AS-level is equivalent to half an A-level and is assessed in conjunction with A-level. The first examinations were set in 1989, and in 1991 there were 50,000 entries (compared with a total of 700,000 entries for A-level subjects).

AS-level is intended to broaden A-level studies. Syllabuses produced so far have adopted three approaches. Some are based on A-level syllabuses with less content; others are based on the now discontinued AO examinations enhanced by additional work, others take a fresh approach, placing emphasis on skills rather than content and requiring research and coursework on the part of the pupil and continuous assessment of the pupil's progress.

AS-levels count for entry to higher and further education: for example, students can offer two passes in subjects at AS-level in place of one required A-level pass, and the universities and polytechnics accept two AS-levels in place of a third A-level. Among some combinations that are being implemented are:

A-levels		AS-levels		
		complementary		*contrasting*
Maths and physics	*plus*	chemistry	*and*	German
History and English	*plus*	French	*and*	maths
Geography and economics	*plus*	statistics	*and*	design and technology

Studying for A-levels

A-level courses usually last for two years with examinations taken after six terms of academic study. Colleges of further education sometimes offer intensive one-year courses for older students. Part-time students may take several years preparing for the examinations.

If the aim is to go to university or polytechnic afterwards, it is wise to take three subjects. Some schools start students off on three subjects, with the option of dropping one after the first year. Other schools prefer students who are not going on to university to take two A-levels, or one plus GCSE subjects. Many schools add General Studies at GCSE level or at A-level as a cultural extra, but like any other A-level subject it has to be taken seriously and worked for.

The vast majority of students take their A-levels in June, although the AEB and Cambridge Board offer a limited number of subjects in November, and the London Board provides examinations in January.

Adding to GCSE subjects

Before a student goes on to A-levels, it is important for him or her to have a solid grounding of GCSE subjects to build on. A-level is much more difficult than GCSE, more intensive and demanding. It involves more reading and essay-writing, the grasp of more specialised knowledge and a more analytical approach to a subject. A student who has obtained only grades C to E at GCSE is likely to find A-level work very difficult. Some schools insist that students have five GCSEs at grades A to C before taking an A-level course. Others have no restrictions, and colleges of further education usually take anyone as long as he or she indicates a willingness to work hard.

The range of the GCSE subjects is also very important. It is very useful, although not essential, to have passes in English language, mathematics and a science subject. These subjects provide a basis for a wide range of course and career possibilities.

The decision about whether or not to go on to A-levels should be discussed with teachers, and this is why most schools have parents' evenings. However, the decision may have to be made immediately after the GCSE results come out, usually in September. Parents should ask to see the teachers involved if the results at GCSE have been poor. The student may be wiser to abandon thoughts of studying A-levels. One possibility is to consolidate GCSE before proceeding to A-level, although this will mean another year spent on GCSE studies. Another possibility is to leave school and enrol at a college of further education on a City and Guilds or a BTEC course, providing that there are still vacancies and the college will take the student. This can be a very positive step: for example, a BTEC National Diploma course (two years full time, entry depending on three or four GCSE passes at A to C grades) is generally regarded by polytechnics and universities as equivalent to two A-levels.

Bridging courses

It is possible that the college or school will provide a bridging course, perhaps for as long as a term. This has always been a common practice and will continue to be necessary for some subjects. In geography, for example, some syllabuses at GCSE do not require the student to study physical geography and if that area of study is called for at A-level, it may form the introduction to the course. In English, an A-level group may be made up of students from a number of GCSE groups, among whom the range of texts studied in coursework will be very wide. A-level teachers may decide to prepare a brief course to give a common basis of study before approaching the set books.

Benefits of GCSE

After GCSE students proceed to A-level and AS-level with some advantages. The active discovery methods of learning used in GCSE help them, as an enquiring cast of mind is expected of an A-level student. The practical and experimental work done in science is certainly of benefit in a further course of study. Students may have had to carry out investigations by use of resource material or by library study – exactly the sort of preparation needed for A-level. Students therefore need to be familiar with such study skills as note-taking, summarising, illustrating by quotations, evidencing work by reference to authorities, presenting work with use of diagrams or graphs, and addressing their work to a particular audience. These features of competence at GCSE are exactly the tools of an A-level student.

However, not all GCSE pupils are skilled in these techniques which is one reason for the failure of some students to move from success at GCSE to A-level work.

Choosing sciences or arts

When picking their A-level subjects, most students select arts and humanities or science subjects. However, a mixed group of A-levels is becoming more common, and there are advantages in having a mixture.

The reason for specialisation is usually because the student already has a view of future career plans. On the science side, most science degree courses will require two science A-levels, so a student who takes three science subjects will have a much better choice of careers. For example, the most common combinations are maths, physics and chemistry or physics, chemistry and biology. Both these groups open up a very wide range of possible degree courses and careers.

If, on the other hand, a student selects maths, physics and history, all careers involving chemistry would be eliminated. Equally, a student who takes chemistry, art and sociology would certainly study a broad range of subjects, but they would not lead to science degree courses. If biology and chemistry were taken together, the range of possible jobs and courses would be much wider.

On the arts and humanities side, English, economics, history, French and geography are popular subjects and any of them can be grouped together. Students who intend to go on to a degree course involving foreign languages should take two languages at A-level but one of them could be Latin. A foreign language is useful but not essential for people wanting to take a history or an English degree. In general terms, there is a lot more flexibility on the arts side, for very few courses have strong vocational links. When students come to select their course at university or polytechnic, they will find that on the humanities side there are very few required A-levels. It is possible therefore to experiment and to choose unusual subjects alongside the more traditional ones: career opportunities will not be hurt by doing so.

Balance

If A-levels were to be chosen on the grounds of career opportunities, there is no doubt that the best group is maths, physics and chemistry. Apart from science careers, many of the professional careers such as accountancy, journalism, business management and insurance welcome students with science A-levels.

However, if everyone studied only science subjects, the world would be a very dull place. In addition, students who are not strong in sciences at GCSE level and have no great interest in sciences would be most unwise to choose them. After all, a tremendous range of jobs and careers is open to people with A-levels in arts subjects, including technical careers. In making the final choice, therefore, students must be advised to base their selection on:

- academic interests
- personal interests, skills and aptitudes
- entry requirements for degree courses or careers
- the subjects available at the school or college.

Changing fashions

Over 85 per cent of the A-level examinations taken each year are in traditional school subjects – maths, physics, English, and so on. On the other hand, there are some popular subjects that were not found in the 'top ten' a few years ago. Economics and sociology are two of these, and computer studies, accounting, law, government and politics, history of art and theatre studies are becoming more popular each year. General studies is often included as an extra subject on a two or three A-level course making a third or fourth A-level and acting as a general educational experience. General studies is a good subject to take, but only if it can be easily accommodated with the other work. If it is going to add to the load of a struggling student, it should not be taken. A popular misconception is that students who intend to take a degree in a certain subject, for example business studies, law or economics, should study that subject at A-level. This is not necessarily the case. Many subjects – computer studies, psychology, law, accounting, statistics, archaeology and many more – do not require an A-level pass in the same subject. Indeed, as it would be very difficult to get into a degree course in statistics without A-level mathematics, or archaeology without history, for instance, the implications may be that in many cases the traditional subjects are preferable to the newer ones as they allow for a wider range of choices and allow a student to keep his or her options open. Only the more traditional subjects such as mathematics, English, chemistry and physics are 'required' A-level subjects for degree courses in these subjects.

Taking three new subjects at A-level could therefore seriously limit career and course opportunities. It is vitally important to check in *University Entrance, The Official Guide* (see Chapter 21) which A-levels are required for certain degree courses. Perhaps the best advice is: check the required subjects for a particular career or degree course, and place it/them first in the A-level package and then see if there is room/time for the non-traditional subjects. An A-level science package could then be maths, physics and statistics (or electronics, surveying or engineering science); an arts package could be English, history and one from the large number of subjects listed earlier which include photography, psychology, sociology, and so on.

However, this advice may be too cautious for some students. If they have no particular career or degree course in mind, then a free choice (constrained by the school's timetabling problems) could be made:

government and politics, German and computer science; or home economics, history of art and biology . . . and so on.

Entry to careers

For young people going straight into jobs, passes in A-level subjects are extremely useful. Two A-levels with a group of good GCSE passes are the minimum requirement for entry to a wide selection of professional and semi-professional careers. For students with one A-level rather than two, the range of jobs is more limited.

It is noticeable that the entry requirements to some courses and careers are raised from time to time. Employers who ten years ago would have been quite satisfied to accept applicants with O-levels now demand A-levels. For some courses, the A-level grades are on a rising curve of expectation. For example, to gain entry to a degree course in medicine, accounting, law, dentistry and some other subjects, admissions tutors specify three A-levels with grades of A and B. A very useful guide to careers and courses is *Jobs and Careers After A-levels* by Mary Munro. This book, which is published by Hobsons, explains the connections between A-level subjects and degree and diploma courses.

Alternatives to A-levels

Before finally deciding whether or not to take A-levels, students who want to stay in full-time education should consider the other alternatives. The local college of further education is likely to have a range of BTEC National Certificate and National Diploma courses. These courses may be in art and design, graphic design, computing, engineering, business studies, printing and many other vocational subjects. These BTEC courses lead directly into careers in all kinds of industries including catering, building, the media, design, engineering, transport, retail trade and office work. BTEC National Diplomas are recognised by most polytechnics and universities as equivalent to A-levels for entrance to HND courses and some degree courses.

The local college of further education may also have full-time courses in hairdressing, secretarial studies, catering, shop work and other subjects leading to City and Guilds, BTEC, SCOTVEC or other awards. These may be much more suitable than A-levels for students who are keen to take a vocational course from 16 to 18 rather than continue with academic studies.

Students should not be made to feel that full-time courses are the only route into a career. Many employers prefer to take on 16-year-olds, or trainees of 17 who have been on a Youth Training course. It might therefore be a better idea to look for a job at 16 or 17, or enter a course of training and work experience offered by a Youth Training programme. This would be a far more sensible route to take for students who are unlikely to get good A-level results or who would find A-level work very difficult.

In some jobs, particularly engineering, there is a strong tradition of entry at 16 or 17. However, this has been drastically changed by several factors, including the decline of the engineering industry, the lack of jobs and the expansion of Youth Training which gives a thorough training *before* a person takes a full-time job.

A-level grades

There are five levels of pass in A-levels, A, B, C, D and E. Other grades awarded are N which is one grade less than a pass and U which is 'unclassified', that is a firm fail. AS-levels have a similar system. Grades are decided as the result of marks awarded for scripts, oral work and projects where the syllabuses permit or require them. The distribution of marks of all entrants is checked by the senior examiners for the particular subject and the grades are then finally awarded. The Examination Board has a panel of experienced examiners to set the dividing lines between grades. When the results are published in August or September, the student's school or centre has the right of appeal to the Examination Board for a revision or check if it is felt that the result is inaccurate. In practice, very few of these appeals lead to a regrading, and generally schools and colleges are reluctant to appeal unless they feel there is a very good case.

The balancing act

When deciding to stay on for A-levels, and then choosing the subjects to study, all students should attempt to balance their personal interests with later career and course implications. This is where parents can help. They usually have a wider view of careers and jobs, and should not be affected by the considerations that their son or daughter will put forward as personal priorities. For example, a student thinking of a technological degree course may be keen to give up maths and/or physics. From the information given in this book it should be clear that most technology (computing, engineering, construction, etc.) courses require A-level physics or mathematics (or both), so if it is possible to take (and survive) an A-level course in these subjects, the student should be advised to select one or other, or both.

Whatever advice is offered and heeded, the wisest course must be to select the subjects and the package which fit the projected career or degree/HND or any other course. Where this planning has not been done or where the student is uncertain of his or her career or course direction, almost any combination is possible. In the last resort, the best choice of A-levels must be in subjects where there is keen student interest: two years is a long time to survive a subject that is taken reluctantly or inadvisedly.

CHAPTER 14

SCOTLAND

SCOTLAND has always had a different system of education from England and Wales. Furthermore, in recent years the Scots have been reviewing the structure of their secondary and further education courses and examinations, and have introduced radical changes. The Scottish system of courses and examinations is therefore substantially different from the rest of the UK, and if you live in or are about to move to Scotland it is essential to grasp these differences.

Control of schools

In the first place, Scottish schools (which are co-educational and comprehensive) and colleges are controlled from Edinburgh by the Scottish Education Department (SED). The SED uses its power and authority more directly than the Department of Education and Science (DES) does in England and Wales. The SED, through its officials, published guidelines, committees and HM Inspectors, has traditionally enjoyed more authority over what actually happens in education than its English and Welsh equivalents.

Throughout the UK, schools and colleges are administered and paid for by the Local Education Authorities. In Scotland there are nine Regional Councils and three Island Councils, which are also known as Local Education Authorities. These authorities appoint and pay teachers and lecturers and have officials similar to those in England and Wales, such as directors of education and advisers. However, the Scots have a tradition of heeding what central government says, and when the SED commissions and then publishes major reports on education, the reports are not put on a shelf and forgotten but are generally acted on promptly.

Organisation of secondary school courses

In Scotland 90 per cent of the 434 secondary schools follow a six-year course (seven years in England and Wales). Entering the secondary school at 12, a year later than south of the border, pupils take a two-year broad curriculum course across a wide range of subjects. These years are usually called S1 and S2. At the end of the second year pupils choose the subjects they will follow in later years. This is a two-year course (S3 and S4) which leads to O-grade (equivalent to O-level in England and Wales) and Standard Grade at around the age of 16. This is followed by a one-year course for Higher Grade (S5), with the possibility of staying on for a further year (S6) to take the Certificate of Sixth-Year Studies, retake H-grades, or take new H-grades or some other courses. But this system is in the process of change.

Standard Grade

In 1984, Scotland introduced a change to the examinations taken at 16, and a new school examination designed to give a more accurate picture of pupils' education and abilities is being rapidly implemented. The new courses are designed for pupils of all abilities, not just those interested in academic subjects.

The major change is that now everyone has the opportunity to gain a certificate at the age of 16. Like the O-grade which it is fast replacing, the new Standard Grade is open to all school students and to older students.

The first of the new courses, in English, mathematics, science, and social and vocational skills, started in 1984 with the first examinations in 1986. Courses leading to Standard Grade are now available in all the main school subjects and some new multi-disciplinary subjects. O-grade examinations continue to be available for the present but are to be phased out as the Standard Grade courses are fully established by 1992, except for a handful of subjects.

The new Standard Grade shows grades for different aspects of each subject. For example, it is possible to separate ability in speaking and reading English, so the certificate reflects a pupil's achievement in each of these two areas. There are separate grades of award in the scheme, each representing a different level of achievement.

The Standard Grade examination system is part of a series of developments which are intended to change the Scottish education

132

system. More changes are planned. Consult *Factsheet 29* on Standard Grade examinations, published by the Scottish Information Office.

The Dunning and Munn reports

In recent years the Scottish secondary school system has come under very close scrutiny. There was some dissatisfaction with the treatment of pupils who were not taking O-grade courses. Scotland had never had a CSE examination system. Many of the non-O-graders took a variety of 'non-certificate' courses which carried little status. Other pupils took technical and vocational examination courses leading to City and Guilds, SCOTBEC and SCOTEC awards.

In 1974 the Secretary of State for Scotland set up a committee under the chairmanship of Joseph Dunning, then Principal of Napier College, Edinburgh. The Dunning Committee's report, *Assessment for All,* was published in 1977. The report suggested sweeping changes in the examination system and work was started to put the suggestions into effect.

At much the same time, another government committee under the chairmanship of Dr James Munn, Rector of Cathkin High School, Glasgow, was at work on the structure of the Scottish third- and fourth-year courses. The Munn Committee presented its report, *The Structure of the Curriculum in the Third and Fourth Years of the Scottish Secondary School*, in 1977. The introduction of Standard Grade in 1984 was a direct result of this report.

The school curriculum

The delivery of the school curriculum is the responsibility of the twelve education authorities and individual schools. In practice, the existence of much national guidance on the content of the curriculum and of a single examining body has led to a broad agreement of what should be taught. Central guidance to education authorities and schools is issued in the form of circulars from the Scottish Education Department, reports by HM Inspectors of Schools and advice from the Scottish Consultative Council on the Curriculum (SCCC). The SCCC keeps under review the curriculum of schools, issuing guidance on the curriculum to education authorities and schools and promoting and keeping under review a programme of curriculum development work in conjunction

Mode	Language and Communication		Mathematical Studies and Applications		Scientific Studies and Applications		Social and Environmental Studies
TIME (minimum requirement over two years)	360 hours[1]		200 hours[1]		160 hours[1]		160 hours[1]
CORE Courses fully meeting requirements of the mode	English with French German Italian Russian or Spanish	S S S S S S	Mathematics	S	Biology Chemistry Physics Science	S S S S	Classical Studies Contemporary Social Studies Economics Geography History Modern Studies
ENRICHMENT Examples of additional courses/activities selected from							
(a) two-year courses	Classical Studies Gaelic Greek Latin	S S S S	Accounting and Finance	S			Social and Vocational Skills
(b) fields of study (SCE short courses/ NC Modules)[3]	Other Languages Media Studies		Accounting Money Management Navigation Statistics		Biotechnology Electronics Geology Health Studies		Community Stud● Consumer Studie● Economic Aware● Geography Industrial Studies Media Studies
(c) school programmes	Scottish/ Celtic Studies				Energy Studies		Environmental St● European Awaren● International and Multicultural Stud● Scottish/Celtic St●

Notes: 1. Full courses of 160–200 hours, normally SCE Standard Grade
2. 160 hours where full S Grade selected, otherwise combinations of SCE short courses, NC Modules, half modules or school programmes

Technological Activities and Applications		Creative and Aesthetic Activities		Physical Education		Religious and Moral Education	
80 hours[1]		80 hours[1]		80 hours[1]		80 hours[1]	
Computing Studies	S	Art & Design	S	Physical		Religious Studies	S
Craft & Design	S	Drama	S	Education	S	or relevant short	
Home Economics	S	Music	S	or relevant		courses or	
Office and		or relevant short		short courses		appropriate activities	
Information Studies	S	courses or		or appropriate		from above courses	
Technological		appropriate activities		activities from		or others below	
Studies	S	from above courses		above courses			
or relevant short		or others below		or others below			
courses or appropriate							
activities from above							
courses or others below							
Accounting and		Craft & Design	S				
Finance	S	Home Economics	S				
Art & Design	S	Physical					
Physics	S	Education	S				
Social and							
Vocational Skills	S						
Technical Drawing	S						
Agriculture/		Art & Design		Dance and		Religious and	
Horticulture		Dance & Movement		Movement		Moral Studies	
Community Care		Drama Activities		Health & Fitness			
Computer Applications		Media Studies		Physical			
Craft Technology		Musical Activities		Recreation and			
Electronics		Photography		Sport			
Enterprise							
Fabric Technology							
Food Technology							
Graphical							
Communications							
Nautical Studies							
Office & Information							
Technology							
Technological Activity							
Technological							
Applications							
						Related aspects of	
						personal and social	
						development	

3. This is a simplified version of a table appearing in Appendix B of the SCCC publication
Curriculum Design for the Secondary Stages: Guidelines for Headteachers First

Reproduced by permission of The Scottish Office

with the education authorities. Its members are appointed by the Secretary of State for Scotland from a variety of educational backgrounds, including schools, universities, colleges and education authorities as well as representatives of parents, industry and commerce.

A cynic might say that after all the discussion and the flood of publications, there is not a great deal of difference between the new system and the old subjects of English, maths, science, and so on. The big difference, however, is that pupils are expected to study all the subjects listed in the Scottish equivalent of the National Curriculum and not concentrate too much on a few. The new system of courses will adequately cover major subjects. So now, instead of a narrow selection of subjects (as in the past), which might omit something important (such as science), all pupils will have a balanced course covering all the Scottish National Curriculum subjects.

Choices

Pupils are offered some choice in the range of subjects needed to fulfil the minimum requirements for the broad-based curriculum.

Different levels

When the new system was devised it was suggested that courses would be available at three levels – foundation, general and credit. The situation now is something like this. A major aspect of the new system is that courses are available at up to three levels, leading to seven possible grades of award (grades 1 to 7). There are courses suited to all pupils, from those who would previously have followed a non-certificate course to the high-flyers at the top of the academic ability range of 14- to 16-year-olds. Pupils are able to take different levels of study in different courses, so they can tackle a subject according to their ability in it.

The syllabuses for the different levels overlap, but this helps pupils to find their level of ability. To take an example: computer studies can be taken at one of three levels. Where one level ends and another begins, there is some overlap. This means that every pupil, whatever his or her ability, is able to take a suitable course in computer studies and gain something of value from it.

The 14 to 16 curriculum

Scotland effectively has a national curriculum for the 14 to 16 age-group in that all schools are expected to follow guiding principles based on the recommendations of the Munn Report as subsequently qualified by the Scottish Consultative Council on the Curriculum and approved by the Secretary of State for Scotland. In particular, all schools are to include English, mathematics and a science course in the curriculum of every pupil at S3 and S4, and schools are asked to ensure that pupils select additional full or short courses meeting the requirements of eight 'modes' as shown in the table on pages 134-5. The SED has also made it clear that pupils should study a modern European language in S3 and S4.

Traditionally, Scottish secondary schools are organised in separate subject departments and the curriculum for each pupil has tended to be made up of a number of subject-related courses. In S3 and S4 the intention is to ensure that the various courses included in the curriculum of each pupil give adequate experience in all the modes. The matching of Standard Grade courses to modes is not yet completed, nor is it exact, and a single course can contribute to several modes.

Standard Grade

The first of the new Standard Grade courses began in August 1984. There are several stages of development: for the latest position parents should write to the Scottish Examination Board (address on page 207). Phase 1 for some subjects was introduced in 1984 with certification in 1986. The Phase 2 subjects were introduced in 1986 for examinations in 1988. Phases 3 and 4 are to be introduced from 1988-91, completing the schedule for all subjects at a future date.

Advantages of Standard Grade

Standard Grade has more to offer pupils in S3 and S4 because in nearly all curricular areas the courses have been designed to suit every level of ability. In some areas, such as mathematics, pupils follow courses at three levels. In other areas, such as English, the course is the same for all, but the skills to be acquired are designed to suit the different ability groups. For most courses, there are three separate examination papers at the end of the two years. They are set as credit (leading to awards at grade 1 or 2), General (leading to awards at grade 3 or 4) and Foundation (leading to awards at grade 5 or 6). A grade 7 is also available for those who complete the course but provide no evidence of significant attainment on it. Normally, pupils will take examinations covering two pairs of grades, either grades 1 to 4 or grades 3 to 6. This gives every pupil the maximum chance to gain an award which reflects his or her achievements.

Assessment and certification

In Standard Grade courses pupils are assessed against performance standards related to the three levels of award. Criteria for achievement at Foundation, General and Credit levels have been set out which give a description of what candidates achieving the award should know and be able to do. At Credit Level a grade 1 award indicates a high degree of mastery of Credit Level Criteria, while grade 2 indicates a satisfactory degree of mastery and similarly at General and Foundation. The award is based on the achievements of the individual, measured against stated standards, rather than on how his or her achievements compare with those of other candidates. Within a level, e.g. Credit, on all courses candidates have to give evidence of achievement in all the basic elements of the subject. For example in English, candidates receive separate assessments for reading, writing and talking as well as an overall grade. A profile of performance stating the grade obtained in each element will appear on the Certificate beside the overall award for the course.

Ordinary Grade

The O-grade courses and examinations continue for a few subjects. O-grade will be phased out by the end of 1992 as the new Standard Grade courses are introduced. However, there will be some optional subjects available, so O-grade will therefore be around for a few years yet. The Scottish Examination Board has announced that for the moment the Scottish Certificate of Education will still be offered at three grades – Standard (but only for some subjects), Ordinary and Higher – until the Ordinary Grade completely disappears.

Higher Grade

After the fourth year, Scottish pupils move into S5, the fifth year, to take subject courses leading to H-grade. This is the target for most 16- to 17-year-olds who stay on at school, which means the most academically able pupils. H-grade will not be affected by the introduction of Standard Grade, although some adjustments are to be made. The Scottish Examination Board has issued proposals to introduce revised syllabuses and assessment guidelines for some subjects. The first of these revised Higher Grades (in mathematics, English, home economics and Latin) have already been introduced.

'Highers' are normally taken after one year of study. However, some pupils take two years. Pupils who obtain an award at level 1 or 2 of the Standard Grade are expected to be of one-year calibre.

When applying to university, the usual request is that pupils should have passed four or five H-grade subjects. For English universities and polytechnics, three Highers are regarded as the equivalents of two A-levels and four Highers as the equivalents of three A-levels. A-level is reckoned to be of a higher standard than H-grade because A-level studies go into more depth and it usually takes two years to cover the course. On the other hand, because Scottish pupils usually take five H-grades they have a broader range of subjects than their more specialised English counterparts.

The Certificate of Sixth-Year Studies

The Certificate of Sixth-Year Studies (CSYS) is a course available for pupils who get a pass at H-grade in their fifth year at school and want to continue with these studies for a sixth year. At present the CSYS is still available, but the Scottish Examination Board has proposed a new course that will be designed as the second part of a two-year course after H-grade. Another proposal is that pupils will take H-grade and the new examination at the end of the sixth year.

These are only proposals. At the moment, the CSYS is a one-year course, and after it Scottish pupils go straight on to university or a centrally funded institution (Scotland's equivalent of a polytechnic).

The National Certificate

In 1984 a new National Certificate of the Scottish Vocational Education Council was introduced in Scotland and replaced all previous non-advanced vocational education courses. The courses which lead to the Certificate are offered in schools, colleges of further education and other institutions.

The National Certificate has been devised for different groups of students. They may be on Youth Training schemes, or full-time students, trainees sent from their companies on a part-time basis, or adults who need extra knowledge and training. The National Certificate is intended to be a step on the ladder to a qualification, for it can lead into National Diploma and HNC or HND courses. After that, the ladder could take students to degree courses and to professional status. To decide on the content of the modules that make up the National Certificate, the former bodies SCOTEC and SCOTBEC amalgamated to form SCOTVEC – the Scottish Vocational Education Council.

In the majority of instances, pupils and students following the National Certificate are aged 16-plus. Most school-based pupils take SCE Standard Grade, Standard Grade or H-grade courses. It is also possible for pupils in the later years of secondary schooling to obtain the National Curriculum.

The main methods of studying for the Certificate are therefore:

- on a full-time course or a part-time course at a college of further education
- as part of the two-year Youth Training programme
- in the last two years of secondary schooling
- by adults who want to improve their skills or learn new skills.

The courses are built around 'programmes of study'. Programmes are made up of *modules of study*. Most modules are of 40 hours' duration. An essential feature of each module is a statement of the learning objectives, an explanation of what the student can or is expected to do.

The National Certificate has been devised with the help of employers and the modules have been grouped into nine categories, describing the kind of work or employment:

Interdisciplinary studies
This includes English language and communication studies.

Other subjects are maths, statistics, computing, industrial studies, drama, physical education, languages, arts subjects, fashion, photography.

Business and administration
The modules include clerical and secretarial subjects, information processing, hotel work, accounting, costing and estimating, law, travel and tourism, insurance, housing and local government.

Distribution food services and personal services
This course includes topics such as transport and distribution, display, selling and marketing, food services, personal services (such as hairdressing) and retail trading which includes shop work.

Engineering
All the engineering technologies from electronics through to vehicle body building are included.

Built environment
Building crafts from bricklaying to tiling.

Caring
The courses deal with the care of the sick, handicapped, young children, elderly and family work.

Industrial processing
Included in this group are many different courses, among them printing, textile production, cleaning services, cookery and food preparation.

Land and sea-based industries
Forestry, farming, gardening, shipping and landscaping subjects.

Pure and applied sciences
Includes applied science, physics, chemistry, biology, human biology, dental repairs, laboratory work with animals and many other subjects.

This new system of vocational education provides a more flexible and co-ordinated scheme which takes full account of the impact of new technology and the essential skills required by industry. Furthermore, the Scottish Vocational Qualification (SVQ) is being introduced to combine SCOTVEC National Certificate or HND qualifications with those obtained in the workplace; the SVQ is similar to the NVQ operation elsewhere in the UK.

Information about the National Certificate is available from the Scottish Vocational Education Council, 38 Queen Street, Glasgow G1 3DY.

The editor acknowledges the assistance given by the Scottish Education Department, SCOTVEC and Scottish Examination Board staff in the preparation of this chapter.

CHAPTER 15

NATIONAL VOCATIONAL QUALIFICATIONS

NATIONAL Vocational Qualifications (NVQs) is a new system of qualifications and credits that directly apply to people's jobs. Instead of a qualification obtained *before* going to work (such as GCSE, A-level or BTEC diplomas and HNDs), NVQs are applied to the jobs people are doing. An example is given in an NVQ leaflet: 'If you get an NVQ qualification in hairdressing, it means that you can actually cut hair and know what a good hairdresser needs to know.'

NVQs are at five levels: a Level 1 NVQ is the simplest basic level; Level 3 is A-level standard; Level 5 would be the qualification for a manager or director of a large hairdressing salon business with a substantial turnover, for instance.

NVQs are not normally acquired at school but as part of one's employment pattern. It is possible to obtain a dual qualification of an NVQ with a City and Guilds certificate (or some other awards) if the course and the assessment of competence have been approved by the National Council for Vocational Qualifications (NCVQ). Some NVQs have been approved by the NCVQ, but not sufficient for the Government who have announced that they want to see eighty per cent of all vocational courses carrying an NVQ sticker by the end of 1992. This is a tall order, because so few have yet been approved.

Setting standards

The basic philosophy underpinning NVQs is that they recognise people's achievements. And this means achievements at work, performing the tasks of the job, and calling on the knowledge and skills needed to complete these tasks effectively.

The important point is that NVQs are based on *standards*. This means national standards set by employers' organisations in industry and commerce. NVQs, since they are defined by employers, should be widely accepted by employers: that's the theory.

Standards are based on what people can do. Each NVQ is made up of a number of units which set out the standards that must be reached. A unit is like a part-qualification towards, say, a Level 2 qualification in printing. People can choose which units they work for, and they are awarded certificates to show the unit credits that they have achieved. This record of unit credits is carried from one job to another. NVQ-holders therefore carry with them their own personal guarantees of the standards they have achieved, and they can work towards the extra credits they need for a full NVQ or a more advanced one at a higher level.

Back to standards. To fix these, the employers' group first of all identifies the different jobs in the particular industry and breaks them down into closely defined *units of competence*. Having done that, the next task is to decide on the criteria by which the performance of these competences and skills can be measured.

So far, all this is paperwork – defining skills and competences, fixing the performance levels and deciding how to measure them. The next stage is a practical one. Independent examiners called 'verifiers' go into companies or organisations where people are being assessed for NVQs. They assess the skill in doing a particular job in terms of the definition of the skill or competence and the person's performance in doing it.

Are NVQs really important?

Yes. If the promises made for NVQs are fulfilled, they should set national standards of occupational competence and performance based on jobs. This is important for employers who can feel they are a guarantee of the level of performance expected of an employee or someone who is being interviewed for a job. It is a measure of the extent to which an employee is able to do his or her job effectively.

And, because these standards are *national* ones, one company or or-ganisation can compare their standards with other people being inter-viewed.

The importance to individuals is that they have qualifications which say that they can do a job to a nationally agreed and assessed standard.

And you should appreciate that school- and college-based awards such as GCSE, A-level, HND and degrees don't do this. They are standards of educational achievement *prior to* employment; they do not guarantee any kind of standard in performing a job.

However, NVQs have yet to be proved: time will tell whether or not all industries will be able to write, develop, apply and measure them.

NVQs – an example

You might ask, 'but to get an NVQ, what do you have to do?'. To answer it, let's take an example. There is a City and Guilds certificate course in Business Administration. This course is taken by young people (and by mature staff, too) who work in offices.

The City and Guilds course has been in existence for many years, regularly revised to keep it up to date. It deals with topics such as filing, data processing, mail handling, stock control, photocopying, text processing, using a typewriter and a word processor, processing payments, liaising with customers, communicating information, and so on.

In the past, students obtained a City and Guilds certificate if they successfully completed the course. Now it's NVQ-approved. What that means is that an employers' group (called a Lead Body) sets the standards for business, administrative and commercial staff working in offices. It was decided that the course, the skills and the competences were at two Levels:

- Level 1: the skills and competence needed by young people working in an office for the first time.
- Level 2: these standards are appropriate for people who have progressed beyond this initial stage of work and training.

Structure of awards

This chart shows the structure of awards, that is the way the content or 'title' of the full course has been divided into units. To achieve an award at Level 1, students need to take nine units, plus another six or seven units for Level 2.

Assessing knowledge and competence

Students attend college, perhaps on a day-release basis, and, by theoretical and practical work, cover the course and obtain their City and Guilds certificate. Alongside this is the assessment for NVQ purposes.

What is 'competence'?

The instruction for this NVQ says that '. . . Assessment of an individual's performance should be based upon situations which require demonstration of competence, requiring a combination of skills and related knowledge, in purposeful and recognisable tasks. It is the successful day-to-day, consistent demonstration of competence, which is of prime importance in determining that occupational competence has been achieved . . .'

In assessing competence, the City and Guilds requires that evidence of achievement is obtained in a valid, reliable and efficient manner and that achievement is recorded in the candidate's logbook.

Methods of assessing skill and related knowledge

Most of the units are assessed through observation of performance in the workplace. Where this is not possible, realistic simulation needs to be arranged in accordance with the requirements for each part of the syllabus.

In assessing a candidate's competence, consistency of performance is a prime consideration; assessment has to be carried out more than once to ensure that competence is firmly established.

There are three main assessment methods. At least two combine to assemble sufficient evidence to show that the candidate has met, or can meet, the requirements of the syllabus.

They are:

- observation of performance over time or on specified occasions in the workplace or in a simulated workplace
- setting assignments, projects, and practical tasks
- questioning in written or oral form.

The assessment of related knowledge and understanding

There are various methods of assessing knowledge and understanding. These may be drawn from:

- written tests
- assignments/projects
- oral questions.

Logbooks

Each student has a logbook in which his or her progress is noted and monitored. The logbook records progress and achievements towards the certificate and thus towards the NVQ.

Here is a *Summary of Achievement* showing how each aspect or element of the syllabus is assessed, and who has done the assessing.

SUMMARY OF ACHIEVEMENT

Unit	Title	Date Achieved	Assessor	Candidate
002	Communicating information			
003	Data processing			
004	Processing petty cash and invoices			
005	Stockhandling			
006	Mail handling			
007	Reprographics			
008	Liaising with callers and colleagues			
009	Health and safety			
010	Creating and maintaining business relationships			
011	Providing information to customers/clients			
012	Storing and supplying information			
013	Information processing			
014	Telecommunications and data transmission			
015	Reception			
019	Arranging travel and meetings			
020	Processing payments			

Assessing activities

This is the statement of the activities that have to be assessed. 'Arranging travel and meetings' is one 'element' or topic in the full course. As you see, what the student has to do is set out.

Arranging travel and meetings
Element
Arrange meetings involving three or more people.

Assessed activities and performance criteria
In a real or simulated work environment the candidate has:

- checked availability of participants and facilities against proposed meeting dates
- agreed date of meeting and confirmed arrangements
- informed participants of arrangements in advance of meeting
- despatched all necessary papers in advance of the meeting and/or provided them at the meeting as directed
- maintained security and confidentiality of information at all times.

Range of variables to which the element applies

- meetings which involve at least one external participant
- internal and external venues
- supply of the following equipment: flipchart, OH projector and screen, video equipment, refreshments
- distribution of materials prior to meeting on at least one occasion
- informal and formal meetings.

Assessment methods used

_____

_____

_____ Internal Assessor

_____ Candidate

Element achieved _____ Date _____

This example is provided to give you an idea of how NVQ assessment is applied to a course of study and the assessment of skills, knowledge and understanding in the workplace. This kind of assessment is already in existence in other parts of Western Europe, but its introduction in the UK is slow (because of the careful analysis and documentation needed). On the other hand, NVQs are on the way and will become more and more significant in the 1990s.

This example and extracts are reproduced by permission of the City and Guilds of London Institute: the publishers acknowledge the assistance of the City and Guilds in reproducing these examples.

For further information, booklets and leaflets on NVQs, write to NCVQ, 222 Euston Road, London NW1 2BZ.

CHAPTER **16**

THE DIPLOMA IN VOCATIONAL EDUCATION

PARENTS, schools and colleges could say that they are in a state of severe shock on vocational courses. For three years' running, there have been changes, and yet another initiative is now being talked about.

The sequence has been something like this:

- During the 1980s, schools provided TVEI (the Technical and Vocational Education Initiative) courses for 14- to 18-year-olds
- From 1985, courses leading to the City and Guilds/BTEC qualification, the Certificate in Pre-Vocational Education (CPVE) for 16+ students in schools and colleges ran alongside
- TVEI was largely overtaken in 1989-91 by the CGLI/BTEC course and by the Foundation programme which in the period 1992-4 is likely to be dismantled and replaced by the promised Diploma in Vocational Education for 16- to 19-year-olds which will not come in fully until 1994, if the consultations now going ahead lead to new legislation
- In 1991, the Government announced that schools could prepare and enter pupils for BTEC First Diplomas in vocational subjects; these courses are currently offered at further education colleges but the intention is to encourage schools to provide more vocational education.

What does all of this mean for parents? It means that the present Government is very keen to extend vocational courses and is pushing on all fronts – in schools as well as FE colleges – to provide a range of vocational offerings without being quite clear about the priorities and front runners.

150

Looking ahead to 1994

The preferred scenario for the Government would almost certainly be to leave A-levels as a core skill free zone, but to make it desirable to add evidence of competence in communication, problem solving, personal skills, numeracy, information technology and modern languages, recognised through a Diploma in Vocational Studies, which would be at two levels, ordinary and advanced.

Will it work? Will it help to produce a generation of young people eager to show that they are both competent and clever, educated and trained to set Britain's economic and technological future to rights? A tall order, and it could be that your children are part of the experiment to find an effective new form of vocational education. This master-plan, designed to be implemented by 1994, will be based on Ordinary and Advanced Diplomas of a new Diploma in Vocational Education.

Ordinary and Advanced Diplomas

The plans announced in 1991 in the Government White Paper, *Education and Training for the 21st Century* describe how education and training for the 16- to 19-year-old age-group will be adapted to meet future needs.

'The basic aim is to engage more youngsters in education and training and so raise their level of attainment.

'Changes in the labour market are putting an even greater emphasis on the acquisition of skills, making it important for young people to be qualified to higher levels. The proposals say that not only do we need a stronger base of general competences at all levels, but we also need more people with higher skills at management, technician and professional levels. One of the prime aims in introducing the Ordinary and Advanced Diploma, therefore, is to encourage and recognise the attainment of knowledge, skills and understanding at both the basic and higher levels. In doing this the Government recognises that these can be acquired through both academic and vocational routes or combinations of them.'

The Government's plans for 16- to 19-year-olds build on the various changes already being implemented in schools: notably the introduction of the National Curriculum, which will require all pupils to study a broad and balanced curriculum, and the development within that framework of more vocational courses for 14- to l6-year-olds.

The Government considers that increased take up of vocational qualifications would make a big contribution to achieving its aims for 16 to l9 education. However, vocational qualifications are currently often poorly understood and undervalued in comparison with academic qualifications. They say that a system of Ordinary and Advanced Diplomas, covering academic and vocational qualifications whether separately or in combination, should establish a common understanding of the quality and demands of vocational qualifications and lead to equal achievements being given equal value, whatever the route to them or their component parts. Their main purposes are therefore to:

- encourage young people to continue with education or training, irrespective of whether this is via an academic route, adopting a wholly or partially vocationally related route while staying in full-time education, or through entering employment with training towards a vocational qualification appropriate to the job
- provide a simple method for comparing vocational and academic qualifications, by employers, providers of further or higher education, parents and young people themselves.

These Diplomas are not *new* qualifications. They are to be based on existing qualifications (and National Vocational Qualifications currently being developed), which will be recognised by employers, higher education, young people, their parents and teachers alike. They would certify the acquisition, at a given level, of skills, knowledge and understanding.

The Ordinary Diploma

The Government believes that the Ordinary Diploma would give its holder the range of basic, essential skills and knowledge which is necessary for the pursuit of further education and training or progression in employment. It would be pitched broadly at NVQ Level 2. Attainment could be demonstrated through GCSEs and/or equivalent vocational qualifications.

The Ordinary Diploma will not only be awarded to 16-year-olds: it will be possible to accumulate credits towards it over a period of time. It will also be a stepping stone to the Advanced Diploma, as well as being of value in its own right.

The White Paper says that the Ordinary Diploma might be awarded for GCSEs in four or five subjects at National Curriculum levels 7 to 10, for equivalent vocational qualifications, or a combination of these.

The Advanced Diploma

Higher level skills at technician, management and professional level are said to be essential to meet the growing challenge from competitors in overseas markets.

The skills, knowledge and understanding essential to these occupations can be developed through both the academic and vocational routes, through education and training. The Government thinks that the Advanced Diploma will give public recognition to those who have demonstrated the skills, knowledge and understanding which form a sound basis for progression to technician, management or professional levels, whether through the academic or vocational route, in education or employment.

Assessment

From 1994, all 16-year-old pupils (except those in 'special' categories) will be assessed through GCSEs or equivalent in the core subjects of the National Curriculum: mathematics, science (in most cases qualifying for a double award) and English. They will also be assessed through full or 'half' GCSEs (or equivalent in technology) from 1995, and in a modern foreign language and history and/or geography from 1996. The Government's policies are intended to ensure that 14- to 16-year-olds (in Key Stage 4 of the National Curriculum) also have significant opportunities to take other subjects: these too should be able to contribute towards the Ordinary Diploma. From 1996 onwards all 16-year-olds will have covered a broad and balanced curriculum in their compulsory education.

These proposals are now for consultation and discussion, but they give a fair indication of the direction that the present Government is heading in planning the future of vocational education.

CHAPTER **17**

Moving into higher education

'Higher education' is usually taken to mean post A-level courses that lead to degrees, diplomas of higher education (DipHE), HNDs and similar awards. The courses are run by universities, polytechnics, institutes and colleges of higher education, and specialist colleges, such as colleges of art and design, building, agriculture or printing, and in some colleges of further education. Entry is usually at 18 years of age or older.

Applying for and getting into higher education is a crucial time in a student's progress through secondary school, because so much depends on the choice of subject, course and institution. Most parents understand this importance and try to help their children make sensible choices. This occasionally causes problems when teenagers feel their parents are interfering in areas the parents know nothing about, or on which they do not want advice because they want to assert their independence.

Parents, on the other hand, may be confused and uncertain in the jargon-ridden minefield of university and college applications. In this situation the pupil who needs and would welcome advice gets none. Most parents fall back on the school: 'Why don't you see the careers teacher and ask about these courses . . . ?' That can be good advice, but not all schools have knowledgeable careers teachers, even if they have a careers teacher. In these circumstances the parents and the students have to fall back on published material. There are plenty of excellent publications, and they are widely used by the experts as well as by potential students and their parents. The best of these publications are listed in Chapter 21 and some are discussed in detail in the following pages. First, however, why is it that decisions at 17- to 18-plus are so important?

Key decisions

It is not easy to obtain a place in a higher education institution, so a student would be wise to analyse his or her motives for wanting to move on to higher education. First think about the reasons for this choice. Forethought is essential not only to guide the choice of course and place but as a rehearsal for an interview when these questions are likely to be asked by admissions tutors.

Is the reason for going on to a course in higher education:

- Knowledge – to carry on the study of a subject to a higher level (as in choosing a degree course in history, having enjoyed it at A-level or H-grade)?
- A fresh stimulus – to make a new start with a subject never previously studied, such as landscape architecture, nautical studies, psychology, sports studies, biotechnology?
- A career choice – where the subject is a vocational one leading directly to a career, as with medicine, dentistry, dietetics, surveying?
- Intellectual stimulus and academic interest – classics and philosophy, which are not directly career linked, could be said to come into this category?
- Escape – as a means of getting away from home, friends, parents, school or other connections or responsibilities?
- To postpone making a decision about a job or a career until the course is over?
- The pressure and expectations of parents, teachers and friends – some pupils are carried along by the wave of expectation that has built up since they were about 12 and which they are terrified to challenge?
- Indifference – 'I can't think of anything else to do' is a not uncommon motive?

Parents and applicants should be clear about the motives that precede the decision-making stage. Many pupils drift along, bolstered by the expectations of teachers and parents, carried on by their showing in GCSE (O-grade) and A-level (H-grade) examinations, and thus apply to a university or polytechnic for a particular course without really discussing or considering carefully their reasons for wanting to do so.

It might be helpful if a prospective applicant thought about these questions and listed the 'yes' or 'no' answers. This could provide the basis for a discussion with parents, teachers and friends about the decisions to apply or not, and which courses, subjects and institutions should be shortlisted.

Institutions

Before any application form for a higher education course is completed, it is vitally important to consider the type of institution. Is the choice to be from:

● universities – there are over 60 universities and university colleges to choose from. Some of them – the University of London, for instance – have a number of colleges within the university
● polytechnics – there are over 30 throughout the UK
● specialist colleges of building, printing, art and design, agriculture, furniture, etc.
● colleges or institutes of higher education, some of which provide teacher-training courses and all of which have a range of other work, including degree courses
● preliminary course at a college before applying to a university, such as in a one-year foundation course in design before applying for a degree course in design.

Parents and students who do not know the differences between these institutions and what they offer should ask the school careers staff or careers advisers in Local Education Authority careers offices and read the relevant chapters in books such as *Your Choice of Degree and Diploma* (Hobsons) and *The Student Book* (Macmillan).

Place

Having decided on the type of institution, it is important to consider the question of place. Is the choice to be based on:

● size? This varies enormously: the University of Manchester has 12,700 full-time students while the University of Keele has about 3,400
● distance? Does the student want to be able to live at home and travel in daily, or be far from home – University of Aberdeen for a Devonian, University of Exeter for a Shetlander?

- location? The University of Newcastle upon Tyne and Newcastle upon Tyne Polytechnic are both in the centre of a large and lively city; the University of East Anglia is outside a small, old city; the University of Lancaster is in the countryside three miles from a market town
- prestige? Is the applicant likely to be academically a high-flyer with ambitions for Oxford or Cambridge?
- atmosphere? Which appeals most, living on a campus, separate from a city; in a small college; or at the centre of a city with access to city life?

Again, it is worth taking time to think about these factors and to work out which institutions and places are more attractive to the student's attitude and preferences for environmental considerations.

Courses

Careful choice of the subject and the course is vitally important. Should the student:

- continue with a familiar subject, previously taken to A-level or H-grade
- study a new subject
- take a combined studies course which leaves options open for a later choice of the final-year subject: 'combined sciences' and 'combined studies' are two such courses, and modular programmes at polytechnics offer much the same kind of arrangement, allowing for later choice and specialisation
- go for a subject with direct career links, such as business studies, finance and accounting, engineering
- pick a sandwich course mixing periods of full-time study at college with work experience placements in industry or commerce.

A further consideration in choosing a subject or a course is the likely result in A-level, H-grade, BTEC or any other pre-entry examinations. For example, three good A-level passes are likely to win a place on a university course. Lower grades of pass in two or three A-levels will probably secure a place at a polytechnic, depending on the A-level subjects and the grades. One A-level pass or two H-grades could lead to an offer of a place on an HND course at a polytechnic, college of higher education or specialist college.

Qualifications

In assessing a student's chances of getting a place at a higher education institution, his or her A-level or H-grade results or anticipated results have to be weighed.

It is well known, for example, that it is fiendishly difficult to get on to a degree course in medicine or veterinary science. The reason is that there are a restricted number of places on first-degree courses in these subjects and the number of potential applicants far outnumbers the available places. Therefore the universities, teaching hospitals and veterinary colleges can ask for and expect the highest grades. Three grade A passes in three science A-levels are generally demanded for degree courses in medicine and veterinary science, and equally high grades are now expected for courses, such as law, which are very popular, as well as for entry to Oxford or Cambridge for almost any course.

It is wise to have some idea of the A-level or H-grade requirements expected for the course that a student has in view. Clearly, if the applicant's expectations of A-level grades are modest (perhaps three passes at grade C or D) it would be impractical to apply for a degree course in a popular subject at a university. The guidebook for A-level grades linked to degree courses is *Degree Course Offers*, published annually by Careers Consultants.

So, before taking the first step in applying, every candidate must check whether he or she has the correct entry qualifications in terms of passes. The guide below gives an indication of the match between A-level and GCSE qualifications and higher education courses.

Two or more A-levels

With passes at any grade in two A-level subjects, students are eligible to apply for:

- degree courses (BA, BSc, BD, BEd, etc.) at honours and ordinary degree levels at universities, polytechnics and colleges. (But note that two A-levels and three GCSEs is the *minimum* requirement and students should aim for good (grades A to C) A-level grades.)
- Diploma of Higher Education (DipHE) courses available at colleges and institutes of higher education

- professional courses (accountancy, surveying and many others) which lead to exemptions from the examinations of professional institutions
- advanced courses at polytechnics and colleges, leading to college diplomas and certificates
- teaching. The way into teaching is either by taking a degree in a subject (say geography), followed by a further one-year course for a Postgraduate Certificate in Education, or by taking a BEd degree course. For entry to a BEd course, at least two A-levels are needed, with good O-level or GCSE passes in three other subjects, including English language and mathematics.

One A-level

Students with one A-level pass, plus three GCSEs at grades A, B or C, have the following open to them at polytechnics and colleges:

- HNC and HND (BTEC) in a wide range of subjects. For these courses, students are normally expected to have studied two A-level subjects and to have passed in one.

Non-GCSE entry qualifications

It is possible to qualify for university, polytechnic or college courses without A-levels or GCSEs. Those who left school at 16 and studied for qualifications such as a BTEC or SCOTVEC National Certificate or National Diploma and the HNC or HND by attending evening classes or part-time day-release classes at a local technical college have sufficient academic qualifications to gain entry.

The BTEC National Certificate or National Diploma is accepted as an alternative to the A-level component. However, all candidates for degree courses hoping to use BTEC awards as alternatives to A-level/ GCSE should write to the relevant university or polytechnic department before making a firm application.

Qualifications such as National Certificate and National Diploma are generally acceptable as equivalents to A-levels, as long as a pass grade at a high enough standard has been obtained.

Scottish qualifications

People who have been educated in Scotland may have awards of the Scottish Certificate of Education Examination Board at O-grade, S-grade and H-grade and in the CSYS (the Certificate of Sixth-Year Studies). Universities, polytechnics and colleges in England, Wales and Northern Ireland accept Scottish qualifications, generally working to equivalents such as:

- O-grades and S-grades are equal to O-levels or GCSE passes at grades A to C
- H-grades A and B are equal to A-level pass grades A to E
- three H-grade passes are equal to two A-level passes
- four H-grade passes are equal to three A-level passes
- a pass in the Certificate of Sixth-Year Studies is equal to an A-level pass, although some universities specify that the CSYS pass should be at grade A, B or C.

Applicants should check the situation with the university or college before making a formal application.

Overseas qualifications

All institutions accept overseas qualifications. However, there is no hard and fast rule, and applicants from overseas countries should check on the acceptability of their particular qualifications with admissions tutors or departments, or with the Qualifications Branch of the British Council.

A-level subjects and careers

In Part 3 of this book are details of over 200 careers. In most cases the relevant school subjects are mentioned, and if A-levels are needed, they are included. However, another way of looking at A-levels and careers is to list the careers that are possible if a certain group of A-levels – sciences, arts, business studies, for example – is selected. It could happen, for instance, that a student who is considering a group of science A-levels had no idea that possible careers options could be in rubber technology, packaging, fibre sciences, paint, timber, transport and other technical careers. In the following lists some possible careers are suggested: a student could tick the boxes for careers that at this stage look fairly appealing. If interested, the next stage should be to read the appropriate entry in Part 3. Ticking, or even just considering the careers in the following lists, the connections between subjects and future jobs will begin to show up. Another point to make is that these careers *depend* on the science/arts/business connections, which again underlines the importance of making the right choice of A-levels in the first place.

POSSIBLE CAREER CHOICES: SCIENCE AND TECHNOLOGY

- Acoustics
- Aeronautical engineering
- Agriculture
- Air transport
- Astronomy
- Audiology
- Automobile engineering
- Biochemistry
- Biological sciences
- Brewing
- Building
- Chemical engineering
- Chemistry
- Civil engineering
- Computing
- Dentistry
- Dietetics
- Electrical engineering
- Electronics
- Engineering
- Farming
- Fibre technology
- Finance
- Fishing technology
- Food production
- Food technology
- Forestry
- Fuel technology
- Gas technology
- Geology
- Glass technology
- Health visiting
- Home economics
- Horticulture
- Industrial design
- Information technology
- Instrument technology
- Investment
- Leather technology
- Mathematics
- Mechanical engineering
- Medical work
- Metallurgy
- Meteorology
- Military careers
- Mining
- Mining surveying
- Mineral exploration
- Nautical science
- Naval architecture
- Nursing
- Nutrition
- Ophthalmic optics/optician
- Packaging technology
- Paint technology
- Paper technology
- Pharmaceuticals
- Pharmacy
- Photography
- Physics
- Physiotherapy
- Plastics technology
- Polymer technology
- Printing
- Psychology
- Quantity surveying
- Rubber technology
- Shipping and shipbuilding
- Statistics
- Surveying
- Systems analysis
- Taxation
- Tele-communications
- Teaching
- Television
- Textiles
- Town and country planning
- Transport
- Timber trade
- Traffic operations
- Veterinary science
- Water industry
- Wildlife management
- Zoology

POSSIBLE CAREER CHOICES: ARTS, BUSINESS STUDIES AND SOCIAL SCIENCES

- Accountancy
- Administration
- Advertising
- Anthropology
- Archaeology
- Architecture
- Art and design
- Banking
- Broadcasting
- Building society work
- Business
- Cartography
- Catering
- Child care
- Church work
- Civil service
- Clerical work
- Community work
- Company secretary
- Computing
- Conservation
- Customs and Excise
- Dairy farming
- Design
- Drama
- Dressmaking
- Economics
- Education
- Entertainment
- Environmental health
- Estate management
- Exhibition work
- Exporting
- Farming
- Fashion
- Film production
- Finance
- Forestry
- Garage work
- Government service
- Health service
- Home economics
- Hospitals
- Hotel and catering
- Housing management
- Industrial design
- Industrial relations
- Information technology
- Insurance
- Investment
- Journalism
- Land management
- Languages
- Landscape work
- Law
- Libraries
- Local government
- Management
- Marketing
- Military careers
- Music
- Newspapers
- Nursing
- Optician
- Packaging industry
- Personnel work
- Photography
- Physiotherapy
- Pilot
- Police service
- Post Office
- Probation service
- Psychiatric social work
- Public relations
- Publishing
- Purchasing
- Radio
- Radiography
- Rail transport
- Rating and valuation surveying
- Religion
- Retail management
- Sales
- Secretarial work
- Social work
- Speech therapy
- Sport
- Stock Exchange
- Systems analysis
- Tax inspector
- Teaching: arts, business studies, social sciences
- Television
- Textile design
- Theatre
- Town and country planning
- Tourism
- Transport work
- Welfare work
- Youth and community work

CHAPTER 18

HIGHER EDUCATION COURSES

THERE ARE hundreds of different courses and subject combinations at degree level in higher education institutions. It is difficult for an A-level or H-grade student contemplating Universities Central Council on Admissions (UCCA) or Polytechnics Central Admissions System (PCAS) or other application forms to know where to start.

A survey published in 1990 showed that over 82 per cent of school-leavers holding two or more A-levels or three Scottish H-grades intended to go on to a course in higher education. These courses are available in universities, polytechnics, colleges and institutes of higher education, art colleges and in some specialist and further education colleges.

Degrees

These include Bachelor of Arts (BA), Bachelor of Science (BSc), Bachelor of Engineering (BEng), Bachelor of Commerce (BComm) and Bachelor of Education (BEd). Degree courses come in various forms and with different requirements. These are some of them:

- they usually last three years, or four years if they are of the sandwich type, mixing work experience in industry or a year abroad with full-time study at college
- they normally require a minimum of two A-levels and another three subjects at GCSE. Realistic entry requirements are usually much higher than the minimum
- courses can be vocational, such as engineering, or non-vocational, such as philosophy, history, English literature
- they can be single subject (geography, say) or two subjects of roughly

equal weight (such as French and Spanish), or combined studies which could include a group of subjects (such as English, history, archaeology and media studies)

● courses can be modular: modules are units of study and a student builds up a package of modules equal to three- or four- year courses.

The costs of taking a degree course can be broken down into two parts: tuition fees and maintenance or living costs. Degree courses qualify for Local Education Authority mandatory awards which are usually called 'county major awards'. The maintenance part of a grant depends on the income of a student's parents. The tuition fees are generally paid by the student's own Local Education Authority, even if the student does not qualify for a maintenance grant. Students therefore need to discuss with their parents at an early stage what, if any, contribution they can make to the son's or daughter's maintenance.

For details of individual degree courses, the differences between them, entry requirements and special aspects, consult CRAC's *Degree Course Guides* which are available for all degree subjects.

Diploma of Higher Education (DipHE)

● two years in duration, although many DipHE courses allow students to continue for a further one or two years for a degree

● requires a minimum of two A-levels and appropriate GCSE passes at grades A to C

● is usually non-vocational

● usually involves the study of more than one subject. Students may be able to develop an individual course of study from the options or 'modules' available

● can include both familiar and new subjects

● available in polytechnics, and colleges and institutes of further and higher education

● qualifies for a mandatory award (see page 201) from the Local Education Authority.

For more information consult the *Compendium of Advanced Courses in Colleges of Further and Higher Education*.

Business and Technician Education Council, Higher National Diploma (BTEC HND)

- usually two years in duration when full time, three years if a work placement is included as part of a sandwich course
- requires a minimum of one A-level pass with, usually, one other A-level subject to have been studied
- has vocational bias
- usually offered as a single subject (for example, applied physics) but can involve study of several elements under a single-subject heading (for example, business studies, which can incorporate law, accounts, economics, marketing, sociology, statistics, psychology and a foreign language)
- where a traditional school subject is offered (for example, maths) it will be taught in a manner relevant to the needs of employers
- available in polytechnics and colleges and institutes of further and higher education
- qualifies for a mandatory award (see page 201) from the Local Education Authority.

For more information consult the *Compendium of Advanced Courses in Colleges of Further and Higher Education.*

Other advanced courses

- will vary both in duration and in entrance requirements
- are usually concerned with a particular career (radiography, chiropody, languages for business) or a range of careers (for example, communications studies), or preparation for a career such as design, music or drama
- courses may offer part or full professional qualifications
- may draw on knowledge from a variety of disciplines (for example, radiography includes a study of both biology and physics)
- available in polytechnics, colleges and institutes of further and higher education, or specialist institutions such as teaching hospitals, colleges of art and design and drama schools
- for some courses students may be eligible for a mandatory award. More often, any award will be at the discretion of the Local Education Authority (see page 201). In the case of certain paramedical courses the grant is paid by the Department of Health.

For details of many of these courses consult the *Compendium of Advanced Courses in Colleges of Further and Higher Education*.

What is the best course?

This question, regularly asked by pupils, parents, schools' careers teachers and other careers advisers, is impossible to answer. Best for whom? Best for what? But one way of attempting to provide an answer is to say that the choice of a course must be based on the criteria defined in the previous chapter, namely:

● choosing the right subject
● choosing the right course which incorporates this subject or subjects
● choosing the right institution.

All these factors depend on personal attitudes, opinions and needs. The best institution will not necessarily be the one with the highest academic reputation: a student may instinctively or logically decide that another place would be more suited to his or her personality and needs. The best subject may not be the one in which the student achieved the best grade at A-level, or even the subjects *taken* at A-level. The best course may not be an academic one but a vocational one. And so on.

There are therefore many factors to be borne in mind when thinking of the 'best' course and place. The important consideration is to think about the options, and not make a judgement based on inadequate research and enquiries or on hearsay and other people's judgements.

Methods of study

Having made a choice of subject, the next step is to establish the way in which it is studied. Again, it is wrong to suppose that courses with the same title have the same content. If, for instance, the choice is English, the potential student should obtain the prospectuses of six different universities to see what is actually involved in English studies at each one. The wide variation in content may well come as a surprise.

The prospectus should explain how the subject is taught: use will be made of words such as 'tutorial', 'seminar', 'dissertation', 'fieldwork', 'workshop practice', and 'case studies'. Applicants should discuss the teaching methods with the teachers at school.

Another important consideration is whether a single subject is to be taken throughout the three- or four-year course, or if a combined or joint course would be more attractive. Four years of German might be a heavy burden for someone not too keen on linguistics, language and literature, but a course mixing German language and literature with business studies and history might be more attractive.

Recent developments in higher education

In recent years the Government's policy has been to encourage universities, polytechnics and colleges to take more students, but not to increase their costs beyond the rate of inflation.

This has meant that there are more places available in higher education. The reverse side of the coin is that students are likely to be taught in larger groups and have less lecturer contact time than in previous years.

The expansion of places in higher education has coincided with a greater demand for places from young people. The economic recession of 1989-91 has had a lot to do with this increase: students see higher education as a key to careers and jobs and even if they hoped to get a job at 16 or 18, they often had to face up to disappointment. In effect, then, we are postponing the entry of many young people to the job market; the benefit is that when they do look for jobs two, three or four years on, they will be far better qualified.

Between 1988 and 1991 over a thousand additional places were offered for first degree and HND courses, a substantial increase. The Government was keen to expand in scientific areas – physics, engineering, chemistry, information technology, biotechnology, etc – but the demand was as great (if not greater) from arts and business studies applicants.

For A-level and other applicants, therefore, the reality is that it is easier to obtain a place on a science-based first degree or HND course than it is on a business studies or arts course: this is reflected in expected A-level grades – A, B and C grades are essential for arts/business/social studies courses, but lower A-level grades, such as C, D and E, are more widely accepted by admissions tutors for science and maths-based courses.

Look at it another way. In 1988-9, only 32 per cent of 16-year-olds obtained good GCSE grades (A, B or C passes) in mathematics. At A-level and H-grade, 7 per cent of *all* 18-year-olds got a pass *at any grade* in mathematics. Only 5 per cent passed A-level (or H-grade) physics. Therefore, the field of A-level maths and physics applicants is small. The range of potential is huge: the universities and polytechnics are desperately eager to find candidates with science A-levels, simply because these students are so rare, and the institutions have to fill their student 'quotas'.

Students with science and maths A-levels can therefore pick and choose from a wide selection of interesting courses, and be strongly confident of obtaining a place, even though they may have only modest A-level grades. And when it comes to looking for a job later on, or even at 18 immediately after A-levels, they will have more opportunities then, too.

This does not mean that arts, business and other non-science based post-A-level applicants should despair. Far from it. Their brains are equally lively, and their knowledge, skills and spark are just as eagerly looked for by admissions tutors. The range of arts courses is equally wide, and just as stimulating in variety and depth. The point being made here is, however, that it's harder for a non-science A-level candidate to get a place, and a great deal harder to get a job on graduation. But no one should ever despair. Perseverance and determination are wonderful personal qualities, and they are often far more effective than paperweight A-level grades.

Graduate employment

When assessing whether or not to embark on a degree course it is worth considering graduates' job prospects. More and more jobs are now advertised for people with degrees. A degree, an HNC or HND or another qualification gives a much better chance of obtaining a job.

Furthermore, more and more companies are employing graduates. Companies that formerly took no part in the annual recruitment of graduates have joined the race to enrol them. When questioned, employers respond by saying that they feel graduates are more adaptable to change and this is important in a volatile commercial market. Graduates also tend to be mobile, to be willing to take jobs in different parts of the UK or abroad. Finally, employers believe that graduates are the cream of the employment market and their intelligence and liveliness will pay off once they are trained and useful to the business. This view was borne out by the 1991 survey into *What Do Graduates Do?* which revealed that for an increasing number of professions, entry is now mainly at graduate level.

Consequently, if at all possible, students should aim to achieve the best qualifications they are capable of. It may be that these qualifications are obtained before employment, that is by taking a full-time course for a degree, HND or diploma before seeking a job. Or it may be that entry to a job at 17, 18 or older can be combined with part-time study for a BTEC HNC, perhaps leading later to a full-time course. Many technical and commercial managers have taken this route: first, training and work experience, followed by a period of full-time education in their twenties leading to a degree, HND, a diploma in management, personnel or other professional qualification.

Graduate unemployment

A major factor in graduate employment is that employers are looking for graduates or well-qualified staff in science, business studies and engineering. The supply of science and technology graduates does not match demand, which is why job prospects for these graduates are so good. In 1989 there was almost full employment for graduates of civil, manufacturing and software engineering although in 1990 jobs were more difficult to acquire because of the recession. It can be argued that there is an over-supply of arts graduates and a limited number of job places for them. Some science graduates, particularly those who study biology, botany, environmental science, find it difficult to get a job after graduation without undertaking a postgraduate training course.

From the analysis of what graduates do after leaving university or polytechnic and moving into employment, it is possible to make some judgements about where jobs are or are not to be found.

The best prospects

The graduate employment figures reveal that:

- subjects with a numerical content (maths, statistics, etc.) tend to have the best employment rate
- the 1980s boom in computers – their manufacture, design, sales and use in business – stimulated a great demand for computer science graduates and underlined the need, already well known, for physics, electrical engineering, electronics and systems design staff

- other technologies within industries such as engineering, textiles, construction, packaging, printing and road transport offer very good career prospects except in periods of recession
- the growth of commerce and business, especially in the financial, leisure and banking sectors of commerce has maintained a demand for graduates with knowledge, skills and enterprise in these areas, which means that graduates with qualifications in accounting, finance, law, business studies, marketing, advertising and economics also have good job prospects
- there is a very worrying shortfall in the number of science graduates going into teaching: physics, mathematics and chemistry teachers are particularly needed. In addition, the reduction in the number of people applying to take teacher-training courses indicates that prospects are also good for arts graduates, and for students proposing to take BEd degree courses which equip them for teaching posts
- students on sandwich courses or those with good work experience (such as language students who have worked abroad) have a better chance of employment than graduates from full-time courses with no work experience.

Less-good prospects

Employment opportunities are not so encouraging for arts graduates and for some science graduates, unless they have additional qualifications, such as a postgraduate course in advertising, publishing, computing and so on, or varied work experience, or the kind of winning personality that brings them the offer of a job however many applicants there are for it.

There are fewer opportunities than in previous years for arts graduates seeking jobs in administrative posts in local and central government. However, if graduates are prepared to take jobs in civil service departments at executive level, or as trainees in all kinds of offices, there are openings.

Graduates from some science courses such as chemistry, biology, biochemistry, zoology and environmental science may have to take additional postgraduate courses and training to improve their job prospects.

Art and design and media studies graduates are difficult to place. As with arts graduates in general, it may be that additional training is needed, such as a one-year or shorter course in some aspects of business or commercial studies to improve employment prospects.

For more information about graduate employment, consult Hobsons *The Job Book*, which is published annually and lists employers who enrol graduates. Another useful book is *What Do Graduates Do?* which analyses in some detail the graduate employment scene; it is also published by Hobsons.

Job prospects – a summary

From this analysis it must be clear that a graduate has far better job opportunities than a non-graduate. In general, then, the better qualified the person, the more likely it is that he or she will be able to make a start in a job not long after graduation. In all the talk about graduate unemployment, it should be remembered that 90 per cent of all graduates are employed within six months of taking a degree or have proceeded to further training or a higher degree course.

On the other hand, a degree or diploma is not an automatic passport to a job. In some careers, a graduate has little advantage over school-leavers and is expected to make up the leeway very quickly. A graduate is also likely to be required to undertake the same training and take the same professional examinations as a school-leaver, gaining perhaps the advantage of some exemptions from the early stages of professional examinations. A degree, however, does not normally open many doors closed to non-graduates.

Most degree courses do not prepare people for jobs. Every year, about a third of all new graduates go on to further study or training. Even those who move directly into a job will be viewed as trainees and will be expected to complete one or more in-company or at-college training programmes.

About one-third of all jobs that require degree entrants are open to graduates of *any discipline*. This means that the degree subject may not be all that important. A student with a degree in philosophy or zoology may be a much better prospect in the eyes of a graduate recruitment officer than someone with a business studies degree. Personnel or recruitment specialists interviewing candidates for a job start with the applicant's degree course and university and/or polytechnic academic record, but they also consider personality, ambition, ideas and attitudes and it is these rather than the nature of the degree subject that are most likely to tip the balance in a candidate's favour.

Some degree courses may seem vocational, but in fact offer few job opportunities. Zoology is one of these. The reason is that there are very few career openings, and a graduate in zoology must therefore be prepared to make his or her career in a quite different field of work.

Choosing a course – the final decision

It is clear that a lot of thought must go into choosing a post-18 course at any institution. At age 17 or 18, career prospects at 22 or 23 are not a major preoccupation. What tends to influence 17-year-olds is their experience of A-level or H-grade work ('There's no way I'm going to do any more geography'); their views on subjects and courses for a degree ('I've heard that so-and-so is an interesting course'), and second-hand accounts of an institution ('Leeds is big and friendly, Bristol is full of Oxford rejects'). None of these instant opinions is satisfactory as a basis for the choice of a degree course and every applicant, helped by his or her parents, must do some preliminary research and make personal enquiries and visit possible institutions of higher education.

CHAPTER 19

GETTING IN

Student life

There is much more to being a student than taking a degree or diploma course. Some of the questions prospective students have to answer are:

- Do they want to live away from home and, if so, how far?
- Do they want to live in a hall of residence, at least for the first year, and then perhaps during other years?
- Do they want to share a flat with friends?
- Do they want an active social/sporting/intellectual life?

Parental opinion on all these topics can be misguided. Parents may want their children close to home (or as far away as possible). They think a hall of residence will be 'safe' and so on. Students' viewpoints are likely to be very different. So the best advice for parents who want to help is: lay out the advantages and disadvantages of each institution, and then leave the choice to your son or daughter.

A good source of information is *Student Eye*, which gives the student viewpoint of each university and polytechnic. *The Student Book*, published by Macmillan, is another lively guide.

Having selected, say, six to eight institutions, write for the official prospectuses and also for a copy of the 'alternative prospectus' produced by the students' union in some institutions.

Social and leisure facilities vary enormously. Some places are lively, active, dynamic. Others suffer from the 'weekend away' syndrome – where the majority of students return home at weekends. You won't know which is which unless you consult some of the books and ask around. When the final selection is to be made, try to visit the places:

you will get a much better idea from a personal visit, and it may be possible to speak to some students.

As an indication of how important this reconnaissance is you should be aware that one in ten students fails to complete the course. This means that some serious errors have been made in the choice of place as well as the choice of course.

Perhaps the best rule for students to apply when selecting higher education courses is:

- choose the subject to study after careful thought, research and discussion with parents and teachers
- decide on the way or method by which you wish to study this subject, such as by taking a full-time or sandwich course, a combined studies programme, a joint honours course or a single subject
- look at the merits of different institutions by reading what they say about themselves in the prospectuses, and what students say about them in the student guides and alternative prospectuses.

Universities

There are 53 universities, plus the university colleges, spread throughout the UK. Universities, by tradition and the nature of their work, concentrate on academic quality. They are deeply concerned with scholarship and research. Lecturers specialise in a subject or a topic, and study it in depth. Apart from their scholarly and research interests, they are also teachers, and that is what affects undergraduates most. Lecturers seek to pass on the results of their studies through teaching.

University lecturers, especially those in the science, engineering and technology faculties, also assert that they work closely with industry, and are not remote from industrial concerns. Some university researchers/ teachers are deeply involved in practical projects with an industrial or business connection, and this link illuminates their teaching. On the other hand, many university teachers are not concerned with industry, either because their subjects have no direct links with it or because they have no great interest in industry or commerce.

Another factor to bear in mind is that universities create their own courses and award their own degrees. Each university is independent and makes its own rules, working to an annual budget and grants. They therefore have a great deal of independence in deciding how the institution should be organised and administered.

There are other considerations for a potential university student. For instance, some courses are severely non-vocational. It may be very interesting to study an esoteric subject for three years, but the job opportunities at the end of the course are limited. A degree is now generally regarded as a starting-point for entry to a career, and not as a finishing line. The exception to this generalisation is, of course, the vocational course. Studying medicine, engineering or computing for several years does mean that a student is more ready to take up immediate employment than an arts graduate. But, like every generalisation, there is another side to it. Many employers look for arts graduates because they feel the students will have benefited from the discipline of having to collect, assess and use evidence, which is part of the training of an arts graduate. However, an arts graduate must expect to take an extra course – postgraduate or post-experience – in order to have some additional skills to present to an employer. The course could be a crash programme in accounting, publishing, printing, computing or other subjects.

Finally, the universities have outstanding sporting, recreational, social and cultural opportunities. These are unrivalled and it is an unwise or very introspective undergraduate who ignores them.

THE LOCATION OF UNIVERSITIES IN THE UK (see map on page 176)

ENGLAND:
1 University of Aston
2 University of Bath
3 University of Birmingham
4 University of Bradford
5 University of Bristol
6 Brunel University
7 The University of Buckingham
8 University of Cambridge
9 City University
10 Cranfield Institute of Technology
11 University of Durham
12 University of East Anglia
13 University of Essex
14 University of Exeter
15 University of Hull
16 University of Keele
17 University of Kent
18 University of Lancaster
19 University of Leeds
20 University of Leicester
21 University of Liverpool
22 University of London
23 Loughborough University of Technology
24 University of Manchester Institute of Science and Technology
25 University of Manchester
26 University of Newcastle upon Tyne
27 University of Nottingham
28 University of Oxford
29 University of Reading
30 University of Salford
31 University of Sheffield
32 University of Southampton
33 University of Surrey
34 University of Sussex
35 University of Warwick
36 University of York
37 Open University

SCOTLAND:
38 University of Aberdeen
39 University of Dundee
40 University of Edinburgh
41 University of Glasgow
42 Heriot-Watt University
43 University of St Andrews
44 University of Stirling
45 University of Strathclyde

WALES:
46 University College of Wales, Aberystwyth

47 University College of
   North Wales, Bangor
48 University of Wales
   College of Cardiff
49 University College of
   Swansea

50 University of Wales
   College of Medicine
51 St David's University
   College, Lampeter

NORTHERN IRELAND:
52 Queen's University of
   Belfast
53 University of
   Ulster

Polytechnics

There are 34 polytechnics in England, Wales and Northern Ireland, and 18 central institutions in Scotland. Like universities, they are concerned with scholarship, research and teaching. They offer a tremendous range of courses at degree and postgraduate levels, and also a wide selection of non-degree courses. In the past, most polytechnic work was vocational, which meant that job opportunities were (and are still likely to be) very good. But today the polytechnics also offer courses similar to universities, such as history, geography, languages, social sciences and economics. They also include schools or art and design, and provide courses leading to professional qualifications for teaching, social work, nursing, banking, advertising and a host of other careers.

One of the reasons for the great success of the polytechnics is the wide selection of courses. Another is their closeness to industry and commerce. They attract young people (and older people wanting to retrain in new skills) because they offer degree, diploma, certificate and all kinds of professional and vocational courses.

Polytechnic degrees are awarded by the Council for National Academic Awards (CNAA). This organisation closely validates and checks on degree standards. It scrutinises courses by sending teams of people (drawn from other institutions) to talk to staff and to assess the quality of the institution and the course. If the CNAA is not satisfied, the course is not approved. The standards expected of polytechnic degrees are therefore as high as university degrees. Indeed, the CNAA has a policy whereby polytechnics validate their own courses, just like universities. Furthermore, the Government has announced that polytechnics will, by 1994, be given university status and that the CNAA will be dissolved.

In Scotland there are 18 central institutions which offer courses similar to polytechnics. Napier, in Edinburgh, and Glasgow call themselves polytechnics. The others have, so far, retained the name of colleges.

In general, polytechnic courses tend to be more vocational than university courses. For instance, there are courses in hotel and catering studies, textile studies, all kinds of technology subjects, business studies including marketing, accounting and business information technology, aeronautical engineering, and many more. This is not to say that there are no university courses in these subjects, but generally speaking the polytechnics tend to concentrate on vocational studies.

Entry to a degree course at university or polytechnic (or college) depends on A-level or H-grade results. Because of their reputations some universities, such as Oxford and Cambridge, set high A-level expectations, with grades of A and B in three A-levels. Similarly, the other universities will look for high grades. However, some technology and science degree courses find it difficult to reach their student entry targets. For this reason, applicants with lower A-level (H-grade) grades can often obtain a place on a university or polytechnic degree course. One advantage that polytechnics possess is that alongside a degree course in a subject such as engineering, they will have an HND course with an entry requirement level of one A-level. A student from school who expected or hoped to obtain three good A-levels and then, disappointingly, gets only one or two indifferent passes is not barred from higher education. He or she can go on to an HND course at a polytechnic, from where it may be possible to transfer to the degree course. Applications for entry to first degree and HND courses at polytechnics is through the Polytechnics Central Admissions System (PCAS). See later section for details of entry.

THE LOCATION OF POLYTECHNICS IN ENGLAND AND WALES

1 Anglia Polytechnic
2 Birmingham Polytechnic
3 Bournemouth Polytechnic
4 Brighton Polytechnic
5 Bristol Polytechnic
6 Coventry Polytechnic
7 Hatfield Polytechnic
8 Huddersfield Polytechnic
9 Humberside Polytechnic
10 Kingston Polytechnic
11 Lancashire Polytechnic
12 Leeds Polytechnic
13 Leicester Polytechnic
14 Liverpool Polytechnic
15 Polytechnic of Central London
16 City of London Polytechnic
17 Polytechnic of East London
18 Polytechnic of North London
19 South Bank Polytechnic
20 Thames Polytechnic
21 West London Polytechnic
22 Manchester Polytechnic
23 Middlesex Polytechnic
24 Newcastle upon Tyne Polytechnic
25 Nottingham Polytechnic
26 Oxford Polytechnic
27 Portsmouth Polytechnic
28 Sheffield City Polytechnic
29 Polytechnic South-West
30 Staffordshire Polytechnic
31 Sunderland Polytechnic
32 Teesside Polytechnic
33 The Polytechnic of Wales
34 Wolverhampton Polytechnic

Colleges and institutes of higher education

The colleges and institutes of higher education offer courses leading to degrees (BA, BSc, BEd and B Humanities), the DipHE, qualifications in accountancy, social work, personnel management, secretarial work, and so on.

Many of these colleges developed from colleges of education whose

original function was to train teachers. Now they offer a much wider range of courses. Others were colleges of technology with a high proportion of advanced work, and some were colleges of art. Reorganised in the 1970s, these colleges and institutes provide an alternative form of higher education, separate from universities and polytechnics.

Apart from the subjects mentioned above, there are courses in photography, business studies, art and design, computer studies, languages, maths and sciences, technical and craft studies and physical education.

Why choose a college or institute of higher education?

Among the reasons given by the colleges are these:

- BEd courses, which prepare teachers for posts in primary and secondary education, are largely based here (although polytechnics also provide these courses).
- Some BA, B Humanities and B Combined Studies courses are unique in that they often allow students to build up a modular or course unit structure, permitting wide flexibility of choice.
- Apart from traditional subjects, there are unusual degree or other courses in subjects such as dance, drama, film and television, sports studies, community studies, etc.
- There is a wide range of professional courses in subjects such as building, art and design, management studies, etc.
- Many of these courses can be combined with education studies, helping students towards finding jobs in education.
- The colleges have a good reputation academically and for their sound teaching methods.
- They are small in size compared with polytechnics and universities; many are in pleasant rural or town environments; and have attractive residential accommodation.
- They have a reputation as 'caring' places, providing individual help and assistance, small teaching groups, and excellent counselling and careers education services.
- They have good sporting, cultural and recreational facilities.

Entry requirements and places

For degree courses (three or four years, depending on whether they are for ordinary or honours degrees and include some industrial training) the entry requirement is five GCSE passes, including two passes at A-level. Comparable BTEC National Certificate/National Diploma qualifications are acceptable. For the DipHE, the entry requirement is the same as for degree courses; for HNDs, students need one A-level and three GCSEs in different subjects.

The colleges, like the polytechnics, pride themselves on providing courses for people who have not been academic high-flyers, but who mature later. They also assist people who have missed an earlier opportunity. As a result of their perseverance and the encouragement of tutors, many of these students achieve excellent standards of work and personal achievement. Applications for entry to degree and HND courses at these institutions is through the PCAS system.

Art and design colleges

There is a distinctive group of art and design colleges that offers courses in many aspects of fine art, sculpture, media production and the various kinds of design – graphic, fashion, furniture, 3-D, display and others. Among the range of courses are BTEC first and national diplomas, HND, foundation and first degree courses. There is a catalogue of institutions and their degree and HND courses published by the design admissions registry, ADAR. The address is ADAR, Art and Design Admissions Registry, Penn House, 9 Broad Street, Hereford HR4 9AP.

Other colleges

There are colleges that are not in the same mould as colleges and institutes of higher education. These colleges go under various titles, such as colleges of technology, further education colleges, art and design colleges, agricultural colleges and so on.

Their degree and HND courses tend to be in vocational and/or specialist subjects such as transport, photography, drama, catering, transport studies and so on, as well as more familiar subjects such as business studies, design, combined studies, management and engineering. Applicants have to apply direct to the individual college for entry. Details of these colleges and the first degree courses they offer are in the PCAS *Guide for Applicants,* Appendix II.

Applying for a place

Applying for a place in higher education can be both time-consuming and confusing. Before getting involved in the detail of the various procedures it may be helpful to note these general points:

- applications are usually required nine months before the course begins. Nothing is gained by delaying an application
- it would be wise to make some decisions about the choice of course while still in the first year of A-levels
- applications for many courses are made through centralised application procedures. The list of these includes applications for first degree courses at university (made through the Universities Central Council on Admissions, UCCA), first degree, Diploma of Higher Education and teacher training (BEd) courses at polytechnics (through the Polytechnics Central Admissions System, PCAS), art and design degrees and Higher National Diplomas (Art and Design Admissions Registry, ADAR), and training for physiotherapy and occupational therapy (their respective clearing houses)
- offers of places are usually conditional upon a specified level of performance at A-level. The grades required vary from course to course and institution to institution
- as a general rule, and this is only a *general* rule, polytechnics and colleges will demand lower grades than universities for comparable courses
- while academic achievement is usually the major criterion used by admissions tutors, other factors such as motivation, interests and any relevant work experience will be taken into account
- it is possible to make applications after the A-level results have been published, but there are fewer vacancies and the grades required will generally be higher.

Applications

University and polytechnic applications are now breaking all records. In 1990–1 UCCA received over 130,000 applications compared with 109,000 in 1988–9; PCAS for the polytechnics handles 60,000 applications compared with 50,000 in 1988–9. So, although there is a demographic fall in the number of 16- to 19-year-olds, more and more of this age-group are seeking places at institutions of higher education.

Universities

Applications for courses at UK universities are made through the Universities Central Council on Admissions (UCCA) using a single common application form. The UCCA form and *Handbook* should be obtained from the school or college early in the fourth term of the two-year A-level course. Anyone who has left full-time education can get the documents direct from UCCA by writing to UCCA, PO Box 28, Cheltenham, Gloucestershire GL50 3SA.

All completed application forms must reach UCCA with the fee between 1 September and 15 December each year, i.e. nine to twelve months before the applicant's course is due to start.

University Entrance, The Official Guide, which has already been mentioned, lists the courses and gives their minimum entrance requirements, and the UCCA *Handbook* is very straightforward about the courses and methods of applying.

There is another database, currently with over 60,000 higher and further education courses on it, called ECCTIS, which is accessed via a CD-ROM computer. For details, write to ECCTIS, Fulton House, Jessop Avenue, Cheltenham, Gloucestershire GL50 3SH.

Oxford and Cambridge

Cambridge

Students can apply to Cambridge University by sending a direct application to one of the colleges or by sending an open application to the Cambridge Intercollegiate Applications Office (CIAO). Before doing so, however, they should send for a copy of the *Cambridge Admissions Prospectus*, which gives all the details and a lot of information about the colleges: obtained from CIAO, Kellet Lodge, Tennis Court Road, Cambridge CB2 1QJ.

There are 27 colleges that admit undergraduates. They do not specialise in any particular subject, which means that applications can be made to any college to read any subject. Of the 27, Lucy Cavendish (for women only), St Edmund's House (men and women) and Wolfson College (also men and women) admit mature students as undergraduates.

UCCA

For entry to Cambridge, a student should name Cambridge on the UCCA form as one of the choices and the form should be sent to UCCA between 1 September and 15 October. In Section 3 of the UCCA form students should make only one entry and name the college as first preference (the UCCA *Handbook* gives full details).

PAF

In addition to an UCCA application, students must also submit a Preliminary Application Form (PAF). The PAF goes direct to the Cambridge college or, in the case of an open application, direct to CIAO. On the PAF form, an applicant names the college of first preference and names two other colleges by which he or she would like to be considered if not successful with the first-choice college. PAF forms are usually held by schools or one can be obtained from CIAO: the form should be returned to the college of first preference by 31 July if possible and certainly no later than 15 October. Students cannot apply to Cambridge and Oxford in the same admissions year unless they wish to apply for an Organ and/or Choral award at both universities.

There are no faculty or course requirements at Cambridge except for candidates intending to read medicine or veterinary science. The requirements for these courses are given in the *Prospectus*.

Similarly, there is no 'standard offer' on A-level grades for a particular subject. Offers vary from college to college, from subject to subject and also in the light of individual circumstances. Some guidance is given in the *Prospectus*, but it can be said that, in general, the grades required are somewhere between ABB and AAA.

For pre-A-level candidates, other conditions may be set in addition to A-levels. If so, they will be either grades in S-level papers or grades in the new Sixth Term Examination Papers (STEP).

The *Cambridge University Handbook* gives much greater detail about the courses. It is published by Cambridge University Press and can be ordered from bookshops or direct from Cambridge University Press, Edinburgh Building, Shaftesbury Road, Cambridge CB2 2RU. The students' *Alternative Prospectus* can be obtained from 4 Round Church Street, Cambridge CB5 8AD.

Oxford

Admission to Oxford University is direct to one of the colleges. For admission, it is necessary to:

- be accepted by one of the colleges or halls
- satisfy the entrance requirements of the university.

To find out the exact details of entry requirements and the colleges and courses, applicants should send for the *University of Oxford Undergraduate Prospectus,* available from the Admissions Office, University Offices, Wellington Square, Oxford OX1 2JD.

UCCA

An applicant must submit to UCCA between 1 September and 15 October the UCCA/PCAS form naming Oxford as one of the choices. Oxford does not have to be the first choice, although (like Cambridge) it would be sensible to make it so. On the UCCA form an applicant may, if he or she wishes, name up to three colleges in order of preference by entering the college abbreviations in the spaces provided. The entry must coincide with the entry on the Oxford card (see below).

The Oxford card

In addition to the UCCA application form applicants must send a 'card' to Oxford. The application cards, which are common to all the colleges, are obtained from the Admissions Office (address above). These cards must be returned to the Admissions Office by 15 October. For a full list of the courses, consult the UCCA *Handbook*, and, for opinions on what students think about Oxford and its colleges, send for the *Alternative Prospectus* (from the Students' Union) or *Student Eye*, the alternative guide to universities.

UCCA forms

The UCCA *Handbook* gives all the details on how to complete the UCCA forms. UCCA and PCAS have agreed that with effect from the applications cycle leading to entry in October 1992, they will use a single, common application form on which candidates show both their UCCA and PCAS choices. Five choices of university can be made on the UCCA section of the form. These can be made in order of preference or some (or all) bracketed together as equal preferences.

Although the universities are expected to consider bracketed choices as genuinely equal preferences, some regard them as signs of indecision or lack of commitment by the applicant. Therefore, it is best to put them in strict order, one to five. How universities select and decide on the basis of UCCA applications is one of the great mysteries of education. The admissions tutors are the arbiters. Some of them (or the departmental admissions staff who review the applications) automatically reject applicants who place the institution lower than third preference on the UCCA form. For a very popular course, such as English, a rejection may automatically occur if the institution is not put in first or second place. This applies particularly to popular universities.

On the other hand, some universities and university colleges are glad to receive applications from students who put them in third, fourth or fifth place on the UCCA form.

Offers

UCCA photocopies the form and then sends it off to all five choices. A university may decide to offer an applicant a place entirely on the information provided on the form. That is, there may be no interview, only an offer through the post. On the other hand, some universities invite candidates for interview.

If an offer is made it will either be 'conditional' on obtaining certain grades at A-level or 'unconditional', which means it is a firm offer, if the grades have already been obtained.

The applicant then accepts the place 'provisionally' or 'firmly'. Provisional acceptances can be declined at a later date in favour of other offers, but a firm acceptance is binding. Although the application form is considered by all five choices, and theoretically the candidate may receive up to five offers, he or she cannot 'hold' more than two offers at any one time. By 15 May, the candidate must decide which offers to accept and informs UCCA accordingly.

Parental help

There is no reason why parents cannot be closely involved in these immensely important thoughts, discussions and decisions, but to assist in the decision-making may require tact. In the first place, the school staff are giving (or should be giving) advice. They know the academic record of the pupil and will be asked by UCCA or the institutions to give a frank estimate both of expected A-level or H-grade results and of the candidate's potential for a degree or any other course.

On the other hand, some schools are remiss in their provision of careers' advice. Even in schools where good advice is given, teachers cannot know everything. Choosing a higher education course requires a lot of research. This is where parents can help. They can do some of the quiet reading of books on higher education, starting with the UCCA *Handbook*, and looking at the digests and summaries of courses, including Hobsons' Degree Course Guides for each subject, *Student Eye* on institutions, and *University Entrance – The Official Guide* both for institutions and courses.

Passing on this information and knowledge to a sixth-form student may well be difficult. Parental advice often does not appeal to 17-year-olds, who enjoy their independent opinions and suspect a parent's views as prejudiced (which they are — in favour of the child) or out of date. Even if the parent is a graduate, the universities and polytechnics have changed radically over the last 18 years or so, so advice could be dated. Perhaps the most useful ways that parents can help in the process of choosing a higher education course are these:

● helping with the research by obtaining the reference books (listed in Chapter 21) from the library or by buying them, finding out about the courses and the institutions, and drawing them to the attention of the applicant

● attending the school's careers evening that is concerned with applications for higher education (every school should have an evening for this purpose: it is a poor school that does not) and talking to the teachers about the progress and potential of the student

● when an institution is provisionally chosen as first or second choice, try to arrange for the applicant to visit it, to see its environment and to sample the atmosphere and to talk to students there

● when it is time to make the final choice and complete the UCCA, PCAS or college application form, to review again the choices with the applicant.

No offers

If no offers are received from the original five choices, UCCA sends the applicant details of something called the Continuing Application Procedure (CAP). This effectively allows a sixth choice. If this application is also unsuccessful, there is a fall-back. This is 'Clearing', which gives the candidate an opportunity to apply after the A-level results are out. However, most universities have filled their places by the end of the summer term for a start the following October, so Clearing does not bring good news to many.

In these circumstances, when there is no offer, a radical rethink is needed. One possibility is to delay going to university for a year, and take a year off as an interim. Another is to think quickly about polytechnics and to apply to them, if this has not already been done.

A year off

This can be a good idea or a bad idea. It is a good idea if the year off is spent sensibly, getting work experience (paid or unpaid) as a preliminary to a degree or diploma course. It is a bad idea if the year is spent loafing around. For the pros and cons of a year off, and for a long list of institutions and places that offer work to students, consult Hobsons' *A Year Off . . a Year On,* a booklet which gives these details.

Polytechnics

Applications for first degree, HND, and Diploma of Higher Education (DipHE) courses in polytechnics are made through the Polytechnics Central Admissions System (PCAS). BA courses in art and design, courses that lead to the Certificate of Qualification in Social Work (CQSW), and occupational therapy and physiotherapy courses are dealt with by separate admissions systems, see below.

PCAS forms

Applications to polytechnics in England and Wales for first degree and DipHE courses, except those listed above, are made through PCAS on a single standard form, which, from 1992, is the same common application form for UCCA and PCAS applications. The UCCA/PCAS form and *Guide for Applicants* are available in schools and colleges during the summer of the year before the proposed entry into higher education (i.e. some 15 months in advance). Students who have left full-time education should write direct to PCAS (PO Box 67, Cheltenham, Gloucestershire GL50 3SH), which will send the application form.

The completed application form and the applicant's fee must reach PCAS between 1 September and 15 December (i.e. some nine to twelve months before the course starts).

Up to four courses may be chosen for inclusion on the form. It is not necessary to enter courses in order of preference, and each nominated polytechnic will give the application equal consideration. Polytechnics will infer no order of priority from the listing of courses providing they are nominated alphabetically as indicated in the PCAS *Guide for Applicants*.

PCAS photocopies the application form before sending it simultaneously to all the nominated polytechnics. A polytechnic wishing to offer a place may do so solely on the basis of the information on the PCAS form, or it may ask the applicant to attend for an interview.

If an offer is made it will either be 'conditional' on obtaining certain grades at A-level or 'unconditional' if the required grades have already been obtained. An offer can be either 'provisionally' or 'firmly' accepted. Provisional acceptances may be declined at a later date in favour of other offers, but a firm acceptance is binding. Although the application may be considered by four polytechnics, a candidate is not allowed to hold more than two offers at any one time. Eventually, by mid–May at the latest, a decision must be made on which of the two offers is the first choice. This must be accepted firmly with the remaining provisional acceptance held as a reserve offer.

If no offers are received, PCAS sends details of the Continuing Application Procedure (CAP). This effectively allows candidates to make a fifth choice.

A second scheme, Clearing, gives students the chance to re-apply after their A-level results have been published. This scheme applies if candidates have not received any offers or if they have not received the grades specified in the offers.

If a student accepts an offer and reaches the required grades, he or she is expected to honour the acceptance of the offer or withdraw from PCAS for that year.

Applications for other polytechnic courses

Students who want to take any other polytechnic course, apart from a first degree, HND or DipHE, should apply direct to the polytechnic. A different form should be used for each application. The form is different from the PCAS form because it originates within the institution.

There is no limit to the number of applications that can be made, and there is no opening or closing date for the arrival of applications, which can be made even though the course may have started.

PCAS does not deal *only* with polytechnics. It handles applications for first degree, HND and DipHE courses at colleges and institutes of higher education, specialist colleges (such as Camborne School of Mines), Welsh higher education colleges, and two of the Scottish central institutions (Paisley and The Robert Gordon Institute, Aberdeen). For degree and HND courses at these institutions, use the PCAS procedures.

For other non degree/HND at these colleges, and for courses at other colleges and Scottish central institutions that are *not* part of the PCAS scheme, apply direct to the colleges.

Clearing houses for other courses

As well as the two clearing houses for degree and HND courses (UCCA and PCAS), applications for other kinds of courses must be made through clearing houses.

Art and design

The entrance system to art and design courses resembles a Chinese puzzle. There are hurdles and complications which differ from one Local Education Authority to another, and from one college to another. However, it is generally agreed that there are three main types of art and design course:

- foundation courses
- degree courses
- vocational courses which can lead to a BTEC, SCOTVEC, City and Guilds or other qualifications.

Foundation courses are the most usual route to a degree course. These courses last one or two years and are taught in colleges or schools of art and design and in polytechnic design departments. In general, students who obtain a grant from their Local Education Authority are required to attend the local college. The minimum entry requirements are three GCSE passes for a two-year course and five GCSEs at grades A to C for a one-year course: for the latter a candidate must be 17. To be sure of a place, however, qualifications often have to be better than the minimum.

Degree courses in art and design can be taken at colleges of art, polytechnics and universities. For some university courses entry is through the UCCA system. Otherwise, application to art schools and colleges is through the clearing house. This is the Art and Design Admissions Registry (ADAR), Penn House, 9 Broad Street, Hereford HR4 9AP. ADAR processes all applications for first degree, HND and art and design courses that are validated by the Council for National Academic Awards (CNAA) and by BTEC for HNDs. For a degree course, applicants should be 18 and have at least five GCSEs (O-grades) or three GCSEs and one A-level (two H-grades), or two A-levels (three H-grades) and two GCSEs, or three A-levels (four H-grades), but many polytechnics and colleges ask for more than the minimum qualifications. For HND courses, a minimum of one A-level plus a good portfolio of work is looked for. ADAR's application forms must be returned by 31 March for courses due to start in September. For details, candidates should consult the college of their choice.

Vocational courses lead to BTEC and SCOTVEC awards at National Diploma/Certificate and HND/HNC levels. Details can be obtained from ADAR and individual colleges.

Social work

The Certificate of Qualification in Social Work (CQSW) awarded by the Central Council for Education and Training in Social Work (CCETSW) is the basic qualification for all professional social workers in the UK. Training is open to applicants from widely differing social backgrounds and qualifications. Early application is essential because recruitment begins a year before the courses start. Details of the routes to qualification are given in the section on *social work* in Part 3. The clearing house system for applications is explained by leaflets from the CCETSW, Information Service, Derbyshire House, St Chad's Street, London WC1H 2BW.

Occupational therapy

The entry requirements for a course in occupational therapy are at least six passes at GCSE, one of which must be at A-level. However, such is the competition for places that two A-levels plus three GCSEs are looked for. Details of the career are given in the entry on *occupational therapy* in Part 3. For details of how to apply for training write to the Occupational Therapy Training Clearing House, 20 Rede Place, Bayswater, London W2 4TU.

191

Physiotherapy

Applications have to be made from 1 September for courses in the following year. For details of the career read *physiotherapy* in Part 3. Write to the Clearing House, The Chartered Society of Physiotherapy, 14 Bedford Row, London WC1R 4ED for information about how to apply.

How applicants are selected

Selection procedures vary. Some places interview, others do not. Some use A-level results or expected results as their main guide, and some try to balance personal characteristics alongside assessments of potential academic quality. All the same, there are generally agreed criteria for selection. These are:

- performance or potential in A-levels or other qualifications
- the school report on the applicant (plus reports from employers, if applicable)
- interview.

There is little doubt – and all admissions tutors generally agree on this point – that academic achievement and promise are the vital factors.

Exam results and other criteria

A-levels and H-grades

Whatever the shortcomings of A-levels and H-grades, the crude method of distinguishing between applicants is on the basis of results in these examinations. Conditional offers are made on the basis of the A-level grades expected by the candidates. The grades of A-level pass are A, B, C, D and E, and admissions tutors in every institution will generally begin the process of selection by defining the grades required for entry, such as 'three Bs' or 'BCC'.

Single sitting

The university may also state 'all at one sitting', meaning that the three A-levels must be taken all at the same time. However, polytechnics and colleges are more reasonable: they will judge A-levels taken at any time to be satisfactory; three A-levels over three years may after all show signs of determination and resilience.

O-levels and GCSEs

Admissions tutors will also look at the range of subjects taken at GCSE and the grades obtained in them. Obviously, a good selection of As and Bs in GCSE subjects is worth having on anyone's form.

Subjects

The subjects taken at A-level and at GCSE will be closely examined. For instance, for most engineering, science and computing degree courses, admissions tutors will be looking for good A-level or H-grade passes in mathematics and physics. For almost any course, arts or science, the institutions will expect GCSE passes in English language and mathematics. For other courses the A-level subjects have to be suitable for the particular degree course. For example, to enter a degree course in dietetics, chemistry at A level is essential, plus at least one other science subject at A-level.

Academic record

Any other evidence of academic attainment is a plus – prizes, special awards, or high marks or grades throughout the last four years of a candidate's school (or prior college) career.

Forecasts

It is worth mentioning again because it is important that admissions tutors look closely at the school's forecasts of A-level results and of the candidate's general suitability for a course of higher education.

Any other awards

BTEC awards, City and Guilds, anything extra is valuable in a competitive situation.

Intellect

Admissions tutors look for evidence, assisted by school reports, exam results and personal impressions at an interview, of intellect and mental ability and the qualities that support them.

Interests

Evidence of the range of a candidate's interests is looked for – sporting, social, intellectual, recreational.

Work experience

Any, including holiday or weekend jobs, may be considered – in fact, any evidence of working with adults or travel abroad or any variation that distinguishes the candidate.

Personality

Among the qualities looked for are determination, readiness to work, adaptability, friendliness, liveliness.

Interviews

Selection interviews are not compulsory. Some institutions will make a decision without an interview because they do not want to ask the candidate to make a long journey, or because they feel they can make a judgement based on the application and the head-teacher's report.

However, other universities, polytechnics and colleges regard the interview as an important part of the selection procedure. Being asked for interview shows that the candidate has passed the first test: the admissions tutor has made a tentative opinion in favour of the person and wants to assess his or her suitability at first hand.

On the other hand, some interviews are arranged after an offer has been made, and this generally follows the pattern of a 'getting to know you' routine on both sides, with the tutors perhaps meeting a group of students to discuss matters concerning the university or college and their future course.

Whatever the form and purpose of the interview, it allows candidates to look at the institution and its environment and to talk to resident students in the union, the department or the bars.

An interview of the formal type rarely exceeds thirty minutes. It is an ordeal for most young people. What the interviewer is looking for is evidence of the quality of the candidate and this can be assessed in various ways – by conversation, by oral questioning, by written test, or by group sessions. For applicants, the interview is an eye-opener as well as a mind-opener. Sometimes they are impressed, sometimes not. Most students now at college give this advice: 'It is essential to visit your chosen universities or polytechnics. Insist on seeing the appropriate department. Walk about, talk to other students, visit the halls of residence for first-years. And when you are grilled, be honest! Keep a conversation going, keep calm and don't be afraid to ask questions.'

There are ways of assisting candidates to prepare for what can be a very daunting and worrying experience. Some schools arrange practice sessions with pupils and staff in role-play situations. Alternatively, the role-playing can be arranged so that pupils take it in turns to be interviewer and interviewee. However, many schools give no help whatsoever with interview preparation and techniques. This is where parents and friends can help. They can arrange these 'trial' interviews, thus strengthening a candidate's resolve in a real interview, and giving valuable practice in thinking out and formulating answers in advance of the 'real thing'. Parents can also assist by helping with travel and accommodation. Part of this preparation might be to make it easy to get to the institution – by bus, rail, car. Overnight accommodation may be needed, and this can be arranged in advance.

Failing an interview

If a candidate fails an interview, i.e. if he or she does not get an offer, a realistic assessment has to be made. The applicant would not have been asked for interview unless the institution thought the applicant's basic qualifications and expected A-level or H-grade results would be satisfactory. For one or more reasons, the interviewer(s) and the candidate did not hit it off. Why? Did the candidate make mistakes, either in factual answers to questions, or in mistaking the intention of the interviewer? Did the candidate fail to present his or her case effectively? There are many explanations for lack of success at an interview.

Advanced Further Education Information Service

Students who need advice on places available within higher education should contact their Local Education Authority careers service. The normal time for urgent enquiries is after A-level results have been published, i.e. from mid-August onwards. LEAs are part of the Advanced Further Education Information Service (AFEIS), and their careers officers provide up-to-date information on current vacancies.

In addition, ECCTIS has an on-line telephone service linked to its CD-ROM computerised system of courses and vacancies: it operates from mid-August to October. Write to ECCTIS for details; its address is on page 183.

CHAPTER 20

SPONSORSHIP AND GRANTS

Sponsorship

There are various kinds of sponsorship designed to assist students taking first degrees, postgraduate degrees, HND and other courses.

Industrial and commercial organisations

The most common form of sponsorship (the one which most people are familiar with) is financial support during a university or polytechnic course. Most of these sponsorships come from industrial and commercial organisations which offer students a financial incentive to study a particular subject (such as engineering) with the opportunity to take up a job with the sponsor on graduation.

Some firms pay students a full salary throughout the whole of the sponsorship, both when they are studying and during the periods of industrial experience. However, most organisations pay a salary only during the periods of industrial training, topping up the students' normal maintenance grant during term-time with an additional allowance.

The advantages of this kind of sponsorship are:

● it provides finance to supplement, or replace, the student grant
● if a student does well there will probably be a job on graduation, although this would not necessarily be guaranteed at the outset
● students do not have to worry about organising practical training and employment if they are on a sandwich course.

The disadvantages of this kind of sponsorship are:

● a student is usually committed to the sponsoring organisation for industrial training. This could be a problem if the sponsor does not offer practical training placements to complement the interests that a student is developing on his or her course

- sponsored students feel that they have a moral obligation to remain with their sponsoring company for two years after graduation
- when sponsored students rejoin their firms for the long vacation their colleagues normally have the summer vacation for their own concerns.

Sponsorship is definitely a good idea for a student who is committed to a particular career. It can be very rewarding financially – who wouldn't be glad of an extra £1,000 or so a year? It can also be very useful for the work experience and training. If a sponsorship can be obtained, the advantages must outweigh any possible disadvantages. However, the academic choice of a course should come first: it would be foolish to take the wrong course for the sake of the money.

Armed Services

Students can apply formally as part of a sponsorship scheme organised by the Armed Services. For example, young men and women can apply for RAF cadetships: they are commissioned as acting pilot officers and remain in the rank (with pay and allowances) until they graduate. Pay includes an allowance equivalent to a Local Authority grant. After graduation they go on to take initial officer training degree courses relevant to the RAF's needs. Degree courses such as engineering or science are preferred, but other subjects are acceptable. Technical education bursaries and other kinds of help are available, too, for BTEC Higher National Diplomas (HND) and other courses.

Similarly, the Royal Navy and Royal Marines, the Ministry of Defence and the Army offer various kinds of sponsorships – i.e. cadetships and bursaries paid while taking a university, polytechnic or college course.

Public corporations

Some public corporations and large companies formed from privatised corporations have generous sponsorship schemes. For example, British Coal provides bursaries of up to £1,000-plus to supplement Local Education Authority grants for selected students on mining, electrical and electronic engineering courses. Similarly, British Steel supports sandwich course students on engineering, metallurgy, materials science and computer science courses. British Rail and British Telecom have comparable schemes.

Financial organisations

In the financial field, there are some attractive sponsorship schemes offered by major clearing banks (Nat West, TSB, Midland, Barclays, Lloyds). The way these work is that the banks have selected degree courses that suit their needs and sponsor students through them. For example, Nat West's programme is to put a post-A-level student through a 12-month accelerated training programme in the bank, followed by support during a degree course (such as BSc or BA courses in banking and finance at University College of North Wales, Bangor). Barclays sponsors A-level students on *any* degree course: they provide an annual bursary to bolster LEA or parental grants (if any), and expect the student to spend 12 paid weeks a year training and working in the bank.

Professional or employers' associations

Some professional or employers associations have special schemes. For example, the British Paper and Board Industry Federation gives students an annual bursary if selected for the BSc Paper Science Course at UMIST: this can be augmented by company sponsorship. The Institutions of Marine, Civil, Electrical and Mechanical Engineers arrange help in various ways, such as bursaries, paid vacation work, scholarships, travel grants, etc. Obviously their support is directly applicable and open to students on linked engineering courses.

Universities and polytechnics

Some university and polytechnic departments arrange their own sponsorship schemes with friendly, supportive companies. For example, the BEng and MEng courses at University College, Cardiff, are backed by several companies that give bursaries, well-paid vacation jobs and training with travel costs, and the companies also pay students' fees on special short courses. Most science, technology and business studies departments in universities, polytechnics and colleges operate a register of supportive companies willing to give modest (or in some cases, very generous) financial assistance.

Companies

Books on sponsorship (see page 210) list companies that have well-organised, long-running schemes of financial bursaries and sponsorships. Among the list of over 100 famous companies that operate schemes are (a random sample): Ove Arup, Rover Group, Boots, British Aerospace, BBC, Courtaulds, Dowty, Ferranti, Ford, GEC, ICI, Jaguar, Kodak, Lucas, Marley, Michelin Tyre, Philips, Pilkington, Pirelli, Racal, Rank Xerox, Rolls-Royce, Rowntree, Shell, Smiths Industries, Thorn EMI, Unilever, United Biscuits, Westland Helicopters, Wimpey.

What do they offer?

Offers vary from company to company. Sometimes, an offer is linked to a special course, for example, Rank Xerox has picked out three- and four-year engineering courses at Cambridge and Southampton Universities and Imperial College, London. Students get substantial annual grants ranging from £600 to £1,600 for each year of the course.

Students can get paid placements for industrial training (if on a sandwich course). They can benefit from special training on short courses and travel in the UK or overseas, and the commitment to the company is not for life. Sponsoring companies can reasonably expect students (if good enough) to join them on graduation for one, two or more years, but there can be no legally enforceable contract, if the student is unwilling to make any commitment.

Training placements

Financial sponsorship for the whole (or part) of a higher education course is only one form of sponsorship. There are other ways of benefiting from commercial and industrial support. One way is by work placements for students on sandwich courses. This widens the net enormously. All students on any kind of course from business studies to packaging technology need to find industrial training placements for three, six or twelve months. Most higher education course tutors have a register of supportive companies. These companies provide paid placements plus (in most cases) training and excellent commercial or industrial experience.

Local sponsorship

Another possibility is local sponsorship. There are all kinds of local schemes, not on any register, where students from City A or County B or whose parents work locally in industry can apply for a grant, bursary or travel costs. The only way to get this information is through the local Chamber of Commerce, the Round Table or from parents' or their friends' employers or professional organisations.

Further reading

An essential guide for dealing with sponsorship is *The Which? Guide to Sponsorship in Higher Education* published by Consumers' Association and Hodder & Stoughton which lists over 200 sponsoring companies and gives details of sponsored courses.

How to apply

In most cases, the candidate, not the organisation, makes the first approach. Students should ask the Admissions Tutor of a particular course if there is a list of potential sponsors. Or they can consult the lists provided in the sponsorship directories. After that, it's up to you: how good your written application is; how you perform at an interview; which course you select, or what kind of person you are.

Sponsors do not necessarily offer permanent employment at the end of the course, unless the student is already an employee of the particular company. Now, as mentioned, it is not compulsory to take up employment after graduation (if a job is offered). There is an unwritten gentleman's (or woman's) agreement that the company and student will match up, but if either side feels unhappy about taking up post-graduation employment, the unwritten agreement is ended.

Grants

The vast majority of students in higher education receive financial assistance from their Local Education Authority in the form of a grant. This normally has two parts: *tuition fees,* which are paid direct to the college, and *maintenance* (i.e. living expenses), which is paid to the student. Fees are usually paid in full; maintenance is assessed on a sliding scale in accordance with parental income.

The grant is either 'mandatory' (which the Authority must pay to students attending 'designated' courses) or 'discretionary' (which the Authority awards at its own discretion). A mandatory award is available for degree, BTEC HND, Diplomas of Higher Education and a limited range of other courses, designated by the Department of Education and Science (DES). Formal application for both mandatory and discretionary awards should normally be made after an offer of a place has been received, whether it is conditional or unconditional.

A number of organisations other than the Local Education Authority also provide a limited number of grants. For example, the Department of Health is responsible for awarding grants to students on certain medical courses. See *Grants to Students – a Brief Guide* published by the Department of Education and Science.

Student loans

Student loans were introduced by the Government in 1990. They are Government-funded loans which contribute towards a student's living costs. They are paid as an addition to the maintenance grants.

Students can decide whether or not to apply for a student loan. At first, few students applied, but recently more and more students have taken up these loans, simply because they need the cash to survive. Loans are available alongside grants. Indeed, Local Education Authority grants are now frozen, so that it's inevitable that an increasing number of students will apply for loans to make up the shortfall. Students can also decide *how much* they wish to borrow, up to the maximum amount specified each year. The same courses that qualify for grants also apply for student loans, and so it is important for students to check to see if they are eligible.

To be eligible to apply for a student loan a student must be in full-time education on a designated course (as for LEA grants) and have a bank or building society account.

Students cannot take out a student loan for more than one year at a time (they apply anew in each year of their course).

How much are the loans for?

Student loans are administered by a separate agency, set up by the Government. This is the Student Loans Company (see below for address). There are rules that govern application procedures, but students can apply at any time, once their course has started.

The 1991-2 maximum loan figures were as follows:

	Full year	Final year
Students who live away from their parental home and are studying		
in London	£660	£480
outside London	£580	£425
Students living at their parental home	£460	£335

The final year loan rates are lower because the final summer term isn't included.

Unlike grants, loans are *not* means-tested. A student can get the full amount, no matter what his or her parents or spouse earn, or how much could be earned in vacation work. Nor does it matter if a student has a mandatory or discretionary grant – they can still get the full loan.

Applying for a student loan

Students can apply at any time once they are attending a higher education course. The university, polytechnic or college which they attend has the necessary forms; and also has to verify that the student is in full-time education.

A loan is a loan – it has to be paid back. Students are asked to start paying back from the April after completing their course but they could volunteer to start paying earlier, if they so wish. Most students seem to think that student loans are interest-free. They are not. Interest is charged by the Student Loans Company at the rate of inflation – 9, 7, 5, 4 per cent – whatever the annual rate of inflation is at the time. The Government, which fixed these terms, points out that the value of the money repaid is the same, *in real terms,* as the sum originally borrowed. The amount of the loan not yet re-paid is adjusted each year in line with the Retail Prices Index (RPI). For most borrowers, repayments must be made in equal monthly amounts over five years, although it is possible to pay off earlier. The monthly amounts are adjusted annually, to take account of the RPI. Repayments are tied down in other ways – repayment is by direct debit from a bank or building society account.

What if you can't repay . . . .

If a student is out of work or on a low income, repayments can be deferred. 'Low incomes' are defined as less than 85 per cent of national average earnings. In 1991-2, deferment was allowed on gross incomes of £1,055 per month or less.

Disabled students

There are special terms, conditions and allowances for disabled students who wish to apply for a grant or a student loan. Information is available from the LEA (for information on grants) and the Student Loans Company (for loans).

Information

For additional information on loans, contact the Student Loans Company Limited, 100 Bothwell Street, Glasgow G2 7JD   Tel (0345) 300900.

Money problems

There is no minimum grant. Parents are expected to pay maintenance up to the maximum maintenance grant rate suggested by the DES. Some parents are both able and willing to pay. Other parents, for various reasons, do not make up the difference between what the Local Education Authority pays and the recommended maximum. A survey of undergraduates' income by the National Union of Students in 1990 indicated that half the total number of students received less than the amount recommended to be paid by parents to aid students' maintenance needs.

The result is that many students have to scrape by on what the Local Education Authority provides and what their parents are prepared to give. Since 1986 students have not been entitled to claim Supplementary Benefit or Income Support (which replaced Supplementary Benefit), and can no longer claim Housing Benefit. Consequently, the burden of student support is now firmly on the family and on the individual student. Some students already follow the American pattern of working their way through college by taking all kinds of jobs during the vacations and even during term-time. Students work in cafés and kitchens, as drivers, in offices, and in all kinds of temporary jobs while full-time employees are on holiday.

CHAPTER 21

FURTHER INFORMATION

Hobsons titles are published by Hobsons Publishing, Bateman Street, Cambridge CD2 1LZ

Careers and Occupational Information Centre (COIC) titles are available from COIC, Room W1108, Moorfoot, Sheffield S1 4PQ

The National Curriculum

A Guide to the National Curriculum, by Bob Moon, Oxford University Press, Walton Street, Oxford OX2 6DP

The Technical and Vocational Education Initiative (TVEI)

For further information about TVEI, write to: TVEI Unit, Training Agency, 214 Gray's Inn Road, London WC1X 8HL

For your local scheme, write to the Director of Education at County Hall, asking for the address and details of the local TVEI scheme

A useful guidebook to TVEI is *Introducing Technical and Vocational Education,* by R G Wallace, published by Macmillan, 4 Little Essex Street, London WC2R 3LF

GCSE

Guidance for parents and students on GCSE, A-level and AS-level courses is provided in:

Decisions at 13/14+, by Michael Smith and Veronica Matthew, Hobsons
Decisions at 15/16+, by Michael Smith and Veronica Matthew, Hobsons

Further education

Useful books and pamphlets on changes affecting further educational courses are:
Your Choice of Degree and Diploma, which includes information about ECCTIS, the course information database, Hobsons
Directory of Further Education, Hobsons

For details of local colleges of further education, call in at or phone the careers office, and visit the local colleges

City and Guilds, 76 Portland Place, London W1N 4AA. For course information write to City and Guilds, 46 Britannia Street, London WC1X 9RG

The Business and Technician Education Council, Central House, Upper Woburn Place, London WC1H 0HH, provides information on all BTEC courses

Youth Training

Further information is available from local careers offices, Job-centres or the Training Agency area offices. The addresses and phone numbers are in the telephone directory. Or write to the Training and Education Enterprise Division (TEED), Moorfoot, Sheffield S1 4PQ

A-levels

Your Choice of A-levels, by Mary Munro and Alan Jamieson, Hobsons: a guide to A-level subjects and careers linked to them
Jobs and Careers after A-levels, by Mary Munro, Hobsons
University Entrance, The Official Guide, (see page 208)
Polytechnic Courses Handbook, the Committee of Directors of Polytechnics. Copies from CDP Secretariat, Kirkman House, 12–14 Whitfield Street, London W1P 6AX
Decisions at 15/16+, by Michael Smith and Veronica Matthew, Hobsons
Decisions at 17/18+, by Michael Smith and Peter Marsh, Hobsons

Beyond School, by Michael Smith and Peter Marsh, Hobsons
Directory of Further Education, Hobsons

Scotland

Useful addresses for obtaining copies of documents or other material are:

Scottish Education Department, Room 4/25, New St Andrew's House, St James's Centre, Edinburgh EH1 3SY   Tel 031-556 8400 ext 4542

Consultative Committee on the Curriculum, Room 4/17, New St Andrew's House, St James's Centre, Edinburgh EH1 3SY   Tel 031- 556 8400 ext 4380

Scottish Information Office, Room 2/88, New St Andrew's House, St James's Centre, Edinburgh EH1 3TD   Tel 031-556 8400 ext 5050. They produce *Factsheet 15,* Scottish Education, and *Factsheet 29,* Scottish Certificate of Education, Standard Grade

Scottish Examination Board, Ironmills Road, Dalkeith, Lothian EH22 1LE   Tel 031-663 6601

Scottish Vocational Education Council (SCOTVEC), 22 Great King Street, Edinburgh EH3 6QH   Tel 031-557 4555 and 38 Queen Street, Glasgow G1 3DY   Tel 041-248 7900

Higher education
General

Making the Most of Higher Education is a student's guide to choosing the right course of study, getting the best out of it and finding a job after it. Published by Consumers' Association and Hodder & Stoughton. For copies write to: Consumers' Association, Castlemead, Gascoyne Way, Hertford X, SG14 1LH

Courses and qualifications

Which Degree? is an extensive guide to all full-time and sandwich degree courses at universities, polytechnics and colleges in the UK. There are five volumes: 1: arts, humanities and languages; 2: engineering, technology and the environment; 3: mathematics, medicine and the sciences;

4: business, education and the social sciences; 5: colleges, polytechnics and universities. Newpoint Publishing, 76 St James's Lane, London N10 3DF

Degree Course Guides are written by lecturers of the various degree subjects. The *Guides* provide detailed information on entry, the content of courses and career opportunities. Hobsons

Higher Education – Finding Your Way is a short and very helpful guide-book to assist school students who are going on to higher education. Department of Education and Science, published by HMSO and available from HMSO shops

Degree Course Offers, by Brian Heap. Compiled each year and subtitled 'Winning your place at university, polytechnic and other institutions', it is a guide to admission, with average entry grades for each degree course. Careers Consultants, 12–14 Hill Rise, Richmond Hill, Richmond, Surrey TW10 6UA

University Entrance, The Official Guide is the successor to *The Compendium of University Entrance Requirements* and is the essential starting-point for general and course entry requirements for UK universities. Sheed & Ward Ltd, 2 Creechurch Lane, London EC3A 5AQ

Your Choice of Degree and Diploma (incorporating information about ECCTIS), Hobsons

Sandwich Course Guide, a guide to all sandwich degree and diploma courses. Hobsons

Further information

The various universities, polytechnics and colleges are themselves the best sources of information. Once an initial selection of institutions has been made, write to the Admissions Tutor for a copy of the most recent prospectus, the 'alternative prospectus' (if there is one) produced by students, and any special leaflets about particular courses

The institutions

Directory of First Degree and Diploma of Higher Education Courses. Published annually by the Council for National Academic Awards (CNAA). Free from CNAA, 344–354 Gray's Inn Road, London WC1X 8BP. Information about 400 sandwich, full-time and part-time courses leading to CNAA degrees (BA, BSc, BEd, etc.)

Guide to the Colleges and Institutes of Higher Education. Published free, annually, it lists the institutions and describes the courses. Available from Edge Hill College of Higher Education, Ormskirk, Lancashire L39 4QP
Introducing the Colleges and Institutes of Higher Education. Additional information about the full range of degree and diploma courses. Published by the Standing Conference of Principals and Directors of Colleges and Institutes of Higher Education, and available from Edge Hill College (address above)
Polytechnic Courses Handbook. Published annually, it is a guide to full-time and sandwich courses in England and Wales. From CDP, Kirkman House, 12–14 Whitfield Street, London W1P 6AX
A Compendium of Advanced Courses in Colleges of Further and Higher Education. Published annually on behalf of the Regional Advisory Councils (RACs) by the London and Home Counties RAC for Technological Education, the booklet is available from Tavistock House, Tavistock Square, London WC1H 9LR. It gives details of advanced full-time and sandwich courses. In addition, the regional RACs publish other booklets describing part-time courses in their own areas
Scottish Centrally Funded Colleges, The Secretary, CSCFC, Moray House College, Holyrood Road, Edinburgh EH8 8AQ
Directory of Further Education. Describes over 6,000 courses in polytechnics and colleges. Hobsons
Student Eye. Student views of universities and polytechnics. Hobsons
The Student Book, by Klaus Boehm and Nick Wellings. A guide to UK universities, polytechnics and colleges: where to study, what to study. Macmillan, 4 Little Essex Street, London WC2R 3LF
Mature Students – A Brief Guide to University Entrance. The Committee of Vice-Chancellors and Principals, 29 Tavistock Square, London WC1H 9EZ

Applications for entry

For universities, start with *University Entrance, The Official Guide* (see details above)
How to apply for admission to a university. Published annually by the Universities Central Council on Admissions (UCCA). Free from UCCA, PO Box 28, Cheltenham, Gloucestershire GL50 1HY. Also ask for an application form. (You will get *How to apply* with an application form from your school or college.)

For polytechnics and colleges, consult the *Polytechnics Courses Handbook* and the colleges' *Guide*, listed above. Write to PCAS for a copy of the *Guide for Applicants*: PCAS, PO Box 67, Cheltenham, Gloucestershire GL50 3AP

Scotland: *The Scottish Universities Entrance Guide*. From SUCE, 12 The Links, St Andrews KY16 9JB

Sponsorship and grants

Grants for Students – A Brief Guide. DES, HMSO and obtainable from HMSO or bookshops

Designated Courses. A DES list of courses that have been designated as comparable to first degree courses, and which therefore qualify for grants. DES, Information Division, Elizabeth House, York Road, London SE1 7PH

National Engineering Scholarships: A Guide for Candidates. DES (address above)

The Which? Guide to Sponsorship in Higher Education. A comprehensive guide to sponsorships offered by over 200 companies, and details of sponsored degree courses at universities, polytechnics and colleges. Consumers' Association and Hodder & Stoughton. For copies write to Consumers' Association, Castlemead, Gascoyne Way, Hertford X, SG14 1LH

Training Opportunities in Engineering. Details of undergraduate and graduate training places provided by engineering companies. School Liaison Service, Institution of Mechanical Engineers, PO Box 23, Northgate Avenue, Bury St Edmonds, Suffolk IP32 6BN

The Sandwich Course Guide. Hobsons

For detailed information about degree courses, consult Hobsons' series of *Degree Course Guides*.

Sponsorship Insights is a bi-monthly newsletter, containing details of all kinds of sponsorship in education, i.e. sport, environment and the arts. Hobsons

Alternatives

A Year Off . . . A Year On. A guide for students thinking of work experience or voluntary service before going on to higher education. Hobsons

Careers

Occupations. This government annual careers guide describes over 500 different occupations, professions and careers. COIC

What Do Graduates Do? Hobsons, in association with the Association of Graduate Careers Advisory Services (AGCAS)

Decisions at 15/16+; *Decisions at 17+*; *Your Choice of A-levels*; *Your Choice of Degree and Diploma* and *Surviving Interviews* are careers and educational guides on the implications of choice at decisive times. Hobsons

Jobs and Careers after A-levels, by Mary Munro, Hobsons

Working In series: 40 booklets on careers, COIC

The Careers Book, Macmillan, 4 Little Essex Street, London WC2R 3LF

An A to Z of Careers, ed. by Diane Burston, Kogan Page

Choice of Careers series. Booklets published by COIC

AGCAS Careers Information Sheets. Short guides to a range of careers for graduates. Over 70 titles. Available from Central Services Unit, Crawford House, Precinct Centre, Manchester M13 9EP

GET (Graduate Employment and Training). Details of over 3,000 UK employers who recruit graduates. Hobsons

The Job Book. Published annually, the book lists thousands of jobs that offer training. Hobsons

PART 3

AN A TO Z
OF
CAREERS

An A to Z
of
Careers

Careers in **bold** in the text have their own entries; they can lead directly from the career under discussion or are closely related to it.

The publications listed under Information in the entries should be available from libraries and bookshops or from the organisations that publish them. Hobsons' titles are available from Hobsons Publishing, Bateman Street, Cambridge CB2 1LZ; COIC titles are available from Careers and Occupational Information Centre, Room W1108, Moorfoot, Sheffield S1 4PQ.

In Scotland, Standard Grade has largely replaced Ordinary Grade. Either qualification is equivalent to a GCSE in England and Wales, although for simplicity we quote O-grades only in the examples below. GCSEs are quoted instead of the former O-level, but, again, O-levels should be regarded as an equivalent qualification.

Accountancy

Accountants

Accountants work in private practice, for public authorities, in central or local government, and in large, medium and small industrial and commercial companies. The job of an accountant in private practice is to audit company accounts and present an analysis of the state of the organisation's finances. Accountants advise on record-keeping, taxation, investments and other aspects of finance. Accountants in industry and commerce are involved in the day-to-day running of the business, cash flow forecasting, budgeting, investment appraisal, and so on. Contrary to popular myth, most accountants do not sit at desks poring over ledgers or using pocket calculators to add up and manipulate figures – some do, but most do not.

Accounting is now regarded as a very useful stepping-stone to a wide range of business careers. One recent major survey of company bosses revealed that over a third of them thought that training in finance and accounting was the fastest route to the top in business. On the other hand, accountants have a reputation for being cautious rather than adventurous. Even so, whatever one's view of what accountants are, they dominate business, investment, merchant banking, public sector organisations and industry. In general, they work in one of three broad areas: private practice, the public service, and industry and commerce.

Private practice

Firms of partners or 'principals' function as consultants to all kinds of businesses. Some accounting firms consist of two or three people in a country/town practice; others are of 100-plus partners with portfolios in industrial and international business. In this kind of work, people specialise in, for example, mergers and takeovers, computer systems, corporation finance, VAT and other taxes. However, all firms have a basic workload – the auditing of accounts, the preparation of balance sheets, and tax returns. Audits can be done in a few hours or take several months, depending on the size and complexity of the business for which the audit is being prepared. In general, people who make themselves experts in one of these fields are snapped up by commercial companies, and they can command high salaries.

Public service

Accountants in the public service act as financial managers for local government, in state-owned industries, in the National Health Service and in central government departments. Their main responsibility is to see that public money (grants, taxes, and so on) is spent properly and used efficiently. They work alongside other professional staff and ensure that the financial effects of different policies are understood and followed.

Industry and commerce

In industry and commerce, accountants work in various ways but mainly either as management accountants, assessing the value and contribution to profit of all aspects of the business and making recommendations to improve the company's financial return, or as financial accountants who deal with the day-to-day business of bookkeeping, audits, taxation, VAT payments and wages.

Prospects

Career prospects for young accountants are very good, despite the financial and business problems brought about by the recession of 1990-1. In this period the major accountancy firms cut back on recruitment and indeed some City of London firms that had engaged a substantial number of graduates went out of business or drastically reduced their staff.

At the same time, universities and polytechnics have been steadily increasing the number of students admitted to study finance and accounting subjects. The demand through UCCA and PCAS for these courses is high: to take only three examples, Liverpool University reported 900 applications for 30 places on a degree course in accountancy; East Anglia 640 for 36 places; Glasgow University 600 for 90 places.

As the economy picks up, career opportunities for accountants will no doubt improve; however it is unlikely that all graduates and A-level leavers who hope to go into accountancy will be successful. It is, nevertheless, a subject directly relevant to a much wider range of career opportunities in all kinds of businesses. Because this is well known in schools, the heavy demand for places on degree courses is unlikely to slacken, so students need to be aware of the keen competition to get a place: grades in three A-level subjects ranging from ABB to BCC are required.

Training

There are degree courses in accounting and finance at several universities including Aberdeen, Aberystwyth, Bangor, Belfast, Birmingham, Brunel, Cardiff, City, Dundee, East Anglia, Edinburgh, Essex, Exeter, Glasgow, Heriot-Watt, Hull, Kent, Lancaster, London, Manchester, Newcastle, Salford, Sheffield, Southampton, Strathclyde and Warwick and at most polytechnics. For some courses, A-level maths is preferred but is not essential, but GCSE maths and English language are required.

Training is by full-time, part-time or correspondence courses, mainly at colleges of further education and polytechnics. These lead to the preliminary, professional and final examinations of one of the six professional accountancy bodies: the Institute of Chartered Accountants in England and Wales (or Scotland or Ireland); the Chartered Association of Certified Accountants; the Institute of Cost and Management Accountants; the Chartered Institute of Public Finance and Accountancy. The syllabus differences between them are small but jealously guarded. All courses include economics, statistics, accounting methods, corporate finance, computer systems and applications, law and other topics. In general, graduates train for three or four years: there are various methods of graduate entry, via accountancy degrees or business studies degrees, or with other degree qualifications. Exemptions are given, depending on the prior qualifications, with conversion courses for non-accounting graduates.

Non-graduates train for at least four years, during which time they study for the exams of one of the professional bodies. For entry at 18 to the one-year foundation course, two A-levels and three GCSEs at grades A, B or C are required, including English language and maths at GCSE. For variations in entry requirements, contact the relevant bodies which accept a BTEC National Diploma instead of two A-levels.

Accounting technician

Accounting technicians are the support staff, the desk-workers, on whom the professionals depend. In small companies the technicians work in the accounts office, keeping the day-to-day records of the company and dealing with invoices, payments, tax returns and wages. To train as an accounting technician, there are two-year full-time or three- to four-year part-time courses, starting at 16-plus. The courses (provided at colleges or by correspondence courses) lead to the exams of the Association of Accounting Technicians. For entry to a BTEC National Diploma course, three or four GCSE passes at grade A, B or C, including English language and maths or a numerate subject, are required. Following the BTEC National Diploma in business studies (with accounting options) trainees then study for the AAT final exams. Students need to register with the Association before starting their college courses.

Information

The Institute of Chartered Accountants in England and Wales, PO Box 433, Chartered Accountants' Hall, Moorgate Place, London EC2P 2BJ

The Institute of Chartered Accountants of Scotland, 27 Queen Street, Edinburgh EH2 1LA

The Chartered Association of Certified Accountants, 29 Lincoln's Inn Fields, London WC2A 3EE

The Institute of Cost and Management Accountants, 141–149 Fonthill Road, London N4 3HF

The Chartered Institute of Public Finance and Accountancy, 3 Robert Street, London WC2N 6BH

The Association of Accounting Technicians, 154 Clerkenwell Road, London EC1R 5AD

Working in Accountancy, COIC
The Facts about Chartered Accountancy, Hobsons
Business, Management and Accountancy, Degree Course Guide, Hobsons

The Chartered Association of Certified Accountants (address above) provides an excellent free package of booklets about accountancy as a career

Acoustical engineering

Acoustics or acoustical engineering is concerned with the science of sound. It is closely related to **mechanical engineering** and electronics, and forms a substantial part of some degree courses in these subjects. Electroacoustics is an aspect of **electrical engineering** involving the behaviour and control of sound.

The routes to training and a professional qualification in acoustics follow much the same pattern as other engineering courses: a degree or an HND leading to corporate membership of an engineering institution and the status of a chartered engineer. Another way into the field is by taking a physics degree, and then specialising in acoustics.

Prospects

There are very good career prospects. The **aeronautical**, space and **telecommunications** industries are desperate for young people to work in research and development laboratories in this advanced technology, and there are openings in companies such as GEC, Plessey and

British Telecom for people with manufacturing and research interests.

Training
Courses in acoustics include subjects such as dynamics, electronics, mechanics, structures and engineering drawing (design). Considerable emphasis is placed on practical work: in the lab, degree students are taught experimental and practical skills, as well as studying the subject's underlying scientific principles.

Many mechanical engineering courses include aspects of acoustics. Courses at the following universities offer a final-year project or special course on acoustics: Birmingham, Cambridge, Cardiff, Durham, Imperial College (London), Manchester, UMIST, Nottingham, Reading, Salford, Southampton and East London Polytechnic.

A-level maths is a requirement for 80 per cent of mechanical engineering courses; over 70 per cent require an A-level science subject from a group that includes physics, physical science, chemistry or engineering science. GCSE maths and physics are generally essential, and 30 per cent ask for chemistry at GCSE.

Information
Technology, Degree Course Guide, Hobsons

Acting

Acting is a *very* overcrowded profession. Of the 33,000 members of Equity, the actors' trade union, only about 25 per cent are working at any one time. It is essential that anyone who enters a career in acting has a high degree of mental and physical stamina combined with total commitment. Even with these qualifications there is no guarantee of work. The fact that a school performance has been highly praised does not necessarily indicate a brilliant career as an actor.

Entry to the profession is closely controlled through Equity, which allocates a number of Provisional Membership cards to the Theatre Managers' Association. A Provisional Member has to have had thirty weeks' work before becoming a Full Member. No Provisional Member may work in television, in the West End theatre, in radio or films. Actors on entering the profession therefore have to find work in the regional theatres or in a company working outside London such as the Royal

Shakespeare Company at Stratford. Currently, television provides fifty per cent of all the work for actors. Over the past few years a number of non-Equity companies have been set up but generally these do not survive for any length of time. The salaries paid by such companies are often lower than the already low salaries paid by companies recognised by Equity. In the last few years numbers of 'Community Theatre' and 'Alternative Theatre' companies have been started. These companies spend much of their time 'on the road' appearing in small venues over a wide area.

Prospects
Prospects are poor except for someone who is very lucky or exceptionally talented. There are other opportunities in **drama** and the **theatre** as directors, stage managers, lighting consultants, set designers, costume designers and other back-up services. It is generally easier to find work in these areas.

Training
Anyone who wants to follow a career in acting should try to get into a reputable drama school which has a course validated by the National Council for Drama Training. Talent is the principal requirement for entry to any school, and although most schools do not require academic qualifications a student who has good GCSE and A-level results is more likely to be accepted. Application to a reputable school also provides an opportunity to test one's ability against others hoping to enter the profession. Only about one in fifty women are lucky, and one in twenty men. Courses last for two or three years. There are also a small number of postgraduate courses lasting one year.

Information
National Council for Drama Training, 5 Tavistock Place, London WC1H 9SS
Conference of Drama Schools, c/o Central School of Speech and Drama, Embassy Theatre, Eton Avenue, London NW3 3HY
British Actors' Equity Association, 8 Harley Street, London W1N 2AB

Careers in the Theatre, Kogan Page
Working in the Performing Arts, COIC

Actuarial work

Actuaries are concerned with applying mathematics, statistics and economics to assist in the making of financial recommendations and decisions, especially those concerned with life assurance, pensions and investments. They use probability, interest calculations and statistics to 'work out the odds' for financial institutions, mainly insurance companies and pension funds. From this analysis it is clear that ability and enthusiasm for maths are essential. Two-thirds of actuaries work in insurance companies, while a fifth are concerned with advising companies on their pension arrangements. Other actuaries are involved in government service and the Stock Exchange. However, there are not many actuaries: about 2,500 fully qualified members of the Institute of Actuaries and another 600 of the Faculty of Actuaries in Scotland.

Prospects

Prospects are good. Actuarial science is a profession for a small number of people, but there is a steady demand for their services.

Training

Ninety per cent of entrants are graduates usually, but not necessarily, with qualifications in accounting, finance, mathematics, statistics, or economics with numerate options. Some accountancy degree courses include actuarial studies and there are specialist degree courses at City and Kent Universities in actuarial science. After entry, graduates proceed towards the status of Associate of the Institute of Actuaries (AIA) followed by Fellowship (FIA). This can take several years. In the old days 'seven years' hard' was the loose description of the training period of an actuary. Times have changed, and much has been done to remedy the long haul to Fellowship status, including a postgraduate diploma course and tutorials in addition to correspondence courses, but considerable dedication is required to put in two or three hours of studying at home after a full day's work at the office.

For those who survive the three or more years of study for FIA, there are rewards in the very high salaries paid to good actuaries. Many of the significant number who do not achieve the final qualification nevertheless find niches in the financial world.

Entry is not restricted to graduates: some ten per cent of students make a start after A-levels. High grades in maths (A or B) are looked for at A-level, plus another subject at A-level with A, B or C grade. For these entrants the training period is longer than for graduates.

Of those actuaries in insurance companies, many are senior managers, while of those in the pensions field, many are partners or directors of their firms. On the investment side, some will be involved in investment analysis, portfolio management or other aspects of **stockbroking**, but wherever an actuary works, he or she can achieve a salary level which should satisfy even the most ambitious.

Information
Institute of Actuaries, Staple Inn Hall, High Holborn, London WC1V 7QJ
Faculty of Actuaries, 23 St Andrew Square, Edinburgh EH2 1AQ

The Actuarial Profession, Institute of Actuaries
A Career as an Actuary, Faculty of Actuaries

Administration

'Administration' covers work at many levels, from clerical jobs to senior management. It is used in many different ways and care needs to be taken in understanding how any particular organisation uses it. One fact is certain: every organisation, large or small, in the public or private sector, commercial or non-commercial, requires administration. How administrative tasks are grouped into jobs can vary considerably between organisations. In general terms, and using the word very broadly, administration means jobs in offices, and these can include:

- office work and management – record-keeping, filing, typing
- servicing of production – maintenance, repairs, ordering of goods and equipment
- processing of information – **secretarial**, **computing**, word processing
- planning production and work-flow and the smooth conduct of business
- correspondence – with customers, suppliers, banks
- accounts – invoices, payments, records of transactions.

The list is endless. Ultimately, administration depends on what an organisation needs to operate smoothly. Sometimes it is said that good administration is never seen, that it is noticed only when something has gone wrong.

If all these tasks are taken together, they add up to four million jobs in practically every type of organisation:

- **local government** – education, social services, housing, planning, finance
- **civil service** – departments such as Health, Social Security, Inland Revenue, Trade and Industry
- industry and commerce
- local employers – **estate agents**, stores and garages.

Of these four million jobs some 65 per cent are **clerical** and 20 per cent are **secretarial**. The rest are managerial. There has been some decline in the number of clerical jobs but an increase in demand for managers and for visual display unit operators as offices have adopted new technologies.

Another important factor is the pattern of employment. For instance, 65 per cent of all employees are women, with nine out of ten of them in clerical and secretarial jobs. Women provide three per cent of managers: from any point of view this is a depressing statistic and clearly it is an issue that engages the attention of the Equal Opportunities Commission. An increasing number of women are giving themselves a better chance of competing for management jobs by getting better educational qualifications. Among the professional bodies the Institute of Chartered Secretaries and Administrators reports that nearly 50 per cent of its student intake is made up of women.

A major employer in this field is the Civil Service. It has over 60 departments, some, the DSS for example, with offices in every large town.

Prospects and training

Just as administration is spread across many levels of an organisation, so entry can be from different educational backgrounds. For 16-year-old school-leavers there are openings as accounts clerks, typists and secretaries. It is, however, essential to have some kind of business skill and it is wise to take a City and Guilds, RSA, BTEC business studies, typing, keyboarding or word processing course at a local college of further education before starting the job hunt. For 18-year-olds who have taken A-levels, the same opportunities are there, but again it is essential to have something else to offer in the way of office skills or training. New technology is creating a great deal of unpredictable change in this field so young entrants should be prepared to train and retrain to remain employable in the long term.

Many graduates and holders of BTEC qualifications enter administrative jobs as a route to more senior management roles. Some undertake specialist administrative jobs in, for example, **accountancy** or **personnel**, and may take a specialist professional qualification relating to that field. Others prefer a more general approach and take the qualification of the Institute of Chartered Secretaries and Administrators (ICSA). In the private sector it is very rare to see a job at this level with the title 'administrator'; more often a specialist title is used. In the public sector the job title 'administrator' is used much more commonly and ICSA provides the professional qualification for administrators in local government.

The distinction between administrative and managerial skills is difficult to draw. Both are concerned with people and planning, budgets and paperwork. Qualities required include willingness to pay attention to detail, a methodical mind capable of planning other people's work, a knowledge of office technology and a readiness to deal with members of the public. Administration can be to do with the tasks required, while management is concerned with the level in the organisation at which they are carried out.

For specialist careers, see entries indicated above in bold and also the **Post Office** and **health care**.

Information
Careers in Secretarial and Office Work, Kogan Page
Working in Offices, COIC

Advertising

Advertising is the promotion of goods and services in order to stimulate demand for them. The most obvious kind of commercial advertising is the familiar display of brands in newspapers, magazines and on television. But advertising also includes the promotion of industrial products through trade magazines, exhibitions, mailings and leaflets, special offers, competitions, and all kinds of visual displays – posters, shop windows, stickers, and so on. Non-commercial advertising provides information without the hard-sell buying and selling copy. It includes fund-raising, electoral leaflets, government warnings about smoking, drinking and driving, and job vacancy advertising.

Careers opportunities lie in four main areas: **market research**, advertising agencies, company advertising, and the design and media studios that produce film, video, artwork designs and copy (the writing that describes the product). Market researchers gather facts and opinions on products by means of desk research, questionnaires and interviews. Some large advertising agencies employ over five hundred people but most have ten to fifty employees. Account executives are in charge of several accounts, each concerned with a different product, and link the client with the agency that is planning and designing the ad. Executives use the telephone a lot and travel widely to see clients and suppliers. The account planners and buyers do a similar job but may also have the authority to choose the methods of communication and control the budget for the campaign: they will deal with magazines, television and newspapers and buy the advertising space or airtime.

Other tasks lie within the creative departments – copywriters, designers, art directors, film technicians and so on, all working to tight deadlines and at high speed. There is fierce competition for all these jobs. In companies, the brand managers are responsible for marketing and for placing ads. In addition, each newspaper and magazine has an advertising department with staff responsible for seeking advertising revenue, essential to keep the newspaper or magazine in business. Finally, there are the independent film, video and design studios that create film or printed materials to order.

Prospects

Taken together, there are many different career openings in advertising for people with all kinds of skills – visual, communication, persuading and business skills. Most people work in offices and studios. Career prospects are good: people tend to move from one company to another fairly quickly, and progress for the talented and the businesslike can be swift.

Training

There are no specific entry requirements, although a good all-round education is looked for. For 16-year-olds, five GCSEs are necessary. Better still would be two or three A-levels with English, maths, business studies or art and design among them.

Some large agencies have a graduate trainee scheme where entrants move around between departments. Agencies look for graduates in economics, languages, business studies, English and other subjects. An art and design degree is very useful for designers and programme-makers.

Advertising is a specialist part of many business studies degree and HND courses, particularly courses in business studies, journalism and graphic design at polytechnics and specialist colleges. West Herts College, Watford offers a postgraduate course in advertising.

Training is usually on the job, supplemented by the courses of the Communication, Advertising and Marketing Education Foundation (CAM) and the Institute of Practitioners in Advertising. The CAM Certificate can be prepared for by taking part-time courses at a college of further education, or by correspondence courses. To enter, students must have two A-levels or three H-grades plus three GCSEs at grades A to C (or O-grades), including English language, *or* a BTEC National Diploma in Business Studies, *or* five good GCSE (O-grade) passes including English language and at least a year's practical experience. The course, like the jobs, covers marketing, advertising, public relations, media, market research, business studies and methods of communication. Graduates can negotiate exemptions. After the Certificate students can take a CAM Diploma, which involves a further year's study.

Information

Communication, Advertising and Marketing (CAM) Education Foundation Ltd, Abford House, 15 Wilton Road, London SW1V 1NJ
Institute of Practitioners in Advertising, 44 Belgrave Square, London SW1X 8QS

Working in Advertising, COIC
A Career in Marketing, Advertising and Public Relations, Heinemann
Advertising, Association of Graduate Careers Advisory Services, Central Services Unit, Crawford House, Precinct Centre, Manchester M13 9EP
Getting into Advertising, a careers booklet, from the Advertising Association (same address as CAM, above)

Aeronautics

The aeronautical or aerospace industries are concerned with aircraft design and manufacture. This is specialised work for engineers with high technical skills. Furthermore, the space and satellite industries are desperate for research scientists and engineers. Other jobs are in the administrative, financial, operating and maintenance sides of these businesses. The employers are aircraft manufacturers, airlines, avionics companies and the Ministry of Defence. Some of the UK's most prestigious companies, such as British Aerospace, GEC, Rolls-Royce, and Marconi, are heavily involved in this work.

Engineers specialise in airframe design, manufacture and air engine development. Courses at degree level include dynamics, mechanics, structures, materials, aerodynamics, structural design and systems (heating, lighting, ventilation, radar, flight control, and so on).

Prospects
Prospects are excellent for scientists and engineers with ability. These industries also require substantial support staff – computer personnel, instructors, service engineers, technicians, office staff, etc.

Training
For entry to degree courses in aeronautical engineering, good A-level passes in maths and physics, or engineering science, or physical science, are essential. Chemistry is required in many cases at GCSE or O-grade. Degree courses are provided at the Universities of Bath, Belfast, Bristol, City, Glasgow, Imperial College (London), Queen Mary College (London), Loughborough, Manchester, Salford and Southampton, and at the Polytechnics of Hatfield and Kingston.

Information
Royal Aeronautical Society, 4 Hamilton Place, London W1V 0BQ

Agriculture

Agriculture and **horticulture** include a large number of jobs. There are about 300,000 farmers, and partners and directors in agricultural companies and another 330,000 agricultural workers. Farming is the UK's biggest industry: it employs more than the motor, coal and steel industries added together. On the other hand, jobs are getting fewer. Farming is changing from being a labour-intensive industry to being a capital-intensive one: this means that money, not farmworkers, is the key to the industry's future. Only the very wealthiest people can afford to buy and run a large farm, which means young people entering farming must expect to work not for themselves but for someone else. Sixty per cent of farms are owner-occupied; the remaining 40 per cent are tenanted.

The chief attractions are a healthy, outdoor life, working with animals and freedom from office routine. Again, there is another side to it: technology and good management distinguish an efficient farm from an unsuccessful one, so people with good business skills as well as knowledge of agriculture will do well.

In agriculture, the work divides roughly into these categories:

- livestock: working with beef cattle, dairying, pigs, poultry and sheep
- mechanical production: sowing, harvesting, plus the maintenance of all kinds of farm equipment and transport
- general farm work: tractor-driving, ploughing, and so on.

The range of jobs depends on the size and type of farm, and its ownership. Some farmworkers carry out general duties, others become specialists as farms are attuned to market needs and EC policies.

Prospects

Prospects are not very good: the number of people employed on the land has been steadily falling. There are about 6,000 farm managers in the UK, and to become one it is almost essential to have a degree, HND or some form of specialised training. A significant number of farming people have a family background in the industry. The best job prospects would seem to lie in the application of technology, mechanisation, computers and biology to mass-production. This would take young people towards agricultural sciences or engineering degree courses, and employment with fertilizer, food manufacturing, machinery and supplies companies in the UK. There are also opportunities abroad, particularly in developing countries. At home and overseas there are jobs as specialists in:

- advisory services: the Agricultural Development and Advisory Services (ADAS), Scottish colleges and commercial companies employ advisers to visit growers and farmers to advise on production problems. Among the specialists are horticulturalists, advisers on livestock, and officials of the Milk Marketing Boards. Other advisers suggest equipment, feedstuffs, fertilizers, business methods, etc.

- teaching: in rural schools and technical colleges, and in the agricultural colleges.
- management: the supervision of farmworkers can be the first step on the road towards farm management. Managers are responsible for the day-to-day running of a farm, the marketing of produce, keeping records, dealing with finance, suppliers and government officials, and so on, which usually adds up to a working week of 50 hours or more.
- research is an important aspect of agricultural work, covering crop production, animal husbandry and chemicals. It may involve working in a government research lab or commercial company, observing animal behaviour or plant growth, analysing the effects of climate, studying nutrition, specialising in plant diseases.

Training

For all these jobs, at whatever level, experience and training are required. The experience comes from working on farms: there is nothing like the discipline imposed because a cow calves in the middle of the night and you have to be there. The training comes in various forms:

- for 16-year-old entrants with a general education (GCSEs or O-grades are helpful but not essential) there are the Agricultural Training Board schemes of training. These provide up to three years of practical training with part-time or full-time education at a local college. Courses can lead to craft certificate, or a City and Guilds certificate or the National Certificate in Agriculture. The first year of these (and many other) courses is spent working on a farm. Students who achieve a high standard in the National Certificate (which includes some full-time education at college) can go on to take the Advanced Certificate or the National Certificate in Farm Management.
- BTEC National Diploma in agriculture: this can be a two-year full-time or a three-year part-time course at an agricultural college. To get a place, three or four GCSEs (O-grades) including a science subject are required, plus a year's practical work. The course leads to technician status, and the first step towards farm management.
- BTEC HND in agriculture: a three- or four-year course. To enter, students need at least one science-based A-level and three or four

GCSEs (O-grades), including maths and English language. The courses (which contain more specialised aspects of science) are provided at agricultural colleges.

● a degree course: this lasts three or four years and leads to a BSc in agricultural sciences, provided at many universities. Good grades (A, B or C) are needed in at least two (some ask for three) A-levels including a science subject, plus GCSEs (O-grades). Degree courses cover agricultural science, forest science, agricultural engineering, economics and business management. Graduates, if fortunate, move into jobs in these areas of agricultural work.

Agricultural engineering

Agricultural engineers work in food production, planning and mechanisation: courses include farm machinery design, mechanics, materials science, surveying, soil and water engineering and farm building design. Newcastle upon Tyne University, Wolverhampton Polytechnic and Silsoe College (part of Cranfield Institute of Technology) offer degree courses: A-levels in maths and physics (or physical science) are required.

Information

Agricultural Training Board, Summit House, Glebe Way, West Wickham, Kent BR4 0RF

The Agricultural Education Association, Cleeve Gardens, Oakbank Road, Perth PH1 1HH

The Careers, Education and Training Information Centre, Royal Agricultural Society of England, National Agriculture Centre, Kenilworth, Warwickshire CV8 2LG

Careers in Agriculture, from Agricultural Training Board (see address above)

Agricultural Sciences, Degree Course Guide, Hobsons

Courses in Agriculture in the UK, from AEA Sales, Askham Bryan College of Agriculture, Askham Bryan, York YO2 3PR

Courses in Agriculture, Horticulture and Forestry, National Consultative Committee for Agricultural Education, 2 Looms Lane, Bury St Edmunds, Suffolk IP33 1HE

Working in Agriculture and Horticulture, COIC

Air transport

Freight is carried by most of the airlines that also carry passenger traffic. The UK has over thirty large passenger airlines and about a hundred smaller ones, most of which are air taxi operators. There is, therefore, a substantial business opportunity for specialised staff who want to work in air transport.

Air pilots

Pilots are responsible for all aspects of flying aeroplanes. On large planes such as Boeings and the Airbus, there are two or three pilots on each flight, perhaps accompanied by a flight engineer. The major employers of pilots are the world's airlines and aeroplane-makers. Pilots also test equipment, carrying out aerial surveys and photography, give flying instruction, and spray crops.

Training
Training for these jobs involves attending full-time courses at approved training schools: Oxford and Perth are two of them. These lead to a commercial pilot's licence. Another route is to transfer from the **RAF**.

Entry qualifications for 18-year-olds (the minimum age) are, at the basic level, five GCSEs or equivalents, including maths, English language and a science subject of which physics is the favourite. There are similar courses for helicopter pilots at approved training schools. For graduates, entry is easier (but still highly competitive); graduates in maths and science have a decided advantage. Previous flying experience (perhaps at a local flying school) is a major asset.

Air traffic control officers

Direct the taking-off, approach and landing of air traffic in the UK and elsewhere by means of radio communication to pilots.

Training
To train, there is a two-year course, plus on-the-job training for cadets. For entry as a controller, GCSE (O-grade) passes in five subjects, including English language and mathematics, are required, plus two A-levels, one of which must be maths, geography or a science subject.

Scottish applicants can offer the Scottish Certificate of Education with at least three subjects at H-grade, plus two at O-grade, and one of these subjects should be at grade C or above.

Air cabin staff

Airlines, which generally train staff at their own training centres, look for people (the minimum age is 20) with a good general education and some experience in another job. This could be as a **waiter** or **waitress**, receptionist, shop assistant, **secretary** or **nurse**. Specific GCSE or A-level qualifications are not required, but obviously help. Modern languages are particularly useful, of course.

Aircraft maintenance engineers

Aircraft maintenance engineers work on the maintenance and overhaul of aeroplanes, their equipment and engines. **Mechanical engineers** are concerned with airframes and engines, and avionics engineers maintain electrical instruments, compass, autopilot and radio systems.

Training

There is a BSc course at City University (London) in this subject. A-level maths and physics (or physical science or engineering science) are specified for entry. Some technical colleges, such as Southall College of Technology and Brunel College at Bristol. As well as engineers, there are openings for technicians on maintenance work: most are employed by civil airlines, such as British Airways, flying clubs and air taxi operators.

Information

Civil Aviation Authority, CAA House, 45–59 Kingsway, London WC2B 6TE

Ambulance service

Ambulance crews look after seriously ill and injured people. *Ambulance drivers* take people to and from hospitals, and are trained to give first aid in emergencies. More routine work is in taking infirm or elderly people who cannot use public transport to clinics and hospitals.

Training

The Ambulance Service Institute provides help with private study for the Institute's examinations. The minimum age for entry is 18, and there is a cadet scheme for 16- to 18-year-olds. GCSEs or O-grades are looked for, but are not essential. Candidates must pass a medical test and have a clean driving licence. The National Health Service is the main employer: there are about 20,000 drivers, and for details of vacancies contact the Area Health Authority (the telephone number is in the telephone directory).

Information

Ambulance Service Headquarters, 220 Waterloo Road, London SE1 8SD

Jobs in the Ambulance Service and in Hospitals, Kogan Page

Ancient monuments

The Department of the Environment employs experts who are concerned with the inspection, care and preservation of ancient monuments and historic buildings. An inspector's work includes examining and reporting on the state of monuments, advising on their conservation and restoration, and writing reports to this effect. 'Monuments' include sites and buildings of all kinds dating from neolithic times to the nineteenth century.

Inspectors must have a detailed knowledge of history. In addition, experience of having taken part in archaeological 'digs' and other kinds of fieldwork is required. Knowledge of classical languages, architecture and history of art are very useful. The work of the inspectors takes them all over the UK; some time is also spent in their offices where they write reports and contributions to the guidebooks about the sites, as well as learned articles about the buildings and sites. In this work they are assisted by office staff such as secretaries, and occasionally have an assistant inspector who is being trained.

Prospects and training

There are few vacancies and to become an inspector (which is a senior rank in the **Civil Service**) requires a first- or good second-class honours degree in an appropriate subject, such as history, archaeology or classical languages, plus a postgraduate diploma.

To obtain a place on a university degree course in history (or other subjects useful for an inspector) requires good grades (A, B or C) in three subjects at A-level (or four at H-grade), including history. Other useful A-level (H-grade) subjects are history of art, archaeology, geography and geology.

Animals

The phrase 'working with animals' covers a large number of jobs. Although **agriculture** and **veterinary science** are probably the most obvious fields when thinking about working with animals, there are other possibilities. One of the most popular jobs is to work with a veterinary surgeon. The work and qualifications of a veterinary nurse, which is someone who works with vets, animal welfare societies and zoos, is described in the entry on **veterinary nursing**.

Animal technician

Animal technicians are responsible for the care and welfare of animals being bred for or used in research. Some technicians are involved in experimental work.

Mice, rats, guinea-pigs, rabbits and hamsters are the most usual species to be cared for, though some of the work requires the use of dogs, cats, monkeys, farm animals, amphibians, fish, insects or even exotic animals. The different requirements of these species and the experiments lead to a wide variety of working environments from open fields to hospitals.

A trainee animal technician is taught how to perform routine tasks such as cleaning out cages, washing and cleaning equipment and rooms, feeding, watering and the safe and comfortable ways of handling the animals. Before taking on such responsibilities there are some important questions to be faced:

- Does a love of animals show itself as a mature, caring attitude or does the student merely dote on them?
- Is the student prepared to be inoculated against diseases that may be part of the risks associated with such a job?
- Would the student be prepared to work on 'unsocial' days at weekends and on public holidays?
- Is the student allergic to any of the animals it might be necessary to work with?

An unfavourable reply to any of these questions means that being an animal technician is not a suitable career.

Training

Academic requirements for entry as a trainee animal technician are not standardised, but most employers give preference to those who hold GCSE (O-grade) pass grades or equivalents in English language, mathematics or science subjects as these give a firm basis for training and further education. Animal technology is a practical subject and much training and the learning of necessary skills is undertaken on the job. Technical colleges and colleges of further education offer courses for different levels of qualification under the auspices of The Institute of Animal Technicians (three levels: Intermediate, Associateship and Fellowship, over a period of at least five years), BTEC (two levels, National Certificate and HNC) and SCOTVEC. Good employers encourage further education and most provide day release and financial assistance with fees and travel.

Specialist services: dogs

The work is either the breeding, boarding, quarantine or training of dogs, or the world of dog beauty parlours. Work in kennels is noisy, dirty and tiring. A kennel maid's duties involve cleaning, grooming, feeding, delivering puppies and caring for sick animals. In breeding kennels, dogs are trained and prepared for shows.

Prospects and training

Prospects are not encouraging – there are far more applicants than jobs. To set up on your own requires a lot of money and experience, as well as a 'run' or kennel well away from residential homes. Training involves spending up to 12 months working in a kennel or dogs' home. Because of night and weekend duties, girls (the workforce is almost entirely girls) often stay on the premises, with residential charges added to the bill for training. There are no formal courses or examinations.

Petshops and dog parlours employ girls to clip, groom and train dogs. Pay, as for kennel maids, is low. Prospects, too, are limited. Training is by working in the parlour: clipping and shampooing are practised on less expensive dogs before graduating to parlour work.

Specialist services: cats

There are specialist cats' homes, or catteries. These tend to be run by cat-lovers, caring for cats whose owners are on holiday or who do not want to look after them any longer. As with dogs, there are specialist places where cats are prepared for shows which employ girls as helpers.

Prospects and training
Training is on the job and prospects and pay are generally very poor.

Information
See the separate entry for **horses**

Institute of Animal Technicians, 5 South Parade, Summertown, Oxford OX2 7JL

Royal College of Veterinary Surgeons, 32 Belgrave Square, London SW1X 8QP

Working with Animals, COIC
Careers Working with Animals, Kogan Page

Anthropology

Anthropologists once concentrated mainly on the study of primitive peoples and societies, writing and publishing learned articles about them. However, social anthropologists now study modern society: they look at the reasons for the different development of social groups in various parts of the world, examine the ways that the environment and buildings affect the way people live and behave, and study present-day population trends.

Training
To become involved in this work means taking a degree course at university or polytechnic. A list of these courses is in Hobsons' Degree Course Guide (see below). Another way in is by taking a degree in sociology and then specialising in some aspect of anthropology. The usual entry requirements apply for these courses: the Universities of Cambridge, Durham, Newcastle, London, Oxford and St Andrews ask for three good A-levels or four to five H-grades at A, B or C; the University of Kent and Oxford Polytechnic require C and D grades in three A-level subjects. Any A-level or H-grades are useful, although

sociology and biology would be very appropriate for a degree course. GCSE passes in English language, maths and biology are necessary in some cases. Employment is mainly in research work at universities.

Information
Social Sciences (which includes sociology, social administration and anthropology), Degree Course Guide, Hobsons

Antiques and art dealers

An antique dealer buys furniture, silver, china and/or other objects and sells them to the public. Some antique dealers specialise in certain items, perhaps silver or clocks; others concentrate on periods (eighteenth-century furniture); others are clock repairers as well as dealers, experts on arms and armour, and so on. Full-time dealers usually have a shop, although many work from home. The trade has plenty of part-time dealers who have other jobs.

Antiquarian booksellers, as the name suggests, deal in old books. The books can range from rare and expensive books and documents to quite recent second-hand books. Most of these booksellers specialise, and quite a number work from home, selling by mail catalogue and personal contacts.

Art dealers buy and sell pictures (fine art) and/or objects (the decorative arts). The most prestigious ones are in London, but others have town and country businesses.

For all these jobs expert knowledge is the first essential. The owner or director of the firm will be the chief expert, but the sales and administrative staff in a shop or gallery will also need to have specialist knowledge. Dealers visit trade fairs and house sales. Personal knowledge of the buyers is important, so there is plenty of telephone work.

Prospects
Opportunities are limited. There are probably about 20,000 antique dealers in the UK, with about 1,000 art dealers and 300 antiquarian booksellers. The way in is often via a family connection. Dealers are not keen to train people because the newcomer usually either moves on to another dealer, perhaps a rival, to increase his or her salary, or opens up his or her own business. Pay is not good. On the other hand, once a few items have been collected, it is not difficult to start dealing on your own.

The qualities needed are a good business sense, thorough knowledge of the particular field in which you wish to specialise, artistic appreciation, flair and luck.

Training
There are sometimes jobs in salerooms: the big three are Sotheby, Christie and Phillips in London, but there are salerooms in many towns. Entrants are school-leavers, graduates or older people whose hobby or keen interest leads them to the business. There are no specific qualifications or training. Obviously an interest in history, art, ceramics, metalwork, woodwork and fashion are important, and GCSEs or A-levels or equivalents in some of these subjects are useful. After that, however, it is down to the study of artefacts and books about them.

Information
British Antique Dealers' Association, 20 Rutland Gate, London SW7 1BB
Antiquarian Booksellers' Association, 26 Charing Cross Road, London WC2H 0DG
The Society of London Art Dealers, Fine Art Society, 148 New Bond Street, London W1Y 0JT

Careers in Antiques, Kogan Page

Archaeology

Archaeology is the scientific study of the human past, both through material remains and through the environment in which communities lived. Excavation is only one technique used by archaeologists: they also need to be skilled in ground and aerial surveying, techniques of conservation, the application of scientific techniques, and much more. Modern archaeology is a meticulous scientific discipline, requiring great attention to detail, and it impinges upon many other traditional areas of study.

Prospects
There are career openings in **museums**, central and **local government**, and independent units and trusts, as well as in university teaching. The number of full-time posts in archaeology is small, and opportunities for career advancement are still relatively few. Preference is likely to be given to archaeology graduates with considerable field experience.

Most university courses have a minimum fieldwork requirement, but those seeking a career in field archaeology are urged to gain as much field experience as possible during vacations.

Training

Entry to archaeology is generally through a university degree. Over 20 universities and polytechnics offer archaeology as a course, either as single honours or combined with other subjects, including classics, history and the sciences. Specialist postgraduate courses are also available in museum studies, conservation and the archaeological sciences. It is difficult to generalise about the entry requirements to universities, since courses vary in their emphases. History is not an automatic prerequisite, and Latin is needed only for classical archaeology. Geography and a foreign language are desirable in most cases, and serious consideration should be given to at least one science subject (biology or chemistry for preference).

The Council for British Archaeology organises a Diploma in Archaeological Practice, possession of which can improve career prospects. The Institute of Field Archaeologists is the professional institution for archaeology.

Information

Council for British Archaeology, 112 Kennington Road, London SE11 6RE
Institute of Field Archaeologists, Minerals and Engineering Building, University of Birmingham, PO Box 363, Birmingham B15 2TT

Guide to Undergraduate Courses in Archaeology, Council for British Archaeology
A Job in Archaeology, Council for British Archaeology
History (with Archaeology), Degree Course Guide, Hobsons

Architecture

Architect

The task of an architect is to plan and design buildings that provide for people's needs and also please those who live and work in them. Architects have to study traditional and new building methods and materials, and appreciate their possibilities and limitations. The technical aspects of design have to be matched to a budget, and to the needs of the users and society. As people change their lifestyles and their opinions of what buildings should look like and what they should provide, so architects have to be aware of these changing needs and fashions.

Architects also need to be aware of social problems and be able to respond to them. For example, there is now much public unease about high-rise flats, which were very popular with architects in the 1950s and 1960s, and with the architectural style of many public buildings.

Architects obtain their work from government departments, local authorities, private firms and, to a lesser extent, from private householders. First they must carry out research to find out what people require of the new building. Then comes the design stage, with sketches, revisions, plans and drawings, until the scheme is designed and contract documents have been approved. Then, when the builder begins work, the architect looks after the contractual obligations, visiting the site, keeping a close eye on the budget and what is being spent, checking on materials and construction methods, planning towards the completion date and finally approving the building at the end of the construction period. It is a job that is spent partly in the office and partly on the site, with plenty of travelling between the two places.

Architects are employed by private architectural practices; in the architects' and planning departments of local authorities; by public corporations (such as a New Town); in government departments; by building contractors, and by large industrial and commercial companies. There are good opportunities overseas, particularly in the Middle East, on contract work.

Prospects

Jobs in architecture are difficult to find and are not well paid: income levels are less than half those paid to lawyers or doctors. About 1,000 new architects are registered annually, although the number is diminishing. And yet it is a career that is tempting to young people because it is outdoors, and it mixes arts with science to produce an obvious, tangible end product. Not many professions or jobs have these qualities. However, there is very limited scope for employment, and this, plus the high standard expected of applicants and eventually of qualified architects, means it is difficult to gain entry to a degree course, and even harder to complete it.

The length of training and the relatively few jobs make architecture a difficult career. This is borne out by government plans to reduce the number of architects in training. Young people have to be aware of the problems and be determined to overcome them in order to train as an architect.

Training

Before anyone can practise as an architect, he or she has to obtain educational and practical qualifications. These take at least seven years. The qualifications lead to membership of the Royal Institute of British Architects (RIBA) and to registration as an architect.

The great majority of students enter full-time courses that usually last for five years. All students must also spend at least two years in practical training in addition to the full-time course. One year of this must be after completing the course, with the other year taken at some time during the five-year course. Most schools of architecture have this break between the third and fourth years of the course. Among the subjects studied on a degree course are the history of architecture, building design, materials, construction techniques, town planning, traffic studies, environmental science and economics. During training there is a great deal of practical work that requires students to work long hours. For people worried by a seven-year educational programme, the first three years of a degree course usually lead to an honours degree, and some students then break away into other careers.

Students interested in this career need to find out about the full-time courses at schools of architecture in polytechnics and universities recognised by the Architects Registration Council of the UK or by RIBA. Up-to-date lists of the schools can be obtained from RIBA, and an analysis of the courses is contained in Hobsons' Degree Course Guide (see below).

The basic minimum qualification for a university or polytechnic degree course are five GCSEs (O-grades), ir uding three 'academic' subjects at A-level (or four or five at H-grade). Good grades (A, B or C) at A-level are looked for. Some courses demand A-level maths; others deliberately look for a mixture of arts and science A-levels. GCSE maths is generally demanded, although some schools accept GCSE physics or chemistry in place of maths. However, the requirements of each school should be checked carefully before applying via UCCA or PCAS, because they do vary.

It should be noted that competition for places is very keen: for example, 670 applications for 30 places at University College, London; over 1,000 for 68 places at Newcastle University – so the universities and polytechnics set high A-level grade targets of AAB to BCC.

Architectural technician

A technician assists senior staff. He or she collects and prepares information for the architect, prepares technical drawings, liaises with customers and builders, and supervises work on the site. In some instances the technician carries through small projects from inception to completion, undertaking all design work. However, the number of jobs available makes architecture as difficult a career for the technician as for the architect.

Training

Some technicians train on the job, with day release in order to take a BTEC National Certificate course, or a SCOTVEC course in Scotland. Others take a two-year full-time BTEC course leading to a National Diploma in building studies. After these courses, it is possible to take an HNC by day release and an HND by full-time study, again in building studies. The minimum qualifications for the National Diploma are four GCSEs or their equivalent, and for the HNC and HND either one A-level (two H-grades) plus five GCSEs (O-grades) or the BTEC National Diploma. In all these courses the correct BTEC units have to be taken to qualify as an architectural technician. Alternatively, a student can select different units for qualifications in various aspects of the building industry: surveyor, general builder or quantity surveyor.

In order to qualify as a recognised architectural technician with full membership of SAAT (see below), a further year of study is recommended after completion of the HNC, and a completed logbook showing two years of work is another requirement. Therefore, it all adds up to a minimum period of six years of training after GCSE in order to secure full recognition as an architectural technician.

Information

The Royal Institute of British Architects, 66 Portland Place, London W1N 4AD

The Royal Incorporation of Architects in Scotland, 15 Rutland Square, Edinburgh EH1 2BE

The Society of Architectural and Associated Technicians (SAAT), 397 City Road, London EC1V 1NE (SAAT has free leaflets on architectural technology)

A Career in Architecture, RIBA
A Future in Architecture, RIBA
Schools of Architecture Recognised by the RIBA, RIBA
Architecture, Landscape Architecture and Planning, Degree Course Guide, Hobsons

Archives

Archivists look after documents and other written records of the past in county and city record offices, national libraries, large public libraries and in private libraries and institutions. Their work is to preserve the records of central and local government, the law, and private documents such as diaries, letters, wills, and so on. A major aspect of an archivist's work is to assist students, lecturers, teachers and members of the public who wish to study some aspect of local history, the law or their family. They must enjoy reading about history and like historical research, which is a slow, painstaking business. Increasing numbers of archivists are now involved in records' management, helping with the organisation of current and semi-current records of businesses and other organisations, both to promote efficiency and to make sure the right records are kept for the future.

Prospects and training
There are few vacancies and the total number of archivists is only about 1,000. A good degree is essential: archivists are usually university graduates with degrees in history, Latin or other classical languages, or English. These subjects are very useful at A-level or H-grade; to obtain a place on a university history course or similar course, passes in three A-level subjects (four at H-grade) with grades of A, B or C are required, with history as one of the subjects. After taking a degree, there is a diploma in archive administration – a necessity for most posts.

Information
Society of Archivists, Suffolk Record Office, County Hall, Ipswich

IP4 2JS, and Hampshire Record Office, 20 Southgate Street, Winchester SO23 9EF

Careers in Librarianship and Information Science, Kogan Page

Army

The British Army prides itself on being a modern, highly trained and efficient organisation. A very important factor is that it is made up of volunteers. The job of the Army is to defend and protect Britain's people and overseas interests and responsibilities, which include taking a full part in fulfilling European and United Nations agreements.

About a third of the Army (over 50,000 troops) is based in West Germany as part of NATO but the garrison there is now being reduced. Other regiments are deployed in garrisons from Northern Ireland to the Falklands. The equipment used by the Army is highly technical, including electronic communications systems, guided weapons, armoured vehicles and helicopters. Soldiers of all ranks have to be prepared to work – and fight – using sophisticated weapons: at the same time they have to be very fit, able to march and manoeuvre against opponents on any terrain.

Entry to the Army is at various levels.

For male soldiers the minimum age for entry is 17. The Army sets entrance tests to assess practical and mental skills. In addition, apprentice bandsmen, technicians and craftsmen are taken in from the age of 15 years 8 months.

For male officers there is a scholarship scheme to assist students on sixth-form courses. The age-limits are 16 years to 16½ years.

Welbeck College has a two-year, sixth-form science-based course that prepares students for Regular Commissions. GCSEs or equivalents in English language, maths, physics and at least two other subjects are required, with pass grades of A, B or C. Age-limits are 16 to 17½. This course leads to careers in the technical services branches of the Army.

Regular Commissions are open to applicants with two A-levels or three H-grade passes at A, B or C, plus another three subjects at GCSE or equivalents: these subjects must include English language, maths, a science subject or a foreign language. Age of entry is 17¾ to 22.

Short Service Commissions of three to eight years are open to those between 18 and 26 years (29 in some branches) with at least five GCSEs or equivalents, including English language. For technical work other subjects may be specified.

Graduate entry officers can be given Regular Commissions or Short Service Commissions. Undergraduates can take up a Commission while still studying, or a cadetship. Bursary schemes are available.

Commissions through the ranks is now a popular way of gaining a Commission: spending a period in the ranks before applying for and attending the Regular Commissions Board. Free discharge is available for those who do not satisfy the RCB. Age of entry is $17^1/_2$ to 22 years and up to 29 years for Short Service Commissions. Educational qualifications are the same as for Short Service Commissions. Engineering graduates are encouraged and helped to become chartered engineers.

All candidates for Commissions have to pass the Regular Commissions Board. Candidates are studied over a period of three days of tests which challenge leadership and management qualities in a variety of tasks.

For the WRAC – the Women's Royal Army Corps – the minimum age of entry is $17^1/_4$ for servicewomen. For officers there are Short Service Commissions: five GCSEs or O-grades are required, including English language, maths or a science subject; applications can be made from 17 for training to begin at 18.

For potential female officers there is a scholarship scheme to assist students on sixth-form courses. Age-limits for applications are 16 to 17 years.

Information
Army Careers Information Office in most cities – look in the telephone directory under Army

These three leaflets should be in careers' rooms or libraries:
Army officer. What the job is like and how you an apply for it.
Officer careers in the Army. Methods of entry
The arms and services of the Army
Working in the Armed Services, COIC

Art and design

Industrial design is concerned with matching practical efficiency to good looks. Designers work on cars, televisions and other electrical goods, aeroplanes, computers and a thousand other industrial products. Good, eye-catching design is what often distinguishes and sells one maker's products at the expense of another's. Interior designers work on furniture, houses, offices, shops. Fashion designers may be household names. Graphic design means the style and setting of all printed work – magazines, books, posters – and is a major employment area for young people.

Prospects

Design is fashionable and the morale of people working in all these industrial and commercial fields is high. On the other hand, there is little employment for people with fine art qualifications: they mostly find their way into teaching or fringe areas of design. Prospects are therefore bright in a profession dominated by young people, although there is about a 20 per cent unemployment rate among students a year after taking their degree or diploma. The increasing interest in design is shown in schools by the growth of design as a GCSE option and as an A-level subject. Design, when allied to engineering skills, has high government priority; on the other hand, it is thought that far too many students choose to take fine art qualifications, and attempts are being made to persuade them to opt for the more practical design courses. Nor do all design courses have good career prospects: textile design, for instance, is in the doldrums because of the decline of the textile industry. Computer assisted design (CAD), on the other hand, leads to excellent career opportunities.

Qualifications are important for design, but so too is the portfolio of work that a student accumulates during training: this is often the key to a job offer. Employers are looking for practical skills allied to a good business sense, and artistic ability. Many designers become self-employed, selling their skills to a variety of clients.

Training

Almost everyone starts with formal training and a qualification. Degree courses are offered by most universities and polytechnics, and by schools of art and design and specialist colleges. BTEC and SCOTVEC National Diploma and HND awards are highly regarded by industry. Students can study for these diplomas at polytechnics and colleges. Many of the BTEC and SCOTVEC courses have vocational titles such as 'design – photography, advertising, printing, three-dimensional', and so on. Most of these courses incorporate work experience and so offer better job prospects.

The entry requirements vary according to the course to be taken. For non-degree courses the academic requirements vary considerably. For BTEC and SCOTVEC courses the normal entrance requirements are two or three GCSE passes for the National Certificate, and three or four GCSE (O-grade) passes for the National Diploma courses. Some colleges make particular requirements for subjects at GCSE: *Design Courses in Britain* (see below) gives the details. Most colleges offer diploma courses in general vocational design and/or in graphic design. In addition, there are BTEC and City and Guilds courses in specialised design, such as furniture and fashion.

For degree courses at universities, applications are made via UCCA, as with other degree courses (see Chapter 19). Entry usually follows a one-year full-time foundation course which is provided at many regional art and design colleges. Direct entry from school is possible, but the foundation course allows a student the opportunity to sample different aspects of design and perhaps find an interest that may never have previously occurred to him or her. Degree courses vary, but they generally include four main sections: fine art (painting, sculpture), graphic design (photography, illustration, advertising, film and television design), textiles and fashion, and three-dimensional design (furniture, jewellery, theatre, interior design, etc.).

For other degree courses, BTEC HNDs and foundation courses, the normal route to polytechnics, art schools and colleges is through ADAR, the Art and Design Admissions Registry (see below). ADAR processes all applications for art and design first-degree courses validated by CNAA (the Council for National Academic Awards). For entry, students need five GCSEs, or one A-level and four GCSEs or two A-levels and three GCSEs, and be able to show competence in English, for which a GCSE in English language is sometimes demanded as evidence.

There are many sorts of design courses and students who intend to take a course after the age of 16 or 18 should send for and study the literature to make sure they understand the procedures and have made the correct choice from the many possible options. A good start is the Degree Course Guide on *Art and Design* by Hobsons.

Information
The Design Council, 28 Haymarket, London SW1Y 4SU

Society of Industrial Artists and Designers (SIAD), 12 Carlton House Terrace, London SW1Y 5AH

Chartered Society of Designers, 29 Bedford Square, London WC1B 3EG

Art and Design Admissions Registry (ADAR), Penn House, 9 Broad Street, Hereford HR4 9AP

British Institute of Interior Design, 1 Devonshire Avenue, Beeston, Nottingham NG9 1BS

Careers in Art and Design, Kogan Page
Design Courses in Britain, The Design Council
Working in Art and Design, COIC
Art and Design, Degree Course Guide, Hobsons

Astronomy

Astronomers study the stars and the solar system. Research into satellite communication systems and space agency work is carried out in universities and polytechnics in the UK, and in avionics companies here and in the USA. Other careers are in the **Civil Service** as scientific officers.

Training

Astronomers usually start with a degree in physics or mathematics, or a combination of these subjects. There are, however, special astronomy courses at Glasgow, Newcastle upon Tyne, St Andrews and Sussex universities, and at Queen Mary College and University College (London). Hatfield, Lancashire and South-West polytechnics also have astronomy degree courses. After that, it is a question of getting into university research work: there are few openings and the academic standard is very high. For entry as an Assistant Scientific Officer in the Civil Service, the entry qualifications are more modest: four GCSEs, including maths and English language, are required.

Information

British Astronomical Association, Burlington House, Piccadilly, London W1V 0NL

Astronomy as a Career, British Astronomical Association

Auctioneer

Auctioneering is generally part of the business of a **surveyor** and **estate agent**. However, many auctioneers specialise, for example in the sale of land and of commercial, industrial and residential properties. Others deal with works of art, furniture, motor vehicles and plant and machinery. The famous art auction houses, mostly based in London, are staffed by specialists who advise on the value of an item and who sometimes auction goods as part of their job. Outside London there are firms who operate livestock markets, and they may also be called upon to auction the contents of houses. Others specialise in the sale by auction of the equipment and stock of bankrupt or liquidated companies.

Auctioneers do not just sell; they also assess the value of goods and property, compile catalogues and negotiate with dealers and customers.

Training

Training as an auctioneer is part of the work of a surveyor, estate agent or **valuer**. Most people are employed by commercial firms and learn the practical aspects of auctioneering on the job. This may be while studying for professional qualifications or after taking a degree in estate management or general practice surveying.

Candidates who wish to take the Royal Institution of Chartered Surveyors (RICS) professional examinations are required to have passes in five GCSE subjects of which two are at A-level, including mathematics and English language or literature. Full details of the acceptable subjects are available from the Institution.

Universities and polytechnics set their own requirements for entry to quantity surveying degree courses, seeking grades well above the minimum as there is considerable demand for places on these courses. Some also express a preference for certain subjects; for example, mathematics, geography, economics and physics are often preferred A-level subjects.

Information

Royal Institution of Chartered Surveyors (RICS), 12 Great George Street, London SW1P 3AD
Incorporated Society of Valuers and Auctioneers, 3 Cadogan Place, London SW1X 0AS

Careers in Antiques, Kogan Page

Audiology

A dozen or more different professions are associated with the field of audiology; in the UK there is no single profession of 'audiologists'. These various professions are concerned with such matters as the measurement of hearing function and the diagnosis of hearing disorders, the surgical and medical treatment of hearing disorders, the provision of hearing aids, the rehabilitation and counselling of those who have a hearing impairment, and the special education of hearing-impaired children.

Information
Further information about these various professions, together with details of the training requirements, are contained in *Careers in Audiology* available from the British Society of Audiology, Royal National Throat, Nose and Ear Hospital, 330 Gray's Inn Road, London WC1X 8DA

Automobile engineering

Automobile engineers are concerned with all forms of ground transportation, but usually specialise in wheeled vehicles.

Employment can be in:

- manufacturing companies, working on current or new designs and the construction of cars, vans, lorries and other transport
- garages for the sale and servicing of vehicles
- specialist organisations such as the AA, RAC and recovery services
- any organisation with a transport fleet such as the **Post Office**, the **Army**, the **Royal Navy** and the **RAF**, and **road transport** companies.

Jobs are at various levels from apprentice to technician to graduate engineer. Prospects are very good, for automobile engineering is in a constant state of development and change.

Training
Training is probably best through one of the engineering schemes (see **engineering**). Most **mechanical engineering** courses have options in automobile engineering including degree courses, although there is a specialist degree in automotive engineering at Loughborough University and an HND course at Coventry Polytechnic. For other levels of work and courses, contact the local college of further education.

Information
Work with Motor Vehicles, COIC

Bacteriology

Bacteriology is a very specialised branch of microbiology: it is largely concerned with identifying and treating parasitic diseases. Bacteria are studied for their effects on humans and also in the treatment of poisonous waste materials from industry and other sources.

Prospects
After qualifying, bacteriologists are employed in research laboratories of universities and similar institutions, **hospitals** and the **pharmaceutical industry**. There is a demand for their services, for research into and treatment of bacteriological infections is a regular part of hospitals' work.

Training
Courses at degree level in bacteriology include topics such as biology, chemistry, anatomy, physiology and statistics. There are specialist courses at the Universities of Edinburgh, Newcastle and Manchester. To gain entry, three A-levels or four to five H-grades are required, with good pass grades (A, B or C) in three science or maths subjects. Chemistry at A-level is generally essential and biology is very useful.

Information
Bacteriology, Microbiology and Immunology, Degree Course Guide, Hobsons
Microbes and Man, Penguin
Microbes and Men, BBC Publications

Baking

There is more to baking than people realise. Apart from the skills of making, storing and selling bread, there are the special skills of making pies, cakes and all kinds of fancy breads, buns and delicacies.

Most bakers learn their skills on the job, working with experienced tradesmen. In many towns and villages there is still a small bakery, often a family business, with skills handed down from one generation to the next. That is one area of employment: the others are in the large independent bakeries and in food manufacturing companies, many with household names.

The basic working week is the same in baking as in most other industries, although the pattern of working would nowadays be considered by many as unsocial. Shift working is common, and early morning starts are often a feature in all sectors of the industry. One compensation for the latter which many people find attractive is that early starts usually mean free afternoons and evenings.

Many young people enter the industry after attending full-time courses in baking at colleges of technology. There they can obtain either City and Guilds or BTEC qualifications ranging from skills acquisition to more advanced bakery subjects. Opportunities also exist for young people actually employed in the industry to attend bakery schools on a part-time basis, either through day release or in the evening.

Training

For entry at 16-plus, a good all-round education is required without specific educational qualifications. However, to get on to a City and Guilds course, GCSE passes are looked for, and for a BTEC National Diploma, four GCSEs or their equivalent is the general requirement. Among the school subjects that are very useful are sciences, English language, home economics and cookery.

Information

The Federation of Bakers, 20 Bedford Square, London WC1B 3HF
The National Association of Master Bakers, Confectioners and Caterers, 21 Baldock Street, Ware, Hertfordshire SG12 9DH

Jobs in Baking and Confectionery, Kogan Page

Banking

In recent years the world of banking has changed dramatically. Competition for customers between the banks and with other financial institutions is intense. Just as the **building societies** are offering banking services, so the banks too are extending their range of services to include house mortgages, Saturday opening, 'free' banking for students, and are moving into the fields of **estate agency**, **insurance**, leasing and merchant banking. As a result, banks now want more of their staff to study management, business and marketing skills.

These trends are affecting recruitment. Most banks now expect that their GCSE recruits will occupy the clerical positions and that their A-level and graduate entrants will become the managers of the future, but at every level promotion is dependent upon performance. Competition for all places is keen – in the case of graduates the banks receive over 100 applications for each place available. The basic qualifications required for entry are four GCSE passes at grades A to C, which must include English language and a numerate subject. The banks do not specify any particular A-levels other than that they should be academic subjects and, as with degrees, the discipline is not important. However, law, economics, accounts and business studies are useful, particularly as bases for the Institute of Bankers' examinations.

There are four main areas for careers: high-street banks, merchant banks, the Bank of England and overseas banks. They all offer good prospects.

High-street banks

This is the area of banking with which most people are familiar – the branch networks. Financial services are provided to companies and individuals alike – taking deposits, providing loans and overdrafts, offering advice on all financial matters, supplying foreign currency and travellers' cheques for holidaymakers, making payments abroad for importers and exporters, and arranging the purchase and sale of stocks and shares. Those who progress well are unlikely to spend the whole of their careers in branch banking and, in order to gain experience, will spend periods of, say, three years in other sections and departments of the bank. These include personnel, regional head offices and internal audit sections.

Merchant banks

Merchant banks do not offer services to the individual but advise companies on all aspects of corporate finance, both in the UK and internationally, including capital issues, financial structures, acquisitions, takeovers and mergers. They also manage the investment of large funds provided chiefly by institutional investors among whom the pension funds are now the biggest element. Most of the high-street banks now have merchant banking divisions.

Bank of England

The Bank of England is the nation's central bank and, as such, stands at the centre of the British financial system. Its functions include advising the government on monetary policy, note issue, acting as banker to the government and to the commercial banks and managing the nation's reserves of gold and foreign exchange. It has a responsibility for overseeing the financial system as a whole and is a state-owned institution.

Overseas banks

These are branches of banks established in countries abroad, and the opportunities to work in them are mainly in London. Would-be recruits should be deterred from thinking that they would enjoy a jet-setting life around the world, as the opportunities to work abroad are quite limited and are usually open only to those who have reached a fairly high level of seniority within the bank.

Training

Most of the banks undertake their own training which in the junior grades can be either learning from an experienced colleague or training through interactive video. Training for more senior jobs is given on residential courses at a bank's training college. Before progressing into management, staff must pass the professional examinations which are usually those set by the Institute of Bankers. (In the case of merchant banks, staff may instead take the examinations of the Institute of Chartered Secretaries and Administrators or the Association of Certified Accountants depending upon their area of specialisation.)

A minimum of four GCSE passes at grades A to C, including English language, is necessary to take the examinations. Stage 1 is a two-year part-time course leading to the BTEC National Award in Business and Finance which must include the following options: year 1, Elements of Banking Part 1; year 2, Accounting and Elements of Banking Part 2.

A-level entrants complete a one-year conversion course to qualify them for entry to Stage 2, to which graduates have direct entry. Stage 2 takes, at best, three years and successful completion qualifies candidates for the award of Associateship (AIB). Tuition is available at approximately 150 further education colleges in England and Wales and by correspondence course.

For those expected to reach senior management there is a further course of study for the Financial Studies Diploma.

The Institute of Bankers in Scotland conducts the professional examinations in Scotland. The Diploma takes on average between three and four years to complete, and successful candidates are awarded the Diploma of the Institute of Bankers in Scotland (DipIB (Scot)) while those who successfully complete a further three subjects qualify as Associates (AIB (Scot)).

Passing the Institute of Bankers' examinations does not guarantee a successful career; this depends on many factors – performance, willingness to serve in any of the bank's branches, ability, demonstration of management potential as well as being able to work as part of a team and leadership qualities. Although women make up 60 per cent of all banks' staffs, at present there is less than 3 per cent in management, although a further 20 per cent are now in junior management grades. Other than graduates and exceptional A-level entrants, it generally takes a minimum of 15 years before promotion to management can be expected.

There are also specialist degree courses in Banking and Finance at University Colleges of North Wales at Bangor and Cardiff, and at Loughborough University. On some courses students are sponsored by the leading banks.

There is very little interchange between staff of the high-street banks because they are all run along similar lines and there is little to be gained by a member of staff in one bank applying to join another. The overseas banks, in particular the smaller ones, are more inclined to recruit experienced high-street bank staff, as they do not have the same facilities for training their staff.

Information

Banking Information Service, 10 Lombard Street, London EC3V 9AT
The Institute of Bankers, 10 Lombard Street, London EC3V 9AS
The Institute of Bankers in Scotland, 20 Rutland Square, Edinburgh EH1 2DE

Careers in Banking and Finance, Kogan Page

Barrister

In England and Wales the legal profession is divided into two branches, **solicitors** and barristers. There are many more solicitors in practice (in

1990 about 45,000) than there are barristers (in 1989 about 5,000). Approximately 700 practising barristers are women and that figure is increasing.

Solicitors provide the public with a wide general legal service; barristers supply specialised advice in specific areas of the law. A barrister has no direct contact with the public; it is the solicitor who retains, instructs and pays the barrister. The catchment area of the barrister is considerably more extensive than that of most solicitors' firms. The London Bar operates on a countrywide basis; it affords a service that covers every field of law, and which is available to all solicitors, wherever they may practise. The Provincial Bars operate on a regional basis. Advocacy apart, their members tend on the whole to specialise less than their London counterparts.

The barrister is primarily a specialist in advocacy, that is to say, the presentation of his or her client's case to the court or tribunal which has to decide it. Good advocacy depends on mastery of law and fact, good judgement and the ability to present a case cogently and coherently. It also demands conscientious preparation of every case, often by way of opinions on law, advice on evidence, and, perhaps more important than anything, in civil cases, the preparation of written 'pleadings', which define the issues requiring decision. Apart from the conduct of proceedings in court, barristers also advise both orally and in writing and draft documents in connection with virtually every facet of commercial, industrial and domestic life.

Training

There are three steps in the process of becoming a barrister. A student must:

- be admitted to one of the four Inns of Court in London: Gray's Inn, Inner Temple, Lincoln's Inn and Middle Temple
- satisfy the educational and training requirements of the Inns
- be called to the Bar.

Furthermore, a thorough command of the English language, both written and spoken, is an indispensable requirement of practice at the Bar. Failure to attain a reasonable standard of efficiency may well result in disentitlement to practise. In addition, a student must be of good character and not engaged in any occupation regarded as incompatible with practice as a barrister.

Education and training comprises two stages – the academic stage and the vocational stage. Each stage is completed by examination, though some students may qualify for exemption from the academic stage. To qualify academically a student must hold a degree (in any subject at a minimum standard of an upper second-class honours degree) conferred by a university in the UK or the Republic of Ireland or by the Council for National Academic Awards; or by reading for such a degree as an internal student; or by being an overseas graduate or a mature student subject to certain provisions.

The vocational stage consists of attending for one year at the Inns of Court School of Law, participation in the practical exercises, and the passing of the Bar examination. Attendance on this course and participation in the practical exercises is obligatory for those intending to practise at the Bar of England and Wales. Students who do not intend to practise at the Bar of England and Wales may sit for the Bar Examination without attending the Vocational Course at the Inns of Court School of Law. (Provision is generally made here and at a limited number of other institutions for those in this category.)

Having completed these stages the student must be at least 21 years of age, must have passed the Bar examination and must have kept eight terms, that is to say dined in the hall of his or her Inn three times a term for eight terms. A student who dines in the hall of his or her Inn on six separate days in any term ('double dining') can be credited with having kept two terms (since there are four terms a year) and thereby completes his or her pre-Call dining obligations and other requirements in one year.

Pupillage begins when a student has passed the Bar examination and been called to the Bar, or when just about to be called. Pupillage is a form of unpaid apprenticeship under an experienced barrister for a period of one year. For the first six months pupils may not accept briefs themselves, but during the second six months they may begin representing clients and can therefore start earning a little. There are many branches of work at the Bar, the two main ones being Common Law and Chancery. Common Law in this sense covers Criminal Law and Family Law as well as work in the civil courts, while work at the Chancery Bar includes Company Law, wills, settlements and conveyancing. In addition there are smaller specialist Bars. Pupillage is often divided between Common Law and Chancery. The second six months may be spent with a pupil-master in Chambers (the set of rooms from which barristers practise) specialising in that branch of law in which the pupil wishes to practise. Before embarking on a career as a barrister a student should consider very carefully the pros and cons of practice at the Bar together with the financial and other prospects. At the end of his or her pupillage, if the barrister wishes to practise at the Bar, he or she must obtain a seat or tenancy in a set of Chambers. Unfortunately pupillage does not guarantee a tenancy either in the Chambers in which the barrister has served his or her pupillage or in any other Chambers.

The Bar is a profession for the individual. It is highly competitive and the risks are substantial. Although the gross financial rewards can be as high as in most other professions or occupations, a barrister has heavy expenses (such as Chambers' rent and overheads, travelling expenses and clerk's fees) all of which have to be found out of the barrister's own pocket, in addition to providing for a retirement pension. Against all this, the Bar offers the satisfaction that comes from personal achievement in a highly competitive profession, which is mentally and physically demanding, and in which the rewards are dependent upon individual enterprise and skill. It offers some prospect of elevation to the High Court bench, and a relatively greater chance of appointment as circuit judges, stipendiary magistrates, chairmen of various tribunals, and so on.

Some aspiring barristers do not intend to practise at all. Others leave the Bar after gaining experience in pupillage or practice. In each case, their training as barristers affords a valuable qualification for employment in industry, commerce, **finance**, **education**, the **Civil Service** and **local government**. Some barristers move into **politics**. There are more barristers employed in these fields than there are in practice at the Bar.

How much anyone starting at the Bar can expect to earn is impossible to say. It depends on the person concerned, but over and above this, good fortune is apt to play a bigger part in the early years of practice than at any time thereafter: the inevitable vicissitudes of Chambers' work; chance involvement in a lengthy case or in one which happens to attract publicity; the random brief which may secure a new solicitor – and, perhaps, win over an opponent's as well. The early possibilities are many and exciting, but, though the stimulus never dies, it is hard work and dedication that bring the ultimate, lasting rewards.

Information

Council of Legal Education, Inns of Court School of Law, 4 Gray's Inn Place, London WC1R 5DX

The Under-Treasurer, Lincoln's Inn, London WC2A 3TL

The Sub-Treasurer, Inner Temple, London EC4Y 7HL
The Under-Treasurer, Middle Temple, London EC4Y 9AT
The Under-Treasurer, Gray's Inn, London WC1R 5EU
The Secretary, The Senate of The Inns of Court and The Bar, 11 South Square, Gray's Inn, London WC1R 5EL

Law, Connections series, Hobsons
Law, Degree Course Guide, Hobsons
Careers in the Law, Kogan Page

Beauty care

Beauty care describes the wide range of treatments for the face and body. The special skills needed by beauty care staff are the ability to describe and apply treatments in a courteous and sympathetic manner. They must be well groomed themselves and have plenty of tact and common sense. They must know when and how to refer their clients to specialists such as medical staff. There are several kinds of job, but they can be grouped into three categories: beauty therapists, beauticians and beauty consultants.

Beauty therapists

Beauty therapists work in beauty clinics, health farms and in salons. They treat problems such as bad skin, unwanted hair, blemishes, scars, overweight and tension. They advise on diet and exercise, give facials and massage, and recommend make-up and other facial services.

Beauticians

Beauticians specialise in skin care, make-up, manicuring and foot treatments. They work for private salons or run their own practices at home, and may specialise in a particular aspect of care. For example, an electrologist removes hair by using electrolysis, a masseuse gives body massage, and a manicurist is concerned with grooming the hands.

Beauty consultants

Beauty consultants work almost entirely for perfume and cosmetics manufacturers. They help to sell products by demonstrating them. They work in department stores, visit people in their own homes, sometimes work in luxury hotels, and at country clubs and health farms.

Prospects

Prospects are good because of people's interest in exercise, fitness, health and beauty. Most therapists and consultants are women, and there is a constant turnover of staff.

Training

Most young people start by taking a full-time course at a college of further education or at a private school. The age of entry to jobs is generally 17, which means that a one- or two-year course at college is the right kind of preparation. One of the major courses is for a City and Guilds certificate in health and beauty care: this takes two years, full time, so students would move into a junior job at 18. If already in work, the City and Guilds course can be taken part time over a longer period. The entry level is two passes at GCSE or the equivalent, although colleges exercise their discretion in accepting students without the basic GCSE qualification. English language is looked for as one of these subjects, because good communication with customers is essential. Other courses lead to the qualifications of the International Health and Beauty Council (IHBC). These are as beauty receptionist, manicurist, beauty consultant, masseuse, figure correction specialist, electrologist and beauty therapist. For the IHBC courses two or three GCSEs are needed: the IHBC has a complete list of the colleges that provide these courses.

Students can go on to more advanced studies such as a BTEC HND in beauty therapy. The London College of Fashion is one of the few centres to offer this course. The entry requirement is at least one A-level, or two H-grades, supported by four GCSEs or their equivalent, which should include English language and a science subject.

Information

International Health and Beauty Council, PO Box 36, Arundel, West Sussex BN18 0SW

International Therapy Examination Council, 3 The Planes, Bridge Road, Chertsey, Surrey KT16 8LE

Working in Hairdressing and Beauty, COIC
So You Want to be Beauty Therapist?, IHBC

Biochemistry

Biochemists study the chemistry of living cells and tissues. They usually work as part of a team with biologists, doctors, chemists and other staff in hospitals and universities. They are supported by biochemical technicians who assist with all kinds of scientific duties within the laboratories.

Prospects

Employment opportunities are in research labs, with **pharmaceutical**, **brewing** and **food** manufacturing companies, and in **hospitals**.

There are degree courses in biochemistry at most universities. About a third of all graduates go on to take a higher degree (MSc or PhD) in a specialist area. Afterwards they continue with research or go into technical, advisory or production work, and sometimes move into marketing and selling. Statistics provided by the Biochemical Society show that in recent years only about seven per cent of new biochemistry graduates are unemployed six months after graduating. Biochemistry is a broad-based scientific degree involving a good grounding in analytical methodology and scientific techniques. It therefore gives a good basis for careers in various kinds of scientific work. On the other hand, many graduates choose to go into other areas of employment such as **accountancy** and all other kinds of business careers.

Training

For entry to a degree course (the Degree Course Guide mentioned below gives a full list of courses and the content of studies in them), three good A-level or five H-grade passes are required; many courses require a good A-level grade (A or B) in chemistry (sometimes physical science is an alternative). Other useful A-levels are biology, maths, human or social biology, or physics. Two or three of these subjects at GCSE (O-grade) are essential; certainly maths and chemistry must be offered. Some polytechnics offer degree courses in biochemistry or combined degrees with options in biochemistry: among them are Lancashire, Liverpool, East London and Wolverhampton polytechnics. For the full list of polytechnics that offer biochemistry, consult the PCAS *Guide*.

As training for laboratory work, to become biochemical technicians, students should take a specialist course (which can lead to City and Guilds or BTEC awards) at a local college. Passes in three GCSE subjects are the general entry requirement. There is a three-year BTEC National Certificate in sciences which is linked to a lab technician's duties; beyond this is a BTEC National Diploma in sciences.

Information

The Biochemical Society, 59 Portland Place, London W1N 3AJ
Association of Clinical Biochemists, 30 Russell Square, London WC1B 5DT

Careers for Biochemists, Biochemical Society
Biochemistry, Degree Course Guide, Hobsons
Opportunities for Biochemists, COIC
A Career in Clinical Biochemistry in the National Health Service, Association of Clinical Biochemists
The Biochemist: Careers in the Hospital Service, Department of Health

Biological sciences

In recent years biology has become an important science and a very popular subject at A-level and for degree courses. In the past, biology was descriptive, which meant that plants and animals were observed, classified and named. Now biological scientists work with chemists and physicists on new technologies and experimental techniques. For example, biotechnology (which deals with genetics, hormones, proteins, insulin, interferon, penicillin) has become a major UK industry.

The study of plants (**botany**) and of animals (**zoology**) are still the major features of any course. However, marine biology, ecology, immunology, animal behaviour, social biology, entomology (the study of insects), **pharmacology** (the effects of drugs on tissues and organs), pathology (human, animal and plant diseases) and toxicology (poisons) are now very important offshoots of the two basic subjects.

Prospects

It is surprising that this impressive collection of subjects does not bring greater job opportunities. Biological expertise is applied within the **pharmaceutical** (drugs), medical (**hospitals**), **agricultural**, **food** manufacturing, fertilizer and other industries. Biologists need to know a lot of chemistry: they have to be able to apply physical and statistical techniques, and an understanding of business is a big asset in job searching. Even so, biologists have more difficulty in finding jobs than any other group of scientists. The careers services estimate that 15 to 20 per cent of biologists are still looking for a job six months after graduating, and that one in ten moves straight into a scientific job, whereas four in ten go into all kinds of other jobs, from shop management to **teaching**. In order to get into scientific research it is essential to take a higher degree, an MSc or, better, a PhD. Employment prospects for those who have taken zoology or botany degrees are worse.

The major employer is the NHS. Biologists get jobs in pathology departments of teaching hospitals or research institutes, but there are many more scientists than openings. Other major employers are the Ministry of Agriculture, **health service** laboratories, **water** authorities, teaching or researching in universities, polytechnics and schools, and with commercial companies that manufacture drugs, cattle feed, fertilizers and other goods. Of these, the drug industry is the biggest single employer and offers the most intensive research work.

Other biologists add to their skills by taking extra courses and are employed in **business**, as **factory inspectors**, **environmental health officers**, and in **nursing**, **agriculture**, **conservation** and **teaching**.

Training

Entry to jobs is generally via a good honours degree, although biochemistry, biophysics and biotechnology might offer better long-term job prospects than biological sciences. To get on to a university or polytechnic degree course, applicants need three A-levels or five H-grades, with A, B or C grades. A biological subject and chemistry are usually preferred at A-level (H-grade), but in some cases maths or physics are alternatives. For biophysics, an A-level (H-grade) in physics is required; other degrees are in biomedical science, bioscience, cell biology, human biology, microbiology, ecology, applied biology, plant biology and marine biology. For a full list and course descriptions see the Degree Course Guides listed below.

In addition, there are HND courses in applied biology at several polytechnics and colleges, and biology can be studied as part of combined sciences/combined studies courses at polytechnics (see the *Polytechnic Courses Handbook* for details of these courses). One A-level and at least four GCSEs or equivalents are required, and very often chemistry or biology are specified. For *all* these courses, maths and chemistry at GCSE (O-grade) are necessary, and biology is usually required, too.

Professional qualifications for biologists are awarded by the Institute of Biology. To become MIBiol requires a good honours degree or the Institute's own exam, plus three years' experience of responsible work in biology or its applications.

Information
The Biochemical Society, 59 Portland Place, London W1N 3AJ
The Institute of Biology, 20 Queensberry Place, London SW7 2DZ

Careers in Biology, Institute of Biology
Careers Using Biology, Kogan Page
Biological Sciences; Biochemistry; Bacteriology, Microbiology and Immunology; Pharmacy and Pharmacology, Degree Course Guides, Hobsons
Polytechnic Courses Handbook, Committee of Directors of Polytechnics, 12–14 Whitfield Street, London W1P 6AX

Biotechnology

Biotechnology is concerned with the applications of chemistry, biological sciences, genetics and knowledge of living organisms to industrial processes. The main industrial applications – and the source of employment – are in waste systems, antibiotic products, animal feed and fermentation. It is an exciting industry to be involved in because scientific advances continually lead to fresh discoveries. Jobs are limited, and applicants need to have a strong scientific background at degree level.

Training
There are specialist degree courses in genetics, ecology and biotechnology at most universities and polytechnics. Good A-level grades in science subjects (BCC to CDD are quoted) are required for entry. See *University Entrance* and the *Polytechnic Courses Handbook* for a list of courses.

Information
Institute of Biology, 20 Queensberry Place, London SW7 2DZ

Bookselling

The objective of a bookshop is to sell books. End of story? Not quite, for many also sell other printed materials (diaries, wrapping paper, stationery, cards and sometimes toys). The two major requirements are to know about books and to know about business. The manager or owner has to know publishers and their book-lists, bestsellers, educational and children's books, fiction and non-fiction. Customers usually want to browse undisturbed, but when they have a question the assistants are expected to know the answer or where to find the answer.

The main jobs are as sales assistants, who fill the shelves, dust, learn where the stock is situated, deal with customers, write out orders and do some simple bookkeeping. Bookshop work is not easy: it is hard on the feet and there can be quite a bit of lifting and carrying. Bookbuyers work for large shops and stores such as WH Smith, John Menzies and others. They select from the vast number of books published each month; they compile orders, listen to publishers' representatives, and take the blame if they buy in bulk and the shop sells only a few copies. The managers are likely to do all these duties, and more. They are responsible for window displays, invoicing and ordering, selling, keeping proper accounts and stock control. In this respect, bookshop managers are shop managers, differing only in their goods, books, which they are expected to know about.

Prospects

Job prospects are not too bright. There are far more job seekers than jobs. Bookshops are busy at Christmas and often slack for the rest of the year. It is a sad fact that not all towns even possess a bookshop but have only a multiple store with a book department.

Training

There are no formal entry qualifications. A good education, willingness to help people (the customers), a polite manner and a good idea of how the business works are the main essentials. Graduates start on the bookshop floor, like anyone else, but because of their education they would expect to become an assistant manager fairly quickly. A Certificate in Bookselling Skills was introduced by the Booksellers' Association in 1985. It includes new techniques such as computerised stock control and ordering.

Information
Booksellers' Association, 272 Vauxhall Bridge Road SW1V 1BA

Botany

Botanists study plant life. In their work they investigate a wide variety of micro-organisms, and degree courses include subjects such as cell and molecular biology, genetics, physiology, biochemistry and ecology.

Read the entry on **biological sciences,** for what applies to biology graduates is true for botanists. Each year about three hundred botany graduates look for jobs. To use their knowledge, they try to get into careers in **forestry**, garden centres, botanical gardens, research institutes, universities and **water** boards. However, many of these institutions now look for a higher degree (MSc or PhD) from applicants. Other job opportunities lead botanists to the **Civil Service**, **agricultural** and **medical** research, teaching, conservation, and the **pharmaceutical** and **chemical industries**. However, a substantial number of graduates (about 25 per cent) go into careers where botany is not a requirement, i.e. in government work, **business** and commerce, and in **environmental health** services.

Several universities run degree courses in botany, as distinct from biological sciences. Among them are Bristol, Cambridge, Dundee, Edinburgh, London, and Southampton. Three good A-levels are needed at grades varying from ABB to CCC. For a full list, consult the Degree Course Guide.

Information
Institute of Biology, 20 Queensberry Place, London SW7 2DZ

Careers in Biology, Institute of Biology
Biological Sciences, Degree Course Guide, Hobsons

Brewing

Brewers are responsible for the biological processes of malting barley and brewing beer. Beer is made from malted barley, hops, yeast and water. Most brewing is done by large companies – Allied Breweries, Bass, Courage, Scottish and Newcastle, Watney-Mann and Truman, and Whitbreads. There are also some smaller local breweries making a comeback, and about 80 rather larger regional companies.

The four stages of making beer are mashing the malt, fermenting, processing and bottling/packaging. Most of the work is automated. Within the breweries, senior managers select and purchase the raw materials and equipment, supervise production, take samples and make frequent tests, assume responsibility for corrective action, and keep records. They are the responsible managers or technical supervisors who direct the work of other production staff. Alongside the brewers are production workers, and there are the usual support services of office staff, accounts, drivers, packers, and so on.

In the automated plants, most brewing processes are in enclosed tanks. However, there is some noise and the smell of hops and malt is always present. Brewers have to be prepared for these conditions. Further, they need a lot of knowledge and practical skills. These are based on science: chemistry, biochemistry and microbiology in particular. They also need to understand something of the complex machinery of a brewery, and to know about good business methods. Although there are few suitable courses, prospects are quite good for managers, and there are good opportunities to progress from assistant manager to head brewer – the top of the tree.

Training

There is a solitary degree course – at Heriot-Watt University in Edinburgh – which requires two or three A-levels (four H-grades) with pass grades around C for entry. At Birmingham University there is a brewing school, concerned more with short courses and postgraduate training for people with chemistry or biology degrees. The Incorporated Brewers' Guild arranges courses along with the Institute of Brewing: these are largely concerned with new technical developments. Traditional courses for school-leavers are chiefly on-the-job instruction in a brewery, working with an assistant manager. The technical and scientific side of brewing is taught at college on day-release schemes. Because few colleges have any expertise in brewing, students take a BTEC National Certificate or National Diploma in chemistry or biology and add instruction on brewing techniques in the company or on special courses at the Institute. To get on to a BTEC course generally requires four GCSEs or O-grades, including a science subject; chemistry is the most useful. After that, there are BTEC HNC or HND courses in sciences or applied biology, again backed up by part-time study for exams set by the Institute of Brewing.

Information

The Brewers' Society, 42 Portman Square, London W1H 0BB

The Institute of Brewing, 33 Clarges Street, London W1Y 8EE

Brewing as a Career, The Brewers' Society

Broadcasting

The broadcasting industry is an expanding one: cable television, local radio, commercial radio, communication via satellites and other modern developments have increased its scope. However, it is very difficult indeed to get into broadcasting unless people have engineering skills. (Over five hundred people each year are taken on by the BBC's Engineering Department, and it is reported to be difficult to fill these positions with people of A-level or graduate standard.)

It is the more 'glamorous' side of broadcasting – studio work, costume, make-up, outside broadcasts, and so on – which attracts most people. If they are fortunate to get into **radio** or **television** they soon find that a lot of hard work is required of them. The hours are 'unsocial' with shift work; deadlines are relentless, and the BBC, independent television and radio, and other services prefer short-term contracts, so there is some uncertainty about employment.

Broadcasting covers many, many jobs. The people one sees on the TV screen or hears over the radio are the front men and women – the presenters, actors, performers. Behind them are the studio staff – engineers, technicians, **camera operators**, writers, publishers, clerical staff, accounts departments, personnel, secretaries, drivers and managers.

There are various routes into broadcasting. One is to become a specialist in a particular field, and later on in one's career try to break into broadcasting. Into this category come **journalists**, political commentators, **musicians**, writers, computer personnel, and so on. A second route is to take a job as a **secretary**, **personnel** officer or technician and apply for in-company training courses. The third method is by direct entry from college and university: the competition is very fierce and you have to be particularly talented (revealed in drama clubs, music, writing) to succeed. Very few people are employed without some previous experience: what the broadcasting employers are looking for, therefore, are people with talent, knowledge and skills learned elsewhere and which can immediately be put to work in television and radio.

The main employers are the BBC television, radio, local radio, educational broadcasting, overseas services, independent television and radio, and some commercial stations. There are also many independent television production companies that are not part of the broadcast networks but which make commercials for transmission on, the BBC, ITV and also for Channel 4, the cable companies, and other users. On the fringes of the industry are commercial companies that make tape-slide, video and cassette recordings; there is employment here, but again for experienced people with existing skills.

Training

Being a technical industry, the broadcasting authorities are always looking for engineers and technicians: degree-level applicants with engineering skills are eagerly snapped up, and there are opportunities for young people of 18-plus with A-levels (H-grades) in maths and science subjects. Sponsorship is possible for graduates on electrical engineering degree courses. Other openings are for graduates with computer skills; design training (for costumes, sets, studios); statistical knowledge (for audience research); and with some idea of media in order to train as studio managers and technical back-up staff in recording studios. Vacancies as audio assistants are filled by graduates or school-leavers, usually over 22: again, knowledge of music, drama, entertainment, sport or current affairs are assets. Make-up artists are expected to have trained in **hairdressing** or **beauty** work; set designers and graphics artists must have experience and skills in these areas.

Television producers usually come through the ranks from studio managers, production assistants and floor assistants, although some are internally trained and others recruited from theatres or other companies. The BBC takes on about 20 production trainees each year: competition for these openings is very tough.

The ITV companies arrange their own training schemes for journalists, production staff, technicians and engineers. They also take on a few trainees from time to time. Once again, competition is very fierce, although engineers are always in short supply.

Over 80 colleges and polytechnics have media courses, most of them leading to BTEC National Diploma and HNDs and to degrees in media studies and similar subjects. The quality and relevance of the courses vary, but in general they give a useful insight and preparation for media work. In particular the London College of Printing has training courses in radio journalism, and other colleges, such as Ravensbourne College, University of Wales College of Cardiff (for journalism), and Middlesex Polytechnic (television studies), are highly regarded.

Information
Information Officer, IBA, 70 Brompton Road, London SW3 1EY
Head of Appointments, BBC, Broadcasting House, London W1A 1AA
Training Adviser, ITCA, 56 Mortimer Street, London W1N 8AN

BBC Annual Report and Handbook, BBC Publications Shop, 5 Langham Place, London W1A 1AA
IBA Annual Report, IBA, 70 Brompton Road, London SW3 1EY
Film and Television Training, British Film Institute

Building

Modern society needs more and more complex buildings of every kind – homes, schools, shops, hospitals, offices and factories – in which people can work, live or take part in various activities. It is the task of the building industry to satisfy these needs with speed and economy. The work may range from the alteration, repair or maintenance of existing buildings to the erection of complex multi-storey structures.

Among the managerial, technical and craft skills involved are design, erection, engineering, decorating and repair, together with various services such as heating, ventilation, air-conditioning, plumbing, lighting, safety, electrical servicing and the provision of gas and water services. To direct the skills involved in these activities, the building industry must have well-trained and qualified managers, technologists and technicians. All must be committed to providing the nation with high-quality buildings at the quoted price, on time and to the client's satisfaction.

Prospects
The building and construction industries suffered more than most in the recession of 1990-91. However, as the economy recovers, recruitment should improve. The construction industries in the UK employ over a million people, and the value of work carried out is over £40,000 million a year. Over three-quarters of this activity is in building and, therefore, the prospects for jobs are good. The main contractors, such as Wimpey, Taylor Woodrow, Laing, Mowlem, have many thousands

of employees and look for young people with management potential. Jobs generally go to people with degrees and diplomas in building, and the take-up rate for university and polytechnic building graduates is among the highest in the country.

There is scope for trained young builders. Some of the possibilities are:

- *site manager* – in overall charge of site, responsible for co-ordinating work and the profitability of the operation
- *site engineer* – responsible for surveying the site prior to work and subsequently ensuring that the building is correctly positioned
- *estimator* – prepares tenders by calculating the cost of labour, materials and plant
- *planner* – determines the most appropriate method and sequence of operations in the construction programme
- *quantity surveyor* – the person at the centre of the cost control system responsible for ensuring that the contractor is paid on time for the materials and work carried out
- *buyer* – ensures that materials, components, sub-contracted work and other construction resources required for the job are obtained at the most competitive prices and are available at the correct time.

Any one of these options may ultimately lead to building management, which is a creative, highly technical and intensely rewarding career.

Training

At the craft level – bricklayers, **carpenters**, **electricians**, joiners, painters, plasterers, shopfitters, stonemasons, wood-cutting machinists, plumbers, slaters, tilers, and heating and ventilation engineers – there are no specific entry requirements to become an apprentice or trainee. However, employers like to see candidates with a good school record including some GCSE passes, particularly in practical subjects such as woodwork, metalwork, craft, design and technology. The Construction Industry Training Board operates a national Youth Training scheme, where training is combined with work in a company, leading to very good job prospects.

Preparation for a career as a professional builder or as a building technician involves full- or part-time further education with complementary industrial experience and training. There are over two hundred teaching institutions, including universities, polytechnics and colleges of technology, which balance the necessary technical expertise with the development of management skills.

Entrants to courses leading to awards of BTEC at National Certificate and Diploma level normally need four good GCSEs. Maths, physics and science subjects are very useful entry qualifications. Courses leading to BTEC HNDs and HNCs in Building Studies need at least one A-level or two H-grades together with good GCSEs in four more subjects. Most of the degree courses at the universities and polytechnics are four-year sandwich courses and the major companies offer generous sponsorships. Courses are also available for the Chartered Institute of Building's own examinations, which at the final level are the equivalent of an ordinary degree, and for the diplomas in Building Maintenance Management and Site Management.

The Institute, the professional foundation for all who seek a career in building, provides opportunities ranging from technician to professional levels and has 28,000 members dedicated to raising the standards of technical competence and conduct within the industry. The class membership available on entry depends upon academic achievement and an appropriate length of practical experience at the correct level. Corporate members of the Institute are entitled to use the description Chartered Builder and the designation MCIOB or FCIOB as appropriate.

In Scotland there are courses leading to the equivalent SCOTVEC awards. The industrial training may cover a wide range of job functions in order to develop a broad understanding of building and guide the trainee into the most appropriate function for his or her career development.

Information
Information on careers at craft level: The Construction Industry Training Board, Radnor House, London Road, Norbury, London SW16 4EL
Information on careers in building management: The Chartered Institute of Building, Englemere, Kings Ride, Ascot, Berkshire SL5 8BJ. The Institute has several leaflets on careers and courses in building available on request

Building societies

There are currently about 160 building societies, ranging in size from the largest, with total assets of more than £30 billion, to the smallest, with assets of less than £1 million. The degree of concentration of building society assets is staggering: in 1990 between them the six largest (Halifax, Abbey National (no longer termed a building society since 1989), Nationwide, Alliance & Leicester, Leeds Permanent and Woolwich Equitable) accounted for more than 60 per cent of the industry's total assets, with the next largest nine societies accounting for a further 20 per cent.

There are almost 7,000 building society branches throughout the UK. The larger societies have branch networks in all parts of the country, while the smaller societies tend to operate with one branch which doubles as their head office or with a small (under 10) branch network in the area of the head office. Every city and town and most villages have at least one building society branch, and in some busy high streets there can be more than five such offices.

The size of these branches and hence the number of staff vary from those in small rural towns with perhaps three or four members of staff to a large city branch with perhaps a hundred employees. Building societies are major employers: they employ over 60,000 staff, the bulk of whom work in branch offices.

Prospects

Prospects are good, as building societies have expanded their services into financial investment, travel services and insurance as well as their mortgage services. They are looking for young people of high calibre with business acumen and skills and in return offer varied career opportunities, both at branch and head office level.

Branches   The first person you see on entering a branch is the assistant (usually called a cashier, clerk or 'customer service executive') on the front counter. The cashier is the public's first point of contact with the society – so a pleasant manner helps. He or she is responsible for taking investments and paying out withdrawals on demand while the office is open (most larger societies are now fully computerised and investors' transactions are recorded by counter terminals). Work does not, of course, stop when the branch closes to the public – bookkeeping and accounting duties have to be seen to. Also, many societies' training programmes are conducted on the job, outside normal opening hours.

Many counter staff hope to move on to assistant manager and, eventually, manager status. Often they do, although some societies are now looking for graduate trainees to come into the branch to learn quickly the counter skills and then move on. Managerial responsibilities include dealing with mortgage accounts, assessing applicants' financial suitability for mortgage loans, liaising with professional contacts such as surveyors, estate agents, solicitors and accountants, and advising on the society's range of investment accounts.

Head offices   A building society's head office is in the main no different to any institution's head office, although the specialist departments are, of course, geared to the nature of a society's business. There are departments dealing with **administration**, **personnel**, **computers**, stationery and postal services and public relations. Career opportunities are open at levels from typist/**secretary** to lawyer within societies' head offices.

Training

As you would expect, the more qualifications you have, the greater the choice of career will be. Many societies prefer applicants who can offer qualifications at A-level and GCSE. Passes in English language and mathematics are sometimes required. Do not be put off, however, by assuming that all societies require these qualifications – it is always worthwhile asking for information.

Building societies give their staff thorough training at all levels. The following qualifications are well worth achieving as they may result in swifter promotion:

- Certificate in Building Society Practice – aimed at junior staff
- Associateship of the Chartered Building Societies Institute – a professional qualification, for which a longer period of study, and examinations, are needed.

Information

The Chartered Building Societies Institute, 19 Baldock Street, Ware, Hertfordshire SG12 7PZ, is the training body for building societies. Free booklets and information sheets are available on request

The Building Societies Association, 3 Savile Row, London W1Y 3PF, is the trade association representing building societies. The Association publishes a range of general and specialist material explaining the work of the industry and produces teaching aids for schools covering life skills, money management and housing. Further information is available from the Schools Liaison Officer

For information regarding a career with a particular society, write direct to that society's personnel department. The society will probably send you a form to fill in and may ask you to go along for a talk with one of its personnel managers

Bursar

Bursars are concerned with the administration and financial management of many schools, colleges, halls of residence, old people's homes, industrial training centres and many private institutions. Their job is to administer the finances, buildings, catering, security and other systems – in effect they are business managers.

Training

Management knowledge and skills are needed: these can be obtained by studying for them or through experience of responsible posts in the **Armed Forces**, industry or commerce. Relevant training courses are in institutional management.

Information

Hotel, Catering and Institutional Management Association, 191 Trinity Road, London SW17 7HN

Business

'Business' is a word that covers a tremendous range of commercial and management careers. Apart, perhaps, from accountants, most of the jobs are not 'professions' with specified entry requirements. Instead they are 'career or job areas' that attract people with all kinds of skills, qualifications, interests and ambitions. And of these, ambition is perhaps the most significant. People who go into business careers must expect to be set, or set themselves, targets, and if they fail to reach these targets, dismissal or bankruptcy will be the consequence.

Business is very challenging and attitudes to it are changing. A recent Market & Opinion Research International (MORI) survey of a thousand final-year undergraduates showed that 75 per cent believed that 'large companies are essential for the nation's growth and expansion', and that they make a contribution to society; the undergraduates found the idea of working in business and commerce an attractive one. This marks a change from former attitudes when bright students set their sights on law, medicine and science and thought little of business. Now they see commerce as an area of interesting career opportunities, bringing a lot of satisfaction and also contributing to the nation's growth.

Prospects

Within business, entrants can move into such areas as: **personnel** work; **production**; research; **sales**; **marketing**; **purchasing**; **engineering**; **computing**; **advertising**; public relations; **banking**, **finance** and **insurance**; **accountancy** and bookkeeping, and so on. Job and career prospects in all these areas are very good indeed for people with the necessary qualities.

It is not only undergraduates who see commerce as a means to a good career. Today's school-leavers of 16, 17 and 18 see advantages in seeking a career in business and industry. This is reflected in the take-up of places for work-experience placements given to students on BTEC or sandwich-degree courses.

Training

To prepare for jobs in business, candidates need some preliminary training. One way to achieve this is to take a course at a college of further education, either part time (while in a job) or full time (prior to working) to get a BTEC National Certificate or National Diploma in business studies or finance, or in a subject with a strong business emphasis to the course, such as catering, retail trade, design, printing or engineering.

GCSE courses and A-level passes in commerce, business studies, computer studies and technical subjects are also important and useful preliminaries, but are not essential. People come into business and make a success of it from all directions, and with many different qualifications. It is, however, very difficult to get on to the bottom rung of the ladder without a first qualification – City and Guilds, BTEC National Diploma, HNC or HND or a degree. Applications to universities, polytechnics and colleges were, in 1991, at a record level. Business studies (usually with options in advertising, finance, business law and other topics) has become extremely popular for post-16 and post-18 applicants. And to move to the top of the ladder, an MBA degree (Master of Business Administration or a similar title) or other postgraduate diploma is a tremendous asset. Women are slowly making inroads into management, and the number of senior women managers and directors is increasing.

Another contemporary factor is the increase in the number of people who set up their own business, or who go to work in smaller companies. This trend is tackled in most business studies courses at any level, where the complexities of self-employment and forming a company are generally taught in some detail.

Information

British Institute of Management, Management House, Parker Street, London WC2B 5PT

Business Graduates Association, 28 Margaret Street, London W1N 7LB

Business Technician Education Council (BTEC), Central House, Upper Woburn Place, London WC1H 0HH

Business, Management and Accountancy, Degree Course Guide, Hobsons
Working in Offices, COIC

Buyer

All companies and organisations buy. They need equipment, supplies, raw materials, services. People who deal with the purchase of these goods and services are either buyers or **purchasing officers**. Buyers generally work in the retail trade, which means in shops, stores and supermarkets. In other kinds of companies the buyer may be responsible for the purchase of every kind of equipment or material needed for manufacturing a particular product. Buyers therefore operate in manufacturing industry, and are also employed by local authorities, public organisations and private business.

In retail trade there are three main types of buyer:

- specialists in a particular range of goods; it could be children's clothes, furniture or bedding
- departmental buyers who purchase for a single department in a large store, such as the food or the kitchen department
- a buyer in a chain store or multiple which specialises in certain kinds of goods, such as vehicle spares and parts, magazines and books, meat.

The skill and knowledge expected of a buyer is to be aware of market trends, know where to negotiate the best price for the best quality of goods, and know that his or her purchases will be bought by the customers. This is a risky undertaking, for if a buyer makes a mistake the shop will be left with a stock of unwanted, unsold goods.

Buyers may be part of a team or may work alone. They spend some of their time within their own company or shop, and a great deal of time visiting suppliers to assess their services or goods, and to negotiate prices face-to-face.

Prospects
Prospects are very good for people with knowledge of business methods and a sharp eye for trade. The disadvantage is that pay is not particularly good. On the other hand, buyers often move on to become department or shop managers.

Training
There are no formal entrance requirements. The best way into buying is to work in a store or supermarket and to make oneself an expert in a particular kind of produce or goods. Employers look for a good educational background and a sensible, mature attitude to work. They set their sights on people with three or four GCSEs or equivalents, or staff with A-levels (H-grades) and graduates. Students from BTEC business studies courses at polytechnics and colleges are particularly well regarded.

Most firms run their own training programmes. The Institute of Purchasing and Supply (IPS) arranges courses, and its qualifications are looked on as a guarantee of good training. Over a hundred colleges or polytechnics run part-time courses for the IPS. Examinations are in two stages: foundation studies and professional studies (see **purchasing** for details).

Information
Institute of Purchasing and Supply, Easton House, Easton on the Hill, Northamptonshire PE9 3NZ
Association of Print and Packaging Buyers, West Herts College, Hempstead Road, Watford WD1 3EZ

Camera operator

Camera operators work in at least three very different industries: television, printing and photographic.

Television

A camera operator is a member of a team of between two and four highly skilled people who make television programmes both in studios and on outside broadcasts. In the studio the head of the camera-crew is in charge of lighting and camera angles, working closely with the director of the programme. Assistants load and change magazines, ensure the correct equipment is in place and in working order, and learn how to operate the camera and lighting equipment. To get into this work is very difficult: there are few operators, pay is high and the demand for the jobs is very keen. Entry is via courses in film and television production at art schools and polytechnics. A good set of GCSEs or the equivalent is necessary to get on to these courses. No matter how good the student is, for every vacancy there are several hundred applicants.

Printing

The second kind of camera operator works in the printing industry. Here, camera operators control the machines that photograph an image that is to be printed, operate sophisticated colour scanning equipment, and make printing plates. The job can involve calculating exposure times and assembling film before processing. Camera operators are employed throughout the printing industry and particularly in graphic arts studios where film is prepared, mounted and processed before printing. Prospects are good for experienced staff because the technology is constantly being improved, and technical skills are highly regarded. Training is through a printing course, usually as part of a City and Guilds course which complements in-company training for trainees of 16-plus within the industry. Otherwise, there are full-time courses at colleges of further education in printing techniques which can lead to City and Guilds or to BTEC awards at National Certificate or National Diploma levels. Entrants need four GCSE passes for a National Diploma course, rather less for the Certificate.

Photographic industry

The third area in which camera operators work is within the photographic industry. This could be in printing, graphic arts or in the studios that service the magazine, book and media industries. Camera operators learn how to operate all kinds of photographic equipment, from 35mm to rostrum cameras. Entry is through City and Guilds or BTEC courses in photography, or by training within a company or studio. Companies look for people with good basic qualifications: GCSEs, A-levels or equivalents plus, if possible, a course of study in an art college or elsewhere on photographic and printing techniques.

Information
For **printing**, contact the British Printing Industries Federation, 11 Bedford Row, London WC1R 4DX
See **broadcasting** for television addresses
See **photography** for information about camera operators within the photographic industry

Carpenter and joiner

Carpenters and joiners work in the **building** industry. They are employed by all kinds of building contractors, as well as by local government housing and building services, central government departments, and, at the other extreme, by small jobbing builders. In today's climate many carpenters and joiners have set up on their own, hiring out their skills and services to contractors and to private householders.

Work of this sort involves fitting any kind of wood – floors, doors, windows. It includes erecting roof timbers and staircases, putting down floorboards and parquet floors, hanging doors and building their frames, fitting built-in furniture to kitchens and bedrooms, and building outhouses and garden sheds. The work of carpenters and joiners is not the same, although the words are often used loosely to describe the same job. Carpenters are expected to be able to work from architects' and builders' plans. Joiners (certainly in the north of England and in Scotland) are expected to be able to make and repair furniture.

Prospects

There are probably about 250,000 carpenters and joiners in the UK, of whom about 60,000 are self-employed. There is a constant demand for their trade and craft skills. The building industry is an erratic one, but these craftsmen (and women, although still only a few) are needed not only for new house-building but for repairs. People are constantly improving and enlarging their homes, so the demand does not slacken.

Training

The usual way into these crafts is by joining a company or contractor as a trainee and taking a day-release course at a college of further education to obtain City and Guilds qualifications. Another way in is through the Youth Training programme under the control of the Construction Industry Training Board (CITB). This involves on-the-job training, work experience and attendance at college for an off-the-job course. No formal qualifications are needed, but GCSEs in two or three subjects are favoured. Some experience at school in woodwork and metalwork is generally regarded as essential. A route to trade status is to take a three-year apprenticeship which also involves attendance at college for the City and Guilds certificate.

Information

Construction Industry Training Board, Bircham Newton, King's Lynn, Norfolk PE31 6RH

Building Industry Careers Service, 82 New Cavendish Street, London W1N 8AD

Working in Construction, COIC

Cartography

Cartography is the art or business of drawing maps and charts. Cartographers fall into two broad areas, draughtsmen and surveyors. Draughtsmen typically research, evaluate and compile information, design and draw, write, scribe and edit until the draft is ready for printing or reproduction. A 'map' can be a chart, plan, three-dimensional model or printed map.

In recent years, the work has radically changed. Aerial and satellite photography, seismic testing and electrostatic techniques have been introduced, and methods of printing and reproducing maps have been dramatically improved. One of the most significant advances is the use of a computer to store and 'customise' information to users' requirements. The advances that started in the drawing areas have spread to all parts of the cartographic business.

The cartographic surveyor collects the information from the ground and puts it into a usable form for the draughtsmen, either to redraw to prepare for printing or to input to the computer as raw data from which the user can define his requirements. In the Ordnance Survey (the official national mapping organisation of Great Britain, a government department and therefore part of the Civil Service), surveyors are given an area for which they are responsible and have to ensure that the plans of their area are kept up to date. This is outdoor work, probably 70 per cent of time being spent in the field, and contrasts to the indoor life of the draughtsman. In some companies the two tasks may be combined. Recent advances in the recording methods used by surveyors may eventually reduce the importance of draughtsmen in the map-making process.

Prospects

The largest single employer is the Ordnance Survey. Others are government departments such as the Ministry of Defence and the Department of the Environment. The field is not a large one. The employment opportunities are mainly in the south of England, particularly in London and Southampton (where the Ordnance Survey has its headquarters). In all, there are probably about 4,500 cartographers of both types in the UK. Annual recruitment to the Ordnance Survey averages about 100 surveyors and 75 cartographic assistants (a support grade to a draughtsman). Recruitment in this, as in any other government department, is subject to cutbacks.

Training

Surveyors It is best to contact the organisation you wish to work for to find out the requirements regarding qualifications because it is virtually impossible to generalise about employers' requirements. At the moment applicants for posts as cartographic surveyors with the Ordnance Survey must have three good GCSE passes, including maths, before applying. The entry requirements for all Civil Service posts in the Cartographic and Recording Class have been changed. Applicants should apply to the address below. A few graduates are recruited through the Civil Service Commission, which handles vacancies at this level for all government departments. Degrees for entry to Civil Service graduate surveyor posts must be in a subject relevant to land surveying, such as maths, engineering or geography. Geography candidates must have A-level maths or have taken a special and survey option. There is an increasing need for specialisation and therefore computer science may be required.

A-levels for entry to a degree course should include geography and a science subject. Maths is important also, due to the angles and scales involved in surveying. GCSEs should be in these subjects, plus physics. A modular degree course and HND in cartography are available at Oxford Polytechnic.

Draughtsmen The qualification for entry to the Ordnance Survey draughtsman grades are the same as those for surveyors (currently three GCSEs, one being maths). There are unlikely to be any competitions for these grades in the foreseeable future. There are, however, competitions for cartographic assistants when vacancies are available. The qualifications presently required for these posts are two GCSEs, one of which should be English. Applicants for both classes of posts need be 16; there is no upper age-limit. Further education opportunities are available on day release for students under 18, and assistance with part-time study is available for students over 18.

Information
British Cartographic Society, Department of Civil Engineering, Oxford Polytechnic, Headington, Oxford OX3 0BP
Ordnance Survey, Recruitment Section, Romsey Road, Maybush, Southampton SO9 4BH

Careers in Cartography, British Cartographic Society
Geography, Degree Course Guide, Hobsons

Cashier

Cashiers work in shops and stores, **banks** and **building societies** –

indeed any place where cash is handled. The duties of a cashier are to take money, record the payments and, where necessary, to pay it out. Payments can be in money, or in cheques, orders or other paper transactions. In a bank a cashier is in constant contact with customers, cashing cheques and taking credits. Similarly, cashiers transfer money and cheques in building society offices. In shops a cashier may be in a central position, dealing with payments from several shop assistants. At the end of the day or the shift, a cashier counts the money in the tills and balances the book account.

Training

Training is on the job, supplemented by courses. Experience is gained by doing the job, although cashiers have to learn very fast: they cannot afford to make mistakes. To begin work in a bank as a cashier, the same entry requirements apply as for other clerical staff. The same is true of building societies and shops or other kinds of retail sales businesses. The skills needed for this work are swiftness and accuracy in dealing with money: even though the transactions may be on a cash register or a computerised calculator, speed with figures is still necessary. Arithmetic (although it may not be used much), knowledge of accounting systems, bookkeeping and other records are essential skills. To acquire them, cashiers can attend **business studies**, **accounting** or banking courses at various levels. The courses (at colleges of further education) can lead a 16-year-old by various stages into assistant manager's jobs. If not, the cashier will always be an essential and integral part of a business.

Information

Working in the Money Business, COIC
Working in Accountancy, COIC

Catering

Catering is a catch-all term describing the provision of food, drink and accommodation for customers or staff. It covers a vast number of jobs and employs over 2.5 million people. Among the different services are:

- hotels – from the ritzy to the down-at-heel
- bed-and-breakfast accommodation
- restaurants of all types and sites from the takeaway to those in the grandest hotels

- pubs, cocktail bars and night clubs
- industrial catering – staff canteens, transport catering on planes, trains and boats, directors' hospitality suites
- contract catering – where a single large firm supplies food and drink (often in frozen form) to offices, factories and airlines
- hospitals and old people's homes, school meals, university and college canteens.

Caterers move about from one kind of job to another. However, unless they have had training in hotel work, it is unlikely that they will get management jobs involving accommodation. Job titles are also inter-changeable: a 'manager' can be in charge of a large hotel or smart restaurant, or put out a few pies and sandwiches for his or her customers' lunches in the saloon bar of the local pub. Even so, it is possible to categorise the main types of jobs:

- *directors* – the top management of a fast-food company or a hotel chain. They arrive at the top through managerial work or by takeovers and other Stock Exchange manoeuvres
- *managers* – senior staff in charge of a hotel, restaurant, canteen, club or other provider, and assistant managers who are junior staff learn-ing the trade
- *supervisors* – of a college canteen, a kitchen, or of domestic staff in a hotel
- *assistants and craft workers* – cooks, chefs, cashiers, drivers, waiters, receptionists, the army of people who do much of the hard work
- *unskilled workers* – cleaners, people who wash up, packers.

For all these jobs, applicants must expect to work unsocial hours when other people are relaxing; to deal with all kinds of customers, including the rude and the drunk; to be at customers' beck and call; to put up with hard work; and to have to deal swiftly and practically with problems and emergencies. Tutors on degree, HND and other catering courses at colleges say that many students who apply for courses do not realise what is involved in catering, and think it is an extension of the work they did in home economics and cookery classes. In reality the catering business is a very tough one.

The food industry needs people with varied skills. All those outlined above, but also people with technical qualifications too: food can be prepared in vast kitchens in a production company, sealed in trays and packages, frozen or bottled, transported miles and served to customers in bars, hotels, canteens and by an air steward or stewardess working from an aircraft's galley.

Fast food is another rapidly expanding industry. All these businesses require skills, business acumen and willingness to put in long hours of work.

Prospects

The catering industry is an expanding one, demanding more and more staff. There is a lot of scope for the practical producers: chefs, cooks, house-keepers, drivers, packagers. At the management level it is a dynamic life, which means managers never rest, move between one job and another at the drop of a plate, and are promoted or sacked along the way. There is no rigid career structure except in institutional catering, such as colleges, schools and Civil Service canteens. Promotion depends on skill, mobility, personality and luck.

Training

There is a confusing number of different courses and qualifications. For pre-entry courses, there are City and Guilds craft certificates in hotel reception, cookery for the catering industry, food and beverage service to mention only three of many. For supervisors there are the BTEC National Diploma and National Certificate courses in hotels, catering and institutional operations and food technology and even in vegetarian cookery. As well as a 'core' programme, there are optional units to suit different needs. This course, for 16- to 18-year-olds, offered at colleges of further education, leads to junior management jobs. Entry is at the four GCSEs or O-grades level, including English language and a science subject. In Scotland there is a modular scheme leading to the Scottish National Certificate.

For students with A-levels (H-grades) there are two-year full-time or three-year sandwich courses leading to a BTEC or SCOTVEC HND or HNC. These courses are provided at colleges and polytechnics for people with one A-level (two H-grades) plus four to five supporting GCSEs or their equivalents. Degree courses in hotel and catering administration or catering science are offered at the Universities of Cardiff, Dundee, Strathclyde, Surrey and Ulster. Polytechnics and colleges, among them Napier Polytechnic and Queen Margaret College in Edinburgh, Huddersfield, Leeds, North London, Middlesex, Oxford and Portsmouth polytechnics, offer CNAA degree courses. Two or three A-levels (five H-grades) with average passes (C grades) plus four to five GCSEs, including maths, English language and a science subject, are required. In addition there are several one-year postgraduate courses, including the Hotel, Catering and Institutional Management Association's graduate entry course. People already working in the catering industry can study for Part A of the HCIMA award by part-time study, followed by the Association's Part B course which is available full time, part time or by correspondence. More and more colleges are offering other management courses on a part-time basis.

Information

The Hotel, Catering and Institutional Management Association, 191 Trinity Road, London SW17 7IIN

Hotel and Catering Training Company, International House, High Street, London W5 5DB

Leaflets on careers and qualifications are available from HCIMA
Catering and Hotel Keeping as a Career, Barrie and Jenkins
Working in the Hospitality Industry, COIC
Careers in Catering and Hotel Management, Kogan Page
Working in Catering, COIC

Ceramics

Ceramics used to be just cups, glasses and saucers; today it is a dynamic new technology. The reason is that scientists have discovered that ceramic materials can withstand very high temperatures. As the use of metals declines, ceramic materials are replacing them in the electronics and engineering industries.

As its uses spread, it is noticeable that industries concerned with defence (armour-plating, bullet-proof clothing), machine tools (cutting edges), medicine (artificial hip joints), electrical insulators, steelmaking and, of course, tiles, crockery, piping and pottery are becoming more involved with ceramics. The Institute of Ceramics includes in its membership people from all the industries mentioned above, plus designers and manufacturers working with glass, enamel, cement and brick.

Training

It is possible to study ceramics to degree level. The courses are for scientists and technologists with a close understanding of materials. Specialised degree courses are available at the Universities of Leeds and Sheffield and at Staffordshire Polytechnic, which also has an HND in ceramics technology. Some degree courses in materials science have specialised references to ceramics, as at Imperial College, London. To obtain a place, A-levels in physics, chemistry and maths are looked for, although a candidate may get in without all of them. But at least one A-level pass if not two (or equivalent H-grades) are necessary at around grade C in science subjects.

For ceramics technologists, there is a one-year full-time course leading to a BTEC National Certificate in ceramics technology. For this, at least three GCSEs or O-grades are needed, including maths and English language and a science subject. Progression from this is to the full-time HND course.

There are also the craft-based industries, mostly in pottery. Many of these are not high-technology, and employment in glassmaking and in pottery has been steadily declining.

Information

Institute of Ceramics, Shelton House, Stoke Road, Shelton, Stoke-on-Trent ST4 2DR

Technology (for metallurgy, materials science and engineering), Degree Course Guide, Hobsons

Chemical engineering

Chemical engineers are mainly concerned with the design, construction and operation of industrial processing plants. In former days they were involved with the manufacture of chemical materials. Nowadays the processes may not involve substantial chemical changes: chemical engineers working for huge companies such as ICI may spend their time and skill closer to civil or mechanical engineering. Most chemical engineers, however, work in 'unit operations', which means that materials are converted into products via process operations such as chemical reaction, filtration, mixing, distillation and heat transfer. To understand what is happening, and control it, chemical engineers need to know about gases, liquids and solids. Other topics studied in degree or HND courses, the preliminaries to a career as a chemical engineer, include project management, technical and economic evaluation of processes, biochemical processing, automatic control, and uses of computers. All courses contain a large component of engineering design.

To be able to cope with all this technology, there has to be a good foundation of physics and chemistry and also of mathematics. Degree courses in chemical engineering usually require good passes in these three subjects at A-level or at least four at H-grade, plus supporting GCSEs or O-grades. Knowledge of computing is very useful indeed, and A-levels in computing or engineering science are valuable supporting qualifications.

Prospects

There is a strong demand for chemical engineers. They make their careers in a range of industries, in government work, and in research and teaching. The industries that employ them include chemicals, **pharmaceuticals**, petroleum and petrochemicals, plastics, **food** and drink, soap and detergents, **paper**, coal and oil. Each year about 900 chemical engineers graduate: over 50 per cent go straight into the industries listed; the rest continue with research, higher degrees or go into government work or overseas.

Training

As in other branches of engineering, there are three stages of training: academic study, practical training and work experience leading to the status of a chartered engineer. The first stage is achieved by studying chemical engineering at university or polytechnic: see the Degree Course Guide on *Technology* for the courses. Most institutions insist on three good A-levels, preferably in maths, physics and chemistry. HNDs are three-year sandwich courses. There are good possibilities for sponsorship by the major chemical companies. For graduates in related subjects, such as chemistry or mechanical engineering, there are postgraduate conversion courses which may be recognised by the Institution of Chemical Engineers as sufficient to meet its academic requirements. After graduation, those who want to take up corporate membership of the Institution go into a job, spending at least four years acquiring the approved industrial training and engineering experience.

Graduates generally follow a programme which takes in engineering design, research and development, fabrication, construction, plant operations and estimating. The young engineer works on real, practical projects which may take him or her overseas. The engineer should aspire to become a full Member of the Institution of Chemical Engineers (MIChemE), which normally carries with it the general engineering title 'Chartered Engineer'. This is usually achieved later in his or her career, for the minimum age for election as a Member is 25.

Information

The Institution of Chemical Engineers, Careers Department, 12 Gayfere Street, London SW1P 3HP
National Engineering Scholarships, The Engineering Council, 10 Maltravers Street, London WC2R 3ER

Technology, Degree Course Guide, Hobsons
Why Chemical Engineering?, Your Way into Chemical Engineering, The Biochemical Engineering Option and other information sheets are available from the Institution of Chemical Engineers

Chemistry

Chemistry is the study of the composition of materials, their properties and their reactions with other materials. It is an important subject in schools, and is a key to many sciences. Among the industries that employ chemists and require good knowledge of chemistry for most workers are **pharmaceuticals**, petroleum and oil, fertilizers, paints, **paper**, fabrics, dyestuffs, metals, cosmetics and many more. To anyone with an interest in chemistry there is a tremendous range of careers. Apart from industrial jobs, there is **teaching and lecturing**, the **Civil Service** (a major employer), **food science** research and manufacturing, **pharmacy**, **museums**, and (when linked with biology) work involving research into plants and animals. There is no mention in this list of the 'chemist' in a chemist's shop: the man or woman in a white coat preparing drugs is **a pharmacist**, not a chemist.

Training

There are various ways into a chemist's world. At 16 or 17, students can go to a college of further education to take a BTEC or SCOTVEC

National Certificate or National Diploma in sciences. The minimum entry requirements are four GCSEs at pass grades including English language and maths or a science subject. The BTEC/SCOTVEC qualification can lead to a job as a technician in industry, education or government work. Alternatively, students can take an A-level course, including chemistry (preferably with another science) among the three A-levels. At 18, for anyone with three good A-levels or four or five H-grades, there are degree courses in chemistry at universities, polytechnics and some colleges: see the Degree Course Guide for *Chemistry* for an analysis of all degree courses, where they are, and how they compare and differ. If A-level results are disappointing, an HND course in physical science (chemistry) is offered at many polytechnics: these courses require one A-level, but it must be in a science subject, supported (as for degree course applications) by four GCSEs, including English language and maths. Eligible students on a BTEC HND course can elect to take an additional paper for Graduate Membership Part 1 of the Royal Society of Chemistry. This may be followed by study for the Part 2 examinations of the Society. Graduates move to Member and Fellowship status more quickly.

Information
Royal Society of Chemistry, Burlington House, Piccadilly, London
W1V 0BN

Careers with Chemistry, Royal Society of Chemistry
Chemistry, Degree Course Guide, Hobsons

Children

Working with children, either for educational, medical or social reasons, opens up careers in many different areas, as in **teaching**, **medicine**, **psychology** and **social work**. Below are details of some of the careers where the work is almost entirely involved with children.

Careers officer

Careers officers work for Local Education Authorities (except in Northern Ireland, where they are employed by the Department of Economic Development). They advise school and college students on job opportunities, training and courses, and place young people in jobs and youth training schemes. Many careers services also provide an information and guidance service for adults. There are over 3,000 careers officers in the UK and to become one requires a degree in any subject, an HND or National Diploma in social science or social studies, or a Diploma in Higher Education or a similar teaching qualification. Having got this far, careers officers study for the professional qualification of the Diploma in Careers Guidance. The courses that prepare officers for the award are offered at some polytechnics and colleges. The Institute of Careers Officers offers information about the work of the careers service. Since most careers officers enter the service after working in another job, such as teaching, social work, youth work or social services, this is not an immediate career opportunity for school leavers and graduates need some other kind of job experience, especially in industry or commerce, before they become careers officers.

Child guidance

This is a job for social workers, psychiatrists and other staff, including medical personnel, helping to diagnose and treat disturbed children.

Child psychotherapy

Treatment for children with psychological or emotional disturbance is given by a psychotherapist. It is based on an understanding of the relationship that develops between patient and therapist over a period of time. An honours degree in a relevant subject and experience of work with children are required for training, which lasts a minimum of four years.

Educational psychologist

Educational psychologists advise teachers, parents and social workers on children's and young people's learning and behavioural problems. They are employed mainly by local authorities and work in school or county psychological services. A degree in psychology, plus specialist training, and some experience as a schoolteacher are needed.

Librarian

Libraries generally have a children's section where special help and advice is given on anything to do with books, projects, assignments and reading. The qualifications and training are as for a **librarian**.

Nursery nurse

A nursery nurse, nursery officer or nanny (different titles are used) look after children aged under seven. Generally they work with healthy children in nursery schools, centres or private homes, but may also deal with disturbed children, or those who are mentally or physically handicapped. A large proportion of children in day nurseries (run by the social services departments for under-fives who are at risk socially, physically or emotionally) are disturbed, and work in such nurseries is very demanding. There are also residential nurseries, again run by social services departments. The largest number of nursery nurses, however, work in nursery schools for three- to five-year-olds or work in private families as a nanny: this is a recent growth area of jobs due to the increasing number of families where both parents go out to work. It is possible to train for the National Nursery Examination Board's Certificate. There are no entry qualifications, but most nurses have GCSEs/O-levels or A-levels.

Nursing

See separate entry.

Occupational therapy

Therapists treat patients suffering from mental or physical disorders. The main branches of the work are with physically disabled children, either at home or in hospital; teaching handicapped children; visiting patients at home; and working in groups on the rehabilitation of patients through drama, art, music and many other activities. At least one A-level plus four or five GCSEs/O-levels are required to get a place at an occupational therapy school where training is for a three- to four-year period.

Physiotherapy

Physiotherapists use movement, electrotherapy and manipulative techniques in the management of injured, sick and disabled people. Most work in hospitals, although there are openings in industry, sport and private practice. There are good employment prospects for all who qualify. Four or five GCSEs or O-levels plus two A-levels are required for entry to schools whether in the NHS or higher education. Most courses are diploma courses at present, although there are degree courses at Glasgow, Manchester and Ulster universities and at the Polytechnic of East London.

Probation officer

Probation officers are social workers to the courts who work with older children and young people in trouble with the law, as well as with adult offenders. They provide social enquiry reports to help courts understand the background of defendants and determine the most appropriate sentences. Young people appearing before the courts may be placed under the supervision of a probation officer by means of a supervision or community service order, or by being placed in a scheme of intermediate treatment, to help stop the young person re-offending. Probation officers also try to help young people released from detention and youth custody centres to settle into normal life and avoid re-offending. Entry qualifications and training for the **probation service** are the same as those for **social workers.**

Youth and community worker

These workers are involved with community education and work with young people in informal leisure activities. They are usually employed by Local Education Authorities or voluntary youth organisations and work in community centres or youth clubs, or as detached youth workers. If based in a centre they will be involved with the management of the centre as well as with face-to-face work with young people. Detached youth workers work in the community with young people who are not willing or able to join the activities at a centre. Youth and community workers may hold the Certificate of Qualification in Social Work (CQSW) or be qualified teachers who may have taken further training in this field (see **community work**).

School staff

Into this category come school catering services, school secretaries, caretakers, traffic control at crossings, and so on.

Social services

Local authority social services departments (social work departments in Scotland, health and social services boards in Northern Ireland) are responsible for the care of a variety of clients including children. Certain voluntary agencies, such as Barnardo's, also specialise in work with children. Social workers and other staff in the social services may work with children, for example in a children's residential home.

Teaching

See separate entry.

Information
Institute of Careers Officers, 37a High Street, Stourbridge, West Midlands DY8 1DA
The British Psychological Society, St Andrew's House, 48 Princess Road, Leicester LE1 7DR
British Association of Psychotherapists, 121 Hendon Lane, London N3 3PR
Association of Child Psychotherapists, Burgh House, New End Square, London NW3 1LT
National Nursery Nurse Examination Board, Argyle House, 29–31 Euston Road, London NW1 2SD
College of Occupational Therapists, 20 Rede Place, London W2 4TU
The Chartered Society of Physiotherapy, 14 Bedford Row, London WC1R 4ED
Central Council for Education and Training in Social Work, Information Services, Derbyshire House, St Chad's Street, London WC1H 8AD
Home Office, Probation Service Division, 50 Queen Anne's Gate, London SW1H 9AT

Council for Education and Training in Youth and Community Work, Wellington House, Wellington Street, Leicester LE1 6HL

Working with Children, COIC

Chiropody

Chiropodists diagnose and treat problems of the feet. They deal with minor deformities of the feet, and cure ailments such as corns, verrucas, ingrowing toenails and other complaints. A chiropodist's raw material are feet – many of them ugly, sweaty and disfigured. Footcare is nearing big business status: this is apparent from the evidence of the shoe industry, jogging and sport as healthy pursuits, and people's aversion to ugly feet, whether as owners or spectators. As well as treating feet, chiropodists recommend treatments (ointments and dressings), and fit the necessary appliances. They use heat machines and perform minor surgery (removing a toenail, for example).

One problem for chiropodists is that their profession has no glamour, or even recognition. Although a doctor will refer an eye complaint to an optician, he or she is unlikely to recommend a chiropodist in similar circumstances. Even so, there is a constant demand for the services of chiropodists. Most are in private practice, which has its advantages (such as independence and freedom) and its disadvantages (the practice is a business and needs to be run on business principles). The NHS provides work for properly qualified people.

Training
Chiropodists must study for a diploma approved by the Society of Chiropodists. The course – full time for three years – is offered at 12 recognised schools. To get on to a course, two A-levels or three or four H-grades are required, with at least one A-level in a science-based subject, plus at least three other GCSEs or O-grades. All subjects are acceptable. The minimum age is 18.

Information
Society of Chiropodists, 53 Welbeck Street, London W1M 7HE
Institute of Chiropodists, 91 Lord Street, Southport PR8 1SA

Church work

Church work has changed dramatically over the last 30 years. All churches, whatever denomination, have had to face major problems. All the same, there is enormous vitality in the churches at the moment, and the range, scope and impact of their work is substantial, even though church attendance has fallen steadily.

Churches of all denominations are looking for young people willing to take up the challenge. Few clergymen (or women) say that they made a planned choice of a career in church work at an early age. On the other hand, some young people know at school that they want to devote their lives to the church, and they plan their education towards that objective. Many others come to church work after training for another career or as a result of experiences which have led them to rethink their personal objectives.

For details of the entry qualifications and training, it is best to contact the individual churches.

Information

The Methodist Church, Division of Ministries, 1 Central Buildings, London SW1H 9NH

Church of Scotland, Department of Education, 121 George Street, Edinburgh EH2 4YN

The Baptist Union, Baptist Church House, 4 Southampton Row, London WC1B 4AB

Advisory Council for the Church's Ministry, Church House, Dean's Yard, London SW1P 3NZ (Church of England)

Commission for Priestly Formation, Archbishop's House, Westminster, London SW1P 1QJ (Roman Catholic Church)

Theology and Religious Studies, Degree Course Guide, Hobsons
Careers in the Church, Kogan Page

Cinemas

The Odeons, Roxys, Regals and Empires which had their heyday in the 1930s and 1940s are now managed by film distribution companies and are divided up into 2, 3, 4 or more mini-cinemas showing different films. The manager is responsible for all aspects of the cinema – finance, safety, bookings, confectionery and the rest. His or her staff includes projectionists, attendants and the sales team.

Training

There are no formal qualifications. People who want to be managers need to show (and have qualifications in) management skills. Teamwork is essential, and so too is the ability to deal courteously with the public. Training is arranged by the company that owns the cinema.

Civil aviation

Civil aviation is concerned with all aspects of **air transport** for civil (i.e. non-military) purposes. It provides a large number of jobs, because it includes air freight and passenger travel. Apart from **pilots,** there are specialist careers as:

Air traffic control officers

They control and monitor the movement of aircraft taking off, landing and approaching airfields. A few entrants to this work are graduates; many are ex-RAF senior personnel, and some are direct entrants: for this, applicants need two A-levels or three H-grades, of which one must be maths, science or geography, plus at least three GCSEs or the equivalents. To assist them there is a junior rank of air traffic control assistant, minimum age 17, for which five GCSEs or O-grades, including English language, maths or a science subject, are necessary.

Cabin crew

They look after the welfare of passengers on aeroplanes. Minimum age is 21. No entry qualifications are laid down, but the airlines look for GCSE/O-level standard in two or three subjects, and languages are useful, particularly French, German, Spanish or Italian. Catering or nursing experience is also welcomed.

Ground and maintenance staff

There is a tremendous range of jobs here: passenger service (they look after the arrival and departure desks); sales staff in airport and city offices who sell tickets, book connecting flights and do a thousand and one other jobs; flight operations and flight planning – the behind-the-scenes office staff who arrange freight, luggage and passengers, organising the fleet of aeroplanes and supporting services; **pilots** and repair and maintenance staff, including specialised engineers and repair teams.

Prospects
Prospects for careers in civil aviation are very good; there is a constant demand for staff at all levels. British-trained crews and supporting staff (particularly engineers) are well regarded by other airlines which poach staff.

Training
Training is by varied means, and is obviously much more substantial and at a different level for pilots than for sales staff. For air traffic control there are special courses at a college in Bournemouth; cabin crew are trained by the employing company over an eight-week period; flight operations personnel are trained through the airlines' own schemes, on courses lasting two to three years.

Information
Civil Aviation Authority, FCL 3, 45-49 Kingsway, London WC2B 6TE

Civil and structural engineering

Civil engineers plan, design, construct and maintain what has become known as the country's 'infrastructure': the roads, railways, bridges, tunnels, water supplies, sewerage and drainage systems, ports, airports and power stations – all the services that we usually take for granted, but on which commerce, manufacturing and a high standard of living depend. Civil and structural engineers also design the foundations and structural frameworks of buildings such as hospitals, sports stadia and concert halls. Structural engineering is a specialised branch of civil engineering. Structural engineers may work in the civil engineering industry when designing such structures as bridges or in the building industry with architects.

   Civil engineering offers an immense variety of employment. It can be on site in the sun – and the rain – or in the design office with visits to site to check progress. The site may be in the UK, Africa, the Middle East or South America. British firms of consulting engineers and contractors work all over the world.

In the UK the government and local authorities are the main customers for civil engineering works. If money is tight the first thing any government cuts is spending on the infrastructure. The civil engineering industry reacts to cuts at home by finding more work abroad or by tightening its belt. The industry is a major exporter and its ability to remain competitive and profitable internationally shows its inherent strength. Civil engineers also work for private and the nationalised industries and for civil engineering contractors. They work in private practice as consulting engineers. Consulting engineers prepare designs, survey sites, advise on tenders from contractors, check progress and act as troubleshooters. Contractors carry out the actual construction work.

Training

There are two main routes to qualification in civil engineering: as a chartered engineer and as a technician engineer.

Chartered engineer   The first requirement is a degree in civil engineering which has been approved by the Joint Board of Moderators of the Institutions of Civil and Structural Engineers. These are provided at universities and polytechnics and information on the subjects studied and entry requirements is given in the Degree Course Guide on *Technology*. There are some opportunities for sponsorship by major civil engineering and construction companies. In general, three A-levels of at least C grade are needed by the aspiring chartered engineer. Maths and physics (or physical science) are generally specified as essential. Chemistry is desirable at least at GCSE level, as are English and a foreign language.

Technician engineer   Students with GCSEs or one A-level may follow a BTEC National Certificate or HNC course as a first step to becoming technician engineers.

Information

Civil Engineering Careers Service (CECS), 1–7 Great George Street, London SW1P 3AA. CECS is operated jointly by the Institutions of Civil and Structural Engineers, the Societies of Civil Engineering Technicians and Highway and Traffic Technicians, the Association of Consulting Engineers, Federation of Civil Engineering Contractors and Construction Industry Training Board

Technology, Degree Course Guide, Hobsons
Hobsons Engineering Casebook, Hobsons
Careers in Civil and Structural Engineering, Civil Engineering Careers Service

Civil Service

(see also entry for **Government Service**.)
The Civil Service employs around 550,000 people working as clerical officers, typists, secretaries, drivers and so on. The Civil Service, however, is also a big employer of professionals ranging from architects to tax officers, beekeepers to psychologists, plus a significant percentage of the UK's scientists, surveyors, architects, economists, statisticians and engineers. These professionals rarely describe themselves as Civil Servants: that phrase is normally taken to mean the administrators, people who are trained to work in the departments of state, operating the machinery of government. These civil servants work in a variety of departments: including the Ministry of Defence; the Foreign Office; the Departments of the Environment, Social Security, Education; the Home Office; the Inland Revenue, and many more. They also work in the new Executive Agencies, such as HM Stationery Office, Companies House and the Driver and Vehicle Licensing Centre.

Young people thinking of a career are bound to have images culled from popular mythology or from television. At one extreme are television programmes depicting civil servants as shrewd plotters; another image is of tax inspectors, or other enquirers after truth or money; a third is of paper-pushing bureaucrats who are not under commercial pressure. Contrary to these views, the Civil Service recruits the same type of people as commerce and industry. But for many people the idea of public service – and the wish to be at the very heart of government – is still a very powerful motive for joining the Civil Service – and so is the job security.

Job opportunities are therefore numerous and divide into the following categories.

Administrative staff

The high-flyers are administration trainees. They are given jobs to stretch their capabilities and have periods of concentrated training, usually at the Civil Service College. Right from the start they are involved in policy-making and planning, including the drafting of legislation and of replies to parliamentary questions. They are sometimes attached to ministers and their private secretaries to give them an early insight of how things are done at the very top.

The trainees are expected to become principals in their late 20s and assistant secretaries in their early 30s. A few will go on to join one of the 30 or so permanent secretaries. They are responsible for policy and management within the Civil Service departments.

Executive staff

The backbone of junior and middle management are the executive officers. They are directly involved with the nuts and bolts of society – manning the Jobcentres, tax offices and social security offices. The majority work in regional and local offices around the country.

Over 50 per cent of the executive officer entrants are now graduates, recruited from every university and every kind of degree course. After about four years they may be promoted to Higher Executive Officer (HEO) and after that promotion depends on many factors, including mobility. But someone joining as an executive officer can be promoted to the highest levels of the Civil Service.

There is a tradition of equal pay and equal treatment for women, and this is reflected in staff: about half of the executive team are women. But the higher up the hierarchy, the fewer women there are and so the Civil Service loses some of its advantage over industry or commerce.

Supporting the administration trainees and executive officers are clerical officers and assistants, secretarial and other office support staff.

Scientific staff

They are employed in government laboratories and research centres. They are recruited as scientific officers or, if with fewer qualifications, as assistant scientific officers.

Training

For entry to the administration trainee grade, a first- or second-class honours degree is the starting point. For executive officers, five GCSE passes including two at A-level are required. For clerical officers the first hurdle is five GCSEs, and two GCSEs for clerical assistants. Equivalent or higher qualifications are also accepted. A pass in English language is essential. Selection processes involve exams, tests and interviews to measure intelligence, accuracy, good sense and potential. Clerical officers and assistants are recruited locally by individual departments: vacancies are notified to the local Jobcentre and are often advertised in the local press. Once into government work, training begins. About 30 per cent of all executive officers embark on special courses – accounting, computing, tax laws, immigration legislation, employment and social security rules and regulations, depending on their department. Clerical officers and assistants are trained on the job, occasionally with release to colleges for special courses. The Civil Service College runs other courses and specialised training programmes.

Information

The Civil Service Commission, Information Department, Alencon Link, Basingstoke, Hampshire RG21 1JB

The Civil Service publishes a large number of useful booklets and leaflets on careers, among them:
Civil Service Careers – degree-level entry
Accept Society's Challenge (for administration trainees)
Civil Service Careers (GCSE level)
Along Management Lines (executive officer entry)
Providing a Structure for Society (management careers)
Careers in the Civil Service, Kogan Page

Clerical work

Clerical officers and clerical assistants are employed in all government departments to carry out support tasks and duties. There are many responsibilities: among them are filing, drafting replies, answering correspondence from members of the public or other departments of state, advising the public at Jobcentres or DSS offices, making payments, answering the telephone, checking accounts, preparing statistics. In this work they are generally supervised by an executive officer (for fuller details see the entry for **Civil Service**). Entry is five GCSEs or equivalents for officer level, two GCSEs for clerical assistant.

Clerical staff are also the backbone of **local government**. They sort and deliver mail and help senior staff with correspondence, statistics and policy relating to one or other responsibility – education, planning, rents, health, social services, housing. Some clerical workers have to deal directly with the public. As they gain experience, clerical workers are likely to be given more responsibility and move up to supervisory posts. In all these jobs they must know about office procedures, equipment (including word processing, photocopying, and business accounts machines) as well as the rules and regulations governing their work.

The third area of employment for clerks is in every other kind of government or private business organisation. To take a selection, they could work in accounts departments, **banking** services, **building societies**, costing and estimating, the courts, **finance** offices, **insurance**, law courts, support services to managers, medical records, securities, **travel agencies,** wages offices. They may find that their clerical duties shade into other work – bookkeeping, typing, word processing, filing, record-keeping, receptionist and tea-maker.

Prospects

Job prospects are very good. Despite the explosion of machines in the office (the much-reported 'electronic' office) there is still a demand for clerical staff: they must, of course, be capable of being trained to operate the machines, and all good companies or organisations train their operators, otherwise there is no point in buying the equipment. Even so, there is still scope for other skills – dealing politely with the public, running an efficient office, accuracy with figures, files, letters, and so on.

Training

Training can be arranged in-house or at college. Every college of further education has a general studies or business studies department. They offer courses at various levels for clerical staff. The courses can lead to City and Guilds certificates, or to BTEC or SCOTVEC National Certificates and National Diplomas. Apart from these full-time and part-time courses, the colleges are likely to provide short courses in office practice, secretarial studies, computing and word processing, accounts and bookkeeping.

Efficient companies and organisations provide courses of a similar nature within working hours. Young people who are on Youth Training programmes are able to combine their work experience with companies and organisations, with college-based training and then to move on to specialised training or a full-time job. Other recruitment methods are direct from GCSE courses, or from a one-year or two-year full-time City and Guilds or BTEC National Diploma courses.

Information

Civil Service Commission, Alencon Link, Basingstoke, Hampshire RG21 1JB

Local Government Training Board, 4th Floor, Arndale House, Luton, Bedfordshire LU1 2TS

The National Joint Council for Local Authorities' Services, 6 Coates Crescent, Edinburgh EH3 7AL

Working in Offices, COIC

Clothing industry

Clothing is a huge industry: it includes fashion design, manufacturing (in factories and workrooms) and sales (in stores that range from Harrods to cut-price corner shops).

All of these jobs need skills. These skills are in design; in pattern-cutting; in lay-making (that is fitting patterns to make the most economic use of cloth); in cutting, marking, fixing, sewing and pressing. People are also needed for manufacturing processes, and machinists are particularly in demand.

The old skills are still required although technology is now being applied; computer operators for design, pattern-making and cutting demonstrate these new skills. In the future the number of employees will fall; those that remain need to be well-trained in these sophisticated new techniques.

Other jobs are in **marketing, sales, warehousing, distribution, purchasing** and in research into the use of artificial fibres.

Training

Courses leading to City and Guilds qualifications are listed in the *Directory of Further Education*. For managerial positions students need to take BTEC or SCOTVEC national diploma courses; the main centre for these and for higher education qualifications is the London College of Fashion. Leicester Polytechnic and Bolton Institute of Higher Education offer BSc and HND courses in textiles and clothing studies: one or two A-levels (any subjects) are required for entry, depending on the course.

Information
CAPITB, 80 Richardshaw Lane, Pudsey, West Yorkshire LS28 6BN

Community work

Community workers try to help local communities overcome some of the effects of problems such as bad housing or unemployment. They work with local groups such as tenants' associations so that local people can tackle their own problems, negotiate for resources, work effectively with voluntary and statutory organisations and develop a better quality of life for their members. The role of the community worker is not to solve other people's problems for them, but to encourage and enable them to act collectively for themselves. To this end a community worker's tasks may include stimulating neighbourhood interest in particular projects, such as the development of child-minding schemes, the establishment and running of social clubs and centres, obtaining services for groups like the handicapped or elderly, giving advice on welfare rights and encouraging people to claim the benefits to which they are entitled.

Community workers are employed by local authority social services departments or voluntary organisations. Those employed by local authorities can often find themselves in the difficult position of encouraging people to demand services or benefits the local authority is unwilling to provide. The job therefore requires diplomacy, persistence, patience and stamina as well as knowledge of rights and legislation.

Some community workers are employed by local education authorities and are usually referred to as **youth and community workers**. Their jobs are primarily involved with running youth and community centres or detached youth work in the community.

Training
There is no one qualification for community workers. Some may hold the Certificate of Qualification in Social Work (CQSW) awarded by the Central Council for Education and Training in Social Work (CCETSW); others may have taken one of a variety of qualifications or have no formal professional qualifications at all.

Courses leading to the CQSW are available on a full-time basis over two years for non-graduates, one or two years for graduates depending on their degree subject, or four years for those wishing to obtain a degree and the professional qualification. Courses leading to the CQSW cover all areas of social work, but a number emphasise community work.

Other courses available in community work included undergraduate, postgraduate or non-graduate courses at universities, polytechnics and colleges of further or higher education; teacher-training courses with options in youth and community work; courses leading to college diplomas or certificates and courses provided by organisations concerned with community work for staff already employed in this or related fields.

Information

CCETSW Information Service, Derbyshire House, St Chad's Street, London WC1H 8AD

14 Malone Road, Belfast BT9 5BN

9 South St David Street, Edinburgh EH2 2BW

West Wing, St David's House, Cardiff CF1 1ES

The Association of Community Workers, 22 Columbo Street, London SE1 8DP

Council for Education and Training in Youth and Community Work, Wellington House, Wellington Street, Leicester LE1 6HL

Working in Community Care, COIC

Company secretary

A company secretary can have various functions. Among them are keeping the minutes of the board of directors of a company, preparing the agenda and other papers for meetings, making sure that action is taken to implement any decisions, and ensuring that the company complies with the law in all respects. But the job is generally far more extensive than this. The company secretary is often the chief administrator, controlling and co-ordinating the financial, legal, personnel, property, tax, insurance and pensions business of the company. This makes the job a very responsible and important one. To do the job well requires knowledge of legal, accounting and administrative systems, backed up with common sense, good judgement and discretion.

All public companies are required by law to have a company secretary. The Institute of Chartered Secretaries and Administrators (ICSA) offers the best chance of preparing properly for this career. After qualifying, the best routes to an important position within a company with a seat on the board of directors are generally through the financial, legal, personnel and management services departments. There is now a growing demand for ICSA members in local government.

Training
The minimum entry qualifications for the ICSA course are two A-levels (three H-grades) and three GCSEs or a BTEC National Diploma. An increasing number of people, however, are starting after taking a degree or a BTEC or SCOTVEC HND. These usually allow exemption from subjects in the ICSA course. The more relevant the degree or BTEC subject (in, for example, law, business studies or accountancy) the more exemptions can be claimed, amounting sometimes to 50 per cent of the course. A few people study on a full-time course that they complete in one year, but the great majority study part time while at work. Employees may get day release or attend evening classes. Many study in their own time by correspondence course. An increasing number of people are taking some form of 'open or distance learning/study', which is usually a combination of correspondence course and occasional college attendance. A-level choices are not specified, except that English language is required at GCSE or A-level. Other subjects should be academic (languages or science), rather than practical (woodwork or technical drawing). Most students study while at work, thus gaining experience in a relevant job. This may be in an administrative area such as accounts or personnel, moving across to company secretarial work after three or four years of work experience.

On a part-time basis with no exemptions the course may take four or five years. ICSA allows six years for completion. By finishing the course successfully and gaining the necessary experience, the student is eligible for election to membership of ICSA which, while it does not guarantee employment, opens many paths for career development.

Information
Institute of Chartered Secretaries and Administrators (ICSA), 16 Park Crescent, London W1N 4AH

Leaflets and booklets about careers as a company secretary are available from the Institute

Computing

Computers have revolutionised our lives. They have dramatically increased the speed of communication, which has produced a knock-on effect in commerce, industry and every other kind of business or service where computers are used to store information, control machines and direct people's work in many different ways. Advances in the computer field will continue – the next big breakthrough will come with fifth-generation computers that we can talk to – and computing will, like literacy and numeracy, become part of everyone's basic education.

Computing – or, to use a phrase that has a wider meaning, 'information technology' – includes all aspects of generating and transmitting information by electronic means, for computers are now used to handle information of all kinds and to present it in the form of numbers, words and pictures. As a result, information technology is here to stay. Computing therefore is not only a career, it is part of everyone's education, and the use of computers will affect every kind of job, even those far removed from the computer specialist.

Computing or information technology creates jobs. Almost every company has a word processor and laser printer in the office: this means that secretaries need a basic understanding of what the computer can do in order to get the best from the word processor. Some large companies employ specialist staff to computerise accounts, orders, stock, sales, library and office records. Many companies do not employ the specialists themselves but hire computer expertise from a specialist company: either way, new jobs are being created.

Then there are the new businesses that have arisen from the computer revolution: hardware (machine) manufacturers, software (computer programs) publishers, servicing companies, and so on. Another group of jobs is with local and central government departments, which use computers to store information. The jobs could be grouped like this.

- Computer manufacturing, design and research: for this kind of career, a degree in computing, physics or mathematics is very useful. However, IBM, ICL, and other manufacturing companies recruit non-graduates in large numbers and provide their own training programmes
- Computer installation, servicing and maintenance: technical knowledge is essential and qualifications to degree level, or to BTEC or

SCOTVEC HND or HNC levels are useful, although some companies train their own staff

- Computer graphics: this is a major new area of computer technology. Operators work on the graphics needed for film and television production
- Computer sales: computer knowledge is helpful but not essential, as sales firms provide training. Most mainframe computers are sold by the manufacturer, and the staff are usually graduates trained by the company. Sales staff who work for mini- and micro-computer companies are not necessarily graduates. City and Guilds, BTEC or SCOTVEC qualifications in computing are very useful
- Computer programming, systems analysis and computer design: designers and programmers are concerned with writing the software. This is the information on disc or cassette which tells the computer what to do. Systems analysts (who often work on a freelance or consultancy basis) look at a company's needs and devise a computer system to deal with them. They suggest equipment, software and staff. At this level of work a degree in computing is very useful: some programmers do not have degrees but understand computers very well indeed. Analysts need to know their way around both computers and organisations and to deal with managers on equal terms
- Computer operators are generally recruited locally and for specific jobs.

Prospects

It is estimated that the computer applications industry is growing at the rate of 20 per cent annually. As more companies install equipment they are looking for capable computer staff. Computer programmers are in great demand. Programmers progress up the management hierarchy to become senior programmers or are promoted to administration or technical support jobs such as database management or data processing management. Further opportunities lie in consultancy work. There is a great demand for systems analysts, and promotion can lead to data management posts, or consultancy, or into general management jobs. Another job is as a data processing manager, who could be in charge of a mainframe computer installation and of on-line computer equipment kept within the organisation. Such managers are responsible for the day-to-day operations and may be involved in the applications of information technology throughout the company or organisation. For these posts, people need good knowledge of computer technology and management skills. Computer operators, working from a VDU (visual display unit) and a terminal, use software to identify faults and to take action. Promotion can be to operations manager, supervisor or controller.

In many organisations, the computer staff perform many or all these functions: computer jobs are not clearly divided up, and a competent operator or programmer could possibly tackle other jobs. Another group of users are office staff who have desktop micro-computers which are found in an increasing number of commercial companies, often in addition to a central (mainframe) data-processing installation. Micro-computer operators can therefore be clerks, secretaries and managers.

Training

For a computer operator, on-the-job training in the computer room is usually supplemented by off-the-job training at college or using self-teaching manuals or programmed learning packages. Trainees are also sent on manufacturers' courses. A one-year full-time or two-year part-time course can lead to a BTEC National Certificate in computer studies or information technology. A BTEC or SCOTVEC National Diploma in computer studies, over two years full time, requires four GCSEs or the equivalent, including English language or a City and Guilds certificate in computer studies. For a computer programmer, training is usually given by the employer, who may sponsor the student on a BTEC or SCOTVEC HND in computer studies for an A-level or H-grade entry (in any academic subject), and BTEC/SCOTVEC diploma/ certificate courses taken by operators. For a BTEC/SCOTVEC HND in maths, statistics and computing, at least one A-level is needed, and this should be in maths. Alternatives are HND courses in business studies with computing options. Alternatively, for people in a job and attending college on a day-release basis, there are City and Guilds certificate courses in programming.

Most systems analysts are graduates, but not all have computer science degrees. Business studies, maths and statistics are all very useful, especially if computing options have been taken as part of the course. Data-processing managers need a lot of experience, so they may have qualified and been trained by any one of these methods. For details of the colleges and courses in computing engineering, computer studies and electronics, see below.

Degree courses in computer technology or engineering or electronics (all lead into the jobs described) usually require people to have at least two A-levels and generally three good A-levels (three or four H-grades) to secure a place, plus up to three other subjects at GCSE or equivalent. The A-levels or H-grades should include maths, and physics is usually demanded too.

Students wanting to take a computer studies degree course (as distinct from engineering) need similar GCSEs and A-levels, again including maths.

There is a very wide range of courses which includes computer studies as an option, module or other part of the course. This is a good way of getting into computer work for young people not happy with maths. For instance, without A-level maths, it is possible to take a degree in business studies, management science, economics, or combined sciences: computing is included but not at the high level expected of an engineer.

Some universities and polytechnics put on short courses (six months or one year) for postgraduates with arts degrees: these give an insight into information technology and sufficient knowledge and hands-on experience to get someone started in a job, although at a different level from computer science graduates. The National Computing Centre (address below) puts on short courses too, and also encourages colleges to do so.

Information

British Computer Society, 13 Mansfield Street, London W1M 0BP
Computer Services Industry Training Council, Victoria House, Vernon Place, London WC1B 4DP
National Computing Centre, Oxford Road, Manchester M1 7ED

Technology, Degree Course Guide, Hobsons. This book contains a section on *Computer Science*: it is essential reading for anyone considering a degree course in computing because it lists all courses, describes the differences between them in content, length, teaching and examining, and selection requirements.

On bookstalls there are many computer magazines (a substantial business growth area): they should be consulted to give a flavour of what computing is about and the jobs advertised within the industry
Occupations, COIC, has a very good section on computing

Working in Computing, COIC
Facts about the Computing Services Industry, Hobsons
Careers in Computers, Kogan Page
Directory of Further Education, Hobsons. This gives a full list of colleges offering courses at all levels in computer science and computer studies

Conservation

Nature conservation has become a popular area of work for young people, who feel strongly that the environment should be protected. As a consequence, there are hundreds of applications for any job with a hint of conservation about it, even though the pay may be miserable. This is a sign of the deep concern felt by many young people about protecting the environment and animal life.

Employers that provide a career structure include the Nature Conservancy Council (NCC), the Countryside Commission, the Natural Environment Research Council and the Department of the Environment. To get into field operations for one of these requires at least a first degree: biological sciences, zoology, botany, geography and geology are highly appropriate. But most applicants hold a higher degree: an MSc or PhD. They apply for posts as assistants to regional officers within the NCC, as wardens or as researchers. Other jobs come in the private sector, such as Friends of the Earth, Greenpeace, the Royal Society for the Protection of Birds, the National Trust, the Wildfowl Trust, and so on. Vacancies are few and far between, and even then many jobs are in offices as fund raisers and envelope-addressers.

Other areas for jobs include the staff of the wildlife parks and nature reserves: wardens often come from the ranks of estate workers – the fellers of trees, diggers of ditches and other practical skills. Public holidays and weekends are no different from the rest of the week: indeed, they are the busiest times, with visitors demanding more attention than the animals. Other staff are in the back-up teams: secretaries, drivers, accountants. None is well paid: conservation is very lowly paid in comparison with other jobs. On the other hand, it is a career noted for the dedication and conviction of the people who work in it.

Training
To get in, a degree or degrees in the subjects listed above is essential,

apart from estate work. An interest and preferably a qualification in ecology is needed. Practical experience may come only by taking an unpaid job in a nature reserve, or taking a six- month or one-year job, sometimes funded by the Training Agency. After that, training is on the job.

Information

Council for Environmental Conservation, Zoological Society, Regent's Park, London NW1 4RY

Nature Conservancy Council, Northminster House, Peterborough, Cambridgeshire PE1 1UA

Royal Society for the Protection of Birds, The Lodge, Sandy, Bedfordshire SG19 2DL

Construction

'Building and construction' is used as a general phrase to describe work done at all levels within an industry that employs over 400,000 people (see also the entry on **building**). At craft level there are bricklayers, **carpenters and joiners**, plumbers, scaffolders, painters and decorators, plasterers, and so on. At another level are **surveyors, architects**, contractors and c**ivil engineers**. However, it does not end there. A construction site brings another set of jobs: contractors' plant managers, foremen and labourers; demolition workers; road layers; crane drivers and dumper truck drivers, and the construction 'gang', made up of all these and more staff.

Prospects

When the economic recession of 1990-1 lifts, prospects in the construction industry should improve. The road-building programme paid for by the government and local authorities stretches ahead as a continuing commitment; private and public sector housing, although suffering its share of cuts and ups and downs, nationally is a huge programme of work. There is a continuing demand for graduates in building, and skilled plumbers, plasterers, bricklayers, and so on are always needed. Construction work for roads and housing means the preparation of a site: this involves a lot of earth-moving. Then the contractors move in their 'plant' – trucks, equipment, materials. 'Plant operating' in this sense is recognised as part of the building industry but not as building 'trades'. In charge of the construction team are the manager and the foremen. They direct the gangs to work with:

- earth-moving equipment – excavators, machine shovels, graders, wheeled and tracked vehicles
- compaction jobs – involving motorised rollers and compactors for road surfaces
- road-laying equipment – pavers, asphalt-layers, and so on
- lifting equipment – including wheeled, tracked and tower cranes.

The plant operator and his or her managers have to plan and direct this work, using general labourers. A lot of skill and keen judgement goes into road-laying and site preparation. It is certainly an outdoor life – and also a lifting and carrying, shouting and directing life.

Training

There are various ways into the construction industry.

- A graduate of a building and construction course at a polytechnic joins a construction company and learns the business on a site. To get on to a degree course, two or three A-levels are generally required, plus supporting GCSEs: alternatively, a degree in civil engineering or surveying. There are numerous and generous sponsorship schemes, funded by construction companies, for first-degree courses.
- At technician leading to supervisor level there are BTEC and SCOTVEC National Certificate and National Diploma courses in building studies, building, civil engineering and surveying. For the certificate course GCSE passes, including maths and a science, are the basic level, for a National Diploma GCSEs at grades A to C with maths and a science are needed.
- There is a one-year traineeship for school-leavers, sponsored and supported by an employer: this involves training at a centre plus site work on various types of plant machinery.
- The Construction Industry Training Board (CITB), as well as helping with Youth Training placements, also takes trainees from employers for short (two-week) courses on specific machines.
- An employer can send workers already on-site to the CITB training school for specialist training on one or more machines, which can eventually lead to upgrading to foreman, supervisor and manager.

For general labourers there are jobs concerned with pipe and drain laying; using the plant, machines and equipment already listed; taking part in concreting, kerb-laying or piling (driving metal piles into the ground). Other jobs are as demolition workers. Jobs are not plentiful in this area because of the financial cutbacks. On the other hand, construction work of one kind or another is always going on. No formal entry qualifications are necessary and employees learn by experience and by working with someone who knows how the machines operate and learning from them. However, there are courses on specialist areas of work run by the CITB.

Information
Construction Industry Training Board, Bircham Newton, King's Lynn, Norfolk PE31 6RH

Working in Construction, COIC
Jobs in the Building Trade, Kogan Page

Cooks and chefs

Cooking can be an art, as in the creation of a delicious pudding, a science, as in the mass-production of frozen fish, or just a fry-up, as with sausage, egg and beans. But whichever way you view cooking, it requires considerable skill, and few subjects are more absorbing. The evidence of this can be seen in the vast number of cookery books published each year.

There are cooks and there are chefs. Chefs tend to be employed in hotels and pricey restaurants. A *maître chef de cuisine* is the emperor of a kitchen, controlling and directing a large staff, planning menus, ordering supplies. A *sous chef* is his or her assistant, perhaps a specialist in some dishes, perhaps running a section of the kitchen. The *chef de partie* is responsible for a part of the menu – soups, vegetables, roasts, fish, sauces, sweets or pastries. A *commis chef* is a trainee who is learning the trade on the job. *Commis chefs* spend up to six months in each section of the kitchen learning the different skills.

Cooks, on the other hand, do not work in fancy restaurants. Their skills are demonstrated in canteens; in hospital, school and college kitchens; in the staff restaurants of companies; in clubs and pubs. And there is a special group of cooks, too: call-order cooks work to demand in the kitchens of fish shops, burger bars, pizza places and other fast-food outlets, answering the instant orders of hungry, impatient customers.

Training

For all these jobs there are various training schemes. A start can be made by getting a job as an apprentice at 16-plus. No special educational requirements are demanded. GCSEs or O-grades are an advantage, and if these include home economics, cookery and business studies, so much the better. Some knowledge of French is useful too. Prospects at this level are very good. There is a constant demand for cooks and chefs, and opportunities in institutional as well as private catering do not appear to have declined.

Trainees can take City and Guilds courses in food preparation and cookery. Basic educational qualifications are asked for at the colleges of further education that provide these courses, which are on a day- or block-release or full-time basis. All subjects are useful, but GCSEs in home economics and cookery are particularly valuable.

Furthermore, youth training programmes offer good opportunities for students of 16 to 17. The Hotel and Catering Training Board is the largest organiser of Youth Training schemes, along with colleges and employers. Youth Training gives a two-year (one-year for 17-year-olds) basic foundation programme, allied to off-the-job training leading to City and Guilds and other qualifications.

A different level of entry is by taking a full-time course. This could be a BTEC or SCOTVEC National Certificate, National Diploma or HND course. These qualifications lead to careers in hotel work at various levels, and are not specifically about cookery.

Information

Hotel and Catering Training Company, International House, High Street, London W5 5DB

Working in the Hospitality Industry, COIC
Working in Catering, COIC

Curator

Curatorial staff work in museums and art galleries. They are responsible for the administration, conservation, exhibition, acquisition, circulation and explanation of the items within their collections. They are also concerned with identifying and recording the objects, in addition to preparing the museums' publications. In the large national museums there may be less emphasis on administrative tasks and more on research and publications. The most senior curatorial staff, known as keepers, run the departments of larger museums and are responsible to the head, or director, of the museum. A keeper or curator might be a specialist in one of the many fields, such as art, archaeology, botany, coins, ethnography, geology, natural history, local history and weaponry. In one of the smaller local authority-run museums a curator may be responsible for covering many of these areas and so is less likely to be a specialist.

In addition to curatorial staff museums and art galleries employ people in a wide variety of other jobs. These are listed in the entry for **museums and art galleries.**

Prospects

The main employers of curatorial staff are the national museums, local authorities (there are some 450 local authority museums in Britain which vary considerably in size) and private museums, for example the Ironbridge Gorge Museum.

Opportunities for a museum career are comparatively limited. Applicants have to be ready to wait for a suitable vacancy and to move around the country to find one. Competition is intense. Promotion within the national museums is gradual, and staff tend to develop specialist research among their collections. There is greater mobility of personnel among the local authority museums to achieve promotion.

Training

For a curatorial post a degree in one of the following is often required: anthropology, archaeology, art history, botany, chemistry, geography, geology, history, physics or zoology. Experience of work in a museum, either as a volunteer or in a temporary post, is an advantage when applying for a permanent post. The Department of Museum Studies at Leicester University offers two postgraduate courses in Museum Studies. Manchester University Department of Art History also offers a one-year postgraduate Diploma in Art Gallery and Museum Studies. The Museums' Association offers professional qualifications for those working in museums in the curatorial fields.

Information

Museums' Association, 34 Bloomsbury Way, London WC1A 2SF

Museums and Art Galleries, Association of Graduate Careers Advisory Services, Central Services Unit, Crawford House, Precinct Centre, Manchester M13 9EP
Careers in Museums and Art Galleries, Kogan Page
Careers in Museums, Museums' Association
Museums' Bulletin, published monthly by the Museums' Association, is useful for getting an idea of what museum work involves

Customs and Excise

Customs and Excise officers are civil servants. They work on their feet, not behind a desk, as they are on duty at airports and seaports, checking cargoes and passengers, collecting the customs duties (taxes) required by the government, and trying to stop the illegal import of goods, such as drugs. With the vast traffic in goods and people flowing in and out of Britain, HM Customs and Excise officers are very busy.

However, there is another group who are mostly desk-bound. They are the officers who deal with the collection of a particular tax, Value Added Tax (VAT), which is levied on many goods. When not checking the VAT returns in their offices, they are out checking on companies that pay VAT.

Another group of Customs and Excise officers is involved in collecting taxes (called duties) on oil, petrol, tobacco, wine and spirits. Their job is to check the tax returns and follow up by visiting companies: this work takes officers all over the UK.

Qualifications

Competition for jobs is very keen indeed. The various levels of entry and qualifications needed are:

- *clerical assistant*: two GCSEs at grades A, B or C, including English language; all subjects are acceptable
- *clerical officer*: five GCSEs at grades A, B or C, including English language; all subjects are acceptable
- *executive officer*: at least two A-level passes, plus three other subjects at GCSE all obtained at one examination sitting including English language at one of the levels. An increasing number of applicants and

entrants to the executive officer level are graduates. No particular subjects are specified: all seem to be acceptable, so the interview is important. By taking more graduates, it is becoming harder for 18-year-olds with A-levels to get into this career.

Information

Recruitment Office 7W, HM Customs and Excise, New King's Beam House, 22 Upper Ground, London SE1 9PJ

Civil Service Commission, Alencon Link, Basingstoke, Hampshire RG21 1JB

Working in the Customs and Excise, HM Customs and Excise, Dorset House, Stamford Street, London SE1 9PS

Dancing

Dancing, as with **acting** and **music**, is a very difficult career to enter into and to make a living in. Most people have to give up all ideas of being professional dancers, and instead become dance teachers or make dancing a recreational interest. Even so, some determined men and women are successful. For professional dancers there are opportunities in ballet, musical theatre, television, films, cabaret clubs as well as a national and international professional circuit for ballroom and Latin American dancing.

Dancers

For every performance there are hours of preparation. Training, exercising, practising routines, rehearsals – these are constant activities that precede any performance. So dancing is very hard, physical work. If a dancer is part of a team – a troupe, *corps de ballet*, chorus line – there is the discipline of working with other artists. The dancer will have little opportunity to put down roots, since almost all dance companies undertake tours both in this country and abroad.

Prospects

Except for the really successful, pay is not good and is often irregular, so dancers as well as having to practise every day may also have to take on other jobs between engagements. Like acting, dancing is highly competitive and there are more dancers than there are jobs. Only about one in four dancers registered with Equity is in work at any one time. Prospects are therefore poor. These hazards of a dancer's career are well known, and yet it does not deter the determined, so if a child is persistent, the next step is training.

Training

Formal training is essential. This means several years of study, exercise and daily practice. For theatre dance, specialist dance schools take children under 11, but usually it is not until the age of 11 that the 'real' training begins. There are special residential and non-residential schools where dancing is a major part of the curriculum. A list of such schools is available from the Council for Dance Education and Training (address below) who accredit such schools. For social dance, such as ballroom and Latin American, training is more likely to take the form of specialist coaching by highly experienced former professional dancers.

Dance teaching

Dance teaching as a career presents many more opportunities both as a full-time and a part-time occupation. Prospective dance teachers must themselves be good dancers in order to be able to pass on that knowledge to others. Dance teachers have a very wide age-range of pupils from under 8s to people in their 70s. Between 11 and 16, young people who think they might like to be dance teachers should concentrate on achieving the highest possible level of examinations with one of the major dance bodies.

Prospects

A dance teacher will work in one of three major fields. The first and by far the largest is in the private dance school. These vary from the major vocational schools, through smaller studios to teaching part-time classes in hired halls. The second major sector is in community arts, where a number of local authorities provide dance classes as part of their leisure and recreation services. The third major sector is in the state education sector in primary, secondary and tertiary education.

Training

Qualifications for dance teachers are provided by the main examining bodies. In addition, both the Royal Academy of Dancing and the

Imperial Society of Teachers of Dancing have teacher-training colleges for full-time teacher-training. The latter also provides, in conjunction with Bedford College of Higher Education, a BA honours degree in dance and drama. There are a limited number of degree courses and postgraduate courses in dance and movement, but these do not provide any teaching qualifications. It is estimated that there are over 20,000 full-time and part-time dance teachers in the UK. As a social or recreational pursuit, dance in all its forms probably has a larger number of participants than any other sporting or related activity.

Information

The main teaching and examining bodies for dancing are:

Royal Academy of Dancing, 48 Vicarage Crescent, London SW11 3LT

Royal Ballet School, 155 Talgarth Road, London W14 9DE

Imperial Society of Teachers of Dancing, Euston Hall, Birkenhead Street, London WC1H 8BE

International Dance Teachers Association, 76 Bennett Road, Brighton, East Sussex BN2 5JL

Other useful addresses are:

Council for Dance Education and Training, 5 Tavistock Place, London WC1H 9SS

Scottish Council for Dance, PO Box 410, WDO, Edinburgh EH12 6AR

Laban Centre for Movement and Dance, Laurie Grove, New Cross, London SE14 6NH

Dance Council for Wales, Thurgarton House, Longdown Bank, St Dogmaels, Dyfed SA43 3DU

Working in the Performing Arts, COIC
Careers in Dance, Kogan Page

Dentistry

Dentistry includes the whole range of prevention, diagnosis and treatment of diseases and disorders of teeth, mouth, jaws and surrounding tissues. That is the analysis that the General Dental Council like because it corrects the public's view of dentists as the operators of drills and other devices.

Dentist

Dentists are now much concerned with preventive medicine. They also have to be businessmen and women because dentists in general practice are paid not according to the number of their patients but on the number of treatments, a kind of piece-rate calculation. There is to some extent a dilemma in their work: if they persuade patients to look after their teeth properly and avoid tooth decay, their income will drop because there will be fewer visits and fewer treatments.

Dentists offer NHS work in general practice. The others are in hospitals, private practice, the community dental service, industrial clinics, HM Forces, and in university and hospital teaching. Some dentists specialise in orthodontics, which is the study and correction of mouth irregularities, particularly in children. Another group of hospital specialists are dental surgeons who deal with facial injuries, and another group specialises in restorative dentistry.

Competition for places at dental school is very keen. Furthermore, new graduates are taking longer to find positions than they did in the past, and graduates may have to change their ideas about the area of dentistry in which they would like to specialise. Competition, therefore, for jobs after training is as keen as the competition to enter a dental school. Some schools have cut their intake of students by 10 per cent. All the same, young people are very keen to become dentists; the money is good; there is the attraction of working near home (perhaps actually at home with a surgery added to the house or converted from another room); and it is a career with a high public reputation and esteem.

Training

Entry to dental schools at universities and at teaching hospitals is dependent on high A-level or H-grade results. Three A-levels (four or five H-grades) with ABB to BCC grades are generally required, including chemistry as a required or preferred subject. The traditional grouping of maths, chemistry and biology is a popular one, but other science A-levels are acceptable. Some universities offer a year's preliminary course for students with arts A-levels. There are generally 15 to 20 applicants for each place at dental school. Training takes four to five years.

Having qualified, most young graduates begin their careers as associate dentists then look to an established practice as a partner, or they start up on their own or with another dentist in a practice. In hospital work there is a five-stage career path, and promotion depends on experience and additional qualifications. Most dentists aim for a consultancy, which is gained in open competition with other dentists.

Getting a degree in dental surgery is only the first part of qualification for these jobs. Dentists may not practise until they are registered with the General Dental Council or are on the Medical Register.

Dental technician

Dental technicians make and repair dentures, plates, bridges and other bits and pieces. As with dentists, the physical requirements are manual dexterity and good eyesight, patience and a substantial knowledge of the various materials and their properties used for making dentures. Technicians work in the NHS, in clinics, hospitals and dental laboratories. The great majority of technicians, however, work in commercial laboratories, or in laboratories owned by dentists. There are good prospects for jobs and for promotion to posts of senior and chief technician.

Training
Training starts at 16 to 18 for post-GCSE entrants. Applicants must have four GCSEs or O-grades at grades C and above. Chemistry and biology are looked for among these subjects but strictly speaking are not essential, although a good knowledge of these two subjects is expected.

Dental hygienist

A dental hygienist works under the direct personal supervision of the dentist. The job is to scale, clean and polish teeth and advise on preventive dentistry and oral hygiene. Jobs are in hospitals, general practice, the community dental service, HM Forces and in industry. The 17 major dental hospitals that are situated within universities provide the training for dental hygiene work. Applicants have to be at least 17 and must have four or five GCSEs, including at least one science subject. Human biology is probably the most important subject, although chemistry, biology and physical science are very useful. There is now a substantial A-level entry to this work, and therefore candidates with passes in the same subjects at A-level stand a very good chance of being accepted on a course. Most of these last a year, following a period as a dental surgery assistant.

Dental surgery assistant

A dental surgery assistant is the person you see at the dentist's elbow, preparing fillings, selecting instruments, record-keeping, and generally looking after the welfare of the patient as well as the professional needs of the dentist.

Training
Many dentists recruit and train their assistants, although there are courses on a part-time and full-time basis. Training can start at 16 and applicants need to have at least two or three GCSEs or equivalents for courses at colleges of further education. Dental schools also run courses, with biology usually requested among the GCSE subjects. These courses last from one to two years. Similar courses are provided within HM Forces.

Dental therapist

A dental therapist provides yet another back-up service. He or she works in a hospital or community dental service, carrying out treatment on children's teeth and giving oral hygiene instruction both in the surgery and within the community.

Training
Training is given at the Dental Auxiliaries' Training School, which is a part of the London Hospital Dental School. For this work, applicants need four or five GCSEs, including English language and at least one science subject, and must have had experience as a dental surgery assistant for at least two years.

Receptionist

Receptionists welcome patients, make appointments and keep records. The requirements are as for other clerical jobs: a good education, with qualifications at GCSE in English and other subjects.

Information

The General Dental Council, 37 Wimpole Street, London W1M 8DQ
The British Dental Association, 64 Wimpole Street, London W1M 8AL
The Association of British Dental Surgery Assistants, DSA House, 29 London Street, Fleetwood, Lancashire FY7 6JY
British Dental Hygienists Association, 64 Wimpole Street, London W1M 8AL

All the above organisations have booklets and leaflets about careers in dentistry
Careers in Medicine, Dentistry and Mental Health, Kogan Page
Dentistry, Degree Course Guide, Hobsons

Design

See **Art and design**

Dietetics

The study of nutrition and dietetics can extend over four years of a degree course. After successfully completing it, dietitians work along-side doctors and other medical staff in hospitals and clinics. Dietetics is a specialised profession, and before anyone takes a four-year course he or she should find out about the work by spending time in a hospital, observing the activities and gaining experience of the responsibilities of a dietitian. They would discover that the work involves advising patients and medical staff on food, food supplements and additives and the balance of nutrients in special diets. Dietitians carry out research into what people eat and how foods affect health. They work with health visitors, social workers and other paramedical professions assisting the elderly, babies and pregnant women. However, dietitians advise; they cannot force people to accept what they say and therefore powers of communication and personality are important. They also need detailed knowledge of biology, physiology, biochemistry and food science.

Prospects

With the increasing interest in and knowledge of the importance of diet, prospects in this profession are very good. Careers are available with the NHS; food manufacturing companies; the Department of Health; the

Ministry of Agriculture, Fisheries and Food; Medical and Scientific Research Councils; the school meals service; the Milk Marketing Board and National Dairy Council.

Training

There are degree courses at Leeds (dietetics) and North London (food and nutrition science) polytechnics, three Scottish institutions, Cardiff Institute of Higher Education and the Universities of Surrey and Ulster (nutrition). Specified A-levels are chemistry with at least one other science at A-level. In addition, at least three or four GCSEs, including maths and English language, must be attained. Other useful GCSEs are in physics, human biology, social biology, biology and nutrition. For every degree place there are more than ten applicants, so grades have to be good. These degree courses lead to State Registration in Dietetics, which is essential for work in the NHS where most graduates are employed. Graduates of closely related courses, such as biochemistry, nursing or nutrition, can train for a postgraduate diploma and also obtain State Registration.

Information

The British Dietetic Association, Daimler House, Paradise Circus, Queensway, Birmingham B1 2BJ

Directory of Further Education, Hobsons, lists institutions offering courses in dietetics and nutrition
The British Dietetic Association publishes free leaflets

Diplomatic Service

Diplomats represent British interests abroad. In London they are based on the Foreign and Commonwealth Office; abroad they work in embassies and high commissions where they make business contacts, help British exporters, promote British political viewpoints through information services, and collect information helpful to the British government. In the Diplomatic Service overseas postings (which can make up two-thirds of a diplomat's life in the Service) are up to four years in each country. Knowledge of a specific language is not all that important: what is looked for is the ability to learn a language quickly, although a foreign language is a useful bonus. In recent years there have been cuts in the staffing of the Diplomatic Service, so entry prospects are not good. Less time is being spent abroad; longer periods are spent in the London offices.

As with the Home Civil Service, the Diplomatic Service has levels and grades. They are:

- administrative
- executive
- clerical.

Administrative level

Each year about 25 officers are recruited with a first- or second- class honours degree in any subject. These officers are what are generally called the high-flyers. Oxford and Cambridge graduates provide over half of each year's intake. Selection is by tests and extended interviews. Those who get through are intelligent men and women who want to serve their country and who have the tact, polish and shrewdness to deal with people from any and every part of the world. By the time they are in their 40s they should be ambassadors or high commissioners.

Executive level

There are also about 20 to 25 entrants each year at the executive officer level. Theoretically the entry requirements are two A-levels plus GCSEs, but in fact 80 per cent of entrants are graduates, again from many different subjects and a rather wider selection of universities than those recruited for the administrative level. They do a lot of the paperwork abroad – commercial, political, immigration, dispensing information and advice. They can rise to the rank of consul and consul-general.

Clerical level

Next in line are clerical staff, who are required to have at least five GCSEs or equivalents: in practice they tend to be of A-level calibre.

There are special branches dealing with communications and secretarial work; these jobs are filled by clerical staff with the necessary special skills. Good GCSE passes are the first requirement.

Occasionally a vacancy occurs for the post of assistant legal adviser.

Applicants must be qualified barristers or solicitors, preferably with at least a good second-class honours degree.

Information
A Career in the Diplomatic Service, Civil Service Commission, Alencon Link, Basingstoke, Hampshire RG21 1JB

Distribution

Distribution can refer to two (or more) different industries and related careers. For one area see **transport and distribution.** For another, see **retail trade management,** which describes the jobs included in all kinds of trade which is often called 'distribution' in the sense that goods are distributed to customers. In addition, see **warehousing**.

Drama

As well as **acting**, courses in drama at colleges, universities and poly-technics can lead to other careers, such as arts administration and **teaching**. Degrees in drama (some including 'theatre arts') are offered at various universities and colleges, and the Central School of Speech and Drama in London, which puts on all kinds of part-time and full-time courses, has a BTEC HND in stage management. There is another interesting career opening – in the theatre but behind the scenes, working in management, production and back-up. This kind of training leads to jobs in television and films within the production team – a much more stable profession than acting.

Prospects
Graduates of drama courses do a wide variety of work. About 10 per cent go into teaching and another 10 per cent continue with academic work or training. Another 40 per cent are employed in **entertainment**, but that includes the management and administration-type jobs, **person-nel, library, design** and **marketing.** The remainder find their way into employment sometimes far removed from drama work.

Training
For a full list of the institutions providing first-degree drama and theatre studies courses consult the Degree Course Guides on *Music and Drama*

and also *English*. Since the majority of these courses are combined with other subjects, the required A-levels depend on the course. However, the most useful A-levels or H-grades are English and a foreign language. There is an A-level in theatre studies, but few candidates take it because it is not offered in many schools. Art, history and music are useful too, and the same subjects at GCSE or the equivalent are a good preparation.

Information

British Actors' Equity Association, 8 Harley Street, London W1N 2AB
National Council for Drama Training, 5 Tavistock Place, London WC1H 9SS
Conference of Drama Schools, c/o Central School of Speech and Drama, Embassy Theatre, Eton Avenue, London NW3 3HY

Careers in the Theatre, Kogan Page
Working in the Performing Arts, COIC

Drawing office

Drawing office staff work in all industries: among them **building and construction**, vehicles, **engineering**, oil and petroleum and many manufacturing industries. They prepare and present drawings, diagrams and plans containing information and suggestions on how things should be built, maintained or manufactured. In **architecture** and **surveying,** technicians trained in this work operate alongside professional staff on all kinds of projects. There are various job-titles for this group of staff. Draughtsman used to be the accepted title, but now there are draughtswomen and engineering technicians as well as tracers and copy draughtsmen/women, although this last group of employees is being phased out because drawings can be reproduced and changed more quickly by means of computerised graphics.

To do this work effectively requires good drawing skills. In addition, staff need to know about engineering principles and practices, to understand the application of their drawings. They go beyond drawing: they work out the most effective methods of making a particular product, check safety factors and watch over its production. The breakthrough of computers into this work now means that sophisticated methods of computer-aided design (CAD) are being introduced into drawing offices which means that the staff need to know about computers and be trained in CAD.

Prospects

Prospects are not quite as good as they were, say, 20 years ago. There are fewer engineering companies and therefore fewer jobs. And with the arrival of computers and CAD, there is no great need for tracers to do all the repetitive work, for information can be stored in a computer rather than on hundreds of drawings. All the same, there is still a need for people with these skills: the better qualified and more mobile (prepared to change firms to gain promotion), the better the prospects.

Training

The first demand is *not* to be a talented artist. On the other hand, drawing ability is the prime requirement. More important today, however, is scientific and technical ability to know what the drawings are for. Among the school subjects that are particularly useful are engineering science, engineering drawing, technical drawing, graphic communication (the titles differ but the content of the courses is much the same). At A-level, technical drawing, engineering science, and CDT (craft, design and technology) are very helpful indeed. However, maths and physics are often demanded for students entering a drawing office as assistants to engineers.

Entry and training are at various levels. The best firms have a training programme for 16-year-olds who join after GCSEs. This allows them to attend a college of further education for part-time courses which take them to City and Guilds or BTEC qualifications. For City and Guilds certificate level, three good GCSE passes are looked for.

Apprentices in engineering trades do some drawing in the later stages of their training, but only those who are picked out for promotion would go on to BTEC National Diploma or National Certificate level within the Engineering Industry Training Board schemes, and to HNCs and HNDs in engineering.

At graduate level there are jobs in the drawing office for students with physics, maths, engineering and surveying degrees: their work takes them further in a professional sense, for they are the originators of the designs and drawings and direct the work of the draughtsmen/women and technicians.

Information
Engineering Careers Information Service, 54 Clarendon Road, Watford
WD1 1LB
The Council for Engineering Institutions, 2 Little Smith Street, London
SW1P 3DL

ECIS has numerous leaflets on engineering careers including drawing-office work

Dressmakers, dressers and dress designers

There are many different, and varied, jobs that come under the heading of 'dress and design'.

Dressmaker

A dressmaker can be someone who is very skilful at altering and making women's (and men's) clothes and who does it as a part-time interest or as a full-time job working from their own home. A dressmaker can also be employed in the theatre, television and film studios to make costumes under the direction of designers, and to make alterations to costumes that come from stock. A dressmaker who does this kind of work is almost a tailor. To train, some colleges offer full-time courses of up to three years leading to City and Guilds certificates in tailoring or pattern-cutting. Alternatively, the courses can be taken by part-time attendance. The *Directory of Further Education* lists colleges that offer these courses. There are also jobs as sewing machinist, garment cutter, and inspector and tailor within the clothing industry.

Dressers

Dressers work in the theatre, television, films and fashion houses. They look after the costumes – ironing, cleaning, repairing. The same kind of training and experience is looked for, but the job opportunities are much more limited.

Dress designers

Dress design is very big business indeed. Costume designers,

333

fashion designers, wardrobe designers – whatever they are called – manipulate the fast-moving dynamic and prosperous British (and international) fashion industry. Ways into this kind of work are by means of thorough training in fashion design. Courses are at all levels – degree, HND, diploma. One of the major centres is the London College of Fashion, but many polytechnics have specialised fashion courses (see the *Art and Design* Degree Course Guide for a list of colleges providing degree courses, their content and the qualifications that can be achieved). Useful GCSEs and A-levels (or equivalents) are home economics, needlework, fashion and fabrics, and embroidery.

Information
Working in the Clothing Industry, COIC
Jobs in the Textile and Clothing Industries, Kogan Page
Directory of Further Education and *Art and Design*, Degree Course Guide, Hobsons

Driving instructor and examiner

There are over 20 million motor vehicles on roads in the UK, which means that there are a great many drivers. This suggests that there are plenty of jobs for driving instructors.

Driving instructor

To become an instructor is not so very difficult: to become a good one is not easy. Many instructors begin by working at a recognised driving school and progress to a senior position within it. Others eventually break away to start their own business. This kind of move improves the statistics for self-employment but, according to the motor traders, does not improve standards. There are jobs, too, working for public transport firms, local authority bus services, vehicle manufacturers and in testing equipment. The figures show over 28,000 fully qualified instructors, so it is a real job market. The demand is increasing: there are a million new drivers on the road every year.

In addition to practical driving skills, instructors need to know about vehicle maintenance, road craft, the Highway Code and car mechanics. Some schools offer specialised instruction on heavy goods vehicles, high-performance cars and passenger service vehicles (buses). An instructor can also move on to become a driving examiner.

Driving examiner

Examiners are employed by the Department of Transport. They have to be at least 26 years of age, with good driving experience, a clean licence, a considerable knowledge of motoring, transport law and traffic problems.

Training

In order to qualify as an Approved Driving Instructor (ADI), an applicant must have held a licence for four out of the last six years, not have been disqualified from driving in the last four years, be fit, and pass a qualifying examination. It is an offence for a person who is not an ADI or an authorised trainee to give professional instruction. The ADI exams are administered by the Department of Transport, and to prepare for them an instructor must study at home and may also take professional training. Professional training courses last from two to three weeks: they are put on by driving schools. In addition there are longer courses for people who want to train to become the trainers of driving instructors.

Information

Department of Transport, 2 Marsham Street, London SW1P 3EB

Running Your Own Driving School, Kogan Page
The Driving Instructor's Handbook, Kogan Page

Economics

Economics deals with the organisation, use and distribution of resources. It is a very wide and all-embracing subject because it deals with financial and productive resources, both in Britain and internationally. It encompasses politics, social trends and the study of industry.

Another feature of economics is that beliefs and fashions change. Politicians and the press are constantly debating economic policy, though they rarely refer to the views of economists. There are 'laws' of economics: what happens is that academic economists come up with different solutions to much the same problems.

Although economics affects every kind of activity from household budgeting to world trade, there are few career openings for professional economists. As specialists, they work as advisers in government departments, such as the Department of Energy. Their number is small, their influence is great. In addition they work for financial institutions in the City of London, for international companies such as BP, Shell, IBM and in **banks** and **building societies**. They advise on topics such as the use of resources, the planning of production, investment projects, prices, wages, and the cost of living. They often operate in teams, gathering and assessing information, and writing papers setting out their ideas and policies.

If this description makes the job of an economist sound deskbound and Civil Service-dominated, it is. The Civil Service is the largest employer – but even so the total number of economists employed is only around 400. Local authorities take a handful of graduates each year. Banks and companies take about 450 annually. But a graduate who has studied economics for three or four years can move into many kinds of employment. Many are absorbed into business jobs, ranging from store assistant manager to teacher; others join multinational companies based throughout the world.

Prospects

In the Civil Service and elsewhere prospects for professional economists are limited, but those who move into general management may find the world their oyster. However, this may require extra training – a course in accountancy, management or planning. Other economics graduates take new courses to become **company secretaries, personnel officers** or production managers.

Training

There is no single professional body for economists. They generally join the British Institute of Management or a specialist association. Most further training is on the job, with a view to a specialised career in the management of a company which could be involved in the retail trade, transport, manufacturing, the media or any one of many industries.

To take a degree course in economics requires three good A-levels (four or five H-grades). Any subject is suitable: mathematics is a good base because economics involves number work and calculations and is required for some degree courses. An A-level in economics or in statistics is an excellent preparation for a degree course. The GCSEs or equivalents which support the A-levels must include maths and English language, and economics at this level is certainly a must.

There are other, related degree courses. For example, there is agricultural economics for people who want to work in the Ministry of Agriculture or companies in this field. There are degree courses in economics and social studies, and within many combined studies courses at degree level at college and polytechnics economics is usually one of the more popular options. These courses can lead into research work, and to teaching in schools and universities where competition is especially keen.

To assist the professional economists there are people without a degree but who are, nevertheless, keen on the subject: they find their niche as executive officers and clerical staff, or are diverted into other avenues closely related to the subject such as **accounting, sales** and **marketing, market research,** retail distribution and so on. A-levels (H-grades) in economics, maths, statistics and English language are particularly valuable for this work.

Information
The Economics Association, 18 Cedar Road, Sutton, Surrey SM2 5DF

Economics, in Hobsons' Connections series, describes the subject, explains the career possibilities and gives case-histories of people who have done well with economics
Economics, Degree Course Guide, Hobsons

Education

For most people, education means **teaching**. However, that is not the end of the story, as many other people are employed in servicing or assisting teachers and lecturers.

Education welfare officers

Education welfare officers (or social workers in education) are responsible for ensuring the attendance of children at school, helping nonattenders overcome the problems that may have led to their nonattendance and working with children with behavioural or learning problems at school. Education welfare officers are normally employed by local education authorities in England and Wales and Education and Library Boards in Northern Ireland. In Scotland local authority social work departments are responsible for the education welfare service. The qualification for education welfare officers is the Certificate of Qualification in Social Work (CQSW) which can be obtained by taking either a two-year full-time course for non-graduates, a one- or two-year full-time course for graduates, depending on their degree subject, or a four-year course leading to a degree and the professional qualification. Relevant working experience in the social services is usually required for entry to CQSW courses as well as the academic qualifications.

Educational administration

These are the people who staff the education offices of a local authority. They range from the Chief Education Officer and his deputies, assistants and their staff, through the inspectorate and advisory services, to the office staff that back them up. The officers, advisers and inspectors are generally former **teachers** or **lecturers,** and so they arrive at their position by the teachers' routes – by degree or other higher qualification, teacher-training, and experience in school or college. The support staff are **secretaries, clerks** and technicians who have their own skills and career paths.

Educational support staff

These are the people who work in education but are not teachers. They are school catering staff, secretaries, technicians, caretakers, cleaners. They, too, arrive in education by taking specialist training for their particular trade or skill and use this knowledge in the educational world.

Information
Central Council for Education and Training in Social Work (CCETSW) Information Service, Derbyshire House, St Chad's Street, London WC1H 8AD, and at 9 South St David Street, Edinburgh EH2 2BW
Department of Education and Science (DES), Information Services, Elizabeth House, York Road, London SE1 7PT

Electrical engineering

The electrical engineering profession can be divided into three main sectors: power engineering, communications, and computers and automation.

- Power engineering is concerned with generating electricity and then bringing it to heat and light all kinds of buildings, and with providing a constant source of power for equipment for use in homes, schools, hospitals, industry and offices. Electrical engineers design and manufacture the equipment needed for electricity and its use in industry. Power engineers work out new methods of producing electricity when the traditional sources no longer exist.
- Communications is a rapidly expanding industry that includes activities ranging from radio and satellite communication to television broadcasting. Another fast-developing area is micro-electronic technology, which enables engineers to develop complex information systems using computers and other machines.
- Computers and automation is the fastest-moving branch of engineering. New techniques in the manufacture of electronic circuits have meant they are becoming smaller, more reliable and less expensive. Computers are being used more and more in transport, medicine, business and industry to collect and analyse information.

Not surprisingly, within these three areas there is a tremendous variety of careers. For instance, there are jobs in research, working in universities and polytechnics and in companies. Design engineers have to visualise new solutions to practical problems and translate the ideas into products. Production or development engineers work on products or devices, often solving problems through their experience and knowledge, as in the advances in digital watches and miniature radios. One of the jobs of a test engineer in an aerospace company could be to run a series of trials of an automatic landing system for passenger aircraft. All these jobs could lead to **management, marketing, sales** or jobs in education and training.

Training

To qualify as a chartered electrical engineer means working through a tough programme of education taking at least seven years. No chartered electrical engineer is under 25, for it takes this length of time to qualify. There are, however, engineers and technicians working within the industries already described who are younger than 25, but have not yet reached the status of chartered engineer.

For an engineer a degree course and qualification is essential. To prepare for a degree course, students need a broad range of GCSEs or equivalents including arts and science subjects. The minimum requirement for entry to the electrical engineering courses provided at most universities and polytechnics is normally A-levels or H-grades in mathematics and physics. Grades vary: some universities ask for grades of A, B or C in three science subjects, but some polytechnics offer places to candidates with lower grades in two rather than three A-levels. It is not absolutely necessary for the three A-levels to be in science or maths subjects: two must be, but the third could be economics, English, a foreign language or some other subject. There are more sponsorships available from companies for undergraduates on electrical engineering courses than for any other degree course.

To become a chartered engineer requires a minimum of two years' industrial training and two years' career development, which means a full-time job.

As well as electrical engineers, there are opportunities in **engineering** for technician engineers, technicians and **electricians.** Technician engineers are generally qualified to BTEC or SCOTVEC HND/HNC level and should have five years' industrial experience. The technician qualification is a BTEC or SCOTVEC National Diploma or National Certificate with at least two years' experience.

Useful school subjects are: mathematics, science (particularly physics or physical science), chemistry, and at GCSE a good balance of science and arts subjects. Engineering science at A-level is particularly useful too, although few schools offer it.

Information

The Institution of Electrical Engineers, Savoy Place, London WC2R 0BL

Have You Got What it Takes?, Institution of Electrical Engineers
Technology, Degree Course Guide, for all degree courses, and *The Directory of Further Education*, for all colleges and courses in electrical engineering, Hobsons

Electrician

Electricians work in a highly rated craft trade with well-established levels of technical knowledge and training. Their job is to install, replace and repair electrical equipment and wiring: this could be anything from installing a washing-machine to wiring a factory. The work is varied, and it can be challenging and mobile. Above all, electricians have to observe safety: a mistake could, quite literally, be fatal.

Electricians do not always work in ideal conditions. They are likely to be out of doors a lot, erecting and wiring machinery in half-built factories, houses, flats and shops. They therefore need to be quite fit, for there may be a lot of bending, kneeling, standing, crawling and climbing. Allied to these requirements, they certainly need to know about electricity and have the practical skills to work from drawings and plans, often without direct supervision.

Prospects
Job prospects are good: the electrical industry is an expanding one. Promotion is possible, too, to foreman or perhaps into self-employment in one's own business.

Training
No formal entry requirements are normally needed for entry to a traineeship, although most employers are keen to see GCSE passes in two or three relevant subjects. In Scotland, apprentices are expected to have three O-grade passes with a science subject or engineering science among them. Having got into a firm, local authority or electricity board, trainees then enter a training scheme (see below for addresses).

Training involves on-site instruction and work alongside craftsmen and attendance at a college of further education or training centre for practical training and education which lead to a City and Guilds certificate.

Information
Joint Industry Board for the Electrical Contracting Industry, Kingswood House, 47–51 Sidcup Hill, Sidcup, Kent DA14 6HJ
The Joint Training Council for the Electrical Contracting Industry, 23 Heriot Row, Edinburgh EH3 6EW

Education and Training Branch, Room 5Y6, The Electricity Council, 30 Millbank, London SW1P 4RD

Would You Like to be an Electrician?, Construction Industry Training Board

Electronics

The use of electrical and electronic devices is such an integral part of our world that we sometimes forget its importance. In electronics – which is a specialised branch of physics and electrical engineering – people are concerned with four basic activities – designing, making, applying and selling electronic and electrical devices. The most obvious applications are in computers, large and small, but there are hundreds of other aspects of electronics in all the major industries.

Training

There are special – and different – degree courses in electronic science, electronic engineering and electronic communications. Most of the universities and polytechnics have degree combinations that cover these subjects: refer to the Degree Course Guide in *Technology* for details of them. To obtain a place, A-level passes in physics and mathematics are looked for, plus another subject; grades vary with an average of CCC being looked for at universities; lower grades at polytechnics. There is also an A-level in electronics. Job prospects are excellent: electronics is an industry that really needs people and it is likely to expand fast in the future.

Information
Working in Electronics, COIC

Employment

There are specific jobs concerned with finding people employment. The Department of Employment, together with the Training Agency, is directly involved with training and job-finding. These huge departments are part of the **Civil Service.** They employ staff at all levels in Jobcentres and training centres throughout the UK. Although most of the staff are Civil Servants, other employees are on short-term contracts with the Training Agency, working on special projects or services.

Employment advisers

These advisers work within the Department of Employment and Training Agency and act as consultants to both job-seekers and to employers, providing a service that tries to link openings with applicants. Locally based, they are experts in employment opportunities within their region, and search for employers who could provide extra places. They are executive officers within the Civil Service hierarchy and have their own career and promotion structure.

Disablement resettlement officers

These officers provide a specialist guidance service for disabled people.

Careers officers

Careers officers are employed in local education authority careers services. They offer educational and careers guidance to school pupils, students and other young people, plus a job-finding service. Recruitment is of graduates and non-graduates who normally take a Diploma in Careers Guidance. Full-time and some part-time courses are available, for which industrial or teaching experience is generally required.

Employment agents or consultants

This group of advisers works in the private sector of employment. They have to be licensed by the Department of Employment as being competent to give a careers and job placement service. The agents place people in jobs on a permanent or temporary basis. Some run 'temps' (temporary typists or secretaries) placement services; others concentrate on executives who have been made redundant or who want to change their jobs. No specific entry requirements are demanded, but interviewers are expected to be educated at least to GCSE or O-grade standard: consultants would normally have A-level/H-grade qualifications and most probably a degree. There is a professional body, the Institute of Employment Consultants, to which most agencies require their senior staff to belong. Training is on the job, plus specialist tuition in interviewing techniques. To carry out the job of agent/interviewer/adviser/consultant, considerable experience of senior management positions in industry, commerce or public service is expected, so young people would not immediately enter this kind of work.

Academically, any subject or group of subjects is appropriate. Someone with a degree in social science, sociology, business studies, accounting, finance or other commercial/social/business subjects has a head start because they have the theoretical background to appreciate people's problems. GCSEs and A-levels or H-grades in these subjects are just as valuable, and English language skills are essential. But any subject from history to horticulture would not be barred because interviewing techniques, social skills, knowledge of the worlds of commerce, business and employment are the prime requirements, and these come with maturity, after considerable experience of working life.

Information

The Institute of Employment Consultants, 6 Welbeck Street, London W1M 7PB

Local Government Training Board, Arndale House, Arndale Centre, Luton, Bedfordshire LU1 2TS

The Institute of Careers Officers, 2nd Floor, Old Board Chambers, 37a High Street, Stourbridge, West Midlands DY8 1DA

Energy engineering

The energy industries are among the biggest employers in Britain. These industries include electricity, oil, coal and nuclear fuels. Energy engineers are concerned with the design, manufacture and management of all kinds of energy plant. They could therefore work anywhere within the four industries listed above.

Energy engineering is a branch of engineering. On the other hand, it has its own training pattern and specialised ladder of career opportunities.

Prospects

For graduates, prospects are excellent: these industries are looking for high-calibre young people with engineering and scientific interests in energy. The sky is the limit for the ambitious and capable.

Training

To prepare for a career in this form of engineering there are all number of degree courses. In the first place there are courses in **physics, electrical** and **electronic engineering** and other forms of engineering. Graduates can move from a course in physics or engineering to one in energy, or they can specialise from the start. Energy engineers require a thorough knowledge of fuels, energy release and heat transfer. They also need to know about the financial and environmental implications of the various options of manufacturing or releasing energy. To prepare for this work there are more specialised degree courses in fuel and in energy engineering at the University of Leeds and Heriot-Watt University, Edinburgh.

Another group of courses is energy studies. These are based on physical sciences and cover the possible sources of energy supply and the technology that is needed to utilise them. They are part of a group of science and engineering courses, as at Ulster University, and Brighton and Coventry Polytechnics. A degree course at Coventry Polytechnic in physical sciences has a strong energy component. In addition, Farnborough College of Technology has a BTEC HND course in energy management, and several universities have degree courses in engineering that combine electrical and mechanical engineering components. Three good A-levels at grades around C are needed, and A-levels or H-grades are specified in maths, chemistry and/or physics for most of them. Clearly, good GCSEs (O-grades) in these subjects are also needed. Engineering science is another excellent A-level. For the energy studies and electro-mechanical degree courses, maths and physics are usually required, with chemistry at GCSE or its equivalent.

Information

The Engineering Careers Information Service, 54 Clarendon Road, Watford WD1 1LB, publishes leaflets on all branches of engineering

Technology, Degree Course Guide, Hobsons

Engineering

Engineering is not a single career or a single subject. It covers a range of skills and knowledge and opens doors to a tremendous number of jobs. Of all the university and polytechnic degree, HND and diploma courses on offer, across all subjects, engineering is the one with the best career opportunities and carries a 70 per cent of company sponsorship. Seventy-five per cent of graduates go immediately into permanent jobs; others pick and choose, leaving a very low rate of unemployment (presently one per cent) among engineering graduates. And things look even better. As older industries decline, new ones open up: energy, computers, chemicals, biotechnology, the space industries – these are areas of growth where recruitment staff are desperately seeking the skills of good engineers.

But what is engineering? First and foremost, it is an academic discipline just like physics or mathematics, and it borrows from both these subjects. Within this discipline there are common factors and specialist options.

Engineers have to recognise society's needs and then conceive the ideas, solve the problems, design, construct, maintain and improve the products and technology to fulfil those needs. Their inventiveness ranges from the microchip to the Thames Barrier, from sophisticated life-support systems to simple products in the kitchen, from microbiology to ship and aerospace technology.

Job possibilities are vast, too. There are engineers at all levels in all industries. Then there are **army** officers, **factory inspectors,** consultants, **local government** and central government officials, **computing** specialists, top businessmen and women. Engineering is a transferable skill which, with continuing education and training, means that an engineer often makes a very good business executive, an expert on broadcasting and communications systems, a sales and marketing manager, a university or college lecturer.

Despite these opportunities there is a severe shortage of students for engineering courses. Each year, some polytechnic degree courses do not run because of insufficient numbers and others run with a handful of students. Because of financial pressures, these polytechnic courses will no longer run, reducing further the number of options and in the long term the supply of engineering graduates. One of the reasons for this sad picture is the attitude of many teachers to engineering as a career. The excessive regard for the professions of law, medicine and science has deterred many students from considering engineering as a career. This is in dramatic contrast with countries such as Germany and France, where engineers are very highly regarded, aiming for and reaching the most senior posts in industry and commerce.

The Engineering Council, set up in 1981, works with and through many separate engineering institutions to try to deal with the problem. The Council has to persuade bright pupils of both sexes to think first of an engineering course and career, instead of one of the other options available to them. To try to attract more recruits to the industry the WISE (Women into Science and Engineering) campaign encourages young women to go into engineering. About one per cent of registered engineers are women. A brighter picture is that ten per cent of engineering undergraduates are female and the proportion is rising.

Once a pupil has decided on a future in engineering there are three principal groups of trained engineers: craftsmen and women, technicians and chartered engineers.

Craftsmen and women

These staff are taken on at 16-plus and are trained on the job and at colleges of further education on day- or block-release schemes as apprentices. Courses lead to City and Guilds craft qualifications.

Technicians

Technicians also enter jobs at 16-plus, working for BTEC qualifications on a part-time basis, or they may first take a full-time course leading to a BTEC National Diploma and then look for jobs. Within this group are engineering technicians and technician engineers.

Chartered engineers

For students of 18-plus there are courses leading to engineering degrees, HNDs and HNCs. These can be full time, although the majority of courses are of a sandwich type, with work experience as part of the course. To become a chartered engineer means obtaining an accredited degree in a branch of engineering, a training period in industry and some time in a responsible job.

Prospects
Once qualified, opportunities are not confined to the engineering industry. Engineers, whether chartered or not, are employed in almost every sector of industry and commerce including oil, **chemicals,**

pharmaceuticals, food, brewing, agriculture, banking and **in- surance.**

The skills and knowledge are changing too. Every engineer is expected to update his or her skills, adapting to robotics, computing, the automation of industrial processes, new design ideas, the breakthrough in electronic communication, the improvement of materials, and so on. Some of the institutions insist that their members undertake a specified time in retraining each year.

Branches of engineering

There is no one overall degree course: there are hundreds. This list gives the main areas of specialisation, some of which have separate entries in this book. There are degree courses in all of these and also in 'engineering science', which concentrates on the theories of engineering.

Acoustical	Energy	Mechanical
Aeronautical and	Enviromental	Minerals
propulsion	Food processing	Mining
Agricultural	Fuel	Nuclear
Automotive	Geology and	Optoelectronics
Biochemical	geotechnics	Petroleum
Chemical	Human cybernetics	Plant
Civil	Industrial	Polymer
Communication	Information systems	Power
Computer	Instrumentation	Product
Control and systems	Manufacturing	design
Design and manu-	systems	Production
facture	Marine	Software
Electrical and	Materials	Structural
electronic	Mathematical	Textile

Qualifications

At GCSE or O-grade, the essential subjects are mathematics and physics. Chemistry at GCSE is required for some degree courses. English language at GCSE is demanded for most courses. For entry to university, polytechnic or college courses there is a tremendously wide range in the A-level or H-grade requirements. For example, to read engineering at Oxford or Cambridge, three A or B grades at A-level are specified and expected. Some polytechnic degree courses will take applicants with two A-levels, at grades D or E, but maths or physics/physical science is essential for most courses. Other acceptable A-levels and H-grades are in chemistry (required for chemical engineering), engineering science, building, surveying, and environmental science.

Information

Engineering Careers Information Service, 54 Clarendon Road, Watford WD1 1LB

Engineering Council, 10 Maltravers Street, London WC2R 3ER, publishes *A Closer Look at Engineering* and provides a list of individual institutions and also gives general assistance

A special effort is being made to try to persuade more young women to enter engineering. For a list of special courses and general advice write to the Equal Opportunities Commission, Overseas House, Quay Street, Manchester M3 3HN

Occupations, the annual reference sourcebook, COIC

Equal Opportunities, a Careers Guide, Penguin

Engineering Casebook, Hobsons

Technology, Degree Course Guide, Hobsons

Working in Engineering, COIC

Entertainment

The entertainers we hear about through the media seem to live exciting lives and earn vast amounts. They must represent about one per cent of the entertainment industry. For the other 99 per cent it is a struggle to earn a living. Because of the nature of their work entertainers are here today and gone tomorrow. Today may be lucrative: yesterday and tomorrow are unlikely to be. Pay, like work, is erratic. Prospects are miserable except for the very talented and the very lucky. (The entry for **acting** tells a similar tale.)

On the other hand, many young people are determined to be entertainers or work in the industry, and they do not all want to be actors. Taking a wider view of job opportunities, there is a slightly rosier picture. But first the entertainment industry should be divided into two groups:

● the entertainers or artists themselves
● support teams.

In the first category come actors, musicians, comedians, **dancers**, singers. For each of these there are specialised training programmes such as drama, music and dance schools, and progression from repertory theatre and clubs to radio, television and the West End theatres.

The second group are the supporters. They are the backroom staff: make-up, wardrobe, lighting, booking agents, producers and directors, receptionists, clerks, secretaries, agents. They may have come into the entertainment industry because they want to work alongside actors or musicians, and being a booking clerk or secretary is their own planned choice, or perhaps they saw an advertisement for a make-up assistant and moved to Television Centre from a hairdressing salon or fashion house to sample something different. Employment for the supporters is obviously more secure and stable than for the entertainers themselves. Either way, it is an industry that will endure, change and expand as we all enjoy more leisure time, but finding a niche is due to talent, training, luck and determination.

Information
Working in the Performing Arts, COIC
Careers in the Music Business, Kogan Page

Environmental health officer

Young people who want to know about the jobs that are concerned with 'environment' should consider: **farming, horticulture,** market gardening, **conservation, forestry, town and country planning, surveying, cartography** and working with **animals.**

Then there is the specialised job of an 'environmental health officer' (EHO). These officials got their grand title when 'public health inspector' became unfashionable. Both titles describe much the same kind of work, which is to safeguard people's living and working environment. EHOs work with laws on environmental health which have been established by Parliament. Their functions and jobs cover these areas:

- food. In shops, restaurants, cafés, kitchens, factories and slaughter-houses they inspect the premises and make recommendations on safeguarding health. They investigate any cases of food poisoning

- health and safety at work. EHOs check on standards at work and ensure that workplaces operate in a safe way
- housing. EHOs have the power to enter homes uninvited if they have good reason to believe the house is not fit for human habitation or is prejudicial to health. They enforce housing legislation intended to safeguard tenants in rented accommodation and liaise with landlords on how to improve conditions. They also administer renovation grants
- pollution. This is an increasing part of their work, reflecting the increase in pollution. They watch out for illicit dumping on land and may liaise with the waste disposal authorities on the safety of official tips, monitor air and noise pollution, and enforce the laws designed to reduce the release of waste into the atmosphere.

Whatever they do, EHOs are out and about. A large proportion of their time is out of the office, which is usually in a local town hall. They are sometimes in the law courts, when someone is being prosecuted for a breach of the law.

Prospects for these jobs are quite good. There is a fairly constant demand for new staff and at present about 5,500 officers are employed throughout the UK. Most start by dealing with the work outlined above and some then go on to specialise in food, housing or the other categories. Promotion prospects are good – up to chief officer positions.

Training

There are two main types of qualification which are recognised by the Institution of Environmental Health Officers: a degree or a diploma in environmental health. Degrees in this subject are offered at Cardiff Institute of Higher Education, Leeds, Thames, and Manchester Polytechnics (at Manchester it is in association with Salford College of Technology), and at the Universities of London (King's College), and Ulster. These degree courses are not the same as degree courses in environmental sciences or studies, and the two categories should not be confused.

For EHOs there is a three-year sandwich course which leads to the Diploma in Environmental Health.

For entry to degree courses, two or three good A-levels (three or four H-grades) are needed. Competition is keen: Ulster has 200 applications for 18 places. Useful A-levels are chemistry, biology and environmental science, and physics or physical science are highly rated subjects. For the diploma course, the minimum entry requirements are two A-levels or three H-grades, with one of the subjects a science, plus three GCSE passes at grades A to C. Although the different colleges and polytechnics have different requirements, it is clear that the relevant school subjects are sciences at GCSE and at A-level.

Practical training is carried out by the student's sponsoring local authority, if he or she is being sponsored. On the degree courses, the usual pattern is for the third year to be spent with a local authority. For the diploma course, six months of each of the three years is on placement. Both types of course therefore put great stress on work experience, and all students have to complete this training before being awarded a degree or diploma.

Information

Institution of Environmental Health Officers, Chadwick House, Rushworth Street, London SE1 0QT. Booklets are available from the Institution

The Royal Environmental Health Institute of Scotland, Virginia House, 62 Virginia Street, Glasgow G1 1TX. There are different qualifications for EHOs in Scotland

Environmental science

The word environment is now used in many contexts to mean many different things. It is used here to refer to the natural environment – the air we breathe, the water we drink, the seas and the soil and plants and animals. Environmental science as a subject at university or polytechnic is primarily the study of this, the natural environment, and should not be confused with environmental studies, which is generally used in the context of the human, built environment.

Our modern industrial society places a heavy demand on the environment such that pollution is increasingly evident. Few countries in the world have remained immune from this trend, which also affects almost all components of our environment. Resource depletion and pollution are beginning to assume a global scale. At the local and national level they are the subject of legislation and policy.

The study, monitoring and management of the environment as well as the formulation of policy and control legislation are the work of the environmental scientist.

Prospects

Study of the environment has been a preoccupation of mankind since the dawn of civilisation. Scientists of many persuasions, from ecologists to geologists, atmospheric meteorologists to hydrologists, pedologists to zoologists, have all been students of their small part of the environment. However, the phrase 'environmental scientist' is a fairly recent one.

Environmental science is a growth area. The number of jobs is increasing, and so is the breadth of the subject. Most major industrial companies now have environmental departments, large numbers of consultancies in many fields are recruiting environmental scientists because of the demand for environmental impact assessment work. In the state sector there are opportunties in local and national government and in research establishments. Public utilities such as the water authorities also employ environmental scientists. This trend is mirrored in most developed countries, and the demand for environmental work in the Third World is also increasing as part of aid packages. All the signs are that the growth in environmental science posts will continue.

Training

Most environmental scientists have a combination of science A-levels. Environmental science can be read at degree level at many universities, colleges and polytechnics. Alternatively, individual specialisms can be studied for a first degree, and a second degree can be used to specialise in environmental science. Despite the growing market, there are sufficient well-qualified scientists available, and most job vacancies will be taken by candidates with a second degree. With appropriate qualifications, practitioners can apply for membership of the Institute of Environmental Sciences.

Information

Institute of Environmental Sciences, 14 Prince's Gate, London SW7 1PU

Working in the Countryside, COIC

Estate agent

An estate agent is a member of the **surveying** profession which covers a very wide range of employment. The estate agent's most familiar role is as the person who offers for sale houses and flats on behalf of people who wish to move home. But estate agents are not only concerned with the sale of residential property: they deal with shops, offices, factories or farm and building land, and with letting all types of buildings on behalf of their owners. As the proportion of home-ownership is gradually increasing, the amount of let residential accommodation is steadily declining, but the picture is different in the commercial market, where most big new office blocks are owned by large property companies, insurance companies or pension funds, and are let to smaller firms and organisations that wish to occupy the space.

In country towns and rural areas the work of an estate agent is closely allied to that of the agricultural surveyor who advises landowners, farmers and others with interests in the countryside on the use, management, development, marketing and valuation of all rural property, including country estates, farms and livestock.

The work requires a good standard of fitness and mobility, as an agent has to visit clients, inspect properties and negotiate between buyers and sellers. The working day will often be a combination of office work and outside activities. Prospects are generally good as there is a steady demand for the services of estate agents.

Training

The normal methods of entry are to seek recognition by one of the two main professional bodies. These are RICS – the Royal Institution of Chartered Surveyors – and ISVA – the Incorporated Society of Valuers and Auctioneers. Both bodies have up-to-date information on qualifications, courses and prospects, so it is best to write direct to them.

There are two possible ways to obtain professional qualifications. Most entrants now take a degree course in order to obtain full exemption from the RICS examinations. The courses are either full time (three years) or sandwich (four years). Relevant degree courses are offered at Cambridge, Reading, City (London), Aberdeen, Heriot-Watt and Ulster Universities and at about 15 polytechnics. For a full list consult RICS or the Degree Course Guide on *Technology*, which includes a major section on surveying. For graduates in other subjects, RICS offers a graduate entry scheme which is effectively one year shorter than the courses for school-leavers.

The alternative method is to take a job in an estate agent's office and study part time either by correspondence course or by day release at a local college. In addition to the written examinations, practical training and experience are required for the Test of Professional Competence, successful completion of which leads to full membership (ARICS) of the Institution.

It is possible to be an estate agent without professional qualifications but the best prospects lie with the best qualified. About 13,000 estate agents are qualified members of RICS.

To start a course, RICS demands at least five suitable GCSE passes, including English language and mathematics, and then two subjects at A-level. Alternative qualifications are BTEC or SCOTVEC HND or HNC awards.

ISVA (with about 5,000 members) asks for five GCSEs or equivalents including English language and mathematics, or alternative packages including A-level or BTEC/SCOTVEC awards of certificates in estate management and valuation or surveying. Entry to corporate management of the ISVA can be achieved by taking a degree in estate management, which gives complete exemption from ISVA exams, or by taking a BTEC HNC/HND course. Alternatively, for graduates in other subjects, there are special courses (details from ISVA, below). Estate agency is closely linked to auctioneering and valuing – see the entries on **auctioneer** and **valuer**.

Information

The Royal Institution of Chartered Surveyors, 12 Great George Street, Parliament Square, London SW1P 3AD, and 7 Manor Place, Edinburgh EH3 7DN

The Incorporated Society of Valuers and Auctioneers, 3 Cadogan Place, London SW1X 0AS

National Association of Estate Agents, Arbon House, 21 Jury Street, Warwick CV34 4EH

Leaflets and booklets are available from these organisations

Exhibition work

Organising and putting on exhibitions is becoming big business. Think of the national and international exhibitions of manufactured products and equipment, including the boat and motor shows, computers, furniture, fashion, printing, the 'ideal home', and so on. These exhibitions, held in London, other cities and at centres such as the National

Exhibition Centre at Birmingham and Earls Court in London, regularly attract millions of visitors.

To run an exhibition, whether for one day or two weeks, requires a vast amount of preparation, sometimes years ahead of the event. A large company may mount its own exhibition, so the work is done by its own staff. But, increasingly, companies ask a conference and exhibition organiser to do the job for them. In much the same way, national exhibitions at the major centres and hotels are also arranged by these specialist companies.

A career can be made in exhibition work. Entry to it can be at many levels. In the first place it is a business, so the managers need to be trained in business management, which means they are likely to be accountants, graduates of business schools, or managers who have moved over from other kinds of jobs, often the **retail trade.**

Exhibition design is a different kind of expertise. It is a very skilled craft, for the work involves interior design (as in decorating and furnishing a set for a house interior); using flat surfaces for advertising material, arranged artistically; model-making (as in the creation of three-dimensional models); and the use of objects (perhaps items for sale, such as cars or televisions) for display. Exhibition designers also work in museums, although there are few openings compared with commercial business exhibitions.

A third group are the exhibition assemblers: they are the secretaries, advertisers, construction workers, painters, joiners. They may be employed by the organisers, or (more likely) be recruited on a contract basis.

Training

Entry to careers in exhibition organising is via graduate status for the managerial jobs. Any degree course could be appropriate, but business studies and design, or variations of these, are especially suitable. No special training or qualifications are needed, for people learn on the job. Then there is the design route, via a degree, HND or diploma in graphic design. Some courses specialise in exhibition work. Thirdly, for the construction and administrative jobs, the route is via the appropriate training for these particular skills.

Information

Association of Exhibition Organisers, 207 Market Towers, Nine Elms Lane, London SW8 5NQ

Art and Design, Degree Course Guide, Hobsons

Exporting

Exporters are employed in the sales and marketing departments of large and small companies, in special import and export agencies, and in trade houses. What they do is to sell goods overseas, organise the necessary paperwork (which in terms of permissions and negotiations can be formidable), and arrange for the goods to be shipped or freighted. Some exporters work entirely overseas in the territories for which they are responsible. Some large companies, in order to make it easier to overcome import/export controls, set up subsidiary companies abroad. The export staff then commute between the home office and their overseas outpost or (more likely) stay in the outpost.

Exporting has a glamour that attracts graduates and other ambitious young people. The job of being responsible for sales in Germany and France sounds very attractive to someone with a degree in these languages, backed up by a postgraduate course in business studies. Even more than in a UK sales team, the exporter or representative will have a lot of personal responsibility and will have to make decisions on his or her own initiative. The travelling can, however, be a strain on family life.

Prospects

There are good opportunities in exporting: despite the gloom of newspapers about Britain's trade figures, the country exports vast quantities of goods and services.

Training

Particular pre-entry qualifications are not required, although common sense, a quick brain and some experience of selling are generally demanded of applicants. Companies go for high-calibre people, which means that graduates start with an advantage. But there are many opportunities for the less highly qualified as long as they are lively, have business skills and are personable to foreigners. Modern language graduates start off with a decided advantage, as do graduates in any one of the business subjects: business studies, accounting, marketing, and so on. But companies spread a wide net because it is the individual, not the subject, that really counts.

Training is on the job. The two bodies that give professional qualifications are the Institute of Export and the Institute of Sales and Marketing Management. For part-time study for the exams of the Institute of Export, the minimum qualification is four GCSEs or O-grades, including English language. Some colleges of further education provide courses leading to the Institute's Certificate in Export Office Practice, which is suitable for office administration staff who deal with documentation.

For students with A-levels, another route is to take a two-year full-time or sandwich course for a BTEC HND in business studies, taking up options in export or international marketing. For this course, one A-level or two H-grades is the minimum backed by four GCSEs or O-grades. Lastly, there are university and polytechnic degree courses leading to a BA or BSc in business studies: three good A-levels or four H-grades, plus English language and mathematics at GCSE/O-grade are generally specified as necessary subjects. Some courses have options in exporting.

Information

Institute of Export, Export House, 64 Clifton Street, London EC2A 4HB
Institute of Sales and Marketing Management, Georgian House, 31 Upper George Street, Luton, Bedfordshire LU1 2RD

The Institute of Export provides leaflets, such as *As a Professional Exporter*, on request
Directory of Further Education, Hobsons, lists colleges that provide courses leading to the exams of the Institutes of Export, Freight Forwarding and Marketing
Business, Management and Accountancy, Degree Course Guide, Hobsons

Factory inspector

A factory inspector's job is to see that the standards required by the Health and Safety at Work Act and other laws and regulations are followed in factories, shops, offices and other places of work. This is a varied job, taking inspectors into all kinds of places, meeting managers and employees, making recommendations and insisting on changes where dangers to health are spotted. Among the hazards an inspector checks for are fumes, noise, dust, poisonous substances, moving machinery and the social and psychological effects of technology. To some extent the work overlaps with that of an **environmental health officer**. Prospects are quite good.

Training

To become a factory inspector the usual route is to take a degree course first, then to obtain experience in industry, preferably in a production department or workshop, and then to apply to become an inspector. For the first stage, any degree or BTEC HND course would be suitable, although engineering and science-based courses do give insights into mechanics that arts graduates would not have. But inspectors come from a wide range of degree disciplines. After appointment, fairly extensive training is provided, leading to the Diploma in Safety and Hygiene. Factory inspectors are civil servants, so they have the same kind of career pattern and opportunities for promotion as in other branches of the Civil Service. One possible option is to become a specialist inspector, covering, for example, agriculture, explosives, chemicals, mines and quarries, nuclear plants or air pollution.

Information

Health and Safety Executive, St Hugh's House, Stanley Precinct, Bootle, Liverpool L20 3QY

Civil Service Commission, Alencon Link, Basingstoke, Hampshire RG21 1JB

Farming

Farming has probably undergone more radical changes than any other industry. From being a labour-intensive industry a hundred years ago, it has become a capital-intensive one, where finance and not workers is the major resource, and farms continue to increase in size and decrease in number. Mechanisation and specialised farming under EC rules and regulations are the chief criteria for making a profit – or surviving. Running a farm needs the skills of a business manager, but it is unlikely that farmers will be using these skills and knowledge on their own farms.

About a third of UK farms are owned by large companies, and the percentage is increasing. Even so, some 400,000 people are employed on farms, and it is still a major source of employment.

Farming covers various categories of specialist work. Arable farming deals with root crops, cereals and vegetables. Livestock farming covers the raising of cattle, sheep, pigs and poultry. Horticulture is the art of cultivating gardens. Market gardening deals with fruit and flowers. Dairy farmers concentrate on milk and cheese production.

Among the jobs in farming that school-leavers and graduates can hope to obtain are: farm manager, farm worker, farm secretary and farm mechanic.

Farm managers

Farm managers are responsible for the running of a farm owned by someone else, a private individual, company, tenant or a commercial organisation. On very big farms the managers will be helped by assistant or deputy managers. The way into farm management is via an agricultural degree course at university or specialist college. The entry on **agriculture** gives details of degree and HND courses, but three good A-levels or four H-grades in science subjects (preferably including chemistry and biology) are generally required for entry, and competition for places is keen so good grades (A, B or C) are needed. Alternatively, for students with one A-level or two H-grades plus four GCSEs or O-grades, there are HND courses, and for those with four GCSEs or the equivalents there are BTEC National Diploma courses.

Farm workers

Farm workers are employed on all the various kinds of farms. The work is hard – long hours, out of doors, low pay. The prospects for moving from farm worker to supervisor or assistant farm manager are slim, and competition is fierce. The Agricultural Training Board apprenticeship scheme is open to all applicants and there are no formal entry requirements. Most apprentices enter via the farming industry's Youth Training two-year programme of training and work which leads to City and Guilds or SCOTVEC certificates.

Farm secretaries

Farm secretaries need general secretarial skills, substantial knowledge of financial and accounting systems and an understanding of the agricultural industry. They keep accurate records of farm business, wages, contracts, and so on. In order to acquire this knowledge, secretaries can take a one-year, full-time course leading to the National Certificate for Farm Secretaries. The entry requirements are three GCSEs/O-grades in academic subjects including mathematics and English language, and a pass in typing to RSA stage 1. Otherwise, students can take a two-year, full-time course leading to the BTEC National Diploma in Business Studies for Agricultural Secretaries. For this course, four GCSEs or their equivalents are needed, plus a typing award to at least RSA stage 1.

Farm mechanics

Farm mechanics are responsible for maintaining and repairing farm machinery. They can qualify for this work by taking any one of several engineering courses on a part-time or full-time basis at college. The qualifications are at certificate level for City and Guilds awards. There are no specific entry requirements, apart from an interest in machines, engineering and farming, although any practical or technical subjects studied at school are obviously useful.

Information

Agricultural Training Board, Summit House, Glebe Way, West Wickham, Kent BR4 0RF

The Institute of Agricultural Secretaries, The National Agricultural Centre, Stoneleigh, Kenilworth, Warwickshire CV8 2LZ

Agricultural Sciences, Degree Course Guide, Hobsons
Working in Agriculture and Horticulture, COIC

Fashion

Fashion is a very big industry. It is also a form of design, with its own type of originality and skills. Clothes are a necessity and also a source of fascination. On the other hand, not many people in the fashion industry are creating original designs: the vast majority are adapting or translating other people's ideas to suit a market, or are in that market, selling, making, persuading. All this, however, means there are potential careers in all these branches of fashion.

Haute couture

Here are the big names – Chanel, Conran, Dior – and the Paris, Rome and London fashion shows. Behind the scenes are the workrooms with designers, cutters, fitters, hand-stitchers, dressmakers. Out in front are the exhibition organisers, models, financiers and sales staff. Not many career opportunities here. The very talented and the very lucky make fortunes early, but the couture houses employ few staff, preferring to use freelance or part-time workers and make their money by selling designs to the manufacturers.

Ready-to-wear

At one level are the up-market ready-to-wear clothes made individually for a customer who buys the cloth and wants a personal fit. The other 95 per cent of clothes are mass-produced; the most recent fashion trends are reproduced to careful costings and knowledge of the buying market. These garments are sold in their thousands; in some cases in their millions. They are cut on machines and made up by hand. This is the area of major employment in the industry, with designers, dressmakers, cutters, fitters and support staff making and selling before today's fashion is overtaken by tomorrow's.

Entrepreneurs

These are young art and design graduates, unwilling to be sucked into mass-production, who try it alone. With little capital, working from home, sometimes alone, sometimes in pairs or small groups, they make new styles of clothes usually for the young. Occasionally they end up in their own boutiques, or make a breakthrough with a large order from one store, or, heavily in debt, give up.

Sales

By far the biggest employment area: department stores such as Harrods and the John Lewis Partnership, boutiques, chains such as Dunns,

Benetton, Next, and the dozens of independent or group-owned shops in every town and city. Here are jobs for managers, sales staff, tailors (for alterations), cashiers, cleaners, drivers. And the list of products is equally substantial: men's and women's clothes, sportswear, shoes, gloves, lingerie, knitwear, hats, and so on.

Prospects

In recent years the fashion industry has been hard hit by competition from mass-produced clothing imported from Italy, Eastern Europe and the Far East, which sells more cheaply than UK-produced products. However, prospects are improving: over 300 new companies are formed each year, although 200 of them will probably fail within five years. The best career prospects are, however, not within the ranks of the hundreds of designers churned out each year by the colleges, but in production and clothing technology, where the demand for young graduates and qualified supporting staff is real and unsatisfied.

Training

Each year about 1,500 aspiring young people emerge from fashion design courses. There are probably fewer than 200 vacancies, which is why so many designers try it on their own, and hundreds give up and go into other work. There are over 60 fashion design courses in art colleges, polytechnics and universities. To get a place, applicants need two or three good A-levels or three or four H-grades plus three or four GCSEs or equivalents, plus a portfolio of work to show at an interview. Good drawing ability and talent in art generally is looked for. But, taking the over-production of young design graduates, better advice might be to take a course that combines fashion with technological and management skills. There are such courses, and for every technology or business-trained graduate there are eight to ten vacancies. For design courses, therefore, students should choose carefully. If the syllabus includes substantial periods studying technology, production methods and business studies, and if the course has periods of work experience in industry, then it is likely to lead to practical jobs in an area of demand, not one of over supply.

In sales, the training and skills are similar for any other sales job. For example, Marks & Spencer sells a quarter of all garments bought in the UK. Careers are therefore more closely related to retail trade (shop sales) than fashion. Entry to these jobs can be at 16 or older, with fairly basic educational qualifications. The large stores look for young people with GCSE or O-grade passes, particularly in English language and business studies, but personality and keenness can overcome lack of paper qualifications. And the high-street shops and stores, with a fairly high turnover of staff, are constantly on the lookout for new sales staff. Similarly, office personnel, cleaners, drivers, packers and security staff come from very varied backgrounds, using their training and experience in other kinds of work.

The third area for jobs is production. At the top level are managers, probably with a degree or HND in clothing technology. Supporting them are production workers: they can train on the job, and also attend a college of further education on a day- or block-release basis to take courses leading to City and Guilds certificate awards, or courses that lead to professional qualifications such as the Clothing and Footwear Institute examinations. Candidates should have two or three GCSEs at grades A to C or O-grades for BTEC National Diploma courses and two or three GCSEs at lower grades for City and Guilds courses.

The *Directory of Further Education* lists all the courses and the colleges that provide advanced (degree and HND) and other courses in fashion, textile design and production.

Information

Clothing and Allied Products Industry Training Board, 80 Richardshaw Lane, Pudsey, Leeds LS28 6BN

Clothing and Footwear Institute, 71 Brushfield Street, London E1 6AA

The Design Council, 28 Haymarket, London SW1Y 4SU, and the Scottish Design Council, 72 Vincent Street, Glasgow G2 5TN

Careers in Fashion, Kogan Page
Design Courses in Britain, Design Council
Directory of Further Education, Hobsons
Art and Design, Degree Course Guide, Hobsons

Film production

Film-making is one of the most difficult industries in which to make a career – it is small, crowded with talented people, needs money and has a high-risk, low success rate profile – but it is not impossible for the very ambitious. The industry is made up of:

- feature film-makers: these are the large companies, such as MGM, and a larger number of small independents
- television programme-makers: these are companies such as Euston Films and others who make feature films for television, and others who concentrate on video recordings, advertising films, documentaries and educational programmes
- distribution and exhibition: this category includes cinemas and their management, booking films, distributing them, hiring, editing and processing.

There is no formal system of entry or training. People come into film-making from all directions, such as **acting**, the **theatre, television, advertising,** writing, **entertainment** and production fields. Another way is to train.

Training

There are courses at the National Film and Television School, the London International Film School, the Polytechnic of Central London and some colleges. To be accepted, the course has to be recognised by the Association of Cinematograph, Television and Allied Technicians (ACTT). An increasing number of entrants to film-making come from these schools. To get in to a degree course, the minimum is two A-levels (three or four H-grades) or better, plus two or three GCSEs or equivalents. Any subject is suitable, although English, modern languages and drama are highly rated. The training schools tend to look down on theatre studies at A-level, but that is a pose and A-levels, H-grades, GCSEs or O-grades are an indication of a student's keen interest. A small minority of people make it to the level of director or producer by their early thirties. There is a large pool of experienced film-makers who are under-employed or unemployed, so young people have to serve their time in junior work.

Production staff

There are more openings in production work. This category includes such jobs as film camera and sound staff within camera crews; film editors who work in the cutting-rooms, editing material shot earlier in the studio and on location; and assistant film editors who do the practical jobs in the cutting-room under the editor's direction. The sound recordists and technicians are concerned with dubbing, mixing, sound-transfer and editing. They may record on tape, on location, or make and record special effects in the studio. They have their assistants who have to know about equipment, such as microphones, projectors, sound-recording and playback.

Training

To prepare for these technical jobs, there are various courses at college and polytechnics, either as part of art and design degrees or HND courses at a postgraduate level. (The list of books below gives colleges offering these courses.)

It is very difficult to get into film work with the BBC or independent television. The BBC has a film training scheme and reckons there are 500 applicants for every place. There are no specific GCSE requirements, but graduate status and certainly 'a lively interest in film-making techniques' (the BBC's words) are needed. Special knowledge of the cinema, music, sound recording techniques, current affairs and films is highly regarded, and that is *before* any training. Independent television companies look for similarly well-motivated and trained people. For camera and studio work a diploma from a film school or experience in some similar type of work is a substantial advantage. A-levels in physics, maths, theatre studies and music are definite advantages, but the most indefinable quality is a flair for sound and vision, and that is difficult to demonstrate unless you have been involved in film-making or sound recording. This is why a pre-entry course at a polytechnic, college or film school is so valuable.

Information

BBC Appointments, Broadcasting House, Portland Place, London W1A 1AA

Independent Television Companies Association, 56 Mortimer Street, London W1N 8AN

British Film Institute, 21 Stephen Street, London W1P 1PL

Association of Independent Producers, 17 Great Pulteney Street, London W1R 3DG

Music and Drama, Degree Course Guide, Hobsons
Directory of Further Education, Hobsons, lists degree and diploma courses and the colleges that offer them
Film and Television Training, British Film Institute

Finance

Finance has many categories. Among those listed in this book are **banking, accountancy, building societies, insurance, actuaries,** and **stockbroking**, although any job in which money changes hands could be said to be financial. The City of London is the centre of the country's banking system. It is highly specialised, and, under the scrutiny of the government, is changing its ways of doing business. Traditionally, the City stockbroking, investment and trust services have been staffed by graduates of Oxford and Cambridge Universities assisted by people who have risen to the top through banking, accountancy, **law, insurance** and similar fields. All these institutions have their own distinctive modes of entry and career patterns. But apart from bankers there are specialists who work on a freelance basis, or are part of the Stock Exchange, or contribute skills in computing, surveying, law, international trade and management. These people are recruited from outside the world of finance and they may move on to take up new opportunities in manufacturing companies, finance houses and banks.

There are other specialists too. Some are experts in investment services who study stocks and shares and advise private individuals, companies and pension fund administrators on when to buy and sell shares. They operate close to the Stock Exchange in London and other main cities. Some are employed by stockbrokers, unit trusts, merchant banks or investment trusts. This work requires experience and training in finance, generally through a degree course in accountancy, business studies, law or a similar subject, and then through experience in a bank or other kind of financial institution.

Training

To make a start generally requires a degree. Depending on the subject and the university, three good A-levels or four or five H-grades, plus supporting GCSEs or equivalents, are needed for entry. (See the Degree Course Guides, details below, for courses in these areas.) Any degree course could be useful. However, degrees in business studies or accountancy are particularly appropriate, and there are two specialist course in finance and banking at University College of North Wales (Bangor) and at Loughborough University. What is needed after graduation is a period of experience and training, and therefore entry to the specialised world of financial services often comes in the mid-twenties and later, although finance companies in the City recruit graduates straight from university.

Supporting the financial services specialists are **computer** staff, **cashiers, clerks, secretaries** and all the other essential personnel of a busy office.

Information
The International Stock Exchange, London EC2N 1HP
The Society of Investment Analysts, 211–212 High Street, Bromley, Kent BR1 1NY
Unit Trust Association, Park House, 16 Finsbury Circus, London EC2M 7JP
Finance Houses Association, 18 Upper Grosvenor Street, London W1X 9PB

Business, Management and Accountancy and *Law*, Degree Course Guides, Hobsons
The Facts about Finance, Hobsons
Working in the Money Business, COIC

Fire service

The fire service is one of the three main emergency services (the others are the **ambulance** service and the **police**). Fire prevention and control are the responsibility of local fire authorities, with oversight by the Home Office in London and the Scottish Home and Health Department in Edinburgh. Fire officers not only fight fires but also give advice on how to prevent them. They are also called to road, rail and aircraft accidents and help when there are floods, explosions, chemical discharges, and occasional household crises. As well as the local fire authorities, the airports, HM Forces and some large companies have their own fire services.

Not every hour of the day is spent on a ladder squirting water at roaring flames. Much of a fire officer's day is spent at the fire station, cleaning and maintaining equipment and taking part in training exercises as well as carrying out statutory inspection duties. Periods of relative inactivity can be followed by sudden, dangerous and dirty emergencies.

Training

At present, the fire services are well staffed. Competition for any vacancies is fairly fierce. Once into the service, promotion depends on passing interview boards. Training is given at the station and at the Fire Service College, Gloucestershire, and the Scottish Fire Service Training School, East Lothian. For senior staff there are other courses at the Fire Service College.

Applicants must be between 18 and 35, physically fit, willing to accept discipline under pressure, and of course be unafraid of fire or heights. In England, Wales and Scotland the entry requirements are specified as a good general education, but three GCSE passes at grades A to C in England and Wales or O-grades or Standard Grades in Scotland including English language, maths or science would give a substantial advantage. There is also a compulsory entrance test. Once in, training is organised over a two-year probationary period which starts with a residential course lasting 15 weeks. After that, training is constant. It should be pointed out that more fire officers enter the service in their 20s so the fire service is not usually a job that is immediately available to school or college leavers.

Information

Home Office, Fire Department, Queen Anne's Gate, London SW1H 9AT

Scottish Home and Health Department, Fire Service Division, Room 274, St Andrew's House, Edinburgh EH1 3DE

Fishing

The fishing industry has been severely damaged in recent years. The heavy off-shore fishing by large fleets from the USSR, Japan and other nations has reduced fish stocks in all waters but particularly in the once-fruitful North Sea and the Arctic; fish are on the point of becoming an endangered species. Large-scale fishing has taken a knock, but nevertheless Britain still has a fishing industry.

Deep-sea fishing is both dangerous and very uncomfortable. Each year there is the tragedy of at least one trawler lost at sea. And prospects are not good – for every potential recruit there are a dozen experienced men looking for a job. Yet, despite all these hazards, fishing still attracts young people. Most recruits already live in fishing towns and know something of the dangers as well as the attractions. Fishermen themselves seldom admit to any love for the sea: they stress its unpredictability and cruelty, but on the other hand they keep going back.

Fishing is a very localised industry. Although there are no formal entry requirements, entry is a great deal easier for people living in Fleetwood, Grimsby, Tyneside, Cornwall and the east coast of Scotland than in Birmingham, Slough or London. Family connections also play a big part in recruitment. Anyone thinking of fishing in terms of a career should consult the local careers office in a fishing town and listen carefully to the advice. Otherwise, concentrate on fishing for recreation.

Training

For students who want to train to be deck officers on fishing vessels, there are Department of Transport certificate of competency qualifications to aim for; courses leading to these awards are available at some colleges. There is a degree course in fisheries science at Polytechnic South-West (Plymouth) and in fishery studies at Humberside Polytechnic, as well as degree courses in marine or maritime studies at Liverpool and Sunderland Polytechnics and Polytechnic South-West, and elsewhere. For these, two A-levels or three H-grades are looked for with grades of around C or D, plus three or four GCSEs or equivalents. No particular subjects are specified at A-level (H-grade), but clearly those with a science basis, such as physics, chemistry or physical sciences, are most acceptable. Certainly good GCSE passes in maths, a science subject and English language are necessary.

Fish-farming

Breeding and rearing fish for sport or food is something quite different. There are about 400 fish-farms, mostly small businesses, run by people who have come from a background of farming, river-fishing, sea-fishing or food management. What they do is to select a certain type of fish, such as trout, and breed them to stock fishing-pools, lakes and rivers, or for sale to restaurants and hotels.

Information
Ministry of Agriculture, Fisheries and Food, Whitehall Place, London
SW1A 2HH

Directory of Further Education, Hobsons

Floristry

Most florists work in florists' shops, although a small minority are
employed in hotels and large stores. A florist's work involves selecting
flowers, assembling and making-up bouquets, wreaths and displays. As
well as doing this skilled, behind-the-scenes work, the florist is likely to
sell the displays to customers. There is therefore a 'back-room' job in a
cool room, and the counter job of selling and wrapping, as well as
running the business. Florists are likely to buy their flowers by visiting
wholesale markets and market-gardens, and so commercial expertise is
as important as artistic skill. Some florists take on contract work where
they tend the flower displays in office blocks, flats and hotels. Others,
employed in large hotels, look after the table displays and flower
arrangements in the public rooms and bedrooms. A number of people
who set up a high-street shop on their own account learn their skills in
hotels or by working in stores or other florists' shops. There are
estimated to be 5,000 of these shops in the UK, so job opportunities for
trained staff are plentiful – it is estimated that there are 60,000 florists in
employment.

Training
No particular training or entrance requirements are specified, apart from
learning the job by working in a florist's shop. There are two private
floristry schools providing full-time courses and several offering part-
time ones. Full-time courses are provided at the Welsh College of
Horticulture, the Isle of Ely College, Wisbech, and at St Albans College,
Hertfordshire. Otherwise there are part-time courses on a day-release
basis at about 40 colleges of further education. The Society of Floristry
(address below) has an up-to-date list of the colleges. Most courses lead
to a City and Guilds certificate in floristry, Parts 1, 2 and 3, and then to
the Intermediate and Diploma examinations of the Society of Floristry.
The Welsh College offers its own National Diploma in Floristry with
Flower Production, and an interior landscaping course. Useful school

subjects are English language, business studies, maths, and of course the biological subjects such as botany, biology and social biology. Arts and crafts are useful skills, and science subjects in general are very welcome.

Information
The Society of Floristry, The Old Schoolhouse, Payford, Redmarley, Gloucestershire GL19 3HY. The Society publishes a leaflet, *A Career in Floristry,* and has a list of colleges offering courses in floristry
The British Retail Florists Association, The Bothy, Sunningdale Park, Silwood Road, Sunningdale, Berkshire SL5 0QF. The BRFA runs Youth Training schemes at several centres: for details write to BRFA, Youth Training Scheme, 113 St Pancras, Chichester, West Sussex PO19 4LH

Working in Agriculture and Horticulture, COIC

Food science and technology

Food science deals with the nature and behaviour of food materials of all kinds. The basis of the science lies in chemistry and biology, and its applications are within the food processing industries. Food technology is the application of scientific knowledge to the treatment of food materials in order to make them acceptable to consumers. Food engineering, which is also an applied science, is concerned with the design, construction and use of food-processing equipment. In other words, if the food scientists 'create' a new cheese, the technologists process and make it with machines invented or adapted by the engineers. A fourth group of people contribute to the cheese inventing/making/eating process: the marketing and sales professionals who must persuade a fifth group, the consumers, that the new cheese is tasty, healthy, safe and inexpensive. In any large food manufacturing company or combine people from the first four groups will be found working in the research, quality assurance, product development, manufacture and marketing departments.

Prospects
Prospects are excellent: the fast growth of convenience foods, frozen foods, pre-packaged foods and health foods has led to a substantial demand for scientists, technologists and engineers. The job opportunities are mainly with the big food manufacturing groups, the household

names of the supermarket shelves. They search the universities, polytechnics and colleges for potential employees who can work in any one of these areas. Graduates move into research, analysis, production, packaging, quality control or sales.

Training

To make a start, the first step is to obtain a degree or HND. There are specialist degree courses in food science and technology at the Universities of Belfast, King's College and Queen Mary College, London, Ulster, Leeds, Reading, Surrey and Nottingham and at several polytechnics and colleges. There are also degree courses in food chemistry, food distribution, food policy, food manufacture and marketing. The admission requirements are a minimum of two A-levels or three H-grades plus three to four other subjects at GCSE or O-grade. In fact three A-levels with grades B or C at universities and D and E levels for polytechnics and colleges are generally looked for. Special subject requirements are usually chemistry and one or two other science subjects (biology and mathematics are the most useful) at A-level. Other useful A-levels or H-grade subjects are social biology, human biology, physics, botany and zoology. Home economics at A-level may be considered provided that it has been studied with science subjects.

An alternative way into food science is to take a first degree in a science subject and follow it up with a postgraduate course for an MSc or another higher award.

A third method of entry for those without good A-levels is to take an HND course: the minimum requirement is one A-level, although two subjects or three H-grades is a better bet. Again, the same science-based subjects are necessary. For a full list of the colleges that offer degree, BTEC, SCOTVEC and City and Guilds courses (the latter in food processing), consult the *Directory of Further Education*.

Information

The Institute of Food Science and Technology, 5 Cambridge Court, 210 Shepherd's Bush Road, London WC2B 5JJ

Agricultural Sciences, Degree Course Guide, Hobsons
Working in Food Processing, COIC

Forestry

Forestry is the management and care of woodlands. The management objectives include the production of timber, the conservation of a natural heritage, recreational activities, and scientific research. Most jobs are with the Forestry Commission, which owns about 50 per cent of British forests, or with forest management companies. What foresters do is to plan, look after, harvest and market materials produced in the forest, of which wood is only one product. Among the skills they must train for are planting, thinning, felling, conservation and marketing. The managers have to be able to organise both themselves and their business, and to do so miles from towns, often in very remote parts of the country. Another option is a career in 'arboriculture', a grand name for people who grow trees for parks, gardens, exhibition sites, town streets and other locations. With the increase in garden centres, this has become a business in its own right.

There are only limited jobs in forestry. The Forestry Commission, which is part of the Civil Service, takes on a handful of people each year. The input to private companies and garden centres is limited. Opportunities abroad get fewer. Promotion is slow and steady and depends mostly on retirements. Prospects are therefore not very exciting. On the other hand, young people who have sampled working in forest conditions and enjoyed it should not be put off, for they are likely to find a lifetime's interest in this work.

There are three levels or grades of forester: a graduate who hopes to become a manager, the technical support staff, and forestry workers.

Managers

For these posts there are degree courses in forestry at Aberdeen and Edinburgh universities, and at University College of North Wales (Bangor): two or three A-levels or three to four H-grades are required with grades around B or C. The A-levels/H-grades should include chemistry or physics. Competition is keen: Bangor has about 200 applicants for 36 places. Otherwise, a degree course in agriculture (some have specialist options in forestry) could be considered. Following the degree course, graduates can hope to become a forester or a forest officer.

Technical support staff

A second route into a career in forestry is through college courses. These are available at Cumbria College of Agriculture and Forestry and at the Scottish School of Forestry, which is part of Inverness College of Further and Higher Education. At present there are three-year sandwich courses which must be preceded by two years of practical experience. These courses are also much sought after. Students coming out of all these courses would enter the support staff of a district forest manager and hope to be promoted eventually to a senior position.

Training

Suitable school subjects for these careers are chemistry, physics and maths. The degree course at Aberdeen requires A-levels in chemistry or physics, or physical science, or mathematics. GCSEs or O-grades must include English language, mathematics, and a science subject for all courses either at university or college. Bangor makes a requirement for A-level or H-grade biology, or botany or zoology. Other useful A-levels are geography, geology and economics. The special course at Edinburgh University provides a broad education in ecology, with a fourth-year honours option in forestry; the same subjects are very useful, with chemistry or physical science as essential A-levels, and the other two A-levels or H-grades required to be in science or maths subjects.

Whether they have been trained at university or college, foresters need to take a professional qualification. These are in the form of examinations set by the Institute of Chartered Foresters. Normally a degree or diploma from university or college gives exemption from Part 1 of the examination, but everyone has to take Part 2 after a minimum of two years' employment. An alternative professional qualification is the National Diploma in Forestry, awarded by the Forestry Central Examination Board.

Forestry workers

For a forestry worker, no special academic qualifications are required and most staff are recruited locally.

Information

The Forestry Commission, 231 Corstorphine Road, Edinburgh EH12 7AT

Scottish School of Forestry, Inverness College of Further and Higher Education, 3 Longman Road, Inverness IV1 1SA

Cumbria College of Agriculture and Forestry, Newton Rigg, Penrith, Cumbria CA11 0AH

Institute of Chartered Foresters, 22 Walker Street, Edinburgh EH3 7HR

Working in Farms and Forests, COIC

Funeral director

This may not be a career that attracts young people, unless members of their family are already involved in it. Even so, there are careers in funeral work.

Funeral directors prepare bodies for burial or cremation. At the request of the family, the funeral director normally makes all arrangements for the funeral, including the time and place, notices of death in newspapers, the payment of fees and the arrangement of flowers. Directors may also arrange or carry out embalming as well as laying the body to rest in a funeral parlour or church prior to the funeral. Transport of the coffin and mourners to and from the crematorium or cemetery is also arranged. Tact, sympathy and understanding are essential personal qualities.

Training

Beginners can study for the diploma in funeral directing by registering with the National Association of Funeral Directors (NAFD) and can take up student membership of the British Institute of Funeral Directors (BIFD). Prior to the diploma course, students must take a foundation module and have at least a year's experience.

Information

British Institute of Funeral Directors, 11 Regent Street, Kingswood, Bristol BS15 2JX

Furniture

Since 90 per cent of the timber used in the UK is imported, the furniture industry is largely concerned with manufacturing and selling. The starting-point is design, technology or craftsmanship, and there are specialist courses both in design and furniture manufacture. As an industry, it is strongly craft-based, with substantial family interests going back many, many years. Much of today's furniture is made in stages, in component units, using established and new technologies, and manufacturing is generally planned in this way. All the same, there is still a place for the traditional craft skills of machine woodworker, cabinet-maker, polisher and upholsterer.

The industry extends from small restoration workshops employing two or three people, where practical skills are highly respected, to large-scale production, where there is a high and regular demand for designers and all types of technically capable people.

Training

The traditional method of taking up a career in the industry is to become an apprentice to a cabinct-maker or to one of the other furniture craftsmen. Generally no particular academic qualifications are needed, but aptitude at school at woodwork, metalwork or craft, design and technology (CDT) would be looked for. Some employers ask for GCSE passes in craft subjects, English language and maths. Courses at a college of further education on a part-time basis lead to recognised City and Guilds qualifications such as the certificate in furniture crafts. Alternatively, there are BTEC National Diplomas and HNDs for furniture technicians in design, production and restoration. Three GCSEs or equivalent are needed for entry to a BTEC National Diploma course.

Production technologists or managers enter the furniture trade from universities, polytechnics or colleges, plus special training and experience in a company. Designers enter from a design course taken at a polytechnic or college with options or opportunities in furniture.

Information

British Furniture Manufacturers' Federated Associations, 30 Harcourt Street, London W1H 2AA
Furniture Industry Research Association, Maxwell Road, Stevenage, Hertfordshire SG1 2EW
Institute of Wood Science, Premier House, 150 Southampton Row, London WC1B 5AL
London College of Furniture, 41–71 Commercial Road, London E1 1LA

Gardens

Some people find the idea of working in gardens so tempting that they are prepared to do so for low wages. The outdoor life, the yearly round of planting, tending, pruning, flowering, and so on, and the pleasure of working with plants are for them much more satisfying than earning a lot more money in an office or factory. But there is money to be made in gardening. Garden centres are doing very good business indeed, as people spend their money on improving and decorating their homes. Gardening therefore has good business possibilities as well as providing a pleasant way of life for people who like to observe the passing of the seasons while they are digging and planting.

There are various job possibilities in garden work.

Garden contractors

They design and build private gardens. For instance, a purchaser of a newly built house may pay a contractor to plant the whole garden. In summer these contractors often take on jobbing gardeners. Other contractors are specialists such as tree-fellers or tree-pruners, and are engaged by local authorities or private owners to carry out tree surgery or mow lawns.

Market gardeners

Market gardeners grow vegetables, salad crops, tomatoes and flowers and sell them either direct to the public, to shops or to wholesalers. This is a major business which is part of **horticulture.** The work can include planting, harvesting, thinning-out, weeding and transporting to market.

Staff in garden centres

They sell plants to the general public. They also advise about plants, flowers and vegetables, and answer customers' enquiries and undertake contract work, if asked. They tend to be busiest at weekends.

Amenity gardeners

Amenity gardeners work in parks, town gardens, picnic areas and country parks. The job includes planting and tending trees, bushes and flowers, and dealing with customers or visitors. The work often involves the maintenance of ornamental gardens and greenhouses. Another group of gardeners, called greenkeepers or groundsmen, look after bowling-greens, golf courses and tennis courts.

Self-employed gardeners

Perhaps one, two or three people combine to offer a service to private householders. They cut lawns, weed, plant and generally look after a garden on a casual or a contract basis. Sometimes they also agree to look after a garden while a family is away from home.

Training

Prospects are quite good, but more so if entrants take qualifications in horticulture. The major qualification is the Royal Horticultural Society's Master of Horticulture award (described in the **horticulture** entry). There are courses that lead to City and Guilds awards at certificate and advanced certificate level in horticulture. School subjects that are useful are rural studies, chemistry, biology and botany: these can be taken at GCSE or O-grade level, and some, such as biology, botany and social biology, at A-level.

Information

Agricultural Training Board, Summit House, Glebe Way, West Wickham, Kent BR4 0RF

Royal Botanic Gardens, Kew, Richmond, Surrey TW9 3AB

Women's Farm and Garden Association, 175 Gloucester Road, Cirencester, Gloucestershire GL7 2DP

Working in Agriculture and Horticulture, COIC

Gas industry

British Gas is a high-technology business and today uses some 50 mainframe computers and thousands of terminals in a highly sophisticated operation; it has 16.5 million customers. It also employs some 2,000 scientists and engineers on a £70 million a year research and development programme, supporting every part of the industry's operations.

With a turnover of over £8,000 million and an operating profit of well over £1,000 million, British Gas is one of the ten largest businesses in Britain. The largest single supplier of fuel to homes and factories, it is a nationwide marketing and distribution organisation, employing specialists in every field and offering training to graduates from all faculties. It trains service engineers to City and Guilds standards, candidates with GCSEs in maths and physics being the first choice.

British Gas is divided into 12 regions covering the whole of Britain. Each region, and British Gas headquarters in London, recruit for the 90,000-strong industry. Many of the available posts are in the sales and customer service areas. These are involved in assisting in some 14 million service calls to customers every year, or in supporting the marketing drive, including the work of some 800 showrooms.

Training

There are fuel engineering or fuel technology degree courses at Leeds and Sheffield Universities. Otherwise a degree in any branch of engineering, but particularly chemical engineering or in energy studies, would be suitable. For these courses chemistry at A-level is generally specified. Other recommended subjects are A-levels in physics or physical science and maths.

To support the engineers are technicians and other staff. Technicians can train via a full-time BTEC or SCOTVEC course in fuel technology which can be at National Certificate (one year full time or two years part time) or National Diploma (two years full time) levels. Good GCSE or O-grade passes are needed in four subjects for the diploma and in one or two subjects for the certificate, including if possible engineering or science subjects.

For other work in gasworks, foundries, oil-rigs and at storage terminals, the gas industry looks for all kinds of men and women – engineers, technicians, office workers and support staff. Other jobs are at British Gas showrooms, and in the repair and maintenance services. Again, the industry looks for a team of engineers, technicians and supporting staff. To prepare for this work, there are City and Guilds awards in plant operation, gas services, boiler maintenance and so on.

British Gas also has commercial training schemes covering the clerical and administrative skills the business uses. It also runs a scholarship scheme whereby financial assistance is given to undergraduates reading certain subjects.

Information

British Gas PLC, Rivermill House, 152 Grosvenor Road, London SW1V 3JL

Institute of Energy, 18 Devonshire Street, London W1N 2AU

Directory of Further Education, Hobsons, lists colleges that provide BSc courses in energy or gas engineering; the diploma in fuel technology; diploma in energy management; BTEC National Certificate in fuel technology and BTEC National Certificate and National Diploma in gas services. Other courses for City and Guilds certificates in gas installation, gas equipment fault diagnosis, boiler operations and service engineering are also listed in the *Directory*.

Geography

Geography is a very popular course at A-level and H-grade, and as a degree subject. However, it does not lead immediately into many jobs. Perhaps **teaching and lecturing** are the only areas in which graduates can immediately start to use their knowledge. Otherwise, additional study, training and experience are needed. Geography is very close to some science degrees. For example, a geography degree course is likely to include such topics as cartography, geomorphology, climatology, environmental studies. landscape studies, hydrology and regional geography. From this list it is clear that geography can lead to **surveying, cartography, conservation,** shipping, **water** supply, and environmental work. On the other hand, many more geography graduates make their careers in national and **local government, business, banking, insurance** and teaching.

There is virtually no degree course for which geography at A-level is an essential entry requirement apart from geography itself. On the other hand, it is highly valued as a career preparation. So, although prospects as a geographer are very limited, the subject opens doors to many other careers as long as it is topped up with additional training.

Training

There are degree courses at most universities (see the Degree Course Guide for the details of courses, careers and entry requirements). As a subject it can be taken alongside others in combined studies, combined sciences, humanities and social studies courses. For most degree courses geography at A-level is a requirement, and certainly one of the GCSEs or equivalents must be mathematics. Grades for entry vary widely from three As for Oxford and Cambridge Universities to a combination of D and E grades for degree courses at polytechnics and colleges of higher education.

Information
Working in Geography, COIC
Geography, Degree Course Guide, Hobsons
Directory of Further Education, Hobsons

Geology

Geology is the study of the composition, structure and history of the Earth. Among topics included in degree courses are the study of fossils, crystals, minerals, rocks, sediments, the physical and chemical properties of the Earth, and the formation of geological materials. As a degree course it is offered in many universities and polytechnics. (See the Degree Course Guide and the *Directory of Further Education* for details of the courses, their content, entry requirements and career possibilities.) As a degree course geology can be taken with other subjects in combined sciences, combined studies and environmental sciences courses. In order to obtain a place on a degree course, three good A-levels or four or five H-grades are required, and for some of them physics or chemistry may be necessary. Some universities demand mathematics at A-level. All these subjects, plus physics, geography, environmental studies or science, are very useful at A-level or H-grade and certainly at GCSE or its equivalents.

Geology can be studied at GCSE and A-level – if the school can find staff and enough students to make the subject viable – but career openings at 16-plus and 18-plus are virtually nil. It is not much better for graduates. At present, the UK turns out about 1,000 graduate geologists annually. About a quarter remain at university or polytechnic to study for postgraduate qualifications. The rest tend to move out into all kinds of careers from **business** to national and **local government.** Even the PhDs and MScs find it difficult to obtain employment as geologists, for there are many more graduates than jobs. Only one in four geologists find degree-related posts either in the UK or overseas. It has to be said that the rate of unemployment, or temporary unemployment for geology graduates is one of the highest for any subject. The lucky ones get into oil companies, oil-servicing or oil-seeking companies, mining and quarrying concerns and British Coal. The other main openings are in **civil engineer**ing and the public services (waste disposal, **museums**, quarrying and **water supply**) of local authorities.

Information
Institution of Geologists, Burlington House, Piccadilly, London W1V 9AG

Careers for Geologists, Institution of Geologists
Geological and Environmental Sciences, Hobsons
Directory of Further Education, Hobsons

Glass industry

Glass-making is a very old industry. Although other materials, such as plastics, have reduced its use, glass is still an important manufacturing enterprise. The traditional skills are now augmented by new technology and advances in science. All the same, entry to the industry is still wedded to tradition. Sons learn skills from their fathers, and glass-making businesses have been handed down through the generations.

The industry, however, is changing fast. Glass-making, like other old industries, is being taken over by large manufacturing groups. Managers approach the making and selling of glass using much the same management techniques as if they were in engineering, baking or packaging. Managers, therefore, are recruited from business studies and management backgrounds where degree qualifications are important. However, if they can ally business knowledge to an understanding of glass technology, their usefulness is increased. To acquire this kind of knowledge means taking a specialist course.

Training
For foundry workers, technicians and shop-floor managers, some of the relevant courses at colleges of further education lead to City and Guilds awards. One is a certificate in glass manufacture and processing; another is in scientific glassworking (see below for the colleges which offer them). The entry requirements for City and Guilds courses and also for college certificates (as in glass-blowing, kiln firing, glass decoration and glass-making) are 'a good education', which means that two or three

GCSE passes are looked for, but students who have taken physics, chemistry, engineering science and other technical subjects have a head start, although they may not have many GCSEs or their equivalents.

At the next level (16-plus entry for a one- or two-year full- or part-time course) there is a BTEC National Certificate in Glass Technology (at Dudley College of Technology) and part-time courses leading to the Certificate in Glass-blowing awarded by the British Society for Scientific Glass-blowers. Again, there are no particular entry or subject requirements, but chemistry, physics, technical studies and CDT would be very useful preliminaries if taken to GCSE standard.

For a degree course, there is a BSc course in glass science and engineering at Sheffield University; alternatively students can take a BSc in materials science or in ceramics and minerals technology. For these courses two to three A-levels (three to four H-grades) in maths or science subjects are required.

Information
Directory of Further Education, Hobsons
Working in Glass, COIC

Government service

The Civil Service is now smaller than at any time since 1945, but it remains one of the UK's largest employers of graduates. In 1990 over 4,000 graduates entered the Service. For details of the grades and entry qualifications, see the entry on the **Civil Service**. This entry deals with opportunities for posts not at the administrative level.

The Civil Service has always been a career for those who want to serve the public. The concept of public service lies at the heart of government and it is a potent recruitment factor. Another factor that Whitehall stresses is the quiet revolution that has overtaken the Civil Service. The rigid demarcation lines between grades has gone: people can move up the hierarchy and into senior posts without necessarily having a classics degree from Oxford or Cambridge. Better value for money for the taxpayer has become a major consideration, and financial authority is being delegated from central finance units to service providers. That is why the Civil Service now says that its managers actually manage. On the other hand, there is not the commercial pressure one gets in a company. And job security and a pension scheme, which Civil Servants enjoy, are telling factors in recruitment.

Apart from the administrative, executive and clerical staff, there is a place for almost every type of specialist graduate, including scientists, engineers, actuaries, accountants, valuers, economists and lawyers.

Professional and technology group

People from over a hundred different disciplines are employed in the professional and technology group, ranging from **engineers** to **pharmacists**. Whatever their discipline all new entrants are given the training and experience which are valuable to them and valuable to the Civil Service. Staff are encouraged to keep up to date professionally, to become members of their appropriate professional institutions and to develop managerial and administrative skills.

The Civil Service employs about 5,000 professional engineers of one sort or another. They work on research and development, construction and installation, or on procurement and production, either in industry or in government establishments. They ensure that the Tower of London is attractively illuminated as well as overseeing multi-million pound defence contracts. They advise on noise and vibration problems in hospitals, and plan major road networks. Young graduates do not have to wait before getting involved: they are given a high level of responsibility at an early stage.

There are opportunities for anyone with a degree or equivalent in electrical, electronic, mechanical, civil and allied engineering disciplines as well as mathematics, physics, computer studies, etc. There are also career opportunities available for those with HND or pass degree qualifications.

The Civil Service is also the UK's largest employer of **surveyors** and **architects**, and there are wide-ranging opportunities for graduates. They are involved in designing, building or maintaining the thousands of government buildings, or else they are concerned with the valuation, acquisition and management of land and property, or advising ministers and setting national standards.

Scientific Civil Service

There are over 16,000 people in the Scientific Civil Service, and large numbers of graduates are recruited every year. Many posts demand the intellectual qualities of the good honours degree scientist or the person with postgraduate qualifications, whereas there are others that will be more appropriate for the practical man or woman with a sound basic knowledge of scientific or engineering principles.

There are over a hundred research and development establishments, many of them with international reputations. The scope and variety of work is unique – from meteorological research to computer-aided design and manufacture, from biotechnology to electronics. Graduates can continue the learning process using up-to-date equipment and gain experience across the scientific spectrum by working on problems of real scientific interest.

Other general graduate and specialist opportunities

Graduates can apply to be trained as **factory inspectors**, for the **prison service** or as **tax inspectors**. There are also opportunities for a wide variety of graduate specialists – **lawyers, librarians, statisticians, accountants, economists,** linguists, **museum curators,** and so on.

Information
Civil Service Commission, Alencon Link, Basingstoke, Hampshire
RG21 1JB

Hairdressing

Hairdressing is a good job for people with strong legs and feet. That might seem odd, but hairdressers are on their feet all day and the work can be very tiring. A skilful and well-trained hairdresser can usually choose where he or she works – in a shop in town, in a hotel, in a salon in a large city where prices are high and wages are good, or perhaps they will set up their own business. Doing things to people's hair – cutting, washing, styling, tinting – is only part of the job. Hairdressers also have to keep an appointments book, make out bills, maintain a simple bookkeeping system, replenish supplies and advertise. All these are jobs that a small business has to arrange, and therefore some understanding of business methods is very important.

The prospects are reasonable, although much depends on where the salon is. People's spending power is the key factor, so the West End of London is a better place than a town with high unemployment figures.

The best prospects are for the foot-loose – on cruise ships, in airports and abroad, particularly at holiday resorts.

Training
There are several ways in which a hairdresser can train. One is to take a three-year apprenticeship at 16-plus supplemented by attending day-release classes at a local college of further education. Some salons do their own teaching, which is another source of business. At college, the trainees learn the academic aspects of their job – hygiene, some chemistry, business methods, and some of the skills such as tinting, wig-making, and so on. These courses lead to one of several City and Guilds examinations: ladies' hairdressing, men's hairdressing, salon management, wig-making, beauty therapy, manicure, and advanced studies in hairdressing. No particular entry requirements are specified, but salons look for presentable people and if they also have good grades at GCSE or O-grade in home economics, fashion, beauty care, English language and other subjects, they stand a better chance of getting into a salon and making good use of the college course.

There are also college awards and BTEC courses: these tend to be in beauty therapy rather than hairdressing on its own. However, the professional bodies have their own standards. To achieve these, trainees study for certificates of the Royal Institute of Public Health and Hygiene, the Royal Society of Health, and the Incorporated Guild of Hairdressers, Wigmakers and Perfumers. These and other courses are listed in the *Directory of Further Education*.

Another way to become a hairdresser is to take a full-time course in hairdressing and beauty therapy at college and seek a job afterwards at 17 or 18. These courses also lead to City and Guilds exams. A third method is to take a six-month or twelve-month course at a private hairdressing salon. The subjects listed above are suitable. To add to these, science subjects at GCSE grades A to C, especially chemistry, social biology or human biology, are very useful indeed.

Information
Hairdressing Training Board, Silver House, 17 Silver Street, Doncaster DN1 1HL
Incorporated Guild of Hairdressers, 24 Woodbridge Road, Guildford, Surrey GU1 1DY. The Guild publishes leaflets on careers

Directory of Further Education, Hobsons
Working in Hairdressing and Beauty, COIC

Health service

The NHS is Britain's largest employing organisation, with over a million members of staff working in over a hundred distinct professional and occupational groups. Many thousands more in the private sector owe their jobs to supplying and servicing NHS needs.

Successive reorganisations in different areas of the NHS are introducing many changes in its structure and methods of working. New technologies, sharper emphasis on open management and greater dynamism in training policies are all contributing to produce a very challenging working environment in a new-style NHS.

There are great external pressures too. Changing patterns of disease (including alcoholism, drug abuse and AIDS), financial constraints, new philosophies of caring for patients in the community, and the debate on the proper balance of preventive medicine are just some of the forces causing major changes in traditional patterns of working.

Some of the professional and specialist jobs have separate entries in this book: doctor (under **medicine**), **dentist, nurse, midwife, optician, pharmacist, ambulance** driver, **chiropodist, physiotherapist**, **dietitian** and **radiographer**. This entry concentrates on health service administrators who back up the professional staff.

In England and Wales most health services are provided by the 201 District Health Authorities, which are grouped within 14 Regional Health Authority areas in England, and in Wales are accountable to the Welsh Office. In a separate system GPs and their staff (England and Wales) are independent contractors for community health care, organised into Family Practitioner Committee areas.

Both these networks rely on good management and administration. A district general manager, for example, will typically have an annual revenue budget of some £70 million and employ some 8,500 staff in 25 hospitals and 13 health centres. The network of management extends from the Regions, through the Districts to the individual units, where health-care professionals also perform vital management functions. Nurses and administrators are also vital in the Family Practitioner Committees, where work relating to the prescription of drugs is just one of the major activities. Hundreds of thousands of jobs thus require a wide mixture of skills in such areas as computer technology, engineering, finance, administration, personnel, manpower planning and training, catering, construction and maintenance, hospital supplies and sterile services. Substantial salaries are paid at the higher grades, though NHS salary levels more generally have been depressed by financial constraints. Increased emphasis on skill development and career progression now offers better opportunities than ever before, however, for the recognition of individuals with skill, experience and ability.

Training

The National Health Service Training Authority was set up in 1984 to provide, for the first time, a strategic national centre for the planning of training and manpower development policies across England and Wales. The NHSTA aims to attract an intake of new graduates to the NHS each year with equal emphasis on effective talent-scouting among in-service staff ready for greater responsibilities.

Qualifications for NHS professions and occupations are extremely complex, reflecting the variety of professional bodies involved and the possible geographical variations. The best reference book is *The Hospitals and Health Services Year Book,* available at public libraries. Practical advice may also be obtained from the personnel departments of District (or Regional) Health Authorities.

Information

The NHS Training Authority, St Bartholomews Court, 18 Christmas Street, Bristol BS1 5BT
The Institute of Health Service Management, 75 Portland Place, London W1N 4AN

Health visitor

Health visitors are part of the team of people concerned with the mental, physical and social health of people in their own homes and within the local community and are particularly concerned with the promotion of good health. Other members of the team include doctors, district nurses, midwives and school nurses. The health visitor's job entails visiting people in their own homes, for example babies, young children and their families, elderly and handicapped people. In addition, health visitors' work may take them to schools, day nurseries and playgroups, health clinics, surgeries and old people's homes. They assess the health care needs of people and where necessary deal with the situation themselves or call in specialist help. They teach and give advice to individuals, families, community groups and schools.

There are over 11,000 health visitors working throughout the UK. About 900 enter training each year, and the great majority obtain employment. All are employees of the NHS, working for District Health Authorities. The promotion ladder is into teaching in colleges and polytechnics, management of nursing or more general management in the NHS. (There are other routes for people who want to go direct into a management career in the NHS.) Until fairly recently, health visiting was almost entirely a woman's occupation, but now some men have taken up the career.

Training

Candidates must be qualified as Registered General Nurses (formerly called State Registered Nurses) and have successfully completed a recognised obstetric course, or obtained a midwifery qualification. Exceptionally there are one or two direct-entry degree courses that combine nursing and health visiting.

The basic academic entry qualification is five GCSEs or O-grades including English language or Welsh, or alternative educational accomplishments to the same level. Many candidates offer A-levels (H-grades) or degrees. Having secured entry, there are various training routes. One is by taking a full-time course over one year: this is the usual route taken by general nurses who have midwifery or obstetric nursing experience. Three colleges provide part-time courses lasting two years. Graduates with a nursing degree or a science degree and the professional pre-entry qualifications can take a modified course. For details of the specialist nursing degree courses that combine nursing studies with health visiting see the Degree Insights Series book, *Nursing*. School subjects useful for a health visitor are those that provide a broad education such as history, literature, a second language, mathematics, biological and social sciences. Literacy and numeracy are essential, and an understanding of information technology desirable.

Information

English National Board for Nursing, Midwifery and Health Visiting, PO Box 356, Sheffield S8 0SJ

Scottish National Board, 22 Queen Street, Edinburgh EH2 1JX
Welsh National Board, Pearl Assurance House, Greyfriars Road, Cardiff CF1 3AG
Health Visitors' Association, 50 Southwark Street, London SE1 1UN

Education and Training: Health Visiting, from any of the National Boards listed above
Directory of Schools of Medicine and Nursing, Kogan Page
Nursing, Hobsons

History

Many students are attracted by the idea of finding out what happened in the past, of reading about famous men and women, their ideas and achievements, and of the events and circumstances that created the environment and society in which we live. History continues to attract undergraduates to study it at university.

The problems come later – what do you do with an A-level or H-grade or a degree or a postgraduate degree in history? The career prospects are not obvious. On the other hand, many employers, including those in **retail management,** welcome applications from A-level or H-grade school-leavers who have been trained to assess evidence.

Similarly, graduates look for jobs in the **Civil Service, business,** commerce and various administrative jobs. History is quite highly rated by employers for the intellectual qualities required to study it. However, as a direct preparation for a job it is not particularly appropriate, and job-seekers should add a short course on business or whatever career attracts them. Those who want to continue with their interest in history go into **teaching** in schools, colleges and universities. And they need not be restricted to history, for teachers and lecturers in a wide range of subjects from communication studies to sociology often start with a history degree.

Other possibilities are **museum work, libraries, archivist** and **archaeology**, but it is not a long list of opportunities. On the other hand, historians move easily into jobs in **banking, insurance, local government**, the Civil Service and all kinds of commercial companies. They are regarded as having had an education that trains their minds to assemble, organise and present facts and opinions, and this is a very useful quality in many walks of life and careers. Most of the career progressions require additional training and qualification: history graduates have to take the full range of banking, insurance or whatever professional qualifications are needed to progress in their chosen careers. So although prospects for an historian who wants to remain one are rather limited, history is an excellent preparation for very many other jobs.

Training

For those who want to take a degree, almost every university and most of the polytechnics have history courses or combined arts degree courses with history as a major option. To gain entry, history at A-level or H-grade is generally preferred or required, and a foreign language at GCSE or equivalent is often asked for. Otherwise a generous view prevails: almost any subject as part of the three A-levels plus two to three good GCSEs package satisfies admissions tutors.

Information

The Historical Association, 59a Kennington Park Road, London SE11 7JH

History (including archaeology), Degree Course Guide, Hobsons *Working in History*, COIC

Home economics

Home economics is a subject that can be studied for GCSE, O-grade and A-level. It also describes a range of careers and jobs for people who advise on food, nutrition, clothing, health care, home management, household services and work connected with the home and commu-nity. A definition use by the Institute of Home Economics describes the subject as 'a study of the relationships between food, clothing and shelter and people's physical, economic, social and aesthetic needs'. That leaves little out and shows the wide extent of possible duties.

Home economists work as professional advisers, teachers, employees of food manufacturing companies, in the retail industry (developing new products and recipes), in the fuel industry (working for the electricity, gas and solid-fuel producers), in research work and with consumer advice centres and community service organisations. Much of this work is in advising the general public on products and services:

either face to face or by writing product advertising brochures, and in magazine work. For instance, the leading women's magazines employ home economists for articles on cookery, household products and services, equipment and health.

Opportunities and prospects are good: first, there is a shortage of teachers of home economics, secondly, companies, consumer groups, manufacturing companies and the fuel industry are all chasing the limited supply of qualified people. As a career it has been virtually one hundred per cent a women's occupation. It is hoped that more men will consider it, but as yet there is no evidence of this happening. For women (and men) who make it their career, home economics provides excellent opportunities to move into **marketing, advertising,** public relations, **journalism** and other work.

Training
There are no formal entry requirements, but the basic level of quali-fication should be a City and Guilds certificate. A course leading to a City and Guilds certificate in family and community care is an excellent preparation. At a higher level there are BTEC and SCOTVEC awards at National Diploma and HND levels. For the National Diploma course, four GCSEs or equivalents are required, including English language and a science subject. For HND courses in home economics, students need at least one A-level or H-grade, plus four GCSEs or equivalents, in-cluding English language and a science subject. For degree courses students should have two or three A-levels or three to four H-grades, or the BTEC or SCOTVEC Diploma, with a back-up of GCSEs or their equivalents.

There are degree courses in home economics, food science or nutrition at universities, polytechnics and colleges of higher education. A good grouping of GCSEs at grades A, B or C, plus two A-levels, is required. Often home economics at A-level and certainly English language and a science subject at GCSE are needed.

Other subjects useful for these courses are biology, social biology, human biology, chemistry and social studies or sociology, although no subjects are barred as entry qualifications.

Information
Institute of Home Economics, 71-79 Aldwych, London WC2B 4HN. The Institute publishes leaflets on careers in home economics

Careers and Courses in Home Economics, Hobsons
Working in Home Economics, COIC

Horses

People who work with horses tend to be very keen. Among the specialist jobs are those of groom, stable manager, stable-hand, riding instructor and general labourer. Dedication to the work is essential because horses take a lot of looking after. It is a seven-days-a-week job, physically hard, outdoors in all weathers, and dirty. The hours are long, the routine is relentless, and the job is very tiring. Despite these disadvantages there is no lack of volunteers. Indeed, there are more candidates than jobs.

Riding instructors

Instructors teach children and adults, both in classes and in private lessons. The job generally includes looking after horses, cleaning tack (saddles and bridles) and stables, and some management duties.

Training

There are various methods of training for the British Horse Society's Assistant Instructor's certificate and Instructor's certificate. One is by taking part in the two-year Youth Training scheme. Another is taking a course at a private school. Such courses may be anything from 3 to 15 months in length with fees likely to be sky-high. Another form of training is as a working pupil at a stable: a rough division would be three months training to nine months working on all the duties of the stable. Yet another method is to take a one- or two-year course at a college of further education, with a strong emphasis on animal care and business studies. No particular educational entry requirements are specified, but for a college course two or three GCSEs or O-grades would be looked for.

Groom

A groom works in a stable and may eventually become a stable manager with the responsibility for managing horses that hunt, race or are entered for show-jumping competitions. The groom cleans the stables and looks after the horses. This includes feeding and general care and keeping the tack in good condition.

Training

Training is generally by getting a job in a stable (and again there are many more candidates than jobs), and learning from senior people. Students go on to take the BHS Assistant Instructor's examination or the Certificate of Horsemanship examination. At 22 they could then take the BHS Certificate in Stable Management. There is a one-year course in Horse Management at the Warwickshire College of Agriculture. Applicants need to have at least one year's experience with horses. The course is for potential managers and the college therefore looks for two or three GCSEs or equivalents, and four to five GCSEs if students want to go on to a teaching qualification.

As with most other jobs involving horses, far more women than men apply for each job or college place. The majority of stable managers, however, are men. On the other hand, more women are taking the chance of setting up their own riding schools or stables; doing so requires business skills, experience and access to a good deal of money.

Almost any school subject is an adequate preliminary but English language at GCSE or equivalent is often requested. Physical fitness is required, and of course a love of horses, acquired by working with them. This is not a career for anyone who thinks it sounds pleasant but has never been involved in riding or looking after horses. A month or two spent giving animals their first feed, mucking out, riding, and bedding them down at night very quickly divides the dedicated from the disillusioned.

Information

British Horse Society, The British Equestrian Centre, Kenilworth, Warwickshire CV8 2LR

Horticulture

There is no clear, well-defined boundary between **agriculture** and horticulture. Nor do horticulturists like to be described as *gardeners:* they point out that their business is an important part of the countryside's economy, for they grow vegetables, fruit, trees, shrubs and flowers to feed people as well as for display. As far as work is concerned, entrants may find themselves in one of four areas:

- market gardens and vegetable farms – growing for contract work, private purchasers, wholesalers and markets
- nurseries and garden centres which grow and sell trees, shrubs, flowers and plants
- orchards and fruit farms
- glasshouse nurseries.

Since all these are commercial businesses, good skills in sales, marketing, bookkeeping and customer services are needed, as well as detailed knowledge of the plants that are being grown and sold. There is some advisory and research work, mostly done by government departments. Outside the commercial sector there are other jobs in what is called 'amenity horticulture': parks, ornamental gardens, sports fields, and for city and town flower-beds. Most of these jobs are with local authorities. However, jobs are also available with hospitals, the police, transport organisations... in fact any and every large organisation that has gardens, parks or a need for regular flower and plant displays. Prospects for jobs are very good. To qualify for them there is a variety of routes.

Horticultural workers

Horticultural workers can start at 16: there are no formal qualifications for entry, but GCSEs or O-grades in two or three subjects, including a science subject (biology and chemistry are highly rated) and maths would be a big asset because there is keen competition among 16 to 17-year-olds. The usual method of training is by means of an ATB (Agricultural Training Board) apprenticeship. Workers have to pass a number of proficiency tests in their craft skills over a period of three years. Apart from on-the-job instruction, apprentices attend college on a block- or day-release basis to study for one of several possible qualifications. These can include a City and Guilds certificate in horticulture, or a National Certificate in horticulture which is based on a one-year course. Some colleges offer full-time courses over one or two years leading to BTEC and SCOTVEC certificates and diplomas: up to three or four GCSEs or their equivalents are needed, including maths and a science subject such as chemistry or biology.

It is possible to become a manager by obtaining additional qualifications: City and Guilds or BTEC awards and working on specialist qualifications. Among these are certificates in sportsground mainte-nance (Institute of Groundsmanship), the diploma of the Institute of Leisure and Amenity Management, and examinations set by the Royal Horticultural Society.

Horticultural managers

Managers must hold one of the following qualifications. A degree in horticulture – there are courses at Bath, Reading, Nottingham, Strathclyde and London (Wye College) Universities. Two or three good A-levels or H-grades are needed for entry, including chemistry and another subject from maths or the sciences.

The Master of Horticulture or MHort (RHS) qualification is offered by the Royal Horticultural Society.

There is an HND in horticulture, entry to which requires five GCSEs including a science A-level/H-grade.

At school, biology and chemistry are very important. Maths is, too, and rural studies and horticulture (it can be taken to A-level) are excellent.

Information

Institute of Horticulture, Askham Bryan College, York YO2 3PR
Royal Horticultural Society, Wisley, Woking, Surrey GU23 6QB

Agricultural Sciences, Degree Course Guide, Hobsons
Directory of Further Education, Hobsons
Working in Agriculture and Horticulture, COIC
Come into Horticulture, Institute of Horticulture

Hospital work

Hospital work covers many different jobs; most of those listed below have entries in this book giving full details of the necessary training and qualifications.

- **administration** – health service administrators and medical records officers
- **biochemists** and other research staff who work in laboratories and treatment centres
- **catering** staff who cook and serve food and drinks to patients and staff

- **dentists,** doctors (under **medicine**), **opticians** and other specialist medical staff
- **dietitians** and nutrition experts who advise on food
- **home economics** staff who are concerned with advising patients and medical staff on all kinds of topics concerned with the family, community and personal welfare services
- housekeepers and other domestic staff responsible for laundry and other hospital services
- **nursery nurses** who work in the children's wards
- **nurses**
- **pharmacists** concerned with medicine and drugs
- **photographers** who specialise in medical photography and **radiographers** who use the X-ray and other machines
- social workers concerned with patients' welfare in hospital and after leaving it.

This is a substantial list of jobs, careers, professional people and their responsibilities.

Prospects

A wide range of jobs and interesting careers are available within the National Health Service. As well as the information in this book there are many articles and books about careers in the health service where details of the entry levels, degree, diploma or other courses and career openings are given. All together, about a million people in a wide selection of occupations are employed in the health and medical services so there is no lack of job opportunities.

Information

British Medical Association, BMA House, Tavistock Square, London WC1H 9JP

English National Board for Nursing, Midwifery and Health Visiting, PO Box 356, Sheffield S8 0SJ

Department of Health, Richmond House, 79 Whitehall, London SW1A 2NS

Working in Hospitals, COIC

Hotel management

There is a well-known slogan describing hotel management: 'from potato peeler to manager'. If this were ever true in the past, it is unlikely to be the picture in the future. Hotel management and catering are becoming increasingly professional and qualification-conscious. The normal and expected route now to becoming a hotel manager is by taking a degree or a BTEC or SCOTVEC HND course at a university or polytechnic. Most of these are sandwich courses with periods of training in a hotel. By the time students graduate, move into full-time jobs and begin the climb through assistants' jobs to hotel management, they have secured a thorough knowledge and training.

Potential students must have a trial run. Hotel work is not a cosy extension of home economics classes. It involves long hours of work, often on shifts that can start at 3am. There is little opportunity to rest or relax: hotel customers are very demanding and often ill-tempered; on top of the work, there is the studying.

Prospects

Hotels offer very good prospects. There is an expansion of business, largely fuelled by 'welcome to Britain' campaigns, foreign visitors and the increasing amount of leisure. Promotion can come very quickly indeed. Many assistant managers, reception or banqueting managers and other responsible personnel are in their late twenties. Willingness to move around the country, perhaps every two years, is absolutely essential.

Training

There are three principal ways of becoming a hotel manager. One is by taking a full-time course leading to a degree in a hotel and catering subject. The minimum requirements are two A-levels or three H-grades, but three A-levels/four H-grades are preferred. Included in the package should be four additional GCSEs or equivalents with passes in English language and possibly a science subject, although the science is not essential. Alternatively, for graduates who have taken their degree in another subject and are then attracted to hotel work, the first degree is acceptable as long as it is supported by a postgraduate course leading to a diploma.

For non-graduates the entry to managerial jobs is by gaining experience working in a hotel in almost any capacity, and studying for the various examinations of City and Guilds and of the Hotel, Catering and Institutional Management Association (HCIMA). This organisation, which publishes very useful careers information sheets, sets out the entry qualifications for Part A of their courses which can lead to professional status. Part A includes technical knowledge and skills appropriate to all sectors of the industry; Part B is made up of a common core of management subjects, plus elective studies. Part A courses are available on a part-time or a block-release basis over two years; Part B is taken on a sandwich or full-time programme, or on a three-year part-time basis.

The entry requirements are detailed but in general are as follows:

● at 16-plus entrants should have four GCSE (O-grade) passes at grades A, B or C, which include English language and subjects that demonstrate general literacy and numeracy and preferably a science subject
● at 20-plus entrants should have had not less than three years' appropriate full-time employment within the industry and successful completion of a full-time catering course lasting a year (or part-time over two years)
● entrants aged 19-plus should hold other HCIMA-approved mix of craft qualifications and experience, such as completion of a two year full-time craft course (which include City and Guilds courses) plus one year's appropriate experience.

Relevant school subjects have been mentioned: it is clear that science subjects such as biology, human biology, social biology, chemistry and maths are more important than home economics, although this is also an excellent preparatory course, whether at A-level/H-grade or for GCSE/O-grade. Business studies courses at school or at college for BTEC/SCOTVEC awards are useful.

Information
Hotel and Catering Training Company, International House, High Street, London W5 5DB
Hotel, Catering and Institutional Management Association, 191 Trinity Road, London SW17 7HN

HCIMA and the HCTB produce leaflets on careers in hotels and catering work

Handbook of Careers in Tourism and Leisure, Hobsons
Directory of Further Education Hobsons
Working in the Hospitality Industry, COIC
Working in Catering, COIC

Housing management

Helping people to meet their housing needs can be very challenging. Housing management offers a varied and rewarding career with considerable prospects for promotion. The type of work depends largely on the organisation the recruit joins – housing association, local authority, private trust or company, aid or advice centre – and the area in which it is based – inner city, small town, rural. However, it is likely to include a lot of day to day contact with residents, whether in their own homes or in the housing office, and to be concerned with solving problems related to repairs, rents, mortgages, grants and to a range of social issues such as difficulties with neighbours, landlords and others. Housing work is, therefore, about dealing with people. It can, however, be stressful work because it is often difficult to get people the housing they want, whether it is rented from a local authority or association or bought on the private market. So officers have to try to balance the wishes of individual consumers against what they are able to provide.

Much of the time, housing officers act on behalf of residents: sorting out issues with other departments (social services, health, technical, education, and so on) and other professionals. This means that alongside good technical knowledge of housing law, building technology, housing practice and social policy, officers have to be good communicators, both to other professionals and, of course, to the residents themselves.

Typically, a housing career begins with a job involving direct contact with residents of an estate. Promotion will then result in an officer having special reponsibilities for a particular aspect of the work, such as homelessness, grants, empty property or repairs. After a few years' more specialist management, research or financial responsibilities may arise, leading ultimately to senior staff positions running entire housing departments or associations with responsibility for a large number of staff, properties and, of course, the homes of numerous residents.

Training
There are various ways to become a qualified housing manager. One is

to get a job as a housing trainee or junior housing officer and study part time on day-release or correspondence courses for the Institute of Housing's professional qualification. Alternatively, students can study full time to get a recognised degree/postgraduate diploma in housing before joining a housing organisation. These courses generally include an element of practical experience. In addition to these routes to professional qualification, there are a number of relevant BTEC/ SCOTVEC National Certificates and HNCs, for example property management and housing services; public administration with housing option, housing administration. There are also related degrees or diplomas in planning, estate management, building, environmental health and surveying.

To enrol in the Institute of Housing's professional qualification course students must be working in housing, have two A-levels and three GCSEs with English language as one of them. The course can be taken at 18 colleges in the UK and lasts three years. Holders of relevant degrees, diplomas and certificates are allowed subject exemptions. Two or three A-levels are also required to enrol for the housing and housing development degree courses at Bristol and Sheffield Polytechnics. The full-time postgraduate diplomas – at Stirling, Heriot-Watt, the London School of Economics – require a good degree.

Relevant school subjects at GCSE can include social studies, history, geography and, at A-level, law, environmental studies, business studies and economics, though most subjects have some relevance.

Information
Careers Office, Institute of Housing, 12 Upper Belgrave Street, London SW1X 8BA. The Institute provides careers advice, leaflets and other publications

Industrial management

All organisations that provide some kind of service or produce goods have managers. They are the people who carry out the policies of the directors and organise the work of the producers.

'Industry' is just as general a word as management: it can cover anything from agricultural machinery to fashion jewellery, helicopters to hats. Not surprisingly, therefore, within the phrase 'industrial management' there is a vast range of jobs and responsibilities. It is not a career in the same sense as that of an engineer or solicitor, but it is a purposeful activity that offers tremendous scope.

The work itself is difficult to define. However, research shows that industrial managers spend between 70 and 90 per cent of their time talking. That may be a surprise, because most people assume that managers are doers. But managing is organising, and that is done by talking to people – face to face, on the telephone, in meetings and at conferences. And this means that there are management skills, which can also be defined.

In industry, almost all managers start with some kind of specialist knowledge or skill. They may know about and have been trained for steel-making, book publishing, whisky distilling, or whatever. Then to this expertise they add management skills and techniques. These are acquired through experience and by attending courses. These courses may themselves be commercially or industrially based, as in degree, HND and diploma courses in such subjects as business studies, accounting, marketing, engineering, or computing. Or they may graduate in a subject such as history and then take a course that adds a specialisation or gives an insight into business, as in the Diploma of Management Studies, a postgraduate course offered at most polytechnics. A third alternative is to take a course that leads to a management expertise such as personnel, purchasing and supply, marketing or operational research.

Prospects

It would be silly to generalise about prospects because of the vast range. On the other hand, the UK needs good managers, and companies of all kinds are looking for industrial managers who can produce, market, sell and develop products. Competition is very keen indeed for management positions, and graduates stand a better chance than most: certainly in industrial management, graduates with technical knowledge and skills have a tremendous start.

Training

It is very difficult to advise school pupils on how to prepare for a career in industrial management. It is probably best to think of courses at university, polytechnic or college in practical and vocational subjects, such as engineering, computing and technology subjects, and prepare for a mixture of experience plus training after graduation. Students should think about the industry they wish to aim for, but people do move around in industrial management, and having started in textiles a manager could well move on to a quite different industry. An alternative route would be to take a business management degree or similar course at college, and follow that with industrial experience topped up with the additional specialist training already mentioned. School subjects are not much of a guide here: they influence the degree course because A-levels in sciences/maths are essential for an engineering degree and business subjects are useful to take students in the direction of general management or chartered secretary/accountant/personnel, etc. But careers in industrial management can follow any course: personality, vitality, ability and drive are the qualifications needed, not just a pass in A-level maths, English or anything else.

Information
British Institute of Management, Management House, Cottingham Road, Corby, Northamptonshire NN17 1TT

Information technology

Information technology is concerned with all forms of collecting, analysing, storing and retrieving information by various methods but mainly by electronic processes. The electronic information can be in the form of text, pictures, numbers or be vocal (spoken). IT therefore includes computing, computer graphics, telecommunications and database handling – it is very much a late-20th century phenomenon and is set to grow into a major industry in the 21st century.

Training
Since IT has such a wide variety of applications, there is a multitude of jobs. Among them is wordprocessing, with training either as part of a secretarial course or as an extra achieved at college on a full-time or part-time course. For BTEC National Diploma and HND courses and for degree programmes, students need to achieve good GCSE and (for degree courses) A-level results. GCSE and A-level subjects that are particularly useful are computing, business studies, English, mathematics and accounting.

Information
British Computer Society, 13 Mansfield Street, London W1M 0BP

Insurance

It would be difficult to think of anyone who does not need insurance at some point in their lives. Protection against loss or misfortune is based on the principle that one pays into a common fund, drawing on it in emergencies. To offer and manage this there are over 800 insurance companies, making it one of the UK's major industries with huge reserves of money. And the future looks good: a quarter of British homes are said to be uninsured, people are being encouraged to set up their own private pension schemes, and the increase in burglaries and car thefts has made people very insurance-conscious.

Salaries vary between the different sectors and individual employers. Often fringe benefits, such as low-interest loans, company pension schemes, subsidised mortgages and company cars, can add considerably to an individual's basic salary. Promotion depends on experience, mobility and a readiness to move from one company to another. Training is on the job, and employees are encouraged to study for the professional qualifications of the Chartered Insurance Institute. Half-day release may be given for study, and many local colleges offer evening classes.

There are different sectors within the insurance industry. The sellers, or suppliers, of insurance are the big insurance companies, such as the Prudential, Royal, Commercial Union, and Lloyd's of London. Employees in the branch office of the insurance companies deal with over-the-counter enquiries and proposals and deal with customers by telephone and correspondence. If it is a general office, they need to know about life, fire, personal accident and other forms of insurance.

Lloyd's of London is a corporation that provides facilities for its members to transact insurance business. Members form themselves into groups, or 'syndicates', and appoint an underwriter to accept risks on their behalf.

Insurance brokers form a third sector of the industry. These brokers are independent intermediaries who must be registered, and they provide a service of matching their client's insurance needs with the contracts available from Lloyd's or the insurance companies. Clients may also ask the broker for advice on how to reduce the risks they are running.

Sales skills in both sectors are important, for the public often finds it difficult, if not impossible, to judge one company's terms against another, and so it is sales techniques, advertising and publicity that wins business. Salesmen in insurance companies are known as inspectors; their clients include brokers, industry and the general public.

Besides the office and sales staff, insurance companies employ these specialists:

- **actuaries** who calculate rates and returns; they need actuarial or mathematical skills
- underwriters who assess risks; a qualification in law or economics can be a good preparation
- **surveyors** who make reports on buildings; a scientific or engineering qualification is useful but not essential
- loss adjusters and claims assessors who specialise in claims work; maths is a useful subject
- investment and pensions managers; economics or maths graduates are looked for.

Training

Professional trainees for all these sectors are recruited each year. At 16-plus, the minimum entry requirements for most insurance companies are four GCSEs at grades A to C or O-grades, including English language and maths. However, the academic level of entrants is going up: a substantial number come in at 18 with A-level or H-grade passes. More and more graduates are looking to insurance as a career; any subject is appropriate, although business studies or accounting and other commercial or mathematical subjects are very useful, as are law and economics. BTEC and SCOTVEC diplomas and HNDS in these and other subjects are acceptable in lieu of A-levels or degrees. In 1990, over 1,000 graduates entered insurance, and each year the number increases.

Once into a company most people begin studying for a professional qualification. The qualifying examination of the Chartered Insurance Institute (CII) is in two parts, the Associateship and the Fellowship. Exemptions are given to those who have obtained qualifications which are broadly similar to CII subjects. Other professional qualifications include those offered by the Chartered Institute of Loss Adjusters and the Institute of Actuaries for those seeking a career as a loss adjuster or as an actuary.

No single school subject leads directly into insurance work. Perhaps economics and business studies are nearest. However, not much can be done without a knowledge of maths, and English language skills are needed not only for correspondence and telephone sales but for understanding the language of insurance policies. Some universities, colleges and polytechnics have degree and HND courses that include insurance options and which give partial exemption from CII exams. These include a specialist degree course in Banking, Insurance and Finance at University College of North Wales (Bangor), and in Banking and Finance, and Accounting and Financial Management at Loughborough University.

Information

Chartered Insurance Institute, 20 Aldermanbury, London EC2V 7HY
The Chartered Institute of Loss Adjusters, Manfield House, 376 Strand, London WC2R 0LR
British Insurance Brokers' Association, 14 Bevis Marks, London EC3A 7NT
Institute of Actuaries, Staple Inn Hall, High Holborn, London WC1V 7QJ

Careers in Insurance, Kogan Page
Leaflets on careers are available from the four organisations listed above

Interpreting

Interpreting is the act of oral translation between two parties without a common language. It requires not only a high level of fluency in both languages, but also the relevant specialist vocabulary, a fast and agile mind, a pleasant and relaxed manner and a tough and resilient personality, as all work is done virtually under examination conditions.

'Ad hoc' and 'liaison interpreting' are the terms used for interpreting other than in a conference. Apart from that done on a casual basis by non-interpreters, much ad hoc interpreting is carried out by freelancers, who may also undertake written translation. It can be broadly divided into two areas: business orientated and community orientated.

Business-orientated interpreting

This is largely concerned with foreign trade and involves, for example, interpreting at business meetings and accompanying trade delegations. In view of the potential profits, enlightened firms will pay good rates for good interpreters, but will expect, in addition to a high level of interpreting ability, a good understanding of commercial and technical matters and the relevant vocabulary in both languages.

Community interpreters

These are required whenever non-English-speaking members of the community come into contact with the public services, for example when witnesses or suspects are interviewed in police stations or appear in court. Interpreters in this field require a knowledge of the legal system and an understanding of legal terminology as well as a sound colloquial grasp of the foreign language and the ability to write it. Rates of pay are not always good, and some organisations still rely on unpaid volunteers. However, with growing professionalism, standards of training and remuneration can be expected to improve in the near future.

Training
There are as yet no accepted qualifications for ad hoc interpreters, but ideally degree-level proficiency in the foreign language should be supplemented by extensive colloquial practice, acquisition of specialist vocabulary and specialist interpreter training. Some universities and polytechnics run postgraduate courses, and the Institute of Linguists provides a Certificate in Community Interpreting. This is at a somewhat lower level and reflects the minimum standard at which a community interpreter can be regarded as competent.

Information
The Institute of Linguists, 24a Highbury Grove, London N5 2EA
Institute of Translating and Interpreting, 318a Finchley Road, London NW3 5HT

Jewellery

Jewellery is designed in a studio by designers and craftspeople who have had some special training within a design course, allied to practical experience. From this studio-based design, the next step is to move to a workshop where each article is made individually. Glass, jewels, settings, silver and other precious stones and metals are moulded into the final article, whether it is a ring, a brooch, or a grand tiara. These studios are small and the owners are generally self-employed. They sell the jewellery by personal contact to shops or individual customers. It is a job that carries a high degree of risk and uncertainty.

Other jewellers work for larger companies, either designing new items or assisting in their production, which can be rather more mechanised than in a designer-studio environment.

Training

To train for this work a student can take a full-time graphic design course with options in jewellery and ceramics. For instance, the BA three-dimensional design courses at Middlesex, Sheffield and Birmingham Polytechnics and the Central School of Art and Design in London all contain special options in jewellery. Alternatively there are vocational courses leading to BTEC National Diplomas and HNDs which also have jewellery as an option.

Many of these courses are approved by SIAD, the Society of Industrial Artists and Designers, and some of them offer substantial training in ceramics, silversmithing, jewellery and engraving (as at Birmingham Polytechnic).

Having completed such a course, the student then seeks permanent employment with a company, studio or any other kind of employer.

The alternative method is to try to get a job at 16,17 or later and to take a day- or block-release course at a specialist college, leading to a City and Guilds certificate in jewellery, silversmithing, glass or ceramics (see below for course details). At school it would be useful to take art and design at A-level, although this is not essential. Ceramics can also be taken to A-level, but not at many schools or colleges. Otherwise, some knowledge of science, metalwork and crafts is useful. For degree, HND and BTEC National Diploma courses, the usual entry requirements apply in terms of GCSEs, A-levels or H-grades.

Information

Art and Design, Degree Course Guide, Hobsons
Directory of Further Education, Hobsons

Journalism

Journalists work on the big national dailies and Sunday newspapers and also on regional dailies, local weeklies, free newspapers, magazines, trade newspapers and also for radio and television, as well as for international news agencies such as Reuters.

One kind of work is done by a reporter who covers assignments as various as weddings, elections, council meetings and a thousand more 'events'. A story can be set immediately or it may require further research, fact-finding and talking to people. Eventually the copy comes to the sub-editor, who checks copy for grammar, spelling and accuracy; he or she adds headlines, captions to photographs and may reduce the article to fit into the space allocated to it.

The sub-editor, editor or, on large national newspapers, the production editor, places all the stories and pictures on a page layout. At this stage, the page is ready for the printer.

Journalism is not a 9 to 5 job: deadlines and production timings are as relentless as editors. Pay is variable – it can be very good for successful writers and for some London journalists, but it can be very low in the provinces. It is also a very difficult world for a beginner to enter.

Training

There are four main routes into journalism. One is to start early as a school-leaver at 16, 17 or 18 on a provincial newspaper. For up to three years the trainee follows a rigorous training schedule and in addition does everything asked of him or her. During this time there is the opportunity to attend a college on a day- or block- release basis to study typing, word processing and shorthand. Some of the large newspaper groups have their own company training programme.

To get in at 16 or 17, at least five GCSEs or O-grades are needed, including English language. Opportunities are few and the demand is great.

The second method of entry is after A-levels or a degree course: almost any subject or group of subjects could be suitable. This group of entrants completes the training-period in a shorter length of time. First-degree courses in communication studies, English, media and business studies are particularly useful; there are postgraduate one-year courses at City University, University of Wales College of Cardiff, and elsewhere.

The third method is to take a full-time pre-entry course at a college of further education. Entry qualifications are two A-levels or three H-grades, plus two or three GCSEs or O-grades including English language.

These courses do not guarantee a job any more than the fourth route, which is by taking a degree and following it up with a postgraduate course. Again, for those with degree and postgraduate status, the training-period is reduced but certainly not abandoned.

These are the formal routes. However, journalists have entered their chosen profession by other means, including experience on free newspapers, advertising agencies, radio and television (there are different pre-entry courses for radio and television) and as trainees on specialist trade magazines.

The number of entrants to newspapers is low: around 60 newcomers each year in London and 300 or so in the provinces, with another 100 or so for trade press jobs. Once on the road, training is on the job, working with an experienced reporter, plus college attendance and possibly company training schemes.

There are no specially suitable school subjects, although it is obvious that some skill at writing is needed, but accuracy and brevity are what editors look for, not verbose, wordy writers. Reuters' jobs go to graduates with two languages. Magazine and trade press work is helped if the applicant has some specialist knowledge, for example of fashion, sport, finance or current affairs, and this means that graduates have a clear advantage because they have had the time to deepen their interests. Otherwise, virtually any school or undergraduate course could be suitable. To give another example – computer magazines are always looking for journalists with detailed knowledge of computing, and there are not too many of them around.

Information
National Union of Journalists, Acorn House, 314–320 Gray's Inn Road, London WC1X 8DP

National Council for the Training of Journalists, Carlton House, Hemnall Street, Epping, Essex CM16 4NL

Newspaper Society, Training Department, Whitefriars House, 6 Carmelite Street, London EC4Y 0BL

Careers in Journalism, Kogan Page

Working in Journalism, COIC

Directory of Further Education, Hobsons, contains a complete list of courses in journalism, communication studies, media studies, public relations and advertising, and the colleges that offer them. It includes colleges which provide the postgraduate courses mentioned above, the one-year, pre-entry indentured training course for newspaper journalism, and relevant BTEC and SCOTVEC certificate, diploma and modular courses

Knitting

This industry is a hybrid between textiles and clothing because it is the only branch of the textile and clothing industry that is completely vertical. In other words, it takes fibres or yarns – natural and man-made – turns them into fabric and then into garments or other end-use products. The technology in the industry is extremely advanced; perhaps less so at the garment-manufacturing point, but even here new technology is making rapid strides.

The industry has recovered rapidly from the recent recession, and, apart from supplying a huge home market, is a leading exporter of high-class products.

The industry currently employs some 100,000 people and is concentrated in the East Midlands – Leicester, Nottingham, Hinckley, and so on – and in Scotland – largely in Hawick and the Borders and Glasgow and the west of Scotland. These areas have strong supporting educational establishments, notably Leicester Polytechnic, Nottingham Polytechnic, Hinckley College, the Borders College of Galashiels and Cardonald College at Glasgow. Courses are offered at degree, HND and other levels in textile and knitting technology, design, business management, marketing and other relevant disciplines.

There is always a demand from the industry for students, and many are sought internationally, particularly by Italy, the USA and Japan.

The various branches of the industry are quite distinct, although there is an overlap in technology. They include:

- pullovers and cardigans
- stockings and tights
- socks
- leisurewear, sportswear and underwear
- jersey fabrics
- industrial and medical fabrics
- dyeing and finishing of fabrics.

A wide range of careers suitable for all levels of creative and managerial activities is offered. These include designers, technologists, technicians, production managers, chemists and engineers; finance and accountancy staff; export, marketing and sales personnel; training staff; production operatives and warehouse personnel. Apart from the larger companies with household names, there are a host of small companies offering opportunities to young people to develop their creative and entrepreneurial skills. It is also an industry where people with flair can establish their own businesses.

Information

The Knitting and Lace Industries Training Resources Agency, 7 Gregory Boulevard, Nottingham NG7 6LD. The Agency publishes a leaflet, *A Career With a Future*

Directory of Further Education, Hobsons, contains a list of courses, and the colleges which provide them, in clothing and tailoring subjects that include specialist knitwear options

Laboratory work

Laboratory work covers many different possibilities and careers. The first that most people probably think of is the research lab. But the research lab for what objective? Every major manufacturing company, certainly in the area of technology, must have research in hand.

An electronics, computing, food processing, engineering or textile manufacturer must be constantly exploring new technology, the alternative uses of materials, adaptations of scientific ideas to technical processes. If the company is not doing this, it is not likely to last long. The Research and Development (R & D) department is therefore crucial to a firm's development. Another type of laboratory is involved in more basic research.

In the UK there are government-funded Research Councils (SERC, the Science and Engineering Research Council, is one) which support research initiatives in their own research institutes, in universities and polytechnics and also in industry. The research work is done in the university, usually in the departments or in a linked university-industry programme of work. Within these institutions there are laboratories staffed by research workers and support staff, such as technicians.

Then there are the laboratories concerned with medical care. These are usually connected to major hospitals and carry out research and investigations into diseases, drugs and other aspects of medical work. Another group of laboratories are in schools, colleges and universities. These are staffed by laboratory assistants or technicians whose job is to set out apparatus, clear up afterwards and generally maintain equipment and supplies.

Research scientists

The wide range of laboratories means there are many different types of jobs. At one level are the research scientists. A typical team in a university will be led by a professor, with science or engineering graduates as lecturers and research assistants, supported by laboratory technicians. In industry, an R & D department follows much the same pattern, except that the senior staff are often more of a mixture of technologists, scientists and production people, but again they will be backed up by technician support.

Within such teams the research scientists are usually very well qualified indeed. They have obtained a degree, gone on to do research work in a specialised field, and are working for an MSc or a PhD, or have moved on from qualification-acquiring to take part in fixed contracts for government, industry or research council-backed projects. The way to get into this type of laboratory work is therefore via a university or polytechnic course.

Laboratory technicians

Laboratory technicians prepare samples, carry out experiments, report on to and generally help scientific and engineering staff with their research, teaching or developmental work. They work within government departments too, on food storage, the analysis of samples and technical assignments.

Training
Prospects are improved by taking qualifications at City and Guilds or BTEC levels, or by taking the examinations of professional bodies such as the Royal Society of Chemistry, the Institute of Physics, the Institute

of Biology, or technical professional bodies such as the Institute of Animal Technicians. Educational qualifications for entry to this work are generally pitched around GCSEs or O-grades in two or three subjects, including maths and/or a science subject.

Many employers expect technicians to take a part-time BTEC or SCOTEC course leading to a National Certificate, and the basic entry qualification for these courses is at least passes in three GCSEs, including a science. However, for advanced medical and some scientific work, the research laboratories, expect entrants to have three to five GCSEs or equivalents and may also look for A-levels in sciences.

Technicians who have the ambition and ability to go on with their studies can progress to BTEC National Diploma (after the Certificate or with three GCSEs) and to an HND in a science or engineering subject, for which the BTEC National Diploma, or at least one A-level plus four GCSEs, including one or two science subjects, is required.

Clearly, for this kind of work, interest and ability in sciences is fundamental, and laboratory staff at all levels need to have a keen interest in scientific study and exploration.

Information
The Royal Society of Chemistry, Burlington House, London W1V 0BN
The Institute of Physics, 47 Belgrave Square, London SW1X 8QX
The Institute of Biology, 20 Queensberry Place, London SW7 2DZ

Working as a Laboratory Technician, Batsford
Chemistry, Physics, Biological Sciences, Degree Course Guides, Hobsons
Directory of Further Education, Hobsons
Biology, Connections series, Hobsons
Biotechnology in Perspective, Hobsons

Landscaping
Landscape architects

Landscape architects are first and foremost designers; they design in the ever-changing outdoor environment and see their designs implemented. The scope of the work is wide: in towns and cities it is mainly concerned with the integration of the layout of housing areas, road-works, parks and play areas, with public and private gardens and with general urban regeneration; in the country the emphasis is on agricultural, forest and tourist landscapes, on the landscaping of roads and the settings of power stations and other industrial buildings, on reservoirs, land reclamation and the impact of the extraction industries on the landscape. The aim is always to create harmony between what is new and what already exists and to cause minimum damage to the environment. Landscape architects do not normally work in isolation, and are often members of a team which may include architects, planners, civil engineers and quantity surveyors; in addition, they often need to seek specialist advice from landscape managers, landscape scientists, foresters and horticulturists.

They spend approximately two-thirds of their time in the offices; thel remainder is spent on site visits, checking progress of the work often in adverse conditions.

Training

Most landscape architects enter the profession by taking a higher education course. Undergraduate entry courses, which involve four years of academic study, are available at Heriot-Watt and Sheffield Universities, at Leeds, Manchester and Thames Polytechnics, and at Gloucestershire College of Arts and Technology. In all except the last it is mandatory for students to spend a year out undergoing practical training between the third and fourth academic years.

Two-year full-time graduate entry courses are provided at Edinburgh, Manchester, Newcastle, and Sheffield Universities. Part-time graduate entry courses, available at Birmingham and Thames Polytechnics, last three and four years respectively. As entry requirements may change from time to time, applicants should check them with the establishments concerned.

The courses mentioned, with the exception of the part-time course at Thames Polytechnic, qualify those who successfully complete them for graduate membership of the Landscape Institute. Associate membership of the Institute, designated ALI, which is the recognised professional qualification in landscape architecture, can only be obtained after a minimum of two years' experience and then passing the Institute's Part 4 Professional Practice Examination. Students on courses are encouraged to become student members of the Institute on very favourable terms.

Landscape managers

A landscape manager relies on academic degrees and relevant practical experience. People who are well qualified at both degree and postgraduate level may be admitted to graduate membership of the Landscape Institute on academic grounds alone.

Training

The first-degree courses listed above contain aspects of landscape management and Heriot-Watt University has two separate courses in estate management and landscape architecture. Agriculture, forestry or botany degrees are also suitable. Alternatively, other related degrees can form a suitable base when linked with postgraduate courses such as the MSc in Landscape Ecology, Design and Maintenance at Wye College. All these can lead to graduate membership of the Institute when followed by relevant practical experience of up to four years.

Landscape scientists

A landscape scientist requires an appropriate degree followed by a combination of a higher degree and/or two years' relevant experience. The required duration of experience depends on the individual candidate's academic qualifications. More experience, up to a total maximum of four years, is demanded for less well-qualified candidates. Exceptionally, scientists who are particularly well qualified at both degree and postgraduate levels may be admitted to graduate membership of the Landscape Institute on academic grounds alone.

Training

Students can specialise in a variety of areas. The first degree should be scientific in emphasis and a broad-based ecology course would be a good start. Environmental studies or similar broadly based courses are only satisfactory if they have a sufficiently high and rigorous scientific base. Similarly, a course with options or units has attractions, as long as care is taken to develop science in depth throughout the course. Students need to develop skills and experience in applying scientific knowledge to practical problems and have an awareness of design, management, planning, contracts, and legislation, and these are unlikely to have been covered in a science course. In this respect relevant research can be as valuable as relevant practical experience in a local authority, central government agency or private practice. The MSc courses at University College, London (Conservation), and Aberdeen University (Ecology) are examples of appropriate higher degree courses.

Information

Landscape Institute, 12 Carlton House Terrace, London SW1Y 5AH

Professional Careers in Landscape Architecture, Landscape Sciences and Landscape Management, Landscape Institute
Landscape Architecture, Job Outline series, COIC
Careers in the Environment, Council for Environmental Conservation
Working in the Countryside, COIC

Languages

A degree in languages is not in itself an adequate preparation for any career. Indeed, there are only three professions in which fluency in one or more foreign languages is a primary qualification: **teaching, interpreting** and translating.

Teaching

A postgraduate teaching qualification is obligatory in state schools, is in practice required in colleges of further education, and is of advantage in independent schools. Universities and polytechnics demand postgraduate literary or linguistic research, which in turn means proven academic potential. Language teaching in LEA and public schools is one career and teaching English as a foreign language (EFL), often abroad, still has openings; this normally requires a qualification in EFL. Remember that the job is teaching the language, not speaking it, so do not enter school teaching unless strongly committed.

Interpreting

There are few opportunities here; the separate entry on **interpreting** gives the details.

Translating

A knowledge of one or more foreign languages is again not enough. Translators must specialise in subject areas, such as the branches of engineering, information technology, medicine, law or finance, and must acquire relevant expertise by studying or working in the chosen field. Voluntary service abroad could be a way to start, but many translators start out in other professions. There are very few openings for literary translation.

A translator should only translate into his or her mother tongue, and a knowledge of a non-European or a less common European language of commercial importance is a considerable recommendation. The Civil Service, international organisations and major firms employ staff translators. Freelance translators will need persistence to make the contacts necessary to build up a clientele, either direct or through agencies.

Several universities and polytechnics offer postgraduate training in translation and interpreting, with subject specialisation, and it is an element of a few degree courses: check the published guides.

Other occupations

The ability to speak or read more than one language is of benefit in a wide range of careers, and is increasingly mentioned in advertisements for jobs. The most obvious areas in which it helps are secretarial work, commercial management, sales and purchasing, industrial research and training, international law and finance, the diplomatic service, tourism, librarianship, journalism and, particularly in the case of the community languages of the UK, social services and medicine. For these jobs a degree in languages is at least as good a qualification as many others, but the graduate must be prepared to undergo further training in a different profession, either through a postgraduate course or as a trainee in employment.

Information

Institute of Linguists, 24a Highbury Grove, London N5 2EA

Working in Languages, COIC
French; German, including Dutch and Scandinavian Studies; Italian; Hispanic Studies; Oriental and African Studies; Russian; Degree Course Guides, Hobsons

Law

Law has traditionally been regarded by parents as a secure, respectable and profitable career for their children, and the response of young people has been just as enthusiastic: Durham University, for instance, says that it receives 1,100 applications for only 86 places, and Manchester University has 2,000 applicants for 120 places. These figures are typical, and as a result university entry requirements are high: for the three A-levels or four or five H-grades needed for entry, most universities require passes at A or B grade. Oxford and Cambridge simply state 'three As'. Other universities and polytechnics are almost as demanding; certainly grades of B or C in three subjects are expected, although not always achieved.

For students who qualify by one of various routes, there are different opportunities within the law. First there are two legal systems in the UK, one for England and Wales, and a separate one for Scotland. (The judicial system in Northern Ireland closely resembles that of England and Wales.) Both are divided into two branches: there are advocates in Scotland and **barristers** in England and Wales and Northern Ireland; and law agents in Scotland and **solicitors** in England, Wales and Northern Ireland. The laws are administered through the courts, which deal broadly with two types of law: criminal and civil (disputes). These legal systems require trained people to administer them – excluding the police there are about 55,000 people working professionally in the law. This helps to explain why it is so difficult to gain entry to a degree course: few recruits are needed and the competition is intense.

Another important factor that has to be considered by students thinking about a law degree course is the nature of the job. All legal work calls for reliability and trustworthiness. It means close attention to detail and very good communications skills. The tradition and the formality of the law are generally unknown to applicants, some of whom are deterred by it when they begin to study legal practice. For this (and other) reasons, a substantial group of graduates who complete a law degree do not make their careers in law. Instead they go into **business, industry, politics, journalism, finance** and many other kinds of work. However, this adds to the attraction of a law degree and is another reason for the large number of applicants for degree courses.

For the 60 per cent of law graduates who practise the law, the main areas of special training and professional work are:

Barrister

See separate entry.

Barrister's clerk

The clerk acts as an intermediary between barristers and solicitors, acting as office manager and administrative assistant. Starting at 16 or 17 with at least three GCSEs or equivalents, clerks go on to take the examinations of the Barristers' Clerks Association. Such is the competition for places and jobs that most entrants have more than the minimum qualifications.

Justices' clerk

Justices' clerks are either solicitors or barristers. They work in an office attached to a magistrates' court. Promotion can be to court clerk.

Justices' clerks' assistant

These enter with at least three GCSEs or equivalents (most have higher qualifications, including A-levels) including English language.

Legal executive

A legal executive works for a solicitor, looking after part of the business of the practice. It is likely that a legal executive will be asked to specialise in one aspect of legal work, such as conveyancing, probate (wills), or company law. The entry requirement is four GCSEs or equivalents, or A-levels. Applicants with A-levels will find that the period of training is not shortened; however, a pass at A-level in law carries exemption from one of the examinations of the Institute of Legal Executives, and by doubling up on his or her studies a candidate can complete the first stage of the exams in one year rather than two.

Solicitor

See separate entry.

Advocate, law agent and procurator-fiscal

See the Scottish address below to which to write for details of the training needed for Scotland.

For all these jobs some school subjects are of crucial importance. In the first place it is essential to find out the GCSEs or O-grades that are needed for the particular category of work that is listed above. This information can be obtained from the professional bodies and the books listed below. Where GCSEs are required, passes need to be at grades A, B or C. Secondly, as with some other professional careers, some subjects called 'academic subjects' are rated more highly than others. In fact some GCSE and A-level subjects do not count at all for entry to courses: again this needs to be carefully checked. Among the academic subjects are English, languages, sciences, history and so on; the 'non-academic' may include technical or practical subjects.

A frequent question is: 'Do you need to take law at A-level as a preliminary or as an entry requirement to a law degree course?' The answer is an emphatic 'No'. A-level law is accepted by most polytechnics and universities. However, many of them do not regard it as a very useful preliminary qualification because of the differences between A-level and degree-level study.

Information

Council of Legal Education, Inns of Court School of Law, 4 Gray's Inn Place, London WC1R 5DX

The Law Society, 113 Chancery Lane, London WC2A 1PL

The Law Society of Scotland, 26 Drumsheugh Gardens, Edinburgh EH3 7YR

The Law Society of Northern Ireland, Law Society House, 90–106 Victoria Street, Belfast BT1 3JZ

Institute of Legal Executives, Kempston Manor, Kempston, Bedfordshire MK42 7AB

Working in Law, COIC
Law, Degree Course Guide, Hobsons
Directory of Further Education, Hobsons
Law, Connections series, Hobsons

Leisure management

For millions of people leisure means sports, games, indoor and outdoor pursuits, going to and performing in theatres, and many other activities.

Leisure managers therefore work in sports centres, outward-bound schools, theatre and arts centres, historic houses and ancient monuments and at centres that have nature trails, fishing and camping facilities. Managers, as well as being in charge of the leisure activities, are usually responsible for the administrative and financial organisation of the enterprise. Many are employed in local government, but there are also opportunities in private sports centres and clubs.

Training

The Institute of Leisure and Amenity Management (ILAM) has certificate and diploma qualifications in leisure management. These are taken by people already in work who attend part-time courses.

In order to take the certificate, candidates have to be 18 and need the following qualifications: four GCSEs and one A-level (or Scottish equivalents) with English language and maths as two of the subjects; a BTEC/SCOTVEC national certificate or national diploma; a National Examining Board for Supervisory Management (NEBSM) certificate, or a City and Guilds qualification in leisure and recreation studies. Students going for the diploma must hold the certificate or a relevant qualification.

HND courses are available at some polytechnics: the qualification is equivalent to the ILAM certificate. A degree or diploma in leisure studies or recreation management or similar is equivalent to the diploma.

Information

Institute of Leisure and Amenity Management, ILAM House, Lower Basildon, Reading, Berkshire RG8 9NE

Careers in Sport, Kogan Page

Libraries and information science

One of the major impacts of information technology has been on the library service. The distinction between a librarian and an information scientist has become blurred, for libraries have become dominated by the various forms of electronically published material. Traditionally, however, the major function of a library is to make available to the public any kind of published information or fiction, in whatever form. The skills and knowledge of a librarian therefore extend beyond knowledge of books, periodicals and newspapers. In terms of job titles, the ones most commonly used are librarian, library assistant and information officer, although their skills overlap.

Workplaces are in public libraries that provide the widest range of services, lending cassettes, records and books, and with specialist children's, local history and other services, often illustrated by exhibitions backed up with film shows, lectures, plays and occasional concerts.

Librarians

A librarian may be able to specialise in school and children's books (and perhaps work in a school library), in a music library, in a museum or university library where there could be specialist sections, in government libraries and in the great national libraries of London, Aberystwyth, Edinburgh and Belfast and the central libraries of other major cities.

Prospects

Opportunities for jobs come in all parts of the country. On the other hand, there has been little expansion in library posts – restrictions on public spending have affected libraries as well as other services. Therefore applicants with a good knowledge of modern methods of storing, cataloguing and releasing information by electronic means (information sciences) have the best chance of getting a job and being promoted.

Training

There are degree courses in librarianship at the Universities of Aberystwyth and Loughborough and at the Polytechnics of Birmingham, Brighton, Leeds, Liverpool, Manchester, Newcastle and North London, and at some colleges of higher education.

The special requirements are three A-levels or four H-grades with grades in the B to C category backed up by two to three GCSEs or equivalents including English language and maths; a foreign language is also occasionally asked for. A-levels are dependent on the subject option, but English, modern languages, computing and information sciences are highly rated, although no subject is excluded. Some of these courses are of the four-year sandwich type, with a year in a library; others are a straightforward three years' full time. There is also a three- to five-year part-time degree course at Manchester and Leeds Polytechnics for people already in a job. Graduates in other subjects can take a one-year full-time diploma course, or a two- to three-year part-time course.

As well as successfully completing an approved course, students must apply for the licentiateship of the Library Association. After two years as a licentiate, they can apply for chartered status and eventually may be able to put the letters FLA after their name – Fellow of the Library Association.

Library assistants

Training

For library assistants, the minimum entry requirements are four GCSEs/ O-grades or their equivalents, including English language. For posts of information assistant, two A-levels or three H-grades are looked for. Students can go on to take BTEC National Certificate and National Diploma awards in library and information science, and there are SCOTVEC modular courses at some Scottish colleges of technology. Alternatively, there is the City and Guilds library assistant's certificate course which is a part-time programme of studies for people who are already employed in libraries. A substantial number of colleges of further education have this course on their prospectus, and in London there are additional courses leading to a certificate in media resources. For details of all these courses and the colleges, polytechnics and universities that offer them, see the *Directory of Further Education*.

Information officers

Information officers (or information scientists) collect, store, retrieve and disseminate information, largely by electronic means. Besides libraries, there are opportunities for jobs in information offices or centres, particularly in the engineering, pharmaceutical, computing and other high-technology industries. More job opportunities are occurring in banks, insurance offices, building societies and other organisations concerned with information storage.

425

Training

Almost all professionally qualified information scientists are graduates in an information technology/computing subject. Otherwise, for a graduate without this background, the necessary preparation is to take a postgraduate course in information work. A degree and then six years of approved experience can lead to membership of the Institute of Information Scientists (IIS). To prepare for this, there is a three-year full-time BSc degree course at Leeds Polytechnic in information systems, which integrates modern languages and scientific studies. For other graduates, postgraduate courses can last from one to five years and lead to a diploma or a higher degree.

Useful school subjects extend from the arts grouping of languages, English language and literature, history, economics and on to the mathematics, information sciences and computing group.

Information

The Library Association, 7 Ridgmount Street, London WC1E 7AE
ASLIB (Association for Information Management), 26–27 Boswell Street, London WC1N 3JZ
The Institute of Information Scientists, 44 Museum Street, London WC1A 1LY

The organisations above provide free careers leaflets
Careers in Librarianship and Information Science, Kogan Page
Directory of Further Education, Hobsons

Linguist

See **interpreting** and **languages**.

Local government

Local government is one of the biggest categories of jobs, employing 12 per cent of the working population. The jobs themselves are extremely varied: town clerk (the top of the tree), zoo-keeper, **environmental health officer**, municipal refuse collector (dustman), and so on. There is a substantial professional group, including **accountants, solicitors, teachers, architects,** and a tremendous range of services requiring large administrative teams – schools, library services, social services, housing.

Working in local government does not offer much scope for the entrepreneur: the rules and regulations have been devised over the years to protect the interests of the public and these rules are now so complex that it is difficult to take any step before consulting the book of words. Another factor that has to be accepted is that the 'officers' – that is local government staff at senior level – are directed by elected representatives and both the parties and the politicians can change their policies.

Within the hierarchy of the departments – finance, legal, education, planning, housing, social services and so on – are specialists such as accountants and teachers, who have taken vocational courses or special training. Supporting them are administrative staff, working at many different levels of grade and responsibility.

Prospects

Taking England, Wales, Scotland and Northern Ireland together, there are over 500 employers. Generally, the larger County Councils offer the best prospects, although people settle very happily in the smaller District Councils: it all depends on the ambitions and attitudes of the individual, whether he or she is ambitious enough to be willing to move around, or even out of local government.

Entry is at all levels. Training is by day or block release on a variety of courses relevant to the individual's work. Most local authorities are generous with assistance for training and attending courses to improve knowledge and skills. For the officer level, entrants generally need to have a prior qualification, usually at degree level, plus some kind of postgraduate training.

Careers in local government are at four levels:

- Professional careers (including the ones already listed) that can be followed in or out of the town hall – **engineering, horticulture, law,** architecture, planning, education and so on
- Administrative staff responsible for the smooth running of offices and local government services, such as planning, **housing management**, trading standards, roads, environmental health and **social work**
- General clerical work, again capable of being done elsewhere – **secretaries, clerks**, bookkeepers
- Manual workers.

Training

For the individual professions the entrant must take the relevant degree, HND or other kind of academic or professional course and qualification.

For the administrative group, local authorities' requirements vary, but normally two A-levels or three H-grades are asked for, or a BTEC National Diploma. However, the number of graduates seeking jobs in administration – and being offered them – is increasing fast. For top jobs, people have to take the examinations that lead to membership of the Institute of Chartered Secretaries and Administrators (ICSA). It is possible to prepare thoroughly for the job of administrator by taking a degree in public administration at the Universities of Kent and Birmingham or at the Polytechnics of Leicester, Nottingham, Manchester, Sheffield and Wales. No particular A-level subjects are required for entry, but all the institutions want GCSEs or the equivalent in maths and English as part of the two or three A-level and three or four GCSE package.

For the clerical grade there are no minimum qualifications, but nowadays local authorities look for a two or three GCSE or equivalent standard, including English. If clerical officers want to take BTEC qualifications, they need to have the basic entry requirements of three GCSEs at grades A to C for the National Diploma (in business studies, for instance). Maths is also rated highly for this grade.

For manual workers there are no specified educational qualifications.

Information

Local Government Training Board, Arndale House, Arndale Centre, Luton, Bedfordshire LU1 2TS. The Board publishes leaflets, giving the exact professional and educational requirements for a wide range of possible jobs and careers

Careers in Local Government, Kogan Page

Directory of Further Education, Hobsons, lists colleges and courses in government and local administration: for example, many colleges of further education offer the BTEC National Certificate in Public Administration, which is generally regarded as an excellent preparation for work in local government: the colleges offering this course are all listed

Machinist

Engineering machinists use a wide range of machine tools to shape, cut, grind and drill metal. Among this group of jobs within the engineering industry are:

- *turners*, who use lathes to produce cylindrical and tapered components, holes, screw threads, grooves, recesses and eccentrics
- *millers*, who use milling machines to produce flat surfaces, or cut special shapes, curves, slots and grooves to drawings produced by engineers or technicians
- *borers*, who use horizontal or vertical machines to produce diameters, holes and recesses in larger workpieces
- *grinders*, who use machines to produce cylindrical or flat surfaces such as tapers, gears, cams and threads
- *planers* and *shapers*, who cut or plane to produce flat or curved surfaces or required shapes
- *drillers*, who use drilling machines to produce holes.

Machinists have to work to plans or drawings, interpreting and fulfilling the demands made by engineers or designers. They must know the capability of their machines and the sequence of actions to shape, cut or alter metal and must work carefully to exact measurements. Machinists generally work in factories or workshops, sometimes with other people, sometimes on their own. Conditions can vary from a production unit staffed by a small team to a large and noisy factory floor.

Prospects

Prospects have decreased as the engineering industry has gone through a depression, but there are about 400,000 engineering craft workers employed throughout the UK, and machinists form an important part of the team. They are to be found in every kind of manufacturing workshop, factory and plant. The availability of jobs depends on the state of the engineering industry in the particular area in which applicants live – good in some, extremely bad in others. It is now clear that machinists must be prepared to move to other parts of the country to secure a job. The shipbuilding industry, which once employed large numbers of machinists, is now in severe decline, and the steel industry, another once large employer, is also in a state of some distress.

Training

Entrants are usually 16- or 17-year-olds. Employers look for good practical skills, taking account of achievements in school metalwork, woodwork or CDT courses at GCSE level. Some set an aptitude test.

Information

The Engineering Careers Information Service, 54 Clarendon Road, Watford, Hertfordshire WD1 1LB
Engineering Careers Information Service, EITB, Fleming House, Renfrew Street, Glasgow G3 6ST

Working in Engineering, COIC
Directory of Further Education, Hobsons

Magazines

Magazines make up a significant part of the publishing industry, providing employment for journalists, printers and other staff. Broadly speaking, there are four main categories of magazine:

- consumer magazines – women's, teenagers', hobbies, holidays, and specialist interests such as boating, computing and many more
- business magazines which are closely tied to a particular industry or professional interest, such as *Packaging News, Chemical Engineer* and hundreds of others
- in-house magazines – for the employees of a company such as ICI, IBM, Marks & Spencer, and so on, and those for a particular membership such as *The Director*, a magazine of the Institute of Directors
- comics – the world of the *Beano* and other comics and magazines.

All magazines employ writers, artists, designers, journalists, a few photographers and create work and opportunities for advertisers, printers and many other trades. Magazine work creates its own career structure: either within one magazine, or the publishing company that owns it; or by transferring to another magazine published elsewhere; or, for highly specialised staff and some journalists, into newspapers. Magazines are also part of an expanding market, for although some of the weekly and monthly magazines find it difficult to keep their large circulation, newcomers are constantly starting – and sometimes disappearing just as quickly.

Ways into this kind of work are described in the section on **journalism**. What is said there largely applies to magazine work. On the other hand, magazines recruit from a wider group of people and experts than newspapers. For example, they are looking for writers on fashion, entertainment, current affairs and the host of specialist skills which are needed for trade magazines – writers on electronics, holidays, computers, cars, houses, books, gardens, and so on. This advice is true for mature entrants, of course, people who learn their skills and expertise elsewhere and then find their way to journalism. It is possible for young people to take this route, but it is a slow one. A quicker way is to try to get on to the staff of a magazine at 18-plus. To achieve this means following the journalists' routes or by being very lucky in securing a job on a magazine at 18 in a fairly humble position and working up through all the tea-making and general office duties to sub-editing and into writing. However, this door seems to be closing: there is some movement from being a secretary to an editorial assistant and then to a journalist, but fewer and fewer people are making this kind of transition.

Training

In magazine work, as for so many other jobs, the better qualified and trained the candidate, the better the chance of getting a start. A-levels, for example, are necessary, for 75 per cent of new entrants have post-A-level qualifications. After that, some form of pre-entry training is generally essential. If the job-seeker is a graduate (60 per cent of entrants are), the chances are much brighter. If the graduate has taken a training course after his or her degree, the chances are that at least an interview may be possible! Among the directly relevant courses are two at the London College of Printing. One is a postgraduate pre-entry course in periodical journalism, and the other (for A-level students) is a two-year, full-time course leading to a BTEC HND in business studies with a periodical publishing option. In addition, there are private, fee-paying training courses lasting up to 17 weeks run by commercial training organisations.

Most school subjects could be relevant. English language and literature are clearly very important at any level. There is no point in thinking of any kind of career in journalism without good skills in English. However, special knowledge or skills in almost any subject could lead to a career as a writer/journalist. Similarly, an A-level or degree in almost any subject could have potential. But training is essential, either as a pre-entry course before getting a job, or as part of a company training scheme once into a job.

When in a job, training is usually arranged in-company, and on courses arranged by the Periodical Training Council, based in London.

Information

Periodical Training Council, Imperial House, 15–19 Kingsway, London WC2B 6UN

National Council for the Training of Journalists, Carlton House, Hemnall Street, Epping, Essex CM16 4NL

Management

Of all the 200 careers described in this book, it is possible that 'management' is the most important for Britain's future. Managers are the key to success in commercial and industrial businesses. Managers are needed not only in industry. They are required for non-industrial concerns such as educational institutions, local and central government, voluntary organisations, and indeed in any place where people, products, transport and services have to be organised.

Prospects

'Manager' is a loose word, for it applies to personnel managers, advertising managers, training managers, and so on. But the greatest need is for industrial, manufacturing and commercial managers, people who organise production, new products and exports. That is where money is made, and that is where there are careers.

Training

There are various ways into management. One way is to leave school at 16, learn a craft, a trade or acquire knowledge of manufacturing processes and on the basis of this experience and knowledge to move through the ranks of assistant, junior and then senior management. The same route can be taken by an A-level school-leaver, or indeed anyone with determination, ability and the willingness to work in an industrial or commercial setting. Many of Britain's best managers have come via these routes, as craftsmen, technicians, junior managers and production workers.

Another route is to leave school at 16 or 18 and move into a college of technology or further education and take a full-time course leading to a City and Guilds, BTEC or some other kind of qualification, and then look for a job. These courses are in engineering, printing, transport, textiles, catering, construction, computing and a host of other subjects, many of which provide work experience along with college tuition. For those who go to college at 18 with A-levels or H-grades, the route can lead to BTEC or SCOTVEC HNDs or HNCs, again in the manufacturing subjects but also in business studies, which provides the theoretical study and understanding of business on which later knowledge can be built.

For students who have two or three good A-levels or three to four H-grades, there are many possibilities. Among them are degree courses in engineering or technological subjects, or business and commercial subjects, again with possibilities for work experience in companies. Having graduated, the very ambitious might take a postgraduate course, perhaps leading to a further degree or Master of Business Administration (MBA). Another possibility is any one of the science courses, then a job in industry, supported by short courses. There are qualifications to be aimed for, such as the Diploma in Management Studies (DMS) and qualifications such as these provide employers with extra evidence of the student's ambition to rise to the top.

All the courses and the careers share an appreciation that all potential managers have to work their way up from the bottom. With a degree, an HND or another qualification, it is possible to begin a little bit higher up the ladder, but for everyone a lowly start is necessary, simply to understand the nature of the business and the important role that production workers, secretaries, warehouse and transport staff all play in its success – or its failure.

One encouraging aspect of management is that school-leavers see it as important. In the 1960s the social sciences were the boom subjects; in the 1970s it was the turn of law and humanities subjects; now it is business studies and related subjects that attract 18-year-olds. So a first degree or an HND is becoming more and more essential to secure a foothold on the bottom rung of the ladder. Once there, however, the opportunities are exciting, especially for the 'movers'. The British Institute of Management (BIM) estimates that the proportion of managers who spend their working life with one firm has dropped from 34 per cent in 1968 to under 10 per cent today. There is not only mobility *between* companies but also *within* companies.

For people who want to be managers but do not want to operate at the 'sharp end' of commercial enterprises, there are managerial careers in public services and in government: for details, look at the separate entries.

For management careers almost any school subject could be appropriate. The business and commercial subjects are clearly of great use, to GCSE, A-level and degree level. Similarly, the science and maths subjects, which include computing, statistics and technology, are also very important. But so are design subjects, and arts courses to GCSE and beyond can provide the foundation for later courses on management for someone in a job with experience of the commercial and industrial world.

Information
British Institute of Management, Management House, Parker Street, London WC2B 5PT

Business, Management and Accountancy, Degree Course Guide, Hobsons

Marketing

Marketing managers find out what potential customers need and want, and then, when the product is ready to be launched, they plan and co-ordinate the effort to make it available to customers at the right time and at the right price. Marketing is increasingly taking over from **accountancy** and **finance** as the essential grounding necessary for the aspiring managing director. Why? The argument is that the marketing manager sees the product even before it is manufactured, dictates how it should be produced, and watches over its launch on to the market. Managers who have not come up the company ladder via marketing naturally dispute the assumption that the marketplace dominates the business. However, the evidence is that marketing is increasingly influencing the direction of businesses and gives the staff concerned with it a leading role and excellent opportunities for promotion.

A common misconception is that marketing is the same as selling. It is not, although some companies add to the confusion by treating 'sales and marketing' as a single department with the same staff. Sales are one aspect of marketing. The marketing manager's team have other responsibilities which include researching the market, organising and planning: the sales team follows up one part of the master plan. Of course, if the orchestration and the strategy are not right, everything collapses and the first to fall is the marketing manager.

Prospects

Opportunities are very good indeed. One reason for this is that the traditional non-marketing organisations, such as **banks, building societies,** the **law**, and public service industries, have all realised the need to market their services. So there is now scope for staff in other fields, apart from the fast-moving consumer goods areas such as electrical, food, clothing and media products.

Promotion can be fast – in both directions. The fastest movers are in the consumer goods industries – sweets, chocolate, cars, washing-machines, magazines, records. It is slower for those who market, say, oil rigs. Marketing is not for the faint-hearted: pressures are intense and security is non-existent.

Training

To get into this career, a degree is useful but not essential. Personality and flair are important factors, plus a very good business sense and a keen awareness of client needs. This knowledge can come from working one's way through a sales team, entering at 16, 18 or as a graduate, and learning from experience. However, graduates and BTEC HNC/ HND students are increasingly sought after, especially if they have taken courses in business studies, economics, marketing or finance. A techno-logical or scientific background is a big advantage – and sometimes required by companies involved in technology. Into this category come industries marketing machinery, machine tools, computers, building services, vehicles and other technologically based businesses. It is not that technologists have more flair or personality, but their knowledge of the technicalities of the product can be crucially important in understanding and exploiting the business opportunities. On the other hand, graduates and students from arts courses can become excellent marketing managers.

There are specialist degree courses in marketing at Aberystwyth (with economics), Salford (with languages), Stirling, Strathclyde and Lancas-ter (with French or German) Universities, and at the Polytechnics of Bristol, Lancashire, Manchester, Huddersfield and Sheffield. Normally, three A-levels are required for entry to degree courses, with passes in maths and English language at GCSE level as well. A modern language at GCSE or equivalent is useful. Three A-level subjects with C grades should generally secure a place on one of the degree courses. Other routes into marketing are by taking a degree or HNC/HND in virtually any subject, although a marketing option within a management studies or business studies course is very useful indeed.

There are career routes, too, for post-A-level applicants. They can take a part-time, two-year course at a college leading to the qualifying certificate of the Institute of Marketing. Students need at least one A-level or two H-grades and four GCSEs or equivalents, including English language and maths. The certificate can then be followed up with a further year's study for the diploma of the Institute of Marketing. Alternative ways into the diploma course are by taking a BTEC or SCOTVEC HND in business and finance with marketing options. Graduates are also advised to take Institute of Marketing courses, for they give a good theoretical as well as practical basis for work.

Information

The Institute of Marketing, Moor Hall, Cookham, Maidenhead, Berkshire SL6 9QH. The Institute has a complete list of suitable marketing courses at degree level

Business, Management and Accountancy, Degree Course Guide, Hobsons, gives degree courses both in marketing and the wider business and management area

Directory of Further Education, Hobsons, gives details of the courses leading to SCOTVEC, BTEC, the Institute of Marketing and other qualifications, and the colleges that offer them

Working in Marketing, COIC

Market research

Market researchers find out what people want, don't want, and why. They are part of a marketing team, finding out the facts upon which products and the publicity will later depend. Numerically and in terms of opinion, they try to discover what customers or clients require/need/ would be tempted to buy. It is a key job in any business for if the researchers get it wrong the whole business will be sent heading for disaster. Market researchers also need to be aware of what the competition is doing, so the team must keep a wary eye on the marketplace, shops, stores or wherever the rivalry is intense.

To get in to market research really requires a degree – not essential, but three-quarters of marketing researchers are graduates. Economics is the best way in, followed by psychology. Statistics is very useful indeed, although market research is not concerned only with numbers. Appreciating and translating people's opinions is an important asset, more important than swiftness with maths and statistics, and arts graduates are good material. A career in market research can be with a company – any company – that has a structured approach to product development by using a market research team. But there are also 200 or so market research agencies whose business is finding out the facts for companies and organisations. They are specialised businesses and, usually, are on the lookout for women. Over a third of people in this field are women, and the number of them in employment is growing. The very able ones of either sex set up their own agencies, once they have learned the skills in someone else's, and normally they don't look back.

School subjects of relevance are clearly economics, commerce, business studies or any other course linked to business, but most subjects are potentially useful and mathematics/statistics are particularly valuable. A-level or H-grade subjects should be in the same grouping, and degrees in the business/mathematics/statistics area are an excellent preparation but arts and science degrees, depending on the calibre of the person, could be the basis for further study and work. Anyone who is working in marketing or market research can take the Diploma of the Market Research Society. As an alternative back-up for an arts or science graduate, a postgraduate course in business studies for a BTEC or SCOTVEC award would be very useful.

Information
The Market Research Society, 175 Oxford Street, London W1R 1TA

Mathematics

Some people think that mathematics means number-crunching. But computers and pocket calculators crunch numbers: mathematicians are involved in designing those computers and calculators. Mathematicians generally define their work as solving theoretical and practical problems concerned with engineering, economics, marketing, physical sciences, computing and statistics.

As a result, they are much in demand, particularly in **actuarial work**, and in **finance**. There is also a substantial and increasing demand for mathematicians to work in the science and electronics-based industries. If none of those appeals, the UK is desperately short of mathematics teachers both in schools and in further education. For the brightest academics among them, university and research council-inspired projects are other areas of employment.

Training

To prepare for these opportunities a degree in maths or statistics is the first requirement. The *Degree Course Guide* for these subjects gives all the details that applicants need – university and polytechnic courses, the differences between them, and careers after taking a degree. To get a place, two or three A-levels are needed (or three or four H-grades) with grades varying from three As at prestigious universities to Ds and Es in two A-levels at some polytechnics and colleges. A pass in maths at A-level is essential, and physics may be required or preferred. At school, other maths or science-based subjects are generally taken alongside maths, but it is possible to take a maths degree course having taken a mixture of maths and science/arts A-levels.

For those with lesser school-based qualifications, it is possible to take a two-year part-time or full-time course leading to the BTEC HNC/HND in maths, statistics and computing. An A-level pass in maths is required, plus four other subjects at GCSE level.

Information

Institute of Mathematics and its Applications, Maitland House, Warrior Square, Southend-on-Sea, Essex SS1 2JY
Mathematical Association, 259 London Road, Leicester LE2 3BE

Careers in Mathematics and *Routes to Qualification in Mathematics*, Institute of Mathematics and its Applications
Mathematics and Statistics, Degree Course Guide, Hobsons
Working in Mathematics, COIC

Meat industry

Everyone thinks they know what a butcher does but, to be more accurate, we should describe careers and jobs as being in 'the meat industry' because there is a range of jobs and responsibilities. These include local retail shops, buying meat for supermarkets, and buying and preparing meat for hotels, restaurants and caterers. Another group of jobs are with food manufacturing and processing companies which sell to the supermarket chains.

Training
A good all-round education is needed, but there are no formal academic requirements. Training is on-the-job, and there are City and Guilds courses at colleges of further education, leading to examinations of the Institute of Meat.

Information
Institute of Meat, Langford, Bristol BS18 7DY

Mechanical engineering

For many, many years mechanical engineering has had the image of being concerned with noisy, dirty industry, whether steelmills, car factories, foundries, workshops or shipyards. Though once this was an accurate picture it is no longer so. Mechanical engineering is about designing and making machines, and it is very likely that these will incorporate microprocessors and electronics. Indeed, one could say that the 'mechanicals', being involved in every kind of production, are better placed than most people to take advantage of new technology. Even now they are in oil, chemicals, textiles, printing, packaging, aerospace, construction, food and transport, to name a few industries. Degree courses have been radically adapted to include computing as a major element. Therefore, it is true to say that the prospects for mechanical engineers are very promising indeed.

Among the qualities and expertise that engineers are expected to have are an understanding of design, business methods and structures, the scientific and technological aspects of engineering, and marketing. To cope with these wide expectations, degree courses have been revised so that 'engineering applications' are an important element of any course:

this means training in the development of an idea, through production, to marketing and selling the product. In the past, mechanical engineers often became managing directors: with the 'applications' training it is likely that even more of them will be able to reach this level.

Prospects

Each year about 2,000 graduates in mechanical engineering leave higher education and look for jobs. Many have already made their first moves or been offered a secure place as a result of contacts during their period of industrial training or through sponsorship schemes. The figures show that 60 per cent of graduates go straight into a job. Most of these enter engineering/manufacturing industries where they continue learning, aiming for a professional qualification. Another 20 per cent are overseas students. The remainder carry on at universities or polytechnics, taking a higher degree, or they go into other kinds of work. Few are unemployed.

Training

Of all the engineering degree courses, mechanical engineering is the most popular, for students recognise its potential for the future. It also carries many opportunities for sponsorship: 30 per cent of all first-degree mechanical engineering students are sponsored. To get a place, two to three A-levels or four to five H-grades are looked for. The necessary A-level grades vary: Oxford and Cambridge automatically state three As, Imperial College, London (very high reputation), is not much different (ABB), while some polytechnics will accept two Ds or even two Es. The A-levels or H-grades need to be in maths and science subjects, including physics, physical science and chemistry, but engineering itself at A-level is a good preparation. For GCSE or equivalent subjects, the same ones crop up, and colleges also expect English language at GCSE.

Most university and polytechnic courses are of the sandwich type, so students are able to gain industrial experience as they work towards a degree. After graduating, the mechanicals move off into the industries already listed, plus a few more. Graduate status is a help in working towards a professional engineering award, but is not essential. Students who leave school at 16 take a BTEC or SCOTVEC certificate or diploma and become a technician, or join industry at16-plus and train on the job as a craft worker or technician, taking City and Guilds or BTEC qualifications on a part-time day- or block-release basis.

Information

Institution of Mechanical Engineers, 1 Birdcage Walk, London SW1H 9JJ

Mechanical Engineering: The Chartered Engineer and *Training Opportunities in Engineering,* Institution of Mechanical Engineers
Technology, Degree Course Guide, Hobsons
Directory of Further Education, Hobsons, lists courses and colleges leading to degree, BTEC HND, National Certificate and National Diploma and SCOTVEC National Certificate

Medicine

Medicine includes many different careers, but they all have in common the medical care of people who are at home, in hospitals or at special centres. Among the specialist careers are doctor, surgeon, pathologist, gynaecologist, **physiotherapist, nurse, dentist,** medical photographer, radiologist (under **radiography**) and many more.

Doctor

Medicine is one of the most varied professions. Everyone is familiar with doctors in general practice and hospitals, but many others are in industry, the Armed Forces, merchant navy, and civil airlines, in government service, or doing full-time research. Their work varies from the essential day-to-day contact with patients to the most advanced scientific studies. The opportunities for specialisation range from paediatrics to geriatrics, from cardiology to rheumatology, neurosurgery to orthopaedics, obstetrics and gynaecology to chemical pathology, psychotherapy to plastic surgery, among many other branches. A speciality should be chosen within two or three years of graduation.

Learning to be a doctor involves the most expensive – and one of the longest – courses of study for any degree, so it is essential that students who are thinking of medicine as a career are absolutely sure this is what they want to do with their working lives before taking the first step and applying to enter a medical school.

Training

During their first sixth-form year at school, students may begin

441

specialising in science subjects – chemistry, physics and biology – which form the basis of the medical curriculum and will obviously be good preparation for later studies. Students who have specialised in the arts or classics may sometimes be accepted by a university medical school, but an inadequate science background will involve taking a first Bachelor of Medicine (MB) course, something not all medical schools offer. This course lasts a year and does not qualify for a mandatory Local Education Authority grant.

Some minimum academic requirements are common to all medical schools and, under the overall supervision of the General Medical Council (GMC) every university medical faculty and medical school has its own syllabus and regulations for the course of study in medicine. Details of the entry requirements at each university in the UK are published annually in *University Entrance, The Official Guide*. These are summarised in the British Medical Association leaflet *Medical Schools, Requirements for Entry*. Applications for admission to medical schools are handled by UCCA.

The standards of entry for any medical teaching centre are exacting. Applicants called for interview will face searching questions about their motivation, their work at school, hobbies and personal interests, quite apart from having to produce evidence of their academic achievements. A key question will be their reason for wanting to become doctors. The essential personal qualities for a doctor are compassion, resourcefulness, boundless energy and perseverance.

Apart from these personal qualities, excellent A-level or H-grade passes are required. Grades of three As or Bs are generally demanded by medical schools, and this cuts out a large number of applicants. Even so, applications are in the ratio of ten for every place. The long course of study leads to problems, too. The drop-out rate for medicine is around nine per cent, and in any one year about ten per cent of the group has to take resits of examinations not passed the first time.

Accepted students begin their first year's training with the second MB course, which includes instruction in anatomy, physiology, biochemistry, psychology, medical sociology and the basics of pathology and pharmacology. This is followed by the clinical course of approximately three years, during which students are attached to a clinical 'firm', usually consisting of two consultants, senior registrar and newly qualified houseman. They become familiar with working in hospital wards, get their first introduction to patients and learn the techniques of making physical examinations and obtaining the patients' medical histories. Throughout the three years they will attend lectures on all aspects of medical practice.

After qualifying at the end of the fifth year, graduates must complete one pre-registration year as house officers in general hospitals. On the successful conclusion of this, application can be made for full registration with the GMC, and then an area of specialisation can be chosen, if the doctor so wants.

Medical laboratory scientists or scientific officers

These people are the technicians of medicine. They carry out laboratory experiments to diagnose and treat disease. Prospects are good and many are graduates, particularly of biochemistry.

Training
In theory it is possible to start with GCSEs or their equivalents in biology and chemistry and to take courses such as a two-year day-release BTEC National Certificate in science before moving on to an HNC in medical laboratory sciences. But as many MLS personnel have A-levels or degrees, it is becoming very difficult indeed for a 16-year-old to get into this career. Other relevant degrees are in microbiology, biology, chemistry, physics and engineering. Similarly, at A-level these are the subjects to take in order to prepare properly for a career as a medical laboratory scientist.

The entries for **nursing, occupational therapy, dentistry, physiotherapy** and **dietetics** give the details about entry requirements for these careers.

Information
British Medical Association, BMA House, Tavistock Square, London WC1H 9JP

Medical Training – Medical Schools, BMA
Medical Schools –-Requirements for Entry, BMA
Learning Medicine, BMA
Medicine, Degree Course Guide, Hobsons
Directory of Further Education, Hobsons, gives details of colleges offering courses in, for instance, medical information processing, medical

laboratory science, medical photography and medical records and health care

Occupations, COIC, gives detailed analyses of all the medical and para-medical careers

Working in Medicine and Surgery, COIC

Merchant navy

Over the last 10 years, Britain's merchant fleet has declined from over 50 million tonnes to under 15 million, and is still declining. Other shipping fleets including the Japanese, Scandinavian and American have also been reduced as world trade has declined. But the UK's fall has been the most dramatic, and matters are not likely to improve. British shipping-lines now fly the flags of Panama and Liberia to escape the high costs of operating out of Britain and employing highly paid British crews.

Job opportunities are very limited. The ocean fleets, Shell tankers, the Royal Fleet Auxiliary (which supplies Royal Naval vessels) and the other merchant shipping companies recruit some people each year, so it is worthwhile writing to them.

A merchant navy officer can train to be an expert in one of four groups of personnel: deck officer, engineer, radio officer or catering services. Deck ratings and catering staff can achieve promotion from the ranks of rating to officer, and some companies operate a deck-to-officer training course.

Deck and engineer officers

Deck officers are responsible for the loading and discharge of cargoes, navigation and the welfare and discipline of the crew. From their ranks come captains. Engineer officers spend most of their time below decks and are responsible for the operation and maintenance of the ship's machinery and services.

Training

Deck and engineer officers enter as cadets for a training schedule that is divided between periods at sea and time at college. Exams have to be passed to gain promotion. For deck officers the initial training scheme lasts three years. The studying is at an approved nautical college and leads to a BTEC National Diploma in Nautical Science together with the Department of Transport Class 3 Certificate of Competency. For a cadetship, a minimum of four GCSEs or O-grades is needed, including maths, physics and English language. A-level entrants must have studied maths and physics and have passed at least one of these subjects at A-level or H-grade.

Engineer officers take a sandwich course with periods of on-ship training alternating with study at approved colleges. This leads to a BTEC HNC in Marine Engineering – a qualification that gives some exemptions from the Department of Transport's Engineer Class 2 Certificate. The minimum entry level is four GCSEs or equivalents with passes in maths and a science, preferably physics, and English language. Alternatively, students with an A-level pass in maths or physics can take a BTEC HND which gains them Class 1 exemptions.

Deck and marine engineer officers can take a two-year full-time course leading to a BTEC National Diploma in Maritime Technology at specialist marine colleges at Southampton, South Shields, and South Mersey (Liverpool). This is a novel and innovative development in further education which is designed to equip people to go on to HND courses linked to deck and engineer officer senior certificates of competency. In addition, there are HND and degree courses for deck and engineering entrants for which The Marine Society offers scholarships.

Radio officers

These officers are responsible for a ship's radio and communications service. There is a need for more officers to be trained in electronics.

Training

Radio officers take a three-year full-time course at a recognised radio college. After the second year, successful students are awarded the BTEC National Diploma in Marine Radio and Radar, and after the third year there is a BTEC HNC course in marine radio and radar.

To gain entry, three or four GCSEs or equivalents at grades A, B or C are required, including maths, physics and English language. Candidates cannot go to sea until they have completed the course.

Ratings and catering staff

For ratings and for catering staff, entry is normally through the National Sea Training College at Gravesend. There are no formal academic entry requirements, but shipping companies, because of keen competition, normally expect candidates to have been successful in maths and English language at GCSE.

It is clear that essential school subjects are maths and sciences, particularly physics or physical science. For catering, some interest in cookery is expected. For ratings, the companies look for technical or scientific interests and aptitude, physical fitness, and a genuine wish or liking for a life at sea.

Information

Department of Transport, Marine Division, Sunley House, High Holborn, London WC1V 6LP
Institute of Marine Engineers, 76 Mark Lane, London EC3R 7JN
The Marine Society, 202 Lambeth Road, London SE1 7JW

Marine Engineering, A Challenging Career, Institute of Marine Engineers

Metallurgy

Metallurgy comprises a wide range of scientific and engineering disciplines concerned with the study, extraction, refining, alloying and fabrication of metals. Specialised interests range from materials science to extraction of metals from ores, from microchips to oil platform structures, from special alloys for submarines and aeroplanes to metal ceramics for space technology, from superconductors to superinsulators. Metallurgy is continuously developing as a branch of the wider field of materials science and technology. Career opportunities in the future will be related as much to the new materials – alloys, plastics, ceramics – as to the traditional industries based on steel, copper, lead or zinc. The supply of scientists and engineers with appropriate education and training may be affected by reduced demand for metallurgists by traditional manufacturing industries.

Training

There are degree courses in materials science and/or metallurgy at most universities and some polytechnics. For details of these courses, the variations between them, entry requirements and career possibilities, consult the Degree Course Guide on *Technology*. For entry, two or three A-levels or three or four H-grades are needed in mathematics and science subjects. Mathematics is occasionally required at A-level and generally it is necessary to have physics and chemistry at GCSE or equivalent. Professional engineers will aspire to the status of Chartered Engineer through membership of the Institute of Metals or the Institution of Mining and Metallurgy, the qualifying bodies of the Engineering Council. Honours degrees and industrial training form the necessary basic qualifications.

For those who do not take a degree there is a three-year part-time course leading to a BTEC National Certificate in Metallurgy. The minimum entry requirement is at least three GCSE subjects, with two of them in maths and a science subject; people with GCSEs or the equivalents are given exemptions from some units. Following this, there is a two-year part-time course leading to a BTEC HNC in metallurgy or a three-year course for the HND. At this level the work is designated technologist or technician, depending on how far the student goes in acquiring qualifications. For professional status, holders of the BTEC HND qualify for the Associateship of the Institute of Metals or the Institution of Mining and Metallurgy. Successful honours graduates can become full members of these. The essential school subjects at GCSE and A-level are: mathematics, physics, chemistry, physical science or engineering science.

Information

The Institute of Metals, 1 Carlton House Terrace, London SW1Y 5DB
The Institution of Mining and Metallurgy, 44 Portland Place, London W1N 4BR

Technology, Degree Course Guide, Hobsons
Directory of Further Education, Hobsons, for colleges providing the BTEC certificate and diploma courses, as well as City and Guilds and other courses

Meteorology

Meteorologists study the weather. The largest employer is the Meteorological Office, which is responsible for providing meteorological services to central and local government, aviation (both civil and military), public corporations, industry, the media and general public as well as undertaking a wide-ranging meteorological research programme. There are also limited opportunities for employment in industry and universities. Staff in the Meteorological Office are mostly scientific Civil Servants.

Training

Entry as a Scientific Officer or above generally requires a degree or BTEC HNC or HND in a scientific discipline, preferably maths, physics, meteorology (normally with maths or physics), computer science or electronics. For entry as an Assistant Scientific Officer, at least four GCSEs or O-grades are required, which must include English language, maths or physics (preferably both); A-levels or H-grades, particularly in maths or physics, are advantageous. Degree courses in meteorology combined with maths or physics are available at Reading University. There are also BSc courses at East Anglia, Lancaster, London and Newcastle upon Tyne Universities where meteorology is part of the environmental sciences course. Higher degree courses (MSc) are also available at these and some other universities.

Competition for appointment in the Meteorological Office is very keen. Training is provided at the Meteorological Office's own residential college, where courses last between four weeks and five months. There are good career prospects.

School subjects of particular relevance at all levels are maths and physics, while computer studies, electronics and statistics are also very useful. The preferred degree disciplines are mentioned above, while geography, environmental science, chemistry and oceanography are the disciplines least likely to lead to success in the competition for appointment.

Information

Meteorological Office, Met 0 10 Recruitment, London Road, Bracknell, Berkshire RG12 2SZ

Annual Report of the Meteorological Office, HMSO
Mathematics and Physics, Degree Course Guides, Hobsons
Directory of Further Education, Hobsons

Midwifery

Midwifery is the care of women during pregnancy and childbirth and the mother and baby for at least 10 days and up to 28 days following the birth. Midwives are responsible for conducting the delivery of the baby if there are no complications. They work in hospitals, or in health centres, doctors' surgeries and the women's homes. Community midwives working outside the hospital mainly give care to women during pregnancy and to the mother and baby after birth, but occasionally look after a woman during childbirth if she has chosen to have her baby at home. Most community midwives need to have a driving licence.

Prospects

There are over 28,000 midwives currently practising in the UK. There is plenty of demand from the NHS (which employs most of them). The remainder are employed in private clinics and hospitals or work abroad. A few are self-employed and are booked by a woman when she is pregnant to give total care, for which the midwife charges a fee.

Training

The minimum age of entry for persons without nurse training (direct entry) is 17 years. The educational entry qualification is five subjects at GCSE grades A, B or C or equivalents. Subjects must include English language, and maths or a science subject. There is keen competition for places, as at present there is only one training school, which is in England, offering the three-year training for direct entrants. Consequently some applicants wait until A-levels have been taken (and passed). It is expected that in the foreseeable future there will be more training institutions offering midwifery training for direct entrants.

The majority of midwives train after they have become registered general nurses. Midwifery training for these nurses lasts 18 months; for direct entrants, or nurses who are not general nurses, it is three years. Occasionally, mature entrants take up midwifery after a career-break.

Beyond the basic qualification there are advanced midwifery diplomas, and midwives can also qualify as midwife teachers or managers or engage in research.

Midwifery used to be entirely a women's profession. Although a few men enter the profession, the majority of midwives are still women. At school the most useful subjects are: biology, social biology and human biology, with English language, maths and almost any other subject to GCSE grades A, B or C, with A-levels in the biological sciences or other sciences, or a combination of arts and sciences if students intend to take up nursing after A-levels or H-grades.

Information
United Kingdom Central Council for Nursing, Midwifery and Health Visiting, 23 Portland Place, London W1N 3AF

Mining

A fuller title should perhaps be 'mining and minerals engineering and quarrying'. Mining involves extracting from the earth minerals that can be processed into raw materials and fuels to feed other industries, or be manufactured into useful products. The minerals themselves can be metals (copper, iron, lead, zinc, etc.) or non-metals such as sand, clay, gravel, coal, phosphates, etc. Minerals engineering is the separation of the mined material into useful products and waste; its processing, purification and refining. So although coal-mining is what most people think of first when 'mining' is mentioned, it is only one of the many careers within this large area of work.

For mining engineers, employment within the UK is mainly in the coal industry, either with British Coal or with a contractor. Apart from coal, there is a little tin and iron mining, but for other minerals the opportunities are overseas, particularly in South Africa and Zambia. Some graduates join international mining companies, which means they must be prepared to go anywhere in the world, sometimes to inhospitable places.

Companies involved in quarrying supply stone, gravel and sand to building and road construction projects. There are jobs for minerals engineers here, too, plus jobs in local authority and government departments in waste disposal, pollution control, and the reclamation of useful products from industrial waste. The scientifically interested can go into government or company research labs and development units, looking into new processes concerned with waste and pollution.

Prospects
Each year about 260 mining engineers and about 60 minerals engineers emerge on to the job market from universities and polytechnics. They

are generally snapped up, although many go overseas either as employees of UK or international companies or to work for overseas firms. Prospects are therefore good.

Training

To prepare for this work, there are degree courses in mining engineering with company sponsorship (see the Degree Course Guide on *Technology* for a list of the institutions). Generally, three A-levels or four to five H-grades in maths, physics and chemistry, or with physical science or geology as alternatives, are looked for. The courses are three or four years full time or four years sandwich, and some scholarships are available from the Engineering Council and from some employers.

Following the academic course and professional work experience, most engineers aim for professional status within the Institution of Mining Engineers, the Institute of Metals or the Institution of Mining and Metallurgy: write to these bodies for details of how to qualify for membership (addresses below). After that, suitably qualified members of the institutions will be registered with the Engineering Council as chartered engineers (CEng), technician engineers (TEng) or engineering technicians (Tech).

Within these industries are other employees – miners, technicians, managers, metallurgists, drivers and administrative as well as industrial staff. The entry qualifications, training and prospects for these other jobs within the mining, quarrying and related industries vary and should be checked by writing to the institutions or British Coal or other major employers.

The academic subjects that lead to mining and minerals engineering are obviously the sciences, both at GCSE or O-grade and at A-level/H-grade. The subjects have been listed, but to them could be added engineering science and surveying at A-level or equivalent, and technological subjects at GCSE or equivalent.

Information

The Institution of Mining Engineers, Danum House, South Parade, Doncaster DN1 2DY

The Institution of Mining and Metallurgy, 44 Portland Place, London W1N 4BR

The Institute of Metals, 1 Carlton House Terrace, London SW1Y 5DB

International Mining, Mineral Industry Manpower and Careers Unit, Prince Consort Road, London SW7 2BP
Technology, Degree Course Guide, Hobsons

Modelling

In preparing this book, the Association of Model Agents was asked to give an opinion of modelling as a career. Here is the Association's response: 'There are probably fewer than a thousand models in the UK making anything like a decent living, and they are almost all in London. Hardly anyone is suitable for it, and the result of any publicity – television, radio, newspaper, etc., however cautionary – is always that hundreds, probably thousands, of young people get "conned" by their local "model school", "model agent" or "photographer" who thinks that 15 or 20 mediocre pictures, all practically the same, constitute a model's portfolio. The real model business is tiny and unfortunately denied to virtually all young people. You will be doing your readers no favours by putting the idea into their heads.'

A severe opinion, and one that is no doubt accurate. For the 'fewer than a thousand' who are in this work, the two groups are fashion models, who work within the clothing and fashion industry, and advertising models. Fashion modelling can be both photographic and live, as in fashion shows.

Most models are self-employed freelancers, working through agencies that promote, manage and represent the model on an exclusive basis. Beginners find it very difficult indeed to make a start, for a reputable agency will take on only one or two people each year. And yet the agent's approval is the first, and necessary, step to work. A would-be model not yet deterred by this analysis must have the basic entry qualifications. There are no specific educational qualifications: the qualities needed are physical, i.e. a height of at least five feet seven inches (1.70m) and a 34–24–34-inch figure. Qualifications from a 'model school' do not impress agents, and nor does the modelling course offered at the London College of Fashion if the student does not also meet the physical specification.

Information

Association of Model Agents, St Catherine's Mews, Milner Street, London SW3 2PU

Motor mechanic

Mechanics work in garages and other establishments which sell, repair and carry out maintenance on all kinds of vehicles or for organisations that own fleets of vehicles, such as department stores, delivery firms, the AA, RAC and car-hire firms. The job can vary from a small roadside garage where the mechanic deals direct with customers and is expected to know about every kind of vehicle, or a large garage which is the agent for a single manufacturer. Mechanics who are ambitious can move up to supervisor and manager, or if they have the money, open their own garage.

To do this work requires, first of all, a strong and permanent interest in cars, lorries, motor-cycles and so on, because most of a mechanic's life will be spent either head under or head over one, or advising people on what is wrong with their vehicle. The work environment is not cosy: it can be cold, noisy and the work none too clean. But despite these disadvantages there is no lack of keen applicants. Cars fascinate young people and the demand for apprenticeships has always exceeded the number of places available. There are now fewer and fewer traditional apprenticeships because many young people come in after taking part in a youth training programme which includes on- and off-the-job instruction.

Training

When someone is taken on as an apprentice or trainee, the period of training can last from two to four years, depending on the nature of the programme of work and training. While employed the trainee can take a City and Guilds certificate. The courses vary, and for a full list of the courses and the colleges that offer them, consult the *Directory of Further Education* under automobile engineering. If a trainee wants to specialise there are separate modular courses in electrics, brakes, transmission, etc. There are no rigid entry qualifications either for the City and Guilds courses or for a traineeship. On the other hand, because of the demand, employers can be very choosy, and they look for GCSEs, particularly in maths, technical subjects, metalwork, mechanics, sciences and so on.

If a mechanic wishes to take further qualifications, he or she can study for a BTEC or SCOTVEC National Diploma, HNC or HND. By the time that he or she gets to this stage, the mechanic is likely to be looking for a position as a supervisor or manager.

Information

The Motor Agents Association, 201 Great Portland Street, London W1N 6AB

Scottish Motor Trade Association, 3 Palmerston Place, Edinburgh EH12 5AQ

Vehicle Builders and Repairers Association, Belmont House, Finkle Lane, Gildersome, Leeds LS27 7TW

Work with Motor Vehicles, COIC
Directory of Further Education, Hobsons

Museums and art galleries

The work and qualifications required to become a museum keeper or curator are given in the entry **curator**.

To help him or her, a curator may have an assistant curator (or in large museums such as the Science Museum and the British Museum, a group of assistants) aided by research assistants. Another job is that of conservation officer, someone who works on the restoration, repair, protection and conservation of exhibits.

Prospects

Career prospects are not rosy: there are few openings and competition is keen. Promotion is on the wait-and-see basis, and to move up it may be necessary to move to another museum. In the large museums of London, Edinburgh, Cardiff or elsewhere, the staff are part of the Civil Service. Other galleries or museums are run by local authorities, and there are some private institutions.

Conservation officer

Conservation officers are usually required to have scientific qualifications, manual dexterity and patience. It is increasingly common for those entering the field to have taken a specialised course in the restoration or conservation of pictures, archaeological material, textiles, furniture, etc. following completion of a degree, usually in chemistry. A list of such courses is published by the United Kingdom Institute for Conservation.

Education officer

Anyone wishing to work in a museum's educational service should have a degree in one of the following subjects: anthropology, archaeology, art history, botany, chemistry, geography, geology, history, physics or zoology, and additionally a teaching qualification and teaching experience.

Designers

A museum designer would normally hold a degree or equivalent qualification specialising in either three-dimensional work, graphic design, or both.

Technicians

Technicians normally hold A-levels or their equivalents, NDD, or DipAD in sculpture and industrial design. Trade qualifications may be required for appropriate subjects. Much training is in-service, undertaken in the employee's museum.

Training

As well as the qualifications and training mentioned for the various types of museum work, the Museums Association offers professional qualifications to those working in museums in the curatorial, conservation and technical fields.

The Institute of Archaeology at London University has a degree course in conservation; chemistry at A-level is normally required. For assistants, four relevant GCSEs are needed in theory, but in fact most candidates have much higher qualifications.

The relevant school subjects at any level, but particularly at A-level, are: history, history of art, chemistry, geology, zoology, archaeology; other useful subjects are physical science, social history, modern languages and classical languages and civilisation.

Information

Museums Association, 34 Bloomsbury Way, London WC1A 2SF

Careers in Museums, Museums Association
History (which includes archaeology), *Geological and Environmental Sciences,*

455

and *Art and Design* (which includes the history of art), Degree Course Guides, Hobsons

Music

Careers in music can be at several different levels. Listed below are some of the most popular options:

Performing

To be a performer generally requires years of training and then practice and performances throughout one's life. It is therefore a very demanding profession, but one that brings an enormous amount of pleasure both to the performer and the audience, although not many practitioners say so – they just talk about the hard work. Training begins at music college. To gain entry depends on GCSE and A-level qualifications and performance at an audition. The Guildhall School of Music and Drama, the Royal Academy of Music, the Royal College of Music, the Royal Northern College of Music, and other colleges provide full-time courses. Alternatively, students can study at local colleges on a full-time or part-time basis for licentiate diplomas, college awards and graduate diplomas (see the *Directory of Further Education* for a full list of courses and colleges).

London, provincial and BBC orchestras and opera houses employ full-time musicians. However, most people are freelancers, looking for occasional contract work. Television commercials, films, radio, live concerts and recording sessions are other work opportunities. In between is long practice at home or in a studio. Some performers teach part time, or they take a quite different job and are musicians in their spare time. Either way, it is the love of music that keeps them going.

Teaching

Teaching music is a different career. To prepare for a school-teaching job requires a degree or diploma in music (for secondary schools) or a primary education qualification with some specialist studies in music. It is essential to be a performer, and better still to be able to play more than one instrument and to teach choral works. At the best schools (that means those with the best teachers) there is likely to be a school orchestra or band, visits to concerts, a choral society, a good record library, and opportunities for pupils to learn to play instruments and to make their own music.

Sound engineers

Sound engineers (who are not likely to be musicians) are responsible for the quality of sound in a recording studio. Any musician hoping to get into this kind of work needs to understand the electronics of sound reproduction. If the engineer is a musician, he or she might well be called a 'music technologist' and work in recording studios for the broadcasting organisations or for manufacturers.

Music therapy

Another career is in music therapy. Music can help physically and mentally handicapped children and adults to relax, as well as give them a mental and emotional stimulus. To prepare for this work, which is very demanding, there are one-year full-time postgraduate courses: candidates are required to have a degree in music or at least a three-year full-time musical education.

Music administration

Music administration is everything from being the director of an opera house to selling tickets to the audience. At the level of senior administrator, the work demands great skill in business planning, marketing, organising, budgeting. Administrators are employed by orchestras, concert halls, agents and provincial theatres. They need not be musicians themselves, although most administrators have applied for and been appointed to these jobs because they are clearly interested in music. But the theatres look for business acumen before instrumental skills. The route to these jobs is via any kind of business or management training at degree level or BTEC National Diplomas and HNDs, plus experience of work in other businesses. To help them, administrators have a staff which may include an accountant, secretary, sales staff, transport personnel, and so on.

Musical instrument technology

Musical instrument technology is a craft skill: making and repairing instruments. There are two- and three-year courses leading to City and Guilds certificates and to college certificates, and there are BTEC National Diploma and HND courses in musical instrument studies and repair. For the diploma, three GCSEs are required, preferably including maths and a craft subject, and for the HND at least one A-level plus four GCSEs or equivalents are required. Unlike other jobs, craft skills are more important here than musical ability: if the two are combined, the opportunities for the instrument technologist are considerably increased.

Piano tuners come into this category, as do other instrument tuners and repairers. There are City and Guilds courses in string and keyboard instrument manufacture for those who want to learn the skills.

Training

For any of these careers music must feature significantly at school to GCSE or O-grade, A level or H-grade. If this is combined with passes in other subjects, the opportunities open up for degree and diploma courses. English, arts and science subjects are all acceptable, and for the craft careers skills in woodwork, design and technology are clearly very useful indeed.

Information

UK Council for Music Education and Training, University of Reading School of Education, London Road, Reading RG1 5AQ
Music Advisers National Association, County Music Adviser, County Hall, Hertford SG13 8DW

Careers in the Music Business, Kogan Page
British Music Education Yearbook, Rhinegold Publishing
Choosing Your Music Course, Jennifer Anne Lera, Pullen Publications
Music, Degree Course Guide, Hobsons
Directory of Further Education, Hobsons
Working in Music, COIC

Naval architecture

Despite its title, this is an engineering subject. Naval architects are engineers who play a key role as project leaders and specialists in the design, building and marketing of any system which has to move on or under the sea, including merchant ships, warships, drilling platforms, semi-submersibles, submarines, yachts and hovercraft. Some of them are among the most complex and highly valued systems produced by mankind. Today, naval architects have a wider range of employment opportunities than ever before, both in the UK and abroad. The development in the exploration and exploitation of offshore resources has more than compensated for the contraction of shipbuilding and shipping in the UK.

Prospects

Naval architects are concerned with a wide range of work depending on their education, training and experience which also provide the essential background to their major roles as general managers and engineering managers. There are many opportunities for foreign travel. As specialists they are involved in: design and consultancy, production, maintenance and repair; marketing and selling; commissioning, operating and salvaging; regulating and surveying; research, development and testing; education and training. They work for: ship and repair yards, offshore rig fabricators and operators; government departments; classification societies; consultants; equipment manufacturers; small craft and yacht builders; research organisations; universities, polytechnics and colleges; shipping companies.

Training

Fully qualified naval architects are members of the Royal Institution of Naval Architects (RINA) and as such are entitled to be registered with the Engineering Council. The education training and experience required for membership of RINA conform to the standards laid down for all professional engineering institutions who are nominated bodies of the Engineering Council.

At school or college a broad range of subjects should be studied at GCSE level, covering both the arts and sciences and including the essential subjects of maths, physics and English language. These studies should lead to qualifications satisfying the entry requirements for either an accredited degree (BEng) course if corporate membership of RINA is sought, or an accredited certificate (BTEC/SCOTVEC HNC in Engineering) course for associate membership.

The minimum qualifications for entry to an accredited degree (BEng) course are A-levels in maths and physics or their Scottish equivalents. Acceptance on a particular course is normally dependent on an interview as well as the A-level grades achieved, and to have a wide choice of courses it is advisable to take an appropriate third subject at A-level. Bridges between educational routes exist, and students with degree potential taking BTEC/SCOTVEC certificates and diplomas may be considered for entry to accredited degree (BEng) courses if merit passes are obtained in a number of mathematical and science subjects at an appropriate level.

The following universities specialise in naval architecture: Glasgow, Newcastle upon Tyne, Southampton (BEng in ship science), Strathclyde and University College, London. There are also first-degree courses in marine engineering, marine technology and marine processes. Full details of the courses may be obtained from the registrars. Local colleges of technology and institutes of higher education should be consulted on educational routes leading to the award of BTEC/ SCOTVEC HNCs in engineering.

Information
Education and Training Officer, The Royal Institution of Naval Architects, 10 Upper Belgrave Street, London SW1X 8BQ

Nursery nursing

Nursery nurses work with children under seven. They are not 'nurses' in the generally accepted sense of the word, as they deal with healthy children, although specialist work may lead them to care for disturbed and mentally or physically handicapped children. The job involves more than physical care: young children learn through play, communication with adults and other children and by responding to all kinds of stimuli, and it is the job of the nursery nurse to provide and organise these activities.

The work can be in one of several environments: nursery classes in day schools, infant schools, day nurseries run by the social services department, or in private schools. In day nurseries a large proportion of children are disturbed, so the work is very demanding, and the parents can be as demanding as their children. Other jobs are in residential nurseries for the under-fives who cannot be looked after at home, in hospitals, or in private homes as the day or residential 'nanny'.

Prospects

There is a considerable demand for nursery nurses. Among the reasons for this are the increasing number of working mothers, the growth in under-sevens requiring special care, and the ability of some families to engage a nanny. Pay is reasonable in private families but not exciting in public sector work.

Training

No particular entry requirements are laid down for the National Nursery Examination Board's certificate, but some colleges look for at least two GCSEs or equivalents. Most entrants have more than two and it is not uncommon to find applicants with A-level or H-grade passes. The usual method of training is to take a two-year course at a college of further education which leads to the NNEB'S certificate. Two-fifths of the course is spent in nurseries or centres working alongside professional staff. Since the NNEB'S syllabus for this course includes topics such as the social, emotional, physical and intellectual care of children, the GCSE subjects suitable as an introduction to nursery nursing are English language, human and social biology, home economics and social studies. At A-level, biology, psychology and sociology are very useful subjects, although almost any subject is a bonus. This is a career dominated by women (about 97 per cent, according to the NNEB), but men are encouraged to apply both for jobs and courses.

Information

National Nursery Examination Board, Argyle House, 8 Chequer Street, St Albans, Hertfordshire AL1 3XZ

Nursing

Nursing is a very old profession: as a result people think they know what it involves, but they are generally well wide of the mark. Bedside nursing in a hospital is what the public sees. However, they do not appreciate the complex procedures of administering drugs, monitoring the use of sophisticated equipment, the treatment of wounds and the skills and knowledge needed to observe and deal with patients suffering from all kinds of complaints and diseases. The work is very demanding, both physically and mentally, and on top of that nurses have to be good communicators in order to help patients and doctors.

Prospects

Within the nursing profession there are different types of training courses available: general, mental illness and mental handicap. Training can last for two or three years. Once qualified, many opportunities are available. At the top of the tree, senior nurses, together with administrators and doctors, are responsible for running hospital and community health services, and staff nurses can choose whether to stay on wards or go into teaching, administration or specialise in clinical work.

For descriptions of nursing life, the different jobs and specialist training required, students should read careers leaflets – the best ones are listed below.

Training

Entry requirements for training courses vary considerably. The minimum statutory requirement for a Registered (First-Level) three-year training course is five GCSEs at grades A, B or C or equivalent or a pass in a test set by the United Kingdom Central Council (UKCC). Generally speaking, most schools of nursing require evidence of a pass in an English subject, and many specify a pass in a maths or science subject. The better-known training schools look for applicants with evidence of A-level studies, and it is not unusual for them to specify that the GCSEs should have been obtained over no more than two sittings, not added to year by year. Among useful subjects are GCSEs in chemistry, biology, social biology, human biology, physics, sociology and English language. Where applicants have A-levels or H-grades, the same subjects plus psychology are very useful.

A new method of applying for training in England has been put into operation. Anyone wishing to start training in England must apply to the Nurses' Central Clearing House. Details of the application system can be obtained from local careers offices and careers teachers.

Essentially, applicants must be 17 years of age and must already hold the entry requirements for the type of training they wish to follow as laid down in the applicants' handbook which will be available as a reference document in Jobcentres, careers offices and school.

Those wishing to apply to schools of nursing in Scotland, Wales or Northern Ireland should write to the individual institutions.

There are degree courses in nursing: they vary widely and it is essential to obtain the prospectuses and to check on the entry requirements of each course. Hobsons book on *Nursing* (below) is an invaluable guide to all nursing degree courses. Courses vary but last from four to five years, depending on the amount of practical training within the course. They lead to Registered Nurse status and also give a broad training in sciences, social sciences and economics.

Some courses set students on different paths: towards **health visitor, midwifery,** or district nurse training. Each of these has its own form of training and special qualifications. Details of all these courses are contained in *Degrees with Nursing* (below).

Once into a hospital or other kind of nursing job, the range of opportunities for further training is both impressive and complex. The publications of the Careers Advisory Centre explain them clearly.

Information
English National Board for Nursing, Midwifery and Health Visiting, PO Box 356, Sheffield S8 0SJ. The Centre publishes/distributes several leaflets and booklets including *Nursing – Where do I go from here?* and *Degrees with Nursing*

Nursing – the way in to RGN, RNN, RNMH, DoH
Nursing, Degree Insights series, Hobsons
Working in Nursing, COIC

Occupational therapy

The objective of an occupational therapist is to help people who are temporarily or permanently disabled. The work is mainly in hospitals or day centres, helping physically disabled, mentally ill and mentally handicapped patients. Some specialists work in units that concentrate on burns, spinal injuries or drug addiction, and others specialise in children's problems. Occupational therapists also treat people in their own homes.

The work involves teaching social skills, helping patients to use all kinds of aids, organising group activities such as play-readings and dances, and helping patients to learn craft skills such as art or gardening.

Prospects

Seventy-five per cent of jobs are within the NHS and the rest with local authorities. The demand for occupational therapy services is growing, and there is no shortage of jobs. Indeed, there is said to be a thirty per cent under-supply, so it is a good career to consider in terms of employment, if the applicant can fulfil the skills and attitudes needed of a therapist. These include practical skills, perseverance, patience and an outgoing personality.

Training

Entry is by means of a diploma course at a school of occupational therapy. The minimum age of entry to one of the 14 schools in the UK is 18 ($17^1/_2$ in Scotland). Some of the schools are part of colleges of further education. Applications are not direct but go through the Clearing House (see below for address). Applications are accepted from June of the year preceding entry for admission to occupational therapy schools in October. It is essential, therefore, that if any pupil is interested in occupational therapy as a career, the research, enquiries and applications have to be thought out and prepared long in advance of entry. These training schools have around 800 places each year, and 90 per cent of places are sponsored by the Department of Health.

Entry requirements are at least six GCSE passes, one of which should be an 'academic' subject at A-level. However, most schools expect or even require applicants to have two A-levels or three H-grades. These subjects should include English language, a science subject and at least two other 'academic' subjects. Among the GCSE and A-level subjects that are particularly useful are biology, social biology and human biology, crafts and home economics. As part of the entry procedure, applicants are asked about their attitudes to disadvantaged people, so it is essential that applicants should visit an occupational therapy department in a hospital or special centre before appearing before an interview panel at college.

Training lasts for three years and includes a substantial period of clinical experience in hospitals. Among subjects studied on the course are anatomy, physiology, psychology, sociology and other medical and social topics, which should give clues to the most useful A-level or H-grade subjects.

Information

The Occupational Therapy Training Clearing House, and the British Association of Occupational Therapy, both at 20 Rede Place, Bayswater, London W2 4TU. Leaflets are available on careers in occupational therapy and the colleges that provide the training

Optical work

There are a number of career opportunities for school-leavers interested in optical work.

Dispensing optician

A dispensing optician supplies spectacles, contact lenses and other optical aids. To become a dispensing optician, the basic educational qualification is five GCSEs or O-grades, which should include maths or physics, English language and another science subject. In practice, applicants tend to have higher qualifications, including A-levels in science subjects.

Prospects

Prospects for jobs are fair: a dispensing optician usually begins as an assistant and later becomes a manager of a shop or a practice, with the ophthalmic optician doing the eye-testing. In the end, therefore, dispensing opticians are likely to do rather better financially, for they have more chance of ending up as managers.

Training

The training period generally lasts three years – two years on a full-time course at college and a year's practical experience. Alternatively, a trainee can attend college on a day- or block-release basis, spreading the learning over a longer span. Both methods lead to the qualifying examinations of the Fellowship of the Association of British Dispensing Opticians. Since the syllabus covers subjects such as physics, the anatomy and physiology of the eye, and business practice, the relevant school subjects at any level are maths, physics, biology and social and human biology, although other subjects can be included to make up the necessary five GCSEs.

Ophthalmic opticians (optometrists)

Ophthalmic opticians or optometrists examine eyes for defects of vision and for signs of abnormality or disease. To correct defects of vision, they issue prescriptions for spectacles or contact lenses; where signs of abnormality or disease are found they refer the patient for medical investigation and treatment. Ophthalmic opticians/optometrists do not treat patients with diseased eyes: that is the job of doctors and surgeons.

Training

To enter training, two or three science A-levels or three to four H-grades are required, plus two or three GCSEs or the equivalents. The GCSE subjects should include physics and a biological subject if physics and biology are not being taken at A-level. English language is also needed at GCSE and other appropriate subjects are chemistry and physical science.

There are degree courses in ophthalmic optics/optometry at the Universities of Bradford, Aston, UMIST (Manchester), University of Wales College of Cardiff, City (London) and Glasgow College of Technology. The A-level grades should be A to C, because competition for places is very keen indeed. For instance, Bradford University has 450 applications for an annual intake of 35 students. Candidates have to be highly motivated and therefore it is no good applying for an optics course without careful study of the work involved. A lot of prior research should precede any application to university. After the university course, pre-registration ophthalmic opticians/optometrists complete a year's clinical experience and work, during which they take the professional qualifying examination of the British College of Ophthalmic Opticians (Optometrists). Registration with the General Optical Council is necessary before opticians can practise. They do so within the NHS, the hospital eye service and in private practice.

Ophthalmic medical practitioners

Only qualified doctors can become ophthalmic medical practitioners and carry out comprehensive eye examinations and treatment. They work in hospitals, private practice and in some instances in opticians' shops. The most highly qualified of this category is the ophthalmologist, who is often consultant ophthalmologist at a hospital and who carries out eye surgery. This training is the longest of all: a medical degree course plus a long period of postgraduate study, training and examinations.

Orthoptists

Orthoptists work in conjunction with the ophthalmologist and they are concerned with the diagnosis and treatment of squints, disorders of vision and eye movement in addition to vision screening work and other aspects of ophthalmic work. The orthoptist works mainly in hospitals as part of the ophthalmic team, but there are opportunities for private work and in research. A large part of the work is with children and the profession mainly attracts women.

Training
The student entry requirement for the three-year course at a recognised orthoptic training school is five academic subjects at GCSE, including English language, maths and at least one science subject, and two subjects at A-level. The A-level subjects need not be in science, but it is an advantage for them to be in physics, chemistry and/or biology. There are opportunities for study for two post-qualification diplomas.

Information
The Association of British Dispensing Opticians, 22 Nottingham Place, London W1M 4AT
The British College of Ophthalmic Opticians, 10 Knaresborough Place, London SW5 0TG
British Orthoptic Society, Tavistock House, Tavistock Square, London WC1H 9HX

Osteopathy

Osteopaths use manipulative methods of treatment to correct the bone and muscle structures of the body. They deal with bones, joints, ligaments, tendons and muscles. Many people seek treatment for back pain and spinal problems, but osteopaths also treat sports injuries, tension, headaches and respiratory and digestive problems. Osteopathy has a long history as a method of helping people with chronic problems. It only rarely includes the curing of organic disease, but osteopaths do investigate and recommend treatments affecting health, diet, environmental factors and posture, and may thus contribute to reducing organic disease. Osteopaths are not recognised by the NHS, although some have orthodox medical training and qualifications. On the other hand many GPs now advise their patients to go to an osteopath for treatment.

Before making a decision to apply to take the full-time course, applicants should find out about osteopathy, listing its advantages and disadvantages as a career. Many of the applicants for the course are mature people who have become interested through their work in other areas of medical (and non-medical) care. About 35 per cent of osteopaths are women (50 per cent of students in training). Whoever they are, young or mature, men or women, prospective students should visit an osteopath, asking questions and observing his or her work, before applying for a place on the course.

Training

The training period is a four-year full-time course at one of the colleges of osteopathy. These are in Maidstone, Kent, and in Hampstead and Westminster, London. The syllabuses include anatomy, physiology, pathology, osteopath theory and practice, and dietetics. Having taken a course, students are ready to take the qualifying examination for the Diploma of Osteopathy. They thus become eligible for membership of the General Council and Register of Osteopaths (GCRO) and are able to practise as an assistant or open their own practice.

To gain entry to the degree or Diploma in Osteopathy courses, applicants should have at least two A-levels or three H-grades. Among the most suitable subjects are chemistry, biology, social biology, human biology, zoology and psychology. In addition, three GSCEs or equivalents are needed, and these should include English language. Some relaxation of these examination requirements is possible if applicants have other qualifications. Applicants with degrees in medicine, anatomy and physiology, or physiotherapy (including MCSP) are eligible for courses of a reduced length. The courses lead to the Diploma in Osteopathy or a BSc in Osteopathy.

Information

General Council and Register of Osteopaths, 1–4 Suffolk Street, London SW1Y 4HG (Information about the teaching colleges may be obtained from the General Council)

Packaging industry

A career in packaging may not have quite the same attraction as a career in, say, the law, journalism, or medicine, yet packaging offers very good career prospects. Packaging plays an important part in modern life, affecting every industry and commercial activity. Everything is packaged, from supermarket goods to cars. And apart from the advertising and promotional role of packaging, which is what most people notice, there are considerations of safety, protection, security, resistance to damage and other factors, all of which make packaging a challenging business as well as a profitable one.

Training

The traditional route for packaging technologists has been to take a degree in a science or an engineering subject and then specialise when they join a company that has a big interest – commercial or industrial – in packaging. Alternatively, students can take a degree course in packaging at West Herts College, Watford, which is the main centre for training. The college cannot fill its places, and yet estimates that its graduates have a choice of three, four or more jobs. For graduates of other disciplines, the Institute of Packaging provides a correspondence course and part-time courses. Special aspects of packaging, such as biological protection, are offered as part-time courses at some polytechnics. Yet another way into the technology is to take a specialist degree course in one of the materials – paper, plastics, glass, metals – and to apply knowledge and techniques within the research or production departments of major suppliers or users, such as Kodak, Marks & Spencer, Boots, and others.

The educational qualifications for entry to degree courses in packaging, materials science, engineering or pure science generally include science subjects within the necessary A-level or H-grade package. Of these, chemistry and biology are particularly relevant, and so are maths and physics or physical science. Two or three A-levels are needed, and the grades depend on the different institutions.

Information

Institute of Packaging, Sysonby Lodge, Nottingham Road, Melton Mowbray, Leicestershire LE13 0NU

Finding Out About Packaging, Hobsons

Paper industry

The paper industry is a very specialised one, concerned with the production of paper and board for all kinds of purposes, including newspapers and magazines, packaging, advertising and publishing. It is an industry in its own right, with some paper mills owned by UK companies and others owned by international firms that buy, sell and manufacture paper all around the world. It is also a high-technology industry, with scientists and technologists playing key roles in research and in management.

Training

In order to enter the industry at a technical level, it is necessary to take an engineering degree course, or a degree in materials science, or the specialised degree course in paper science at the University of Manchester Institute of Science and Technology (UMIST). The student intake to this course is around 10 people each year: they require two or three A-levels in chemistry, mathematics and/or a physical science subject, with grades around CCD. Only about 20 students apply each year for this course. The reason is that, like courses in printing and packaging, neither the course nor the industry are rated very highly by careers teachers in schools, who probably know very little about paper science, packaging or printing. They are usually unaware that the paper industry offers excellent job prospects for those who qualify at technologist and scientist levels.

For potential managers in the paper industry, a good career route is to take the UMIST (Manchester) degree course or an engineering or materials science degree or a BTEC or SCOTVEC HND course, and then seek employment within the industry. Managers are also recruited from management positions in other industries: they need specialist training in paper technology which has to be acquired at the company's expense. By whatever route the knowledge is obtained, the best managers are those that understand papermaking in some technical detail. For graduates with engineering or science degrees, there are conversion courses at UMIST and elsewhere.

The relevant school subjects are mentioned above: at A-level or H-grade they must be in chemistry, maths/physics/physical science. Engineering science, computing and statistics are also very useful A-levels (H-grades).

Information
British Paper and Board Industry Federation, Papermaker's House, Rivenhall Road, Westlea, Swindon, Wiltshire SN5 7BE

Patents

Patent agent
A patent agent advises inventors and companies concerned with inventions about patents and infringements of patents in the UK and abroad. In order to obtain a patent, an agent will make a search of known techniques or products and will then prepare a detailed specification which describes the invention and is an essential part of any application. Having completed this stage, the agent files the application with the Patent Office and may deal with commercial applications once it is granted. The majority of agents deal with electronics, chemical processes and engineering applications and have a good degree in one of these areas of technology or science although this is not strictly necessary.

Training
To become a patent agent, students train for the examinations of the Chartered Institute of Patent Agents and also of the European Patent Office. To prepare for these examinations, candidates train with a patent agent: the syllabus covers law, the drafting of patents and investigations of European methods of patent registration. For the European examinations, some knowledge of French and German is needed, as some of the exam papers are in these languages. The preparation for the examinations is by private study, assisted by lectures and tutorials arranged by the Chartered Institute. Students who do not make it through the rigorous examination schedule can work as technical assistants to agents. They will not be as well paid and they cannot become partners in a firm of patent agents, but otherwise they can do very well within the business.

This is not an easy career to enter, not least because jobs are difficult to find, and the only way to secure the necessary training is to get a job with a patent agent. A science, engineering or law degree is needed, and then there is the fluency in languages required for the European examinations. Taken together, these are formidable entry requirements, so the supply of applicants is about as limited as the job/training places.

Patent examiner

A patent examiner works in the Patent Office in London, examining and reporting on applications for patents. These examiners are senior Civil Servants and therefore come under the career and training umbrella of government service.

Training

To become an examiner requires, first, a good honours degree in a scientific, engineering or mathematical subject, and the ability to read French or German is very useful. The training is organised within the Patent Office and involves the study of law as well as the practice of specialised fields, such as electronics or mechanical inventions.

Information

Chartered Institute of Patent Agents, Staple Inn Buildings, London WC1V 7PZ

Patent Office, 66–71 High Holborn, London WC1R 4TP

Personnel management

Personnel management is about people at work and their relationships within the employing organisation. It aims to bring people together, to develop them effectively and to help them make their contribution to the success of their organisation. At the same time, personnel management pays attention to the well-being of individuals and working groups of which they form part.

Personnel management falls partly to managers, in their day-to-day responsibilities for their staff, and partly to personnel practitioners; the latter occupy staff positions with basically advisory functions. It is with these latter personnel staff that this entry is particularly concerned.

Personnel management is not for those who are simply good with people, or have a vague desire to work with people, nor is it a form or social work. A general personnel manager must cover a very wide range of subjects and is concerned with paperwork and ideas as well as with people. Some of the more specialist functions within personnel management may deal particularly with one subject. Even personnel specialists, however, will probably have had to study most aspects of personnel work – there is almost no such thing as a typical personnel position. The range and variety of work is very large. Differences between posts depend not only on the content of the job but on the type of industry or enterprise in which it is performed: its size, product, degree of unionisation, whether it is in the public or private sector, and so on.

Some idea of the variety of personnel management work is given by the following list of some of the main topics with which it is concerned:

- recruitment, selection and placement
- training and development, management development, appraisal
- separation from the organisation (redundancy, dismissal, etc.)
- manpower forecasting and planning
- working conditions
- industrial relations and negotiations
- human and social implications of change
- counselling of individual employees
- employee welfare
- consultancy and participation.

In a large organisation, the personnel manager is likely to be a member of the senior management team that directs the business.

Training

There are a number of routes into personnel management:

- directly after graduation
- after a full-time course in personnel management (often at post-graduate level)
- after training in general management
- transferring from another part of the company (usually another form of management).

The professional body for personnel management is the Institute of Personnel Management (IPM), with over 25,000 members. While it is not a legal requirement to be a member of this Institute in order to enter personnel management as a career, an ever-increasing number of employers seek professional personnel management qualifications.

The IPM encourages people to take courses and continue their development throughout their careers. Universities, polytechnics and colleges provide a wide range of initial courses. Full details of methods of qualification and establishments are available from the IPM or from the *Directory of Further Education*.

Stages 1 and 2 of the IPM's professional education scheme normally take three years of part-time study, although there are provisions for concentrating this into two years' part-time study or one year's full-time. The examinations are set at ordinary degree level; entry to the courses is normally as for university entrance.

Stage 1 examinations contain three papers: introduction to organisational behaviour, personnel information and decision-making, and personnel management in context. The Stage 2 examinations also contain three papers: employee relations, employee resourcing, and employee development. Six assignments have to be completed as part of the Stage 2 programme and two two-day residential periods attended by students other than those on full-time courses. There is also a third stage of the education scheme in the form of a report to management or work-based project. Upgrading to full Membership and Fellowship follow with appropriate personnel management experience.

The IPM does not recommend any specific subjects for A-level, but suggests that individuals concentrate on those they find interesting. However, qualifications in psychology, industrial or business studies, law and economics are helpful.

Information

Institute of Personnel Management, IPM House, Camp Road, Wimbledon, London SW19 4UW

Basic Personnel Procedures, IPM
The Practice of Personnel Management, IPM
How to be Your Own Personnel Manager, IPM
Personnel Work, Association of Graduate Careers Advisory Services (AGCAS), Central Services Unit, Crawford House, Precinct Centre, Manchester M13 9EP
Directory of Further Education, Hobsons

Pharmaceutical industry

The pharmaceutical industry is concerned with research into medicines and vaccines and their manufacture and sale. It is a large industry, and includes companies such as Glaxo, Beecham, Boots, Wellcome, ICI and others. Their biggest client in the UK is the NHS which means they supply every pharmacy in the country. They also export their products to over 120 different countries, and currently provide a balance of trade surplus of over £800 million a year.

The industry employs many different kinds of scientist, technologist, researcher and business person. Research into medicines and their effects on people's health goes on all the time, leading to new products. One of the new industries that is having a considerable effect on pharmaceuticals is biotechnology, in which living organisms are used to make commercial products. The making of beer and penicillin are two early examples of biotechnology, which is now expanding rapidly with the development of synthetic proteins, insulin, interferon and other products. Manufacture follows research, and for both these areas the need is for graduates in science – **biology, biochemistry**, biotechnology, **physics**, physical science, **chemistry** – to advance knowledge and to organise manufacturing. The industry also needs **engineers** to build and maintain the manufacturing plants. In addition, it requires **business, accountancy, management, sales and marketing** expertise, and these come from graduates in these subjects who are recruited annually from universities, polytechnics and colleges. Another group of experts needed by the industry are **pharmacists,** who work in research, development and production.

Training

To prepare for this kind of employment applicants have to take a first degree, and in the case of researchers, probably higher degrees to MSc and PhD levels. Unless a student has his or her eyes firmly on the pharmaceutical industry while still considering the choice of A-levels, it does not really matter which combination of A-levels is selected, except of course that they have to be the right selection for an engineering, science or pharmacy course, for which there are special subject requirements.

Within this industry are other categories of employees: they are sales, marketing, production, technician, accounts, distribution staff, all of whom are professionals or employees with specialised knowledge and skills relevant to almost any business, but strengthened by application to the needs of the pharmaceutical industry.

Information

Biochemical Society, 7 Warwick Court, Holborn, London WC1R 5DP

The Pharmaceutical Society, 1 Lambeth High Street, London SE1 7JN, and 36 York Place, Edinburgh EH1 3HU
Association of British Pharmaceutical Industry, 12 Whitehall, London SW1A 2DY

Pharmacology

The academic subject of pharmacy is subdivided into the major disciplines of pharmaceutical chemistry, pharmaceutics and pharmacology. The first two are concerned with the development, production and formulation of drugs. Pharmacology studies the actions of drugs on bodily processes. Although it is based on physiology, biochemistry and chemistry, pharmacology is a science in its own right and is taught not only to students of pharmacy, but also to students on courses in dentistry, medicine and veterinary science. In the past most pharmacologists took their first degree in medicine or pharmacy, biochemistry or zoology, but now it is possible to take a first degree in pharmacology itself. The courses and the institutions that provide them are described in the Degree Course Guide on *Pharmacy and Pharmacology*. In most of the universities and polytechnics that provide these courses there is a three-year course, but in some cases it is four years with one year in industry or hospital services.

Training

One route into this career is to specialise in pharmacology at university. There are good career possibilities for a graduate who could be elected to membership of the British Pharmacological Society after graduating and demonstrating a contribution to pharmacology. An alternative route would be to take a degree course in medicine or a paramedical subject, which opens up other career options later. For pharmacology, the A-level requirements are two or three subjects with good grades in science subjects. Biology (or zoology) and chemistry at A-level are generally required or preferred, and the other A-level(s) or H-grade(s) are expected to be in maths or science subjects. Apart from biology (zoology) and chemistry, the most appropriate A-levels (H-grades) are physics, physical science, biochemistry, biotechnology, botany and psychology. Because of the keen competition for places (about 200 applicants for 15 places, on average) the grades should be in the CCC category, although some universities expect higher grades.

Information

British Pharmacological Society, c/o Dr G. N. Woodruff, MSD Laboratories, Terlings Park, Harlow, Essex CM20 2QR

Pharmacology as a Career, British Pharmacological Society
Pharmacy and Pharmacology, Degree Course Guide, Hobsons

Pharmacy

The vast majority of pharmacists work in what most people call chemists' shops, although a grander modern name is 'community pharmacy'. Pharmacists are experts in medicines, and to qualify for their profession they need to take a degree course in pharmacy. This course is available at several UK universities and polytechnics (the Degree Course Guide on *Pharmacy and Pharmacology* gives a full list of the courses, their length, content and entry requirements and the universities providing them). A degree is only the first stage of a pharmacist's training; it has to be linked with and followed by at least a year's practical experience.

The irony is that a pharmacist cannot live by drugs alone. He or she needs to sell cosmetics, films, perfume, toilet articles and other goods in order to make a living from the shop. This means pharmacists must also be skilful at running a small retail business, and this is likely to be in local competition with branches of Boots and other large stores that employ pharmacists in their dispensing departments. There are about 30,000 pharmacists, with 70 per cent of them working in community pharmacy shops. The other 30 per cent work in hospitals and within the pharmaceutical industry, where they are involved in research, production, manufacturing and sales.

Training

Each school of pharmacy in a university or polytechnic has its own entrance requirements. However, they all require two or three A-levels with a supporting group of two or three GCSEs or O-grades. Chemistry at A-level or H-grade is always demanded, and most institutions require another science subject and/or maths at A-level. Certainly the GCSE group should include maths, physics and biology, so it is obvious that to prepare for this career the school subjects have to be selected carefully. Other subjects that are particularly useful are zoology, biotechnology, botany and physical science, all possible A-level subjects. The required grades vary according to the institution, but a student should aim for a good grades at A and B levels in order to have any chance of success for a university course, where as many as 1,000 applicants may try for about 100 places.

Information
The Pharmaceutical Society, 1 Lambeth High Street, London SE1 7JN
The National Pharmaceutical Association, Mallinson House 40–42 St Peter's Street, St Albans, Hertfordshire AL1 3NP

Pharmacy as a Career, The Pharmaceutical Society
Pharmacy and Pharmacology, Degree Course Guide, Hobsons

Photography

Most people think they know what photography is – the taking, developing and printing of photographs by various methods and for all kinds of social and commercial purposes. What they do not realise is that a core of essential skills and knowledge must be augmented by specialist techniques and by awareness of how to market these skills for commercial use. The reason for the stress in businesslike methods is that there are more photographers than jobs, and professionals need to know how to sell their techniques and their wares.

Jobs are generally in the following areas of work:

● advertising – photographers work for advertising agencies or carry out freelance work on contract or commission. This is a highly competitive area of work
● fashion – employment is within a studio or fashion house, or for a magazine specialising in fashion work, or as a freelance photographer. Again, it is a very difficult field to break into
● publicity, printing, magazines – agencies, publishing, printing and magazine companies and most commercial firms need photographic material. This is created by company photographers and processers or by freelancers
● scientific, technical, medical – industrial, commercial, educational and medical bodies such as hospitals and research organisations all need specialist photographic units
● newspapers and the press – photo-journalism is another com-

petitive and highly skilled business, sometimes leading to television work

● technical services – this includes the processing and printing of film, and there are openings for technicians and other staff

● commercial and local photography – this category includes about half the professional photographers: high-street studios, commercial photographers, and local newspaper work.

Although there are all these areas of opportunity, the competition is fierce, and to break in requires good training, experience and luck, and, for those who want to start their own business, some capital funding.

Training

Working photographers range from school-leavers with a GCSE in photography, to 18-plus leavers with a little more knowledge gained through A-level or evening-class photography, to graduates of degree courses which specialise in photography or which combine it with other kinds of graphic arts skills. Depending on a person's level, age and ambitions, it is possible to choose a course leading to a City and Guilds, BTEC National Diploma and HND, or degree qualification. For details of courses at colleges and polytechnics, consult the *Directory of Further Education*.

One of the main objectives of photography students at any level is to qualify as a member of the British Institute of Professional Photography (BIPP) at one of three levels: Licentiate, Associate or Fellow. There are fairly strict rules about qualifying via college courses, and the BIPP publishes a summary sheet giving details of the routes to membership. The BIPP validates its own PQE – professional qualifying examination – which is offered as a one-year course following BTEC HND courses at some colleges: write to BIPP for details (address below).

School pupils need to think carefully about their GCSE and A-level subjects. For example, for entry to the Central London Polytechnic degree course in photographic sciences, students need good passes at GCSE in physics, chemistry and maths, with a pass at A-level in one of these subjects. For degree courses in photography, film and television at Nottingham Polytechnic and Harrow College of Higher Education and elsewhere, arts A-levels are acceptable as well as sciences. It is certainly useful to have taken and passed GCSE and/or A-level photography, but this is not an essential qualification for entry to a degree course – it cannot be while so few schools and colleges offer it.

Competition for college and polytechnic degree and BTEC/ SCOTVEC HND courses is very keen so good GCSE (O-grade) and A-level (H-grade) grades are needed, plus a portfolio of work done either at school or as part of a leisure interest.

Apart from the school subjects already mentioned, other useful ones are art, design, any technological subject, sciences, history of art and history.

Information

The British Institute of Professional Photography (BIPP), Amwell End, Ware, Hertfordshire SG12 9HN

Routes to BIPP Membership, BIPP
Directory of Further Education, Hobsons

Physics

Physics is the study of the laws governing the behaviour of all the matter and energy in the universe. The principles of physics form the basis of many physical manufacturing processes and also of engineering. Physics is therefore a very important basic subject, central to most **engineering** applications as well as geophysics, **metallurgy**, oil production, aero-space, **computing** and many more subjects. Of all the scientific qualifications, physics is probably the most adaptable. Apart from the employment opportunities already suggested, there are also electronics, space technology, **telecommunications**, laser technology – think of any engineering application and physics will be its core.

Prospects

Not surprisingly, therefore, job possibilities are immense. Physicists are in great demand, and there are not enough of them. Apart from jobs in research and manufacturing, there is a great need for physics teachers to work in schools and colleges, to ensure that the supply of physicists does not dry up. A recent analysis by the Institute of Physics showed that 31 per cent of physicists were working in research and development, either in companies, in government service or with research centres. Another 27 per cent were teaching at universities, schools and elsewhere, while a further 30 per cent were in management – either as general managers of companies, or managing a research and development department, or in some other form of scientific management. Each year, over half the science graduates go straight into permanent jobs, most of them in scientific work concerned with production or product development. As a general rule, another degree at MSc or PhD is not needed to get a job, although each year over 20 per cent go on to study for a higher degree. For graduates who are not inclined to seek a junior management opportunity, there are jobs as technicians and technical support staff in many different fields.

Training

To get anywhere as a physicist an HND or a degree are almost essential. The Degree Course Guide for *Physics* and the Institute of Physics list contain details of the degree courses and the institutions that offer them. To obtain a place the requirements vary from three good science/maths A-levels (or four to five H-grades) with pass grades of AAB to BBC for the top-flight universities, to two A-levels (plus the expected package of GCSEs) with pass grades of D and E for entry to some polytechnic or college courses. As well as physics courses, some universities and polytechnics offer degree courses in physical sciences, biophysics, astrophysics, and applied, theoretical, mathematical and chemical physics, all with their own unique career opportunities.

At school it is essential to take GCSE/O-grade and A-level/H-grade physics and to get good grades. Maths is so essential to an understanding of physics that most university courses also require a pass in one or more of the A-level mathematics subjects. Other useful subjects are engineering science, any technology subject, physical science and chemistry.

Apart from degree courses, many colleges and polytechnics have alternatives. Among them are, for example, HNCs and HNDs in applied physical sciences, applied electronics and vacuum technology; these lead to BTEC or SCOTVEC awards and require at least one A-level or two H-grades for entry to the courses.

Information

Institute of Physics, 47 Belgrave Square, London SW1X 8QX

Working in Physics, COIC
Physics Courses in Higher and Further Education, Institute of Physics
Physics, Degree Course Guide, Hobsons

Directory of Further Education, Hobsons
Physics, Connections series, Hobsons

Physiotherapy

Chartered physiotherapists use exercise, manipulation, massage, thermal and electrotherapy techniques and education to promote health and healing, to rehabilitate patients after injury, strokes, heart attacks and surgery, and to maintain mobility in people with long-term physical and mental handicaps and illnesses.

The largest number of physiotherapists work in the NHS in a wide variety of settings, such as outpatient departments, on the wards, in intensive care units, hydrotherapy pools and visiting patients in their own homes or in residential care. Others work in industrial occupational health centres, sports clubs and private hospitals; a growing number set up in private practice.

Priority areas for future development for physiotherapy are in prevention of disability and the care of the elderly, the mentally handicapped and ill and in community care.

Training

All courses leading to qualification as a chartered physiotherapist are at least three years in length, with two four-year honours degree courses. The courses are either in physiotherapy schools run by a health authority or in a higher education institution. All courses follow a similar curriculum and combine theory with clinical education placements in hospitals, clinics and the community.

Minimum education requirements for those under 25 years of age are five good GCSEs and two A-levels or four H-grades. Minimum entry requirements may not be necessary for mature entrants.

Information

The Chartered Society of Physiotherapy, 14 Bedford Row, London WC1R 4ED. The Society publishes a leaflet giving information on how to apply to, and the individual requirements of, each school

Remedial gymnastics

The Society of Remedial Gymnastics and Recreational Therapy has now merged with the Chartered Society of Physiotherapy. Pinderfields College of Physiotherapy retains a remedial gymnastic bias, but applications for this College should be forwarded through the Central Admissions Unit at the Chartered Society.

Pilot

Pilots work in the **Royal Air Force**, the Women's Royal Air Force, and in **civil aviation**.

RAF

In the RAF and WRAF, pilots fly all kinds of aircraft and also plan and carry out air operations and activities. Since the RAF and WRAF base most of their work on training, equipping and assisting pilots, the flying crew are the elite, and competition for pilot training is particularly intense. For very full and comprehensive information on entry to the RAF, pilot training and the entry requirements, both physical and academic, interested students should get in touch with the nearest RAF Careers Information Office (address and telephone number in the telephone directory).

All officers, and especially pilots, must show initiative, integrity, leadership, intelligence and management abilities in addition to good academic attainments to at least A-level, plus the exacting physical criteria demanded of young officers.

As much of the work involves advanced technical equipment, pilots must have good scientific knowledge and technical aptitude. Applicants are tested to see whether they have these capabilities. In addition, communication skills are important. Apart from the personal qualities already listed, pilots have to be very quick-thinking, have great powers of concentration, and be decisive. No academic subject taken at school would reveal evidence of these personal qualities, but it is obvious that subjects such as physics, maths, statistics, computing, technical or technological subjects, English language and physical education are clear favourites. If some of these subjects are studied to A-level or H-grade, the potential pilot starts with definite advantages.

Training
RAF cadetships and bursaries are awarded by competition to school-

leavers who are about to begin a degree course at university or polytechnic, or to undergraduates in their first, second and third years. Pilot and navigator (direct entry) candidates who qualify for these awards must be under 23 years 5 months and have at least five GCSEs or O-grades. For students taking a degree course, the same entry requirements apply for potential RAF pilots as for any other student.

Those who are selected for pilot training have a four-week course at a flying training school. Then, after a further 48 weeks of intensive training, fast jet pilots go on to the Advanced Flying Training School for another 21 weeks, and then to a Tactical Weapons Unit.

Civil aviation

A professional pilot's licence must be held in order to fly for financial gain (in legal terms, to fly for hire or reward). The only exception to this is the possessor of a private pilot's licence with an instructor's rating included in the licence.

Civil airline pilots fly both fixed-wing and rotary-wing (helicopter) aircraft. There are about 30 UK airline companies employing civil airline pilots. These range from British Airways to small companies. Beside these 30, there are air-taxi companies, freight services, aerial surveying, photography and crop-spraying firms, and private owners who occasionally need a pilot.

There is at present a surplus of qualified commercial pilots. When a vacancy does occur, there is a queue of qualified pilots ready for it. The academic qualifications depend very much on the route chosen to obtain a professional pilot's licence.

Training

In the past, many students were sponsored by an airline. Nowadays, very few are sponsored. A high standard of education is required that is at least two or three A-levels or three to four H-grades and three GCSEs or their equivalents, including English language, maths and either physics, chemistry or a science subject. A degree in any subject is acceptable, although science subjects are preferred. As with the RAF, previous flying experience with a flying-club is a big advantage.

Alternatively, there are commercial pilot's licence training courses at Civil Aviation Authority Approved Course Training Schools. These are very expensive.

Thirdly, a pilot with 700 hours' flying time (fixed wing only) and a private pilot's licence is eligible to sit the appropriate examinations and flight tests for a commercial pilot's licence without having to attend an Approved Course School.

For rotary-wing aircraft (CPL(H)), unless taking an approved course, a PPL(H) licence is necessary, with 400 hours' pilot-in-command experience before the necessary examinations and flight tests can be taken.

Most civil airline pilots in the past came from the RAF, and when recruitment perks up they are likely to do so again.

The relevant school subjects are obviously in the sciences: maths, physics, physical science, engineering science, chemistry, computing, and so on. The educational standard assumed for the commercial pilot's licence full-time approved course is that the student will have obtained the equivalent of at least five GCSEs, including English language, maths and a science subject. The same would apply for learning to fly for a PPL.

Information

Civil Aviation Authority, FCL, 3rd Floor, Aviation House, 129 Kingsway, London WC2B 6NN

RAF Careers Information Service, Government Building, London Road, Stanmore HA7 4PZ, or any local RAF Careers Information Office

Careers in Aviation, Kogan Page

Plumbing

Plumbers fit and repair pipes that supply hot and cold water, central heating and gas. They install and repair domestic appliances such as washing-machines and waste disposal fixtures. They also go outside to fit pipes, gutters and flashings to roofs. Many plumbers are self-employed. Others work for local businesses, or for local authorities, building contractors, property developers and institutions such as colleges.

Training

No formal qualifications are required. Training is usually arranged by the employer, with attendance at a further education college for City and Guilds qualifications. The Institute of Plumbing sets its own examinations and makes its own awards.

Information
Institute of Plumbing, 64 Station Road, Hornchurch, Essex
RM12 6NB

Police service

The main purpose of the police service is the prevention and detection of crime, and to do so police officers need to be self-reliant, quick-thinking and prepared to work in a team under strict discipline. Graduates and school-leavers often find the discipline the hardest part of the job to accept. Self-reliance is important, too, because a constable on the street may be called on to deal with many different kinds of emergency. For instance, only a third of police activity is connected with crime detection: the great majority of the work is dealing with neighbourhood or family disputes or coping with drunks.

Prospects
There are over 50 police forces in the UK and they recruit separately. The Metropolitan Police in London is the largest and the best paid. There is some scope for specialisation, as in dog-handling and road traffic, and most police officers hope or intend to move to detection, where the competition for transfer from everyday work is very keen indeed. The CID offers numerous specialist jobs, such as fingerprinting, photography, criminal records, crime prevention, drug abuse, and so on. Each force has its own CID, but to get into it requires a record of hard work and ability, so the CID tends to be staffed by mature men and women who have served their time on the beat.

Training
Candidates are normally accepted between the ages of $18^1/_2$ and 30. Applicants must be of a good educational standard. Four GCSEs (including English language and maths) or equivalents may exempt an applicant from sitting the Police Standardised Entrance Test.

There is also a graduate recruitment scheme. There were over 5,000 graduates in the police service in 1991, representing four per cent of the service's strength. About 30 candidates are awarded places each year under the Graduate Entry Scheme, which is linked to the Special Course at the Police Staff College, Bramshill. This is a sandwich course, with a three-month course at Bramshill (Part I), followed by one or two years of developmental training in the force and then another six-month course at Bramshill (Part II). Officers selected for the special course are promoted to sergeant six months before joining Part I. If an officer successfully completes Part II of the course – probably five or six years after joining the police service – he or she will be made a substantive inspector, subject to satisfactory completion of one year's probationary service in the rank. A few forces also run a cadet scheme, taking recruits from the age of 16. Women police officers are fully integrated into the force and compete on equal terms with men. One in nine police officers is a woman.

Unlike HM Forces, there is no officer class, and to reach the rank of chief inspector, both men and women must start as constables and work their way up to the top ranks by ability, experience and initiative.

All school subjects are appropriate for the police, and GCSEs could be in any subject. However, English language and maths are important largely because the police have a great deal of paper-work to cope with, and they have to be good communicators in every kind of way – on paper, telephone and face to face.

General fitness is essential, and police officers who are good at sport find that there are great opportunities for team and individual games and sports. It helps if a candidate has studied sociology, economics and politics. However, the police also point out that the brutal and sometimes sordid realities of police work are a far cry from the theoretical aspects of social studies or sociology taught in the class or lecture room.

The regulations for entry to the police in Scotland are rather different, and should be checked by writing to the address below.

Information
Police Recruiting Department, Home Office, Queen Anne's Gate, London SW1H 9AT
Police Division, Scottish Home and Health Department, Room 364a, St Andrew's House, Edinburgh EH1 3DE
For local vacancies and information, contact the chief constable of the local police force (address in the telephone directory)

Working in the Police & Security, COIC

Politics

Not many people decide on a political career while they are still at school or college. Those who do join a political party or take a full part in a college or university political club in order to prepare themselves for a career in politics. But most politicians – either in Parliament or in local government – start by carving out a career in another field, and take up politics first as a part-time interest and then as a full-time job if they are elected MP, or have a responsible job in local government or as a constituency agent.

Students really interested in politics can take a degree in politics, political theory or history with options in modern politics. As a degree subject, politics is often linked with economics, history and philosophy: whatever the course, a substantial part of the syllabus is concerned with political theories, close to the study of philosophy. A degree in politics is not, of course, a necessary preparation for political life. MPs have every kind of qualification, among which politics rates no higher than any other. However, for those who would like to take a degree course in this subject, almost any kind of A-level or H-grade grouping of subjects is acceptable, although the necessary grades depend on the university, polytechnic or college.

The main political parties have full-time constituency agents, almost all of whom have long experience of voluntary party work. Occasionally, a new graduate may be appointed as an agent, but that is because of outstanding work for the National Union of Students or a political party while at university or college. To find out about these posts, interested applicants should write to the head office of the political party in which they are interested.

The parties also have researchers, who are often graduates. They find out about all kinds of subjects, mostly to do with economics, social topics and finance, so graduates in these subjects are particularly suitable. Another category of political staff are the secretaries or administrative assistants to MPs: these jobs are advertised in party magazines or national newspapers. The skills needed are secretarial, plus a keen interest in politics.

Information
Politics, Degree Course Guide, Hobsons

Post Office

In 1969 after 300 years as a government department the Post Office became a public corporation responsible for providing postal, tele-communication, banking and remittance services. A further major change occurred when the corporation was divided into three wholly separate businesses: the Royal Mail is responsible for the delivery of letters; Royal Mail Parcelforce delivers parcels; and Post Office Counters is the organisation that administers the local post offices and their services.

Taken as a whole, the Post Office is one of the country's largest organisations. It handles 55 million letters and a million parcels every working day. Over 200 million parcels are delivered to 22 million individual addresses in the UK each year. In addition, the counter network has over 20,000 offices serving 28 million customers each week. To carry out this huge amount of work, the Post Office employs 175,000 staff in a wide range of grades and types of jobs spread across the various businesses, but with the majority concentrated in mail operations (letters and parcels). Grades include postal officers (including counter clerks), postal assistants, postmen and postwomen and postal executives.

Prospects

The Post Office continues to offer good prospects with clearly defined career development and promotion paths within its separate businesses. For instance, people who begin in a clerical grade can advance to executive and administrative work which means higher pay and prospects. Promotion is based on merit and depends on hard work and ability.

Entry requirements

- Postal executive. Entrants generally have a degree. Any subject qualifies, but the most useful ones are maths, business studies, computer science, economics and statistics.
- Postal officers. These do not need formal academic qualifications as all applicants must pass an aptitude test which measures the skills needed for the job. Successful candidates are then invited for interview.
- Postmen and postwomen do not need any formal educational

qualifications either. However, applicants are required to pass a written test to show that they have basic understanding of English and other communication skills. The Post Office uses Youth Training to give placements, job training and in some cases permanent jobs to 16- and 17-year-olds, thus providing an alternative way of joining the Post Office.

The particular school subjects useful for Post Office work have been mentioned, although any subject may be suitable, depending on the grade or kind of work done within the Post Office. Obviously, to move more quickly into executive officer and management posts, a degree, HNC or HND is very useful, particularly if it is in business subjects, economics or computing, but other subjects and degree courses can be just as useful, depending on the calibre and the aptitude of the applicant.

Information

Post Office Management Recruitment Centre, Freepost, Coton House, Rugby, Warwickshire CV23 0BR
Girobank Recruitment Office, Bridle Road, Bootle, Merseyside G1R 0AA

Printing

Printing, which was once a very traditional industry, is now one of the most technologically advanced of all processes. This is due to the introduction of computerised typesetting, electronic scanning and faster methods of making printing-plates and of preparing and running presses. At the same time the printing industry has been affected by keen overseas competition for business. One consequence of these developments has been a substantial reduction in staffing levels, particularly at the craft and technician grades. Another has been the disruptions in the newspaper industry caused by disputes between managements and the trade unions.

The industry's problems, usually well publicised, do not encourage young people to think of printing as a career. This is a pity, for it is interesting technologically and offers good prospects to managers with technological expertise and a good business-sense. Printing companies print everything from postage stamps to encyclopaedias, birthday cards and envelopes to magazines. Over half the total workforce is employed by general printers; the rest are specialist companies that print books, packaging, posters, brochures, stationery, banknotes and greetings cards. Newspapers are a separate business altogether and often have the printing presses close to the editorial offices. An important point to make is that over 70 per cent of printing companies employ fewer than 50 people: small companies, depending on skilled personnel, dominate the industry.

Training

The industry needs people with knowledge of printing technology. This is acquired at the craft level by entering the industry at 16 or 17, taking a traineeship (the term 'apprentice' is no longer used) in a company, attending a college of further education with printing facilities to take a City and Guilds certificate, and emerging at about 19-plus as a trained worker. No particular educational qualifications are needed for entry to jobs and training, but employers look for GCSE passes in two or three subjects, including maths and a science.

An alternative route into printing is to take a two-year BTEC or SCOTVEC course in printing or a graphic design subject with printing options, and move into a job as a technician or in administration at 18-plus. Another method of preparing for a printing career is to stay on at school or college for A-levels, concentrating on science subjects such as physics, chemistry, maths and/or computing, and then to seek a place on a degree or BTEC HND course in printing technology or graphics technology. For a list of colleges that offer BTEC, SCOTVEC, City and Guilds and degree courses, consult the *Directory of Further Education*.

The number of printing graduates is small, and they are snapped up by an industry that needs technological know-how. Another route for graduates is to take an engineering or a pure science degree and then to add a postgraduate course in printing before taking a junior management or research job with a printing or packaging company, book or magazine publisher, or with a manufacturing company that supplies these industries with equipment and materials such as film, plates, paper and inks. Yet another path is by taking a business management course at diploma, HND or degree level, adding to it a concentrated course in printing technology, and then seeking a job in sales, marketing, distribution or similar business function.

For technologists, the relevant school subjects at GCSE, A-level or H-grade are in the sciences, technology subjects, computing and

491

business studies. The printing degree course at West Herts College, Watford, requires two A-level passes. The degree course at Manchester Polytechnic requires one or two A-level passes in science, and the HND courses require at least one A-level pass in a science subject (for the technology option) or in an arts subject (for the business option). Otherwise, almost any subject is useful.

Another possibility for a career is to concentrate on design by taking an HND or degree course in graphic design or typographic design and to seek a job in a design studio, advertising agency or publishing company.

Information

British Printing Industries Federation, 11 Bedford Row, London WC1R 4DX

Institute of Printing, 8 Lonsdale Gardens, Tunbridge Wells, Kent TN1 1NU

Careers in Printing, Kogan Page
Directory of Further Education, Hobsons
Finding Out About Printing, Hobsons
Working in Printing and Publishing, COIC

Prison service

Most people think that a prison officer's job is to punish. But it is basically social work concerned with people who have problems. Prison staff are no longer called 'warders'; they do not just lock and unlock cell doors, but are expected to take a personal interest in the prisoners and help them towards the day when they return to normal life. On the other hand, some prisoners are violent, abusive, brutal and dangerous: they are in a small minority but are nevertheless present and have to be dealt with. For most of the time, however, prison officers deal with men, women, youths and other offenders who want to finish their sentences as quickly as possible and never see a prison again. It has to be recognised that prison work can be depressing. But, like other forms of social work, it can be rewarding and there is no doubt that it is of value to the community.

Prison officers can be asked to serve in any one of the different kinds of penal institutions: remand centre; local prison; training prison which can be open, closed or maximum security; young offender institutions (for 16- to 21-year-olds). The officers supervise training, control and the routine supervision of prisoners who might work in the institution's laundry, kitchen, gardens, farm or workshop as part of a team made up of prison officers, medical staff, psychologists, welfare officers and instructors.

Prospects

Prospects are very good because there is a shortage of prison staff and because crime is growing. The promotion ladder is from officer to senior officer, principal officer and then chief officer. Assistant governors are promoted from prison officers who take training courses as part of their work. There is no longer any direct entry to officer grades as officer and governor grades have now been unified. There is, however, an accelerated promotion scheme which helps graduates. Almost any prior course or degree is suitable for a candidate, but some qualifications are particularly appropriate and in this category are psychology, social studies or sociology, law, personnel, institutional management and administration.

Training

Training is generally within a prison, plus periods of full-time study and training at a prison officers' training school. Governors and assistant governors must be prepared to move around if they are ambitious to reach the most senior posts.

At school A-levels or H-grades in any of the subjects mentioned for degree courses would be suitable.

Information

The Prison Service, Home Office, Cheland House, Page Street, London SW1P 4LN
Scottish Prison Service, St Margaret's House, London Road, Edinburgh EH8 7PQ

Leaflets and booklets are available from the above organisations

Probation service

Probation officers are social workers to the law courts. Their function is to help young people and adults who have been in trouble with the law to lead more satisfactory, law-abiding lives. The challenge and the satisfaction of the job comes from helping people who have made mistakes of one kind or another to improve their attitude and their way of life. Probation officers have a dual role, which makes their job very difficult: they have to protect society, the local community and individuals from the actions of an offender, and at the same time they must win the respect and co-operation of their client, the offender.

In England and Wales the probation service is the responsibility of the Home Office. Probation officers are employed by local probation committees except in Northern Ireland, where there is a special probation board. In Scotland the local authority social work departments are responsible for social work with offenders which includes probation work.

Day-to-day tasks include carrying out enquiries into an offender's background to help the court to decide on the best method of dealing with the person, interviewing and supervising people who have been put on probation by a court, and supervising offenders required to do work which is of value to the community. Some probation officers work in prisons and in youth custody and detention centres. However, the work is not always with offenders; probation officers also provide social work help in matrimonial disputes and serve as welfare officers in the divorce courts. Whatever the environment or the responsibility, this kind of social work is very demanding and testing, for an officer is likely to have a substantial case-load of offenders, or clients, to cope with.

There is a constant demand for probation officers, as for other categories of **social work**. The entry requirements are the same as for other social workers, which means that a candidate must take the Certificate of Qualification in Social Work (CQSW) awarded by the Central Council for Education and Training in Social Work (CCETSW).

Training
Courses leading to the CQSW are available for graduates, non-graduates and undergraduates. Two-year, non-graduate courses are open to applicants who are at least 20 years old and who, if they are under 25, have at least five GCSEs (grades A, B or C) or equivalents, including English language or Welsh. Most courses prefer applicants to have A-levels. Candidates aged 25 or over require no academic qualifications, but colleges look for evidence or ability to study to an advanced level.

Graduates with a degree in a relevant subject may be eligible to take a one-year graduate CQSW course, while those with a degree in any subject will need to take a two-year qualifying course. Four-year degree courses, which include study leading to the CQSW, are also available.

Most courses require, and all prefer, applicants to have had experience of work in the social services. Applicants to one-year courses must have had at least 12 months' relevant experience. CQSW applicants wishing to become probation officers may well be expected to have had experience of social work with offenders.

A number of CQSW courses provide training specifically aimed at work in the probation service in England and Wales. Some of these graduate and non-graduate courses carry a quota of financial sponsorships from the Home Office. Newly qualified CQSW holders wishing to enter the probation service in England and Wales may be given preference by local probation committees if they have held such sponsorships. Anyone considering a career as a probation officer should check the procedure for obtaining sponsorship with the Home Office.

The school subjects relevant for entry to probation work are: English language or Welsh and passes in other subjects at GCSE or A-level. Among appropriate subjects are law, psychology, social studies or sociology, English and administration: if two or three of these are taken to A-level, the candidate's chances are much improved. However, personal qualities are crucially important; probation officers are expected to be persuasive, firm, sympathetic and helpful, and yet be able to make clear judgements about people. Someone who has studied physics or French is just as likely to have these qualities, or acquire them during training, as someone who has studied sociology or other social science subjects to degree or any other level.

Information
Central Council for Education and Training in Social Work, Information Services, Derbyshire House, St Chad's Street, London WC1H 8AD

Careers in Social Work, Kogan Page
Social Sciences, Degree Course Guide, Hobsons
Working in Social Work, COIC

Production engineering

Production engineers are concerned with the manufacture of all kinds of goods: among them could be cars, electrical goods, communication satellites, aeroplanes, computers and marmalade. It is a vitally important subject because the UK's industrial initiative and prosperity depend on production engineers.

As in other branches of engineering, knowledge of mathematical, statistical and scientific techniques is essential, for the production engineer has to know about the properties of the materials he or she is using, the stresses of the engineering processes, and the methods of making, manufacturing or erecting the finished article. Most engineers therefore work in manufacturing industries; others are employed as consultants and lecturers, and within the construction industry, HM Forces, and local and national government departments.

Prospects

Despite the need for men and women capable of doing this essential work, there are not enough graduates. In 1990, for example, there were about 500 graduates in production engineering and another 300 in manufacturing engineering. This is quite inadequate to cope with the demand, and so mechanical engineers or other specialists are drawn into production work. There are postgraduate courses and special training schemes to provide the specialist skills and knowledge needed for production engineering work: graduates in science, engineering and technological subjects are in most cases suitable for this kind of in-service training or pre-entry course. However, more applicants with A-levels in sciences should consider production engineering as an undergraduate course, for the prospects are excellent and several companies offer good sponsorship arrangements to undergraduates.

Once into industry, production engineers could be employed in many different ways and with all kinds of products or engineering problems. One exciting area of development is in CAD and CAM – computer-aided design and computer-aided manufacture. Another important field is the design and manufacture of machine tools.

Training

The route to professional or chartered status as a production engineer requires the completion of three stages. They are, first, academic study and qualification, which can be in production engineering or another branch of engineering, plus the additional training mentioned above. Then comes practical experience and training within a company or government department. The third stage is professional work and experience and further study in order to qualify as a chartered engineer of the Institution of Production Engineers. The Institution stipulates that its members must hold a degree or its equivalent as well as successfully completing the three specific stages of further training.

To find out about suitable degree courses, applicants should read the relevant section in the Degree Course Guide on *Technology*. The universities and polytechnics which have degree courses in production engineering generally look for two or three good A-levels or three to four H-grades in science and mathematics subjects. GCSEs or their equivalents in English language, chemistry, physics and maths are generally required, too. Because there is a shortage of applicants (in 1990 the universities and polytechnics accepted 800 students for production engineering courses out of a total of over 18,000 applicants for all engineering courses), A-level grades can be modest. Grades of B and C in science subjects are likely to be needed for entry to universities, but grades of D and E might be enough to obtain entry to polytechnic undergraduate courses.

Students not taking a degree course can take a BTEC National Certificate or National Diploma in Engineering (or the SCOTVEC equivalents), and then go on to the additional training and qualifications needed for chartered engineer status.

Information

The Institution of Production Engineers, Rochester House, 66 Little Ealing Lane, London W5 4XX

Technology, Degree Course Guide, Hobsons
Directory of Further Education, Hobsons
Training Opportunities in Engineering, A Career as a Chartered Production Engineer, and *Education for the Potential Chartered Production Engineer,* Institution of Production Engineers
Working in Engineering, COIC

Psychology

Psychology can be defined as the scientific study of human behaviour, thinking and feelings either in their normal or abnormal states. In addition to directly observable behaviour, psychology includes topics like learning, memory, emotions, personality and attitudes and beliefs both in individuals and as shared by groups of people. The study of psychology is based upon observing what people do and what they say. It employs the methods of science in an attempt to derive laws of behaviour that will enable the behaviour of both individuals and groups to be predicted accurately. This means it covers a vast range of subject-matter and is a demanding and stimulating area of study.

Psychology is often confused with other aspects of human study. Philosophy is a subject concerned with the nature of truth and reality, systems of thought and questions of a metaphysical nature. Psychiatry is a branch of medicine which deals with the diagnosis, treatment and management of mental diseases. A psychotherapist is an individual who employs psychological treatment methods originally derived from the theories of Sigmund Freud, though modern techniques have progressed a great deal since then. A psychotherapist is usually a psychiatrist, clinical psychologist or social worker who has sought further and more specialised training in psychological treatment methods. Psychoanalysis is a particular form of psychotherapy which seeks to treat emotional disorders through a process of discussion with the patient.

Each year about 2,000 psychology students graduate from universities and polytechnics. Of these about 10 per cent go on to research and higher degrees, over 50 per cent proceed to careers not directly concerned with psychology (for example, industry, **management**, commerce, the **Civil Service**) leaving about 25 per cent who seek further vocational postgraduate training for entry into careers as professional psychologists. The job destinations of the remainder are unknown.

Of those who enter psychology careers, most go into public service (local and national government). The main government departments employing new graduates are the Home Office (**prison service**), HM Forces, the Ministry of Defence and the Department of Employment. At a local level psychologists are employed in remand centres, community homes, social service departments and the **probation service**. A smaller number are successful in obtaining places on professional training courses and become qualified clinical psychologists employed in the NHS or perhaps enter private practice. Others seek postgraduate training as educational psychologists and work in the local school psychological service or in education departments. A third professional group is composed of those who have trained as occupational psychologists and are employed both by industry and commerce, as well as local and national government, as career advisers, personnel officers or in the occupational guidance and rehabilitation centres.

Most graduates seek careers in industry and commerce and are employed in personnel departments, manpower planning, training, work study and career development. Some go into **market research, advertising,** public relations and promotional work. A somewhat shrinking outlet is **teaching**, either at a secondary or tertiary level. Several schools now offer psychology at A-level, and occasional posts arise in polytechnics and universities. These latter posts require evidence of study at a postgraduate level.

Training

For a list of degree courses, the entry qualifications and details of the course of study in different institutions, consult the Degree Course Guide for *Psychology*. To enter a degree course there are no special A-level subject requirements. Applicants should have two or three A-levels and certainly good passes at GCSE or its equivalent in maths and English language. The entry requirements vary considerably from a university to a college or institute of higher education. The leading universities look for grades in the ABB to BCC category; polytechnics and colleges offer places with more modest grades, but still expect grades of around CCD. Generally speaking, students with arts or science backgrounds are equally welcome. The British Psychological Society suggests that the most appropriate A-levels for entry to undergraduate courses are biology, social biology, human biology, maths, economics, history and psychology. However, other A-levels are acceptable, as long as they are at good grades. It is not necessary to have studied psychology at A-level for entry to a degree course.

Information

British Psychological Society, St Andrews House, 48 Princess Road East, Leicester LE1 7DR
The Clearing House for Postgraduate Clinical Psychology Courses, University of Leeds, 15 Hyde Terrace, Leeds LS2 9LT

Careers in Psychology, Kogan Page
Psychology, Degree Course Guide, Hobsons

Public administration

Public administration is a general title that covers many different jobs and careers and includes some four million employees. Safer, securer, less pressurised than business and industry, the careers are in local and central government. The security, once guaranteed, is no longer quite as secure as it used to be because cutbacks in government spending have meant restrictions on recruiting to local authority services and to the Civil Service. Furthermore, redundancies, such as the abolition of the Greater London Council, have occurred in fields of employment once thought utterly safe.

The occupations generally have fixed salary and wage structures and well-defined job descriptions. Pay depends on grade and length of service; increases in pay come as a result of annual increments and awards and by promotion to the next grade or a new job.

Most people who work in central and local government and other forms of public service say that the job satisfaction comes from working for the public. The objective of the job is to help the community, either locally or nationally. It might be difficult for a taxpayer to think of a tax collector as someone who is serving the community, but it is true, for taxes paid in full and promptly pay for the services we sometimes take for granted, such as the NHS. These careers also have their stress points. Rules and regulations dominate and officials usually have to report to a committee, a council or a superior officer, and paperwork becomes very important within the chain of command. Real management skills are needed for this work, both in terms of arranging and managing a service such as housing, public health or environmental health, or in responding to the requirements of the law and of government policies, as in the Civil Service.

Careers within public administration include all the grades and specialist jobs within the **Civil Service**, in **local government**, in the **diplomatic service,** as a **tax inspector** or **factory inspector,** in **housing** and **hospital management**, in **environmental health** services, and within the NHS. For further information read sections or entries in careers information books under the titles of Civil Service, local government and public administration.

Information
Civil Service Commission, Alencon Link, Basingstoke, Hampshire
RG21 1JB
Civil Service Commission, St Andrew's House, Edinburgh EH1 3BX

Publishing

Publishing has the ring of a glamorous job, and it is very attractive to arts graduates and literate school-leavers. In fact it is a small industry, highly competitive, and very difficult to enter. And there are more jobs in sales, marketing and production than in the editorial or commissioning side of the business.

Publishers range from the giants to small companies that bring out just a few books a year. However, there are other opportunities in **magazine** publishing (anything from *Computer World* to *Cosmopolitan*), and in technology ventures such as software publishing for computer owners and electronic publishing, which involves storing and retrieving data by electronic means. Even so, taking all these together, the market for jobs is still small. It is boosted, however, if **bookselling** is included. To the workforce of only about 20,000 in book publishing could be added the 30,000 people involved in magazines and bookselling

The routes into publishing vary. One method is as a secretary who becomes an editorial assistant. Another is as a publicity assistant or sales rep. For these posts, school-leavers or 18-plus, leavers with GCSEs or A-levels are suitable, especially if they have secretarial skills, sales expertise, or have taken a BTEC course at a college of further education in a subject such as business studies which contains courses on sales, marketing and bookkeeping and other office skills.

Another way into publishing – or bookselling – is with specialist knowledge and skills, such as accounting, purchasing, distribution, warehousing, marketing. From an assistant's job the route is wide open to become a manager or director of these services. The third method is as a graduate and to try to secure a job as an assistant to a designer, editor or sales manager.

Most people are inclined to think that English literature and modern languages must be the best subjects either at A-level or for a graduate. For a few jobs they are very useful. On the other hand, many published books are on technical subjects, science and computing, and publishers claim that finding graduates in these disciplines with the right kind of

501

editorial or business knowledge is very difficult. A technical and specialist background, therefore, is very useful indeed. For design and production work, a formal training course at a graphic arts or printing college is generally essential.

Training
Apart from the various ways into publishing described above, there are degree courses in publishing at Oxford Polytechnic and Napier Polytechnic in Edinburgh; in addition, some polytechnics and colleges such as West Herts College, Watford and the London College of Printing offer postgraduate diploma courses which give training in editorial skills, book production, printing, and publicity, sales and marketing. Companies recruit from these courses and also direct from universities, and then provide the necessary training in-company. Starting salaries – because of the competition – are low, but they can become quite high for the successful. For publishers who have ambitions to be entrepreneurs, company experience and training added to a very good commercial sense is often enough to start up independently.

Information
The Publishers Association, 19 Bedford Square, London WC1B 3HJ
Book Trust, Book House, 45 East Hill, London SW18 2QZ

Careers in Book Publishing, Publishers Association
Working in Printing and Publishing, COIC

Purchasing

Purchasing officers (who are often called 'buyers') buy raw materials, equipment and other goods and services from manufacturers, suppliers and wholesalers. They work in every kind of business or professional organisation, for almost every one of these bodies purchases goods and services of some kind. The officers who specialise in this work are trained and get the best deals possible for their company or organisation. Among the qualities a purchasing officer needs, therefore, are a keen business sense, good communication skills and the ability to get on with people. Purchasing officers have to be able to balance many different factors in making their selection of goods and services, and price is only one of the considerations. The work is closely related to stock control and is increasingly computerised. It is essential, therefore, to obtain knowledge of technical processes or manufacturing methods linked to the business of the purchasing officer's company. Additional accomplishments would be knowledge of one or more foreign languages.

There are good prospects for purchasing officers because central and local government, industrial and commercial companies and organisations all need them.

Training

It is possible to gain entry to a job and then to train as a purchasing officer from the age of 16 onwards. For a 16- or 17-year-old, at least four GCSEs or O-grades are required. Alternatively, by taking A-levels, the same route can be followed by getting a job on the basis of one or two A levels, and then taking training courses on a part-time basis. A more thorough preparation is to take a BTEC or SCOTVEC National Diploma two-year full-time business studies course or a course leading to an HNC or an HND in business studies. Some of these courses have units, modules or options in purchasing. Lastly, graduates are now looking to purchasing and supply as a career in itself or for progression later to other business jobs. Almost any degree is suitable although business and management studies, statistics or a technical subject are clearly the most useful kinds of preparation.

Training is by a combination of theoretical study of purchasing, allied to practical experience. Most employers ask their employees to study for the examinations of the Institute of Purchasing and Supply (IPS). These are normally taken as part of the practical and training aspect of an in-company training programme, or by individuals who want to improve their qualifications.

In 1981 another organisation, the Association of Supervisors in Purchasing and Supply, was set up to look after the interests of people who do not meet the academic qualifications required for registration as an IPS student, which are a minimum of two A-levels and three GCSEs or their equivalents. Like the IPS, the ASPS has its own courses and professional awards.

Information

The Institute of Purchasing and Supply , Easton House, Easton on the Hill, Northamptonshire PE9 3NZ
Association of Supervisors in Purchasing and Supply (ASPS), as above

Purchasing and Supply, a career worth thinking about!, IPS
Directory of Further Education, Hobsons

Quarrying

Quarrying is the extraction of gravel, clay, chalk, slate, sandstone and
other minerals from the ground – it is one of Britain's oldest industries.
Today, quarrying companies use advanced technological equipment
and employees have to know not only about the minerals themselves but
also about how to produce concrete, stone and other materials for roads
and buildings.

Training

People are employed at craft, technician and management levels, and
training is linked to these three areas. Craft workers need few formal
qualifications but if they wish to move to technician, they require formal
qualifications and Institute of Quarrying recognition.

There are HNC courses at several colleges in quarrying and there is
a 3-year sandwich HND course at Doncaster Metropolitan Institute of
Higher Education; from here students can go on to Leeds University for
a one-year course leading to the BSc in Mining or a two-year course for
BSc (Hons) in Mining.

Information

Institute of Quarrying, 7 Regent Street, Nottingham NG1 5BY

Radio

BBC Radio employs people in the five main network radio services and
in over 30 local radio stations. In addition, there are now over 40
independent local radio stations. The BBC and the independent companies are the employers, and it is very difficult to gain entry. The
opportunities are better for technical staff with engineering accomplishments than they are for editors, broadcasters, researchers and producers.
Like publishing, journalism and the media in general, radio has a
glamorous image. The reality is very different, for it is likely to mean
long hours, either chasing after local news stories or in the studio, editing
and taping.

Most people enter radio and television as experts in their particular field. For example, to become a producer generally requires previous experience in journalism, newspapers, education or some other specialist area. Engineers need to be skilled: training is given by the BBC, but the basic skills have to be learnt and practised before applying. Competition is intense for jobs as producers, and the BBC and ILR (independent local radio) prefer to offer writers, researchers and presenters short-term contracts rather than permanent positions on the staff.

Each year about 500 new staff are recruited by the BBC Engineering Department, usually with degree or at least A-level qualifications in science or technology subjects, or electronic engineering degrees. Because of the demand for young people with these qualifications in other industries, the BBC and ILR also take people with BTEC and SCOTVEC National Diplomas and HNDs as long as they have engineering awards. Other entrants go into market research (statistics and psychology at degree level are useful subjects) and into a trainee studio manager's scheme. To have any kind of chance, graduates have to demonstrate some knowledge and experience of sound equipment. Vacancies as audio assistants are filled by school-leavers with good GCSE or A-level qualifications. Knowledge of music, drama, light entertainment or current affairs is essential to aid one's application.

Training
Over 80 colleges and polytechnics offer courses that are linked or lead to the media. They vary in quality and are not always rated by the broadcasting authorities. However, they do provide a starting-point for jobs. The courses range from degrees in visual communication, engineering and design to BTEC and SCOTVEC diplomas and HNCs and HNDs. As has been suggested, however, a more fruitful route to the job would be via a full-time course in electronics, radio or television engineering. There are degree courses in communication engineering and electronics, and BTEC and SCOTVEC courses in telecommunications and electronics, plus City and Guilds certificate courses for radio amateurs, electronics servicing and telecommunications.

At school, a good preparation for the technical jobs would be to take A-levels in maths, physics, electronics or electronic systems. For work as a producer/researcher/presenter in front of the microphone, almost any course at degree or equivalent level could be suitable, depending on the experience a graduate or anyone else obtains before applying for work in radio. Employers also look for a keen interest and knowledge of the output of the radio service.

Information

Appointments Department, BBC, Broadcasting House, London W1A 1AA, for information about all posts except technical or engineering appointments

The Engineering Recruitment Officer, BBC, Broadcasting House, London W1A 1AA, for all technical and engineering posts

Working in Radio and Telecommunications, COIC

Radiography

Diagnostic radiographers produce high-quality images of the human body and sometimes on other media such as video tapes. They acquire the skill during their training to select the optimum demonstration of normal and abnormal body anatomy, pathology and physiology. From these images, a radiologist (a specialist doctor) interprets the patient's normal or abnormal condition, which enables other members of the hospital team to give the patient correct treatment.

Therapy radiographers treat patients (mostly those with cancer) with ionising radiation. They are part of a very highly trained team. Radiotherapists (specialist doctors) prescribe the treatment, but radiographers are responsible for the accurate planning and administration of that treatment on a day-to-day basis. They are also vital in the psychological and physical care of the patient.

There are shortages of both diagnostic and therapy radiographers, despite the cutbacks in the NHS. Promotion is to management jobs or to other, linked, specialist services. Radiographers are required to take regular re-training courses as new equipment and alternative techniques are adopted. Today, much of the new high-tech equipment is computer-controlled, so an understanding of what computers are and what they can do is important.

About 75 per cent of radiographers are women, although most of the managers are men, a characteristic of many careers. Over 90 per cent of radiographers work in the NHS, but an increasing number are employed in private clinics. Overall, there are about 10,000 radiographers in a ratio of ten diagnostic to one therapy radiographers. The Diploma of the College of Radiographers is internationally recognised and takes some staff to jobs overseas, especially if they have a language skill.

Training

Full details of the entry requirements to one of the College's training courses are given in a leaflet available from the address below, but briefly they are: a minimum of seven passes in GCSE, with five subjects at grades A, B or C, including English language, physics or maths, a science subject and an 'academic' arts or humanities subject, plus a minimum of two passes at A-level at grade D or above.

In Scotland, a minimum of nine passes in the Scottish Certificate of Education with five of the subjects at O-grade, including English language, maths or physics, a science subject and an academic arts or humanities subject, and four H-grades (or three H-grades if they are at high grades).

There are variations on these entry requirements, so the leaflet available from The College of Radiographers should be read carefully.

The three-year course over eight terms leads to the Diploma of the College of Radiographers. The course is available at over 70 training schools, most of which are attached to hospitals; a list of the schools can be obtained from the address below. Students must decide which discipline – diagnostic or therapeutic – they want to specialise in before embarking on Part 1 of the course.

The suitable school subjects at GCSE, O-grade, A-level and H-grade are listed above. Other useful subjects are biological sciences, either to degree level or to A-level (biology, human biology, social biology), and psychology.

Information

Society of Radiographers, 14 Upper Wimpole Street, London W1M 8BN
College of Radiographers, 14 Upper Wimpole Street, London W1M 8BN

Rail transport

British Rail (BR) is a nationalised industry, split into four main sectors:

- InterCity services – the fast, direct services linking major cities
- Network SouthEast services – largely catering for the heavy commuter traffic into London

- provincial or local services – operating throughout Britain
- freight and parcels services – including Speedlink, Night Star and Red Star services and special company trains carrying freight.

Within the rail industry are jobs at various levels: train drivers, rail guards, railmen and railwomen, railway technicians and management staff. British Rail is continually looking for new staff at all levels.

Train drivers

No particular academic entry requirements are laid down for train drivers. Applicants have to be between 16 and 22 and in good health with perfect eyesight. If they have GCSE passes in maths, a science subject and English language, so much the better. Training for a driver is on the job, in the cab with experienced drivers, and at British Rail's own training centres.

Guards

Rail guards should be 18, in good health and with good eyesight; no particular academic entry requirements are demanded, but the same good general education as for drivers is looked for, and short tests in arithmetic and comprehension are given to all applicants.

Railmen and railwomen

Railmen and railwomen carry luggage (they are no longer called 'porters'), answer travel enquiries, attend train arrivals and departures, load and unload parcels, make train announcements check doors and tickets, and collect tickets. They are the staff who look after the stations, and this includes cleaning platforms and carriages, operating lifts and driving small trucks. There are promotion prospects to leading and then senior railman/woman and finally to chargehand, who supervises the work of a team of staff. Beyond that is promotion to signalman/woman, guard and supervisor. For the railman/woman posts, applicants have to be 18 or older, with a good general education, as before, and are required to pass a simple literacy and numeracy test. Training for all these posts is at British Rail training centres and at stations.

Technical staff

Railway technicians work for the Signal and Telecommunications Department, which designs, installs and maintains railway signalling or other equipment. Most of the work is outdoors – in all kinds of weather. The number of jobs for technical staff is increasing and job prospects are good, as are promotion opportunities to senior technician posts. Applicants must be 16 to 18 and in good health. They must pass basic English language and arithmetic tests, and have at least four GCSE passes, including maths and a science, or give evidence of a good general education. Applicants with GCSEs or O-grades are therefore in a very good position.

Managerial posts

British Rail also recruits graduates for managerial positions. These can be engineering graduates for technical work at stations, depots and workshops, and graduates in other subjects who are recruited for management trainee jobs. These trainees are expected to rise to senior positions within British Rail. Almost any degree subject is suitable although technological subjects are highly regarded. British Rail is, however, looking for managerial skills and therefore combs widely through different degree subjects. The trainees, who benefit from training courses at British Rail's own centres, are expected to move into senior posts at stations and at the Euston headquarters, with promotion to top managerial positions for the successful.

Information
British Railways Board, Rail House, Euston Square, PO Box 100, London NW1 2DZ. The Board publishes booklets and leaflets on the full range of jobs available

Retail trade management

Retailing is one of the largest industries in the country. It is increasing in scope and in job opportunities as more shops and superstores open, as people have more to spend, and as overseas visitors come to Britain to buy. Another feature is that jobs and careers in retailing do not depend on passing certain examinations.

Retailing is a very dynamic changing industry. Each year fresh fashion or food ideas lead to new chains of shops or departments in shops. Shopping hours are lengthening. Sunday opening has made shopping a seven-day activity. The main outlets at present are in supermarkets (or hypermarkets), department stores, chain stores, the multiples, co-operatives and the corner-shop independents. This last category is declining, as rates and price competition from the superstores makes retail trade difficult for the independent trader. Another feature is that although computerisation has reduced the shopfloor workforce in the large stores, there are increasing opportunities and posts for managers. Other growth areas are in franchising, where a big name (such as Benetton) permits individual businesses to use its name and its image to sell its own-label merchandise in return for a specified fee or percentage of takings. Other fast-developing businesses are mail-order selling, using part-time agents and direct selling by mail or phone, and home computer-linked shopping.

Jobs are at all kinds of levels. Starting with the shopfloor, it is possible for a 16-year-old school-leaver to get a job on the counter, in the distribution section, in the warehouse or offices, and by experience and taking part-time day-release courses at a local college of further education to advance to the manager's chair. Alternatively, many stores have in-house training programmes which do not require college attendance, and these can equally well lead to management positions.

In addition, many department stores and multiples take employees straight from a Youth Training programme into permanent jobs. Most stores do not recruit any young employees direct from school at 16, but require them to take a Youth Training programme, providing employment as part of the training scheme. An alternative route to a job in a store is to take a one- or two-year full-time course at a college of further education, and then, armed with a City and Guilds or BTEC National Diploma, look for a job.

Once into a job, promotion can be to senior sales assistant, supervisor and to **buyer**. After that it is possible to gain promotion to junior or senior management positions within the store.

The fastest movers are likely to be graduates. An increasing number of graduates are now entering retail management as a career, attracted while at university or polytechnic by the recruiters who attend the careers days or who take part in the 'milk-round' of interviews in the undergraduate's last year at college. The recruiters take graduates from a wide variety of subjects, from accounting to zoology. The reason is that they are looking for the qualities that make good store managers, and graduates in any subject could be candidates. On the other hand, those with a good knowledge of business studies, management techniques and finance are likely to have a head start. Even so, it is personality that really counts, and the winners have to be well organised, helpful, considerate, efficient and patient.

Training

There is no one way of training for retail management. Systems vary from one company to another. The better companies have their own well-structured training programmes, and it is essential to take and pass them in order to progress to management jobs. This is as true for 16- to 19-year-old entrants as it is for graduates. A-level applicants need to impress the recruiters with their personal qualities and readiness to undertake training programmes, and although A-level passes in business studies and other subjects are an excellent basis (as is a BTEC National Certificate or National Diploma), the same personal qualities are looked for. Colleges of further education are the providers of most off-the-job training for retail companies. The *Directory of Further Education* lists a great variety of courses and the colleges that offer them, from BA and BSc degrees in applied consumer science and retail marketing, through BTEC and SCOTVEC National Certificates, National Diplomas, HNC and HND courses, to City and Guilds certificates in distribution, consumer studies and retailing. Some colleges also offer their own certificate courses in retail management to match the requirements of local companies: these are on all kinds of modes from block- and day-release to sandwich and full-time.

Selling, buying (particularly fashion buying) and store management are the major objectives for graduates and other entrants. However, there are specialist jobs in personnel work, buying, finance, accounting, marketing, computing and distribution: some of these can be entered direct from school or college, others are only open to experienced and well-qualified people. Adding them all together, the retailing industry employs 1.8 million people in over 350,000 shops. On the other hand, candidates need to be aware of the hours (including Saturdays), the commercial attitude, the crowds, and feet-ache. It is a world where the fast movers can move fast but they have to accept the disadvantages.

The school subjects that could be useful have been suggested, but

English language and maths are by far the most useful and appropriate. Other useful subjects are business studies, home economics, biology, fashion and design, although virtually any subject could be useful. But, as with so many jobs, it is personality and attitude rather than exam passes in defined subjects that are the important factors.

Information
British Retailers Association, Commonwealth House, 1–19 New Oxford Street, London WC1A 1PA
College for the Distributive Trades, 30 Leicester Square, London WC2H 7LE

Working in the Retail Industry, COIC
Careers in Retailing, Kogan Page

Road transport

Road transport is the business of planning, organising and carrying out the handling and transport of freight and passenger traffic in the UK and to overseas destinations. It is therefore a very substantial industry, involving heavy goods traffic, passenger bus services and general haulage work, local and national. Among the employers are large companies and operators such as the National Bus Company, the National Freight Company, London Regional Transport and the Scottish Bus Group. To these should be added the thousands of firms, large and small, that operate bus services or haulage contracts. There are also many career opportunities in transport sections of huge industrial companies, with HM Forces, and with motoring organisations such as the RAC and AA.

The range of jobs is just as varied as the firms. First, there are the drivers – lorry, bus, taxi and car drivers. Then there are the planners – the office staff who deal with contracts, orders, route planning, documentation, loading and delivery, servicing and maintenance. Next there are the technical staff – the engineers, mechanics, electricians. Another substantial group of employees are people who are common to all industries – accountants, personnel officers, computer staff, telephonists, secretaries. Finally, there are men and women who specialise in managing road transport: they are the managers and directors of the companies or those who sport the grander title of road manager or traffic

512

manager. Among their duties are maintaining vehicles, co-ordinating schedules, planning routes, pricing, administering safety policies, investigating complaints, settling claims and a hundred other responsibilities.

Training

Entry to these jobs can be by several methods. Many companies prefer managers to emerge through their own training schemes, such as the Young Driver's Scheme, which is for school-leavers. Recruits gain experience by working with experienced drivers, progress to a Heavy Goods Vehicle (HGV) licence at 18, and then take on responsibilities as the company decides. Direct entry at 18-plus is also possible, and some companies give time off to attend college for a BTEC or SCOTVEC HND or HNC course in business studies, some of which have transport units, modules or options. Alternatively, a student can take a full-time HND course and then seek employment as a junior manager. Another method of entry is by taking a degree, and then joining a company as a management trainee. Competition for all these methods of entry is keen.

Graduates can have degrees in any subject, although business studies and management studies are looked on very favourably. Alternatively, there are specialist degree courses in transport management at the University of Wales College of Cardiff and Loughborough University, and in transport operation and planning at Aston University and Huddersfield Polytechnic. No particular subject requirements are needed, apart from a GCSE or O-grade pass in maths. The job prospects of graduates from these courses are excellent in an industry which is looking for managers. Perhaps the best kind of preparation is to take A-levels in business studies, or science and technology subjects, but entry requirements for these degree courses are fluid.

Information

The Chartered Institute of Transport, 80 Portland Place, London W1N 4DP

The Freight Transport Association, Hermes House, St John's Road, Tunbridge Wells, Kent TN4 9UZ

The Road Haulage Association, 35 Monument Hill, Weybridge, Surrey KT13 8RN

Royal Air Force

There are around 90,000 men and women serving in the Royal Air Force, based on stations throughout the UK and overseas, principally in Germany. The RAF is organised in three commands: Strike Command is the largest and includes all operational forces except those based in Germany; Royal Air Force Germany, the second command, is part of the NATO forces; Support Command is responsible for all flying and ground training and includes maintenance units where major overhauls of aircraft are carried out, and a supply centre to keep every station fully equipped. In addition, there is the Women's Royal Air Force whose personnel make up about 10 per cent of the total.

Officers

Officers serve in many different ways. There are the **pilots** and navigators who fly the supersonic strike aircraft and other planes. Ground staff work in air traffic control which plans RAF flights through busy air space, and in photographic interpretation work. In the engineer branch of the RAF there are aerosystems officers who look after aircraft and weapons, and the communications – electronics group responsible for ground-based radio systems. The supply branch of the Service deals with ordering, storage and distribution of aircraft and equipment, and the administration branch deals with education, catering, secretarial, accounting and other management services. The security branch is divided into the RAF Regiment, whose duties include the defence of airfields, and the security and policing services. Furthermore, the RAF has other specialists such as dentists, medical staff, chaplains, lawyers, nurses and other professionally qualified personnel.

For officer entry to the RAF, the two main types of commission available are a permanent commission and a short-service commission. Serving members of the RAF in non-commissioned ranks may apply for a commission at any time, provided they possess the minimum educational qualifications.

Entry

Entry to the RAF can be direct from school or from university, polytechnic or college, or after a period of work in a civilian occupation. Minimum age of entry for most branches is $17^1/_2$ for men and 18 for women. The upper age-limit is generally 39, but there are variations – notably for pilot duties where the age-limit is $23^1/2$.

Entry to some officer branches requires professional qualifications, but there are many opportunities for those who possess, along with the required personal qualities, a minimum of five GCSEs (grade C or above) or equivalents; these must include English language and maths.

All candidates for commissioned service are required to attend the Officers and Aircrew Selection Centre at RAF Biggin Hill for aptitude tests, medical examination, interview and practical leadership exercises.

There is some variation between branches in the minimum medical standards acceptable; for instance, there are stringent eyesight and hearing requirements for those applying for flying duties.

People can apply for a commission ranging from 3 to 16 years, depending on the branch and vacancies existing at the time of application. Commissions of 16 years (or to the age of 38, whichever is the later) qualify for a pension; all others attract a tax-free gratuity on completion.

Once serving in the RAF, there may be opportunities to apply for a full career (possibly up to the age of 55) on a competitive basis.

The RAF offers sponsorship in many forms. This includes flying scholarships (30 hours of free instruction at a selected flying club), sixth-form scholarships (to give financial assistance through an A-level course) and cadetships and bursaries while undergoing higher education. Selection for all forms of sponsorship takes place at the Officers and Aircrew Selection Centre.

Airmen and airwomen

Entry for most trades is from $16^1/2$ for men and from 17 for women, up to 39 for both. Apprentice entry (men only) is between 16 and $18^1/2$ (exceptionally 21). Those under 18 require the written consent of a parent or guardian.

The majority of trades do not call for any academic or professional qualifications. Those that do may in certain cases attract special terms of entry.

For ground trades selection is carried out at the local Careers Information Office. Aptitude tests and a medical examination are given and, if the applicant meets the requirements, he or she would be invited to make an application (subject to vacancies being available in the trade(s) of his or her choice). Following this, assessment interviews would be arranged.

Candidates for airman/airwoman aircrew are required to attend the Officers and Aircrew Selection Centre at RAF Biggin Hill for these procedures and, if successful this far, for practical leadership exercises.

Candidates must meet the medical standards set by the RAF. These standards, including eyesight, colour perception and hearing, vary between trades.

Length of service counts from the day of enlistment at the Careers Information Office if aged 18 or over. Service before this age does not count for pension grants or bonuses. All engagements are reckoned from the age of 18.

There are two types of engagement:

- fixed: fixed engagements available to men may be for 6, 8 (aircrew), 9, 12 or 15 years dependent on trade – followed by 6 years in the RAF Reserve. Women enlisted as Air Loadmasters are engaged on similar terms.
- notice: women (excluding Air Loadmasters) are enlisted on 9-year notice engagements with the right to leave after 18 months' notice subject to having served for a minimum of three years from age 18 or end of training, whichever is the later.

Men who enlist before the age of $17^1/2$ may, at 18, transfer to a notice engagement on the terms outlined above.

The Armed Forces Youth Training Scheme
The Armed Forces run a scheme under which young men and women with a Youth Training entitlement can apply to do this training in the RAF. At any time during their service they may give two weeks' notice to leave the RAF without any obligation on their part.

Training
Information on training is given in the RAF's own leaflets. The school subjects that are important are English language and maths. Science and engineering subjects from GCSE to graduate level are important for aircrew and for ground staff. However, the arts subjects are useful, too, as GCSE, A-level, or degree subjects, for the RAF casts its net wide to attract suitable recruits.

Information

RAF Careers Information Service, Government Buildings, London Road, Stanmore, Middlesex HA7 4PZ

RAF Careers Information Offices: for the nearest one look in the telephone directory

Leaflets on all aspects of the RAF's work and requirements are available from the Information Offices

Royal Navy

The Royal Navy, with about 65,000 personnel, is not quite the force that it was in Britain's past, but it is still of vital importance in protecting the trading fleet and as part of NATO and other treaty obligations. The conflict in the Falkland Islands in 1982 and the Gulf in 1991 showed that there is a major role for the Royal Navy and its supporting services. These include the Royal Marines, who are the Navy's amphibious soldiers, trained as commandos and using helicopters and other modern transport systems to get to the scene of trouble as quickly as possible. The Women's Royal Naval Service (WRNS) is an integral part of the Navy and its members serve mainly in shore establishments in the UK and abroad, although some go to sea in support ships.

In the Royal Navy the main branches are tactical operations at sea, which is the largest sector, engineering, which looks after marine, aeronautical and weapon maintenance and support, the supply and secretariat branch, which deals with administrative and legal matters, and the instructor group, which provides training at all levels and for all jobs.

Officers

There are two main methods of officer entry to the Royal Navy. One is direct entry, straight from school, college, polytechnic or university, or after a short period of civilian employment. The second is via one of several sponsorship schemes – bursaries, scholarships, cadetships. These routes lead to a commission as an officer. Ratings can enter the service at any time, depending on educational, health and age qualifications. Opportunities for promotion to officer are very good, for 40 per cent of officers start their careers as ratings.

For officers, the age of entry is 17 to 23 (to 26 for graduates; 34 for some instructors). Minimum educational requirements are two A-levels or three H-grades, plus three GCSEs or O-grades, and these must include English language and maths. For engineers, the passes at A-level must include physics and maths. However, many applicants have better qualifications, such as a degree. There are also short- or medium-term commissions, with a lower entry qualification of at least five GCSEs or O-grades, including English language and maths. It is possible to transfer from a short-service commission to a full career commission, although this is a very competitive area.

For the WRNS, the competition is so fierce that a degree is virtually essential for a commission as an officer. Even so, because of the keen competition, many women who meet entry requirements are not selected. For details of the sponsorship and bursary arrangements, send for leaflets to the address below.

Ratings and Marines

For a navy engineering technician apprentice (artificer), three GCSEs or their equivalents, including physics or physical science, maths and English language, give exemption from the written qualifying examinations set by the Royal Navy. For a medical technician, five GCSEs or equivalents are needed, and for some specialist jobs, two A-levels are also required. Other trades and ratings in the Royal Navy do not require any particular GCSE or other qualifications, but because of the competition the Royal Navy looks for good educational accomplishments and by this they mean high GCSE grades.

Ratings in the WRNS are expected to show a good general standard of education, and GCSE maths is looked for. For more specialised jobs in the WRNS, such as dental hygienist, education assistant, air engineering mechanic and radar mechanic, particular requirements are listed, such as GCSE English language and mathematics. Other trades do not require particular GCSE subjects.

To prepare for a career in the Royal Navy, the Marines or the WRNS, a good general education is therefore necessary. In some cases subjects are specified, and for officer entry the GCSEs must include maths and English language. Other school subjects that rate highly at any level are physics, integrated science, chemistry, photography, geography and computing. No particular degree is required for the Royal Navy or the WRNS, so an arts or science degree course could be a good preparation. The Royal Navy, like the other Services, is looking for sound personal qualities such as reliability, initiative and determination, and these rate as highly as educational accomplishments.

Information
The Director, Naval Recruiting, Old Admiralty Building, Whitehall, London SW1A 2BE. Information, leaflets and details of entry for all naval careers are available from this address.

Working in the Armed Services, COIC

Rubber technology

Rubber technologists work in the rubber, plastics and polymer industries. Some years ago they held a key position in industrial technology, but rubber has to some extent been ousted by other materials. The rubber industry's output slowed down throughout the 1970s and 1980s largely because tyres were being made by companies throughout the world, so leading to over-production and stock-piling. This has created major problems for the manufacturing companies, leading to a reduction in the number of jobs within the whole industry.

At the same time new ways to use polymers and plastics were being developed, for instance in printing-plates. Among the plastics that created new industrial and commercial products are nylon, polystyrene, polythene and melamine. The demand is growing steadily for highly qualified scientists and technologists capable of carrying out research into new products and uses.

Training
There is no degree course in rubber technology, although it is possible to take a course in polymer science in which rubber is one of the materials studied. There are degree courses at the Universities of Sussex, London (Queen Mary College), Loughborough and Lancaster and at University of Wales College of Cardiff and UMIST (Manchester), and at the Polytechnics of South Bank (London), North London and Manchester. In addition, there are courses that offer a postgraduate

qualification or an introduction to polymers: some of these courses lead to the Graduateship and Licentiateship qualifications of the Plastics and Rubber Institute, as well as BTEC, SCOTVEC and college awards in polymer processes and technology (see below).

To prepare for these courses, the relevant school subjects are chemistry and other sciences. Degree course entry requirements are two or three A-levels, including chemistry, and because the courses are not generally known or highly regarded (although their industrial and career potential is very good), the grades needed at A-level can be modest. C and D grades in two or three subjects will generally secure a place. Other suitable subjects are maths, physics, physical science and the biological sciences.

Information
Plastics and Rubber Institute, 11 Hobart Place, London SW1W 0HL

Directory of Further Education, Hobsons

Sales

'Sales' is one of those general expressions that covers all kinds of jobs at many different levels. In the first place, there are the sales staff in large and small stores, from Marks & Spencer to the local corner shop. They may be at the counter, on a check-out till, or work in a large department. Whatever the situation, the skills are common to all staff: a helpful attitude to customers, an interest in what is being sold, good communication skills and the ability to persuade. These are skills for any other kind of salesman or saleswoman, too.

Another career opportunity is as a travelling sales representative, visiting customers by car or public transport, persuading, selling, taking orders, describing a new product or special service.

Other sales staff work for insurance companies, banks, building societies, hotels, TV and the thousands of different manufacturing or supply groups, selling anything from matches to Concorde. They are all in sales, although the job may have a different, grander title such as 'marketing executive'. Marketing is different: it is the strategy of selling, and for career descriptions look at the entries for **marketing** and **market research.**

Prospects

Prospects for sales staff are excellent – if you are good at it. Counter-sales staff can become department under-managers and then managers. Successful sales reps become regional managers, and the best of these move on to sales manager and then sales director, taking the final step to managing director in companies which are sales-driven – that is, the business is dependent on sales, and the management know it.

Training

Entry to sales careers and jobs can be at any age and with any qualification. School-leavers with modest educational qualifications can start as a petrol pump attendant, on the counter of a large store, or in a technical job, and gradually move on. Obviously the better qualified the school-leaver, the better the chance of succeeding, but academic success is no guide to success at selling. Personality counts for a lot more, and selling skills are learned through experience as well as training. It is certainly possible to obtain training in sales: large companies that are dependent on sales organise their own in-company training programmes for sales staff. In addition, there are all kinds of courses related to sales offered by colleges and independent training organisations.

Exporting is a specialised branch of sales, and the job of export sales manager or rep calls for personal responsibility and communication skills of a high order, often in a foreign language. Technical sales demand other kinds of knowledge: a salesman/woman who 'travels' in electronic colour scanners requires a more detailed and thorough knowledge and training in the uses of the product than someone who works for a chocolate or washing powder manufacturer.

Increasingly, Britain is obtaining a graduate sales force, particularly in technical and export sales where they are often called 'account executives', and in large companies or organisations. Any degree could be suitable because the qualities of self-confidence, self-discipline and sociability cross subject and course boundaries. However, since knowledge of the product is essential, people with technical knowledge start with an advantage in selling technologically or science-based products. But it is possible to make a very successful career in sales with any kind of educational qualification – A-levels, GCSE, O-grade and H-grade, City and Guilds, BTEC or SCOTVEC.

The entry level for membership of the Institute of Sales and Marketing Management is wide open to encourage all sales staff to seek professional membership. For the Institute of Export, however, there is a minimum requirement of four GCSEs or their equivalent.

Information

Institute of Sales and Marketing Management, Georgian House, 31 Upper George Street, Luton, Bedfordshire LU1 2RD

Institute of Export, Export House, 64 Clifton Street, London EC2A 4HB

Science

Science is a vast area of career potential, for it includes people generally known as scientists, i.e. those with a science degree, and thousands of others who have trained in science or use it as a basis for their work.

Scientists

Among the scientists are doctors (see **medicine**), **physicists, biologists, chemists, mathematicians** and technologists (which in turn includes all kinds of specialist jobs). Among the science support staff are technicians, technical sales staff, laboratory assistants, and many more. The degree course requirements vary from one course to another, but in general the specifications are:

- mathematics – most degree courses ask for A-levels in pure and applied maths
- chemistry – chemistry and physics A-levels are preferred, and/or maths, but other combinations including biological sciences are acceptable
- physics – A-levels must include physics and maths
- applied sciences – degree courses in applied physics, cybernetics, biophysics, biotechnology and other courses usually require an A-level combination of two or three from physics, biology, chemistry and mathematics. For some science degree courses, biology may only be accepted as a third science, i.e. after a combination of physics and chemistry
- biology– the A-levels should include one of the biological sciences, plus chemistry. Other combinations are acceptable
- environmental sciences and other science subjects – consult the specialist Degree Course Guides for the degree subject (see below for details).

The information given here for A-levels also applies to H-grades, but instead of three A-levels, the universities are likely to require four or five H-grades. Polytechnics offer places on science courses to candidates with two A-levels, and at significantly lower grades than the universities.

Prospects

Prospects for scientists are generally good. As usual, however, it all depends. There is a worrying amount of graduate unemployment among biologists, which suggests that too many students are taking this subject. Job prospects for physicists and mathematicians are excellent, and technology/science combined degree courses have a very good job placement record. Scientists can choose too: they can become research-based scientists; they can go into teaching at levels from universities to schools; or they can become 'practical' scientists, working on produc tion or manufacturing problems within companies.

Science technician

Technicians work alongside scientists in educational institutions of all types, helping them with their teaching, demonstration and research duties. They work in hospital labs; in production, research and manu-facturing in industry; within the Civil Service as assistant scientific officers, and in government departments concerned with science, such as the Departments of Industry, Environment and Health.

Entry qualifications are not clearly defined: they vary according to the job and the institution or company offering the job. In some cases, GCSE passes will be asked for, but in other cases no rigid definition is made. For some Civil Service and research council posts, A-levels or even a degree is requested. One guideline is that to enter a BTEC National Diploma in science course – full time over two years – four GCSEs or their equivalent are required, including a science subject and preferably with maths. For a BTEC National Certificate, the entry is at a lower level. For entry to an HNC or HND course in science, one A-level pass is required, supported by four GCSEs or their equivalent, including at least one and sometimes two or three science/maths subjects.

Other specialist careers are in **food science and technology, pharmacy**, forensic science, scientific photography, materials science, information science (which overlaps with computer science), and the great range of technology careers based on knowledge of science. These careers are described in specialist sections of this book, or in other careers publications (see below).

Information

Degree Course Guides for the science and technology subjects such as *Biological Sciences, Mathematics and Statistics, Microbiology and Immunology, Pharmacy, Physics, Physiology, Psychology, Technology*, Hobsons *Occupations*, COIC
Equal Opportunities: A Careers Guide, Penguin

Secretarial work

Every company and organisation needs secretaries. This makes it one of the most varied and flexible of careers. One great advantage is that if a secretary gets bored, dislikes the office, has too much or too little to do, it is easy to change jobs. Secretaries are in great demand, so leaving is the preliminary to taking another job, often for better pay. Pay depends on the employer: there is no career structure and no nationally agreed rates of pay, except in the **Civil Service** or **local government**. In business and commerce, working conditions, pay, prospects and work-loads vary enormously. The work can be highly responsible and very demanding of time, patience and personal skills. On the other hand, for most secretaries it does not lead anywhere except to another secretarial job. Promotion may be to 'personal assistant' to a director, but the same skills will be demanded, plus some added ones, such as supervising typists and clerks and possibly some knowledge of finance, law or the specialist operations of an organisation. In **publishing** and other media industries, a secretary can sometimes move into editorial work or as a production controller. But to move into technical areas or junior management, a secretary would probably find it necessary to add to the office skills already acquired. In this category, a secretary can become a **personnel officer**, office manager, **travel agent**, advertising sales assistant, and so on, but additional qualifications are more likely to be needed to get into and get on in these jobs.

The skills needed are typing, plus some knowledge of shorthand (although this is not always considered essential nowadays) and, if possible, knowledge and skill with a word processor or desktop computer. Familiarity with these micros is increasingly important, and attending a part-time or day or evening course in order to master the skills of word processing adds greatly to a secretary's portfolio of skills and opens up many more opportunities.

There are specialist jobs, such as a linguist-secretary: though the danger here is that one may be only a letter-translator. Farm, legal and school secretaries are often asked to look after records and accounts. A secretary in a university or other educational institution will be expected to cope with the jargon of the educational world, but that is also true of industrial and commercial secretaries who are expected to know about the functions of products or services because they will be answering telephone calls and letters from customers and clients.

Preparation at school is obviously by taking GCSE or RSA courses in typing, computer literacy, office studies and business studies. At A-level, business studies, accounting, communication studies and computing would be very useful. At any level, numeracy and English language need to be cultivated. Some secretaries are graduates: they see the job as an opportunity to get a unique inside view of a company or organisation, and if in publishing, the media, travel or the retail trade, to use the secretarial job as a stepping-stone to junior management or other jobs. If a boss does not delegate or provide an opportunity for personal responsibility, the secretary (whether a graduate or not) will not stay long in that post.

Training

It is possible to take a secretarial course immediately on leaving school, and entry requirements vary from college to college. In many cases three GCSE passes could be required, and usually a qualification indicating that a reasonable standard in English has been achieved. There are more advanced courses for those with A-levels. Alternatively, there is a BTEC National Diploma in business studies with secretarial and office studies as options within the course; the entry requirements are four GCSEs or equivalents, including English language. There are part-time, day-release and other methods of attendance for RSA, Pitman Examination Institute, the London Chamber of Commerce, BTEC, SCOTVEC and other recognised qualifications. For details of these courses, which are very extensive in scope, with all kinds of options and variations, and are offered at colleges throughout the UK, consult the Directory of Further Education (see below).

Information

Institute of Qualified Private Secretaries, 126 Farnham Road, Slough, Berkshire SL1 4HA

RSA Examinations Board, John Adam Street, London WC2N 6EZ

Working in Offices, COIC
Skills for Office Work, COIC
Careers in Secretarial and Office Work, Kogan Page
Directory of Further Education, Hobsons

Shipbuilding, shipbroking, shipping

These three business activities have one thing in common – the word 'ship'. Apart from that, the businesses and the jobs associated with them are very different.

Shipbuilding

Shipbuilding is not, to say the least, one of Britain's brightest industries. The Royal Navy still commissions ships from British yards, but the orders are a fraction of their former volume. British merchant shipping has suffered badly in competition with Japan and with other countries' fleets sailing under 'flags of convenience'. The result has been that the great centres of shipbuilding on the Tyne and the Clyde are struggling to attract orders, further hampered by a world decline in shipping. There are few jobs in shipbuilding, and they are greatly sought after. Among the trades are welders, electricians, shipwrights, joiners, carpenters and many more, but the demand for these skills is no longer guaranteed and unemployment figures in these trades in the north-east, Scotland and Northern Ireland is a substantial deterrent to young people.

New areas of demand are for electronics experts, for all ships are now equipped with sophisticated electronics systems. In addition, there is still a need for some **naval architects** who can design ships and supervise their construction. Degrees in electronics, naval architecture and all the forms of engineering, but particularly mechanical and marine engineering, are the best kind of preparation for these careers.

Shipbroking

Shipbroking is the charter of bulk carriers and other merchant ships to carry cargoes that are bought and sold by international traders. Put simply, the broker arranges a business deal between shipowner and cargo merchant. The shipbroker makes his or her money from the commission of the deal. In addition, brokers acting as port agents arrange to represent the interests of the shipowner while the ship is in port, looking after customs formalities and the loading or discharging of cargo.

Most brokers work in the City of London near the Baltic Exchange, which is the international centre for the chartering of ships, and of which most UK shipbroking companies are members (there are about 700 companies). To be a broker, one has to be elected to membership of the Exchange in order to attend the daily freight market conducted on the Floor of the Exchange.

Openings for new entrants are very scarce. Entry is usually straight from school or after taking a degree by direct application to a shipbroking firm. The academic qualifications vary according to the firm: some companies require GCSEs, others require a degree. To have any chance, three A-levels would now be the minimum expected of most applicants. The ability to handle calculations and an awareness of business are essential, so A-levels in maths, business studies, accounting or other subjects in the areas of maths and business would be best. A knowledge of geography is essential too. For these reasons, graduates now make up 90 per cent of the intake. Jobs, when available, are advertised in the *Lloyd's List*, a daily publication available in most libraries. Otherwise, contact the Baltic Exchange. Once into a job, part-time study at a college of further education or a correspondence course leads to the Associateship Examinations of the Institute of Chartered Shipbrokers, for which at least four GCSEs or their equivalents are needed.

Shipping

Shipping is the movement of goods by sea. This can be arranged in several ways. One is by engaging a shipbroker to do the job. Another is for a company to build its own fleet (as BP built tankers for shipping oil). A third is by making a direct approach to a shipping or freight company: this is a different kind of business, calling for keen business skills.

Entry is again by direct application to shipping companies: they look for graduates with good business acumen, possibly gained from a technical degree course or from a business, marketing, management or science course. Once in a job, or as preliminary to applying for one, it is possible to take courses at colleges leading to awards of the Institute of Export, the Institute of Chartered Shipbrokers, the Institute of Freight Forwarders and the Institute of Marketing.

Information

The Institute of Marine Engineers, 76 Mark Lane, London EC3R 7JN

The Institute of Chartered Shipbrokers, 24 St Mary Axe, London EC3A 8DE

The Baltic Exchange, St Mary Axe, London EC3A 8BU (a booklet on the Exchange and its work is available)

Shipping and Travel Personnel Selection, Lloyds Avenue House, 6 Lloyds Avenue, London EC3N 3ES

Directory of Further Education, Hobsons

Social work

Social workers help individuals, families or groups of people to cope with or overcome all kinds of problems that may arise from family, social or environmental circumstances, such as ill health, disability, old age, bad housing or unemployment.

Even when someone's circumstances cannot be changed, for instance because of permanent disability, he or she can often be encouraged to manage the difficulties more successfully. The kind of aid given will vary according to the needs of clients, but each social worker seeks to build up the self-confidence of his or her client so that together they can examine the difficulties and plan the best remedies. These may include financial aid, better housing, a change in attitudes, learning to behave in new ways and bringing about changes in family or other social relationships. Besides working with people as individuals, social workers also work with families and other groups and in community work with local and minority groups.

Most social workers are employed by local authorities' social services departments (England and Wales), social work departments

(Scotland), area health and social services boards (Northern Ireland) or in education departments. Social workers are also employed as **probation officers** by probation committees (England and Wales) and by the Probation Board for Northern Ireland. In Scotland, the duties of probation officers are included in those of social workers employed by local authorities. Social workers are employed by many voluntary and independent agencies and by some other official bodies.

Many social workers are based in offices in the areas in which their clients live, meeting them at the office or in their homes. Others work in day centres, in offices near the courts, in residential homes or hostels, hospitals, health centres or group medical practices, child guidance clinics, day or boarding schools, or prisons.

Social workers have to be sympathetic and understanding, but also have to be able to stand back and analyse situations dispassionately. They must be able to express opinions and advice in a clear and sensible way without taking sides or being overwhelmed. The work requires maturity, a willingness to take responsibility, and the ability to cope with long hours and stress.

The professional qualification for all social workers is the Certificate of Qualification in Social Work (CQSW) awarded by the Central Council for Education and Training in Social Work (CCETSW). Courses leading to the CQSW are available for graduates, non-graduates and undergraduates.

Training

The main routes to qualification are:

- a four-year university, polytechnic or college course which combines a degree, usually in social sciences, with professional training
- a degree or diploma in social studies or social administration followed by a year's postgraduate CQSW course; all candidates for this route must have at least one year's practical experience
- a degree in any subject followed by a two-year full-time postgraduate course
- a two-year non-graduate CQSW course for people who are 20 and over. To obtain a place on this course, candidates need at least five GCSEs (grades A, B or C) including English language or Welsh. However, A-level passes are normally expected. In Scotland, entry requirements are normally three H-grades and two O-grades. No

formal requirements are laid down for applicants to non-graduate courses who are aged 25 and over.

Most CQSW courses generally require or prefer candidates to have obtained relevant working experience before they apply. The CCETSW has a clearing house scheme for most graduate and non-graduate courses. Application forms have to be sent in by 31 December in the year before the course is due to start.

Other career opportunities

In addition to social work, there are a variety of other caring careers in the personal social services including instructors in adult training centres, care assistants in residential and day services or ancilliaries in the Probation Service. Formal qualifications are not normally required for such posts, but entrants should usually be at least 18 years of age, and would normally be a little older. Staff in such posts may be sent on an in-service course of training lasting two to three years leading to the Certificate in Social Service (CSS). The minimum age of entry to CSS training is 18; students under the age of 21 must have five GCSEs or equivalents. Students are normally in employment in the social services.

A new qualification in social work based on the CQSW and CSS patterns of training is to be introduced by CCETSW beginning in the academic year 1990–1. Training leading to the new qualification will last a minimum of three years. Further details of the new training are under discussion, and in the meantime the CQSW and CSS will continue to be awarded.

Information

Information Service, Central Council for Education and Training in Social Work (CCETSW), Derbyshire House, St Chad's Street, London WC1H 8AD. CCETSW has several leaflets on social work careers and the courses that lead to them

National Council for Voluntary Organisations, 26 Bedford Square, London WC1B 3HU. The Council publishes a directory of voluntary social services

Social Sciences, Degree Course Guide, Hobsons

Soil science

Soil is one of our most valuable natural resources. From it we obtain food, fibre, wood, renewable energy sources and foundations for our buildings. The quality of both ground-water and river-water is influenced by the nature of the soils within catchments. Some soils are used for waste disposal.

Because soil is a vital component of the biosphere, there is concern over the quality of our soils. The European Commission is leading moves to protect our soils from degradation and pollution.

Prospects

Traditionally, soil scientists have mostly worked within the agricultural field, although some research has been far removed from practical applications in the growing of crops. Ten years ago the majority of soil scientists could have been placed in the three categories of soil surveyor, research soil scientist and agricultural soils adviser. The geotechnical aspects of soil as an engineering material have always been the province of the civil engineer.

Jobs in these categories still exist in the UK and abroad, but soil scientists are now beginning to work in environmental science and ecology, pollution and waste management, countryside management, land restoration and reclamation, landscape architecture and land planning; all areas with expanding job prospects.

Training

Prospective soil scientists generally have a combination of science A-levels and need at least one degree to progress beyond scientific assistant level. However, very few universities now offer first degree courses in soil science, but it does form part of a number of combined courses and several departments offer opportunities to study soil science at post-graduate level. There are positions available for field sampling and laboratory staff, but more senior vacancies are filled by candidates with a second degree. In fact, it is not uncommon for scientists from other related disciplines, but with postgraduate degree qualifications in aspects of soil science, to be successful. Thus, many soil scientists in the applied field are geographers, ecologists, chemists and physicists with a soil specialism.

Information
British Society of Soil Science, Department of Soil Science, University of Reading, Reading, Berkshire RG1 5AQ

Solicitor

Solicitors give advice to people with legal problems and act for them in disputes. They have five main areas of employment:

- private practice: 75 per cent of solicitors choose to go into private practice. They join a firm as an assistant solicitor when newly qualified and hope to become a partner. Their practice may be highly specialised or entirely general, but a degree of specialisation is usual. Their work may include accident claims, matrimonial problems, tax, land law, buying and selling a house, making a will, civil litigation (e.g. personal injury claims and divorce work), crime, commercial work (e.g. bankruptcy, insurance, business contracts, banking and company matters).
- local authorities: solicitors working for Local Authorities constitute the largest group of solicitors employed outside private practice. They act as advisers to Local Government Departments and are required to guide them on public health, housing, education and many other matters. There is often much administrative work.
- Civil Service: solicitors advise departments of state and interpret the law for them. They may become Parliamentary Counsel and draft Bills for Parliament which eventually become law.
- industry and commerce: more and more companies have their own legal departments concerned with the company's day-to-day affairs and representing their company's interests.
- organisations such as trade unions, television companies and public bodies all employ solicitors to represent and protect their interests.

Training
The training is lengthy and the standards high. The vast majority of solicitors are graduates. For entry to a law degree course, institutions require three A-levels or four to five H-grades with high grades (AAB to BCC, depending on the university or polytechnic). The course lasts three years. A law graduate must then take a one-year full-time course at one of four Colleges of Law (Guildford, London, Chester and York) leading to the Solicitors' Final Examination. On passing this a student

spends two years serving articles with a firm of solicitors before taking the examinations of the Law Society.

Graduates who have not taken a law degree must, on graduating, enrol at one of the Colleges of Law, or a polytechnic, for a 12-month course leading to the Common Professional Examination (CPE). The next stage is to study for a further year, pass the Solicitors' Final Examinations and finally to serve two years under articles.

A small percentage of legal executives (members of the Institute of Legal Executives), holders of the Justices' Clerks' Assistants Diploma, and school-leavers with additional training and experience can go on to become solicitors. A school-leaver must have at least five GCSE passes, including English language, and two of the passes must also be passed at A-level or H-grade. Almost any combination of GCSE and A-levels is suitable, although at A-level law itself, social sciences and subjects such as history, classics and English are probably more useful than the sciences. Grades are more important than subjects: the scramble to get into law, although it is an overcrowded profession, means that law degree courses are heavily over-subscribed, as are the postgraduate professional courses. Furthermore, almost all entrants are graduates, so the best way to become a solicitor is to secure a place at a university law school.

Information

Law Society, 227-8 The Strand, London WC2R 1BA
Law Society of Scotland, Law Society's Hall, 26–7 Drumsheugh Gardens, Edinburgh EH3 7YR
Law Society of Northern Ireland, 90–106 Victoria Street, Belfast BT1 3JZ

Careers in the Law, Kogan Page
Law, Degree Course Guide, Hobsons

Speech therapy

Speech therapists help children and adults to tackle and overcome problems of communication. There are various reasons why people fail to develop normal language uses, and the consequences can include learning difficulties, social problems and emotional distress – it is these that speech therapists deal with. Speech therapists train to help young and older people to overcome their speech difficulties, being responsible for diagnosing, assessing and treating people with all kinds of communication problems.

Speech therapists therefore have to know about and use alternative forms of communication, such as sign language, and they have to keep detailed records and be able to work effectively in a team alongside social workers, teachers, doctors and psychologists.

Although most therapists work within the NHS, they have an open referral system, accepting patients from medical staff, teachers, parents, or those who refer themselves. Some therapists specialise in a particular condition, such as when speech is impaired by mental handicap, a stroke, impaired hearing from birth, or as a result of an accident, or cerebral palsy.

Prospects

At present, although there is no longer a shortage of speech therapists, job prospects remain good. The work environment may be in hospitals, health centres, special schools for the mentally and physically handicapped, and in people's homes. Promotion prospects are good, and there is scope for part-time work as well as full-time jobs.

Training

The first stage of training for speech therapy is to take a degree course. Courses in speech pathology and therapy are provided at the Universities of Manchester, Reading, Sheffield, City (London), University College, London, and Newcastle, and at the Polytechnics of Leicester, Leeds, Manchester, Birmingham and Ulster, and at some colleges such as South Glamorgan Institute (Cardiff), the Central School of Speech and Drama, London, Jordanhill College (Glasgow) and Queen Margaret College, Edinburgh. Competition for places on these courses is very keen, and A-level and H-grade marks need to be high. For example, the universities look for three A-levels with grades of BBB to CCC, the polytechnics expect three A-levels with grades of C and D, and all require either chemistry or biology as one of the A-levels or H-grades. Certainly, GCSE or equivalent passes in English language, maths, chemistry and/or biology are requested. It is very important to check the entry requirements for an institution before selecting A-levels. The science subjects are clearly the most useful at any level, with maths, chemistry, biology, psychology, social biology, human biology and physical sciences among those most often mentioned. Arts subjects are not totally useless, but A-level/H-grade in the sciences really count. Applicants must also have normal hearing and speech, but this does not exclude people with marked regional accents.

Degree courses which last three or four years include clinical observation and practice as part of the programme of study. The theoretical work includes linguistics, child development, psychology, neurology and speech pathology.

The College of Speech Therapists issues a certificate to practise. This is generally obtained by gaining a degree qualification.

Information

The College of Speech Therapists, Harold Poster House, 6 Lechmere Road, London NW2 5BU

Sport

There are two ways of looking at careers in sport – as a performer and as an administrator/organiser. As a performer, entry depends on one factor alone – ability. To be a professional footballer, ice-skater, golfer or whatever requires skill, ability and fitness. With these qualities, it is success in competing against other athletes or players which decides whether or not the route is to the top in sport.

There are many opportunities as administrators. The training may be in business skills, in science, in sportsground maintenance, in marketing for sport or in teaching and coaching. Using their skills and knowledge, the organisers will supervise the work of others, some of whom are likely to be performers.

The trainers/organisers have skills that may be used in different sports (e.g. if they are sportsground managers) or they may be specific to one sport, such as a professional with a golf club.

To prepare for administration there are four different kinds of degree courses:

- sport and physical recreation is a course basically for people who intend to teach, with a substantial element of sports science in it. At least two A-levels are needed for entry, and an A-level pass in science or maths is preferred. Staffordshire Polytechnic and the higher education colleges at Bradford and Bedford offer this course.
- sport and recreation studies. There are about 1,000 applicants each

535

year for 60 places on this course at Staffordshire Polytechnic. No particular subject requirements for the two or three A-level passes but good physical abilities are needed for this practical course.

- sports science at Loughborough University and Liverpool and Brighton Polytechnics also calls for a high level of sporting achievement for potential teachers, coaches and 'sports scientists'. A-levels can be in any subject, but GCSEs or their equivalent should include at least two science subjects. Again, the demand for the course is so keen that good A-level grades are expected and each year hundreds of applicants are disappointed.
- sports studies is a more general course offered at several polytechnics and colleges. Two to three A-levels in any subject are needed. Careers can lead into management or teaching.

In addition there are other specialised courses closely linked to sport such as degree courses in human movement studies, and physical education options within combined studies courses. Colleges also provide coaching courses for swimming, football, badminton and other sports and games. A further career is in sports medicine, which requires a degree in medicine. At a different level there are jobs in sports centre and sportsground management and maintenance, with courses to train people in the skills needed.

Almost any school subject could be appropriate for careers involving sports. Students with science GCSEs and A-levels will look towards sports medicine and sports science; performers will look to teaching and coaching, for which they could have almost any combination. However, whatever the academic base, anyone who takes one of these courses has to be hooked on sports and physical recreation in one way or another, otherwise it would be better to think of an alternative career.

Information

Sports Council, 16 Upper Woburn Place, London WC1H 0QP
Scottish Sports Council, South Gyle, Edinburgh EH12 9DQ

Careers in Sport, Kogan Page
Directory of Further Education, Hobsons
Working in Sport and Leisure, COIC

Statistics

Statistics has been defined as 'the science of collecting, analysing and interpreting numerical information'. Once statistics have been gathered and analysed, they are used in research and for other purposes, mainly to aid decision-makers to come to conclusions based on hard numerical evidence. Statistics is a relatively new career area, which has developed since the 1950s. Today, government departments, commerce and industry all use statistics as part of the process of planning future policies. It is clear, therefore, that once statisticians are qualified and have gained experience they can be employed across a broad career spectrum – government, education, industry, business – and a qualified statistician is not tied to one area of application.

Statisticians begin by asking 'What information needs to be collected?'; this is usually done in consultation with specialists in the field of application. Having decided, the information is collected from the necessary sources, then the statisticians analyse it, draw conclusions and describe the implications that can be drawn from the statistics. In order to carry out this work, statisticians obviously need clear, logical minds. They must have good mathematical abilities, although the job is far from just adding up columns of figures – statisticians need to know how to use computers and other electronic aids. They also need to be good communicators, for they must describe quite complex sets of facts and figures in writing and must explain, without bias, the results to people who have little grasp of figures.

Prospects

Statisticians are usually office-based. These offices are in the **Civil Service, local government** departments, companies and universities. Opportunities are very good because statisticians are increasingly needed and employed in all sectors of business and government. The Civil Service is the largest employer, particularly the Inland Revenue and the Central Statistical Office. Promotion prospects are good, with opportunities to rise through the ranks to senior posts or move from government to industry and back again.

Training

To become a statistician a degree course is the best route, and more likely to lead to senior posts, although many qualify by taking the examinations of the Institute of Statisticians (equivalent to a good honours degree) while working in a statistical environment. The professional qualification as a practising statistician is Membership of the IOS, which includes a period of responsible relevant work and a pass in the Institute's final examinations, although a number of degrees give exemption from the latter requirement.

There are degree courses at several universities and polytechnics (see the Degree Course Guide in *Mathematics and Statistics* for a full list of courses and the differences between them). For entry to a degree course two or three A-levels or three or four H-grades are needed, with at least one of them in a mathematical subject. It is possible to take statistics at A-level, and if this is combined with another mathematical subject the student is in a very good position for a degree course. But mathematics is not the only subject that is useful: most university statistics departments stress the need for competence in written English. Grades should be in the B and C category, although it is possible to get into a polytechnic degree course with lower grades in two A-levels. Alternatively, several polytechnics and colleges offer a BTEC HNC or HND course in maths, statistics and computing, for which the entry requirement is either a BTEC National Diploma or a package of four GCSEs, or the equivalents, plus at least one A-level or H-grade pass in a mathematical subject.

Some government departments and companies offer jobs to A-level and GCSE entrants. They become trainee statisticians, working alongside senior staff. The GCSE entrants are generally taken on in the Civil Service as clerical assistants and are encouraged to study part time for the examinations of the Institute of Statisticians mentioned above. The minimum requirements for entry to the bottom tier of these examinations (the Ordinary Certificate in Statistics) are two GCSE or O-grade passes in English language and mathematics.

The school subjects directly relevant are mathematical subjects (which include physics), English language and computing. In addition, English language at GCSE is a requirement. Other very useful subjects at any level are economics, business studies and sciences.

Information

Institute of Statisticians, 43 St Peter's Square, Preston, Lancashire PR1 7BX

Royal Statistical Society, 25 Enford Street, London W1H 2BH

Careers in Statistics, Institute of Statisticians
Careers Using Mathematics, Kogan Page
Mathematics and Statistics, Degree Course Guide, Hobsons

Stockbroking and the International Stock Exchange

The Stock Exchange has been known as the International Stock Exchange of the United Kingdom and Republic of Ireland Ltd since November 1986.

Stocks and shares in public companies are bought and sold on the International Stock Exchange. Stockbrokers advise their clients on which to buy and sell and when, and then carry out the transactions. To qualify for this work, a stockbroker or a stockjobber needs to have at least three years' training with a firm that is a member of the International Stock Exchange, and to pass the exams of the Exchange. A broker who wants to become a 'principal', i.e. a senior partner in a stockbroking company, has to pass three more examinations, or serve seven years as a broker and pass exams on the technique of investment.

There are no formal entry qualifications, but in reality most entrants are graduates. There are about 4,000 individual members of the International Stock Exchange, grouped into just over 200 firms. Job vacancies are rarely advertised, and when they are the candidates increasingly come from other financial jobs, such as banks and investment firms. There is now a lot more graduate employment than in the past, but a degree carries no special credit for direct entry. Quickness of brain, particularly in manipulating numbers, business sense, the ability to grasp technical knowledge, and a keen interest in current events, particularly in finance and investment, are the qualities that are highly regarded.

Training

Once into a firm as a trainee (and it is possible to get a job at 16 or 18 after GCSE or A-levels), the major objective is to become a member of the International Stock Exchange in order to become a broker or a jobber. To become a member, trainees study at home in their own time or take a day-release course in order to pass the International Stock Exchange exams. At least five good GCSEs or a qualification in business studies are looked on as the minimum entry to the examinations, but A-levels or a degree are better.

It is likely that changes will affect the work of the International Stock Exchange and recruitment for it. There will be some blurring of the distinction between stockbrokers and other types of institution, such as banks. In the future, therefore, finance houses, merchant banks and clearing banks are likely to move into areas of business once thought to be only the jobs of a stockbroker, carried out on the International Stock Exchange.

To prepare for this kind of work, useful school subjects are business studies, accounting, management, mathematics, statistics and English language. If passed at A-level or H-grade, so much the better. In the future, as for careers in banking and in other areas of the financial services, a degree in one of the subjects listed above would certainly be an excellent introduction. However, as already indicated, entry to the International Stock Exchange is not limited to graduates, and there are opportunities for people with A-levels or a BTEC or SCOTVEC business studies diploma or HND.

Information
The International Stock Exchange, Careers Office, London EC2N 1HP

A Career in the Stock Exchange, International Stock Exchange

Surveying

The surveyor performs an invaluable professional service in the world of land, property and construction. Wherever land or buildings are of importance and require valuation or sale, measurement or development, he or she has a role to play. The profession embraces nearly every aspect of the numerous uses of property, and the demands and skills required are as diverse as the many aspects of land use. The experienced surveyor may as easily sit at a boardroom table planning major investments as on a farm gate discussing crop rotation, or even at an arbitration hearing with judicial authority. There is opportunity for the academic, the consultant and the entrepreneur. Each field of activity demands different personal qualities and everyone will find their own level.

The surveyor's time is divided between the office and field-work. The office may include a house in central London and a hotel in Bahrain, while the field may include a derelict warehouse in Liverpool's dockland or a shopping-centre in San Francisco. Usually a surveyor opts for either an urban or a rural discipline, and the work is generally confined to one operation or region.

Anyone choosing to pursue a career in this diverse profession will need to specialise, but having adopted one field surveyors can still change their preference or alter the extent of their specialisation during their career. Moreover, unlike some other professions, surveying knows no territorial bounds, and qualified people can practise their skills anywhere in the world. As a career it is attractive for its rewards, its challenges and opportunities.

Prospects
All specialisations offer interesting careers for surveyors (and the technicians who support their work) with employers such as local authorities, government departments, estates departments or nationalised industries, banks and large companies, and in private practice either with estate agents, building companies or independent firms. Prospects for entry and for promotion vary according to the employer. There is a fairly constant demand from public bodies, although there is no automatic entry for newly qualified surveyors. With larger firms and in government departments there is a 'promotion ladder': climbing it depends on experience and qualifications.

Training
The normal methods of entry are to seek recognition by one of the two main professional bodies. These are the RICS – the Royal Institution of Chartered Surveyors – and the ISVA – the Incorporated Society of Valuers and Auctioneers. Both bodies have up-to-date information on qualifications, courses and prospects, so it is best to write direct to them.

There are two possible routes to gaining professional qualifications. Most entrants now take a degree course to obtain full exemption from the RICS examinations. The courses are either full time (three years) or sandwich (four years). Degree courses are offered at Cambridge, Reading, City (London), Aberdeen, Heriot-Watt and Ulster Universities and at about 15 polytechnics. (For a full list consult the RICS or the Degree Course Guide on *Technology*, which includes a major section on surveying.) For graduates in other subjects, the RICS offers a Graduate Entry Scheme which is effectively one year shorter than the course for school-leavers.

The alternative method is to take a job and study part time either by correspondence course or by day release at a college. In addition to the written examinations, practical training and experience are required for the Test of Professional Competence, successful completion of which leads to full membership (ARICS) of the Institution.

It is possible to be a surveyor without professional qualifications, but the best prospects lie with the best qualified. To start a course, the RICS demands at least five good GCSE passes including English language and maths and then two subjects at A-level. Alternative qualifications are BTEC or SCOTVEC HNC or HND awards.

ISVA (with about 5,000 members) asks for five GCSEs or equivalents including English language and maths, or alternative packages including A-levels or BTEC/SCOTVEC awards of certificates in estate management and valuation or surveying. Entry to corporate membership of ISVA can be achieved by taking a degree in estate management, which gives complete exemption from ISVA exams, or by taking a BTEC HNC/HND course. Alternatively, for graduates in other subjects there are special courses (details from ISV, below).

To become a surveying technician involves taking BTEC courses, and for these at least four GCSEs or equivalents are needed, including English language and maths, and preferably a science subject.

Information

The Royal Institution of Chartered Surveyors, 12 Great George Street, Parliament Square, London SW1P 3AD, and 7 Manor Place, Edinburgh EH3 7DN

The Incorporated Society of Valuers and Auctioneers, 3 Cadogan Place, London SW1X 0AS

The Society of Surveying Technicians, Drayton House, 30 Gordon Street, London WC1H 0AX

Leaflets and booklets are available from the organisations above
Technology, Degree Course Guide, Hobsons

Tax inspector

The Inland Revenue is responsible for direct taxes – including income tax, corporation tax and capital gains tax – and the job of the tax inspectorate is to determine the tax liabilities of individuals and businesses.

Tax inspectors

Fully trained inspectors have to bring their professional tax expertise to bear across the whole range of business, commerce and finance. They must understand the workings of that complex world and be able to deal on equal terms with all the specialists who operate in it. To do this successfully, inspectors need to have a particular combination of skills – those of an accountant, lawyer, investigator, negotiator, advocate and manager. They have full discretion to negotiate and agree with taxpayers and their professional advisers the amount of tax due, and they are expected to find solutions to their own problems, although they can call upon specialist advice when necessary.

The minimum entry requirements are a second-class honours degree or an equivalent or higher qualification.

Tax officers (higher grade)

These officers are employed in the 700 or so local tax offices throughout the country dealing with the affairs of a variety of taxpayers. They may have personal responsibility for a number of individual cases, including company directors and senior employees, which involves the examination of returns of income tax and capital gains and claims for allowances and expense deductions. They have to make the enquiries necessary to determine an individual's entitlement to allowances, etc. and hence the amount of tax payable. This involves more than numeracy. Tax officers at this level have to apply correctly the knowledge that they gain of taxation law to a wide variety of situations. They deal directly with taxpayers and their accountants or solicitors; although most of the work will be conducted by correspondence, there may also be a significant degree of personal contact with taxpayers or their professional advisers.

Collectors of taxes

The work of collectors is wide ranging and requires initiative, understanding of people and the capacity to take responsibility. Collectors may be responsible for the management of a group of clerical staff dealing with the collection of income tax, corporation tax, capital gains tax and National Insurance contributions. They deal personally with some of the larger and more difficult cases and with taxpayers who request time to pay. They may conduct legal proceedings for the recovery of arrears and may represent the department in County Court proceedings. They interview taxpayers and their professional advisers both in the office and at home and visit employers to inspect their records, checking that the correct amounts of tax are being paid and that the relevant regulations are being operated as required by law. Opportunities also arise for collectors with the necessary aptitudes to specialise.

The minimum entry requirements for these two careers are three GCSE passes with grades of A to C plus at least two subject passes at A-level. One GCSE pass must be in English language and the others must be within a broad list of subjects approved by the Civil Service. Equivalent or higher qualifications are also accepted.

Information
Civil Service Commission, Alencon Link, Basingstoke, Hampshire RG21 1JB

Careers in the Civil Service, Kogan Page

Teaching and lecturing

Teachers work within primary, secondary and tertiary education. Lecturers are employed in further and higher education. Broadly speaking, the institutions in which teachers and lecturers work are:

- nursery and primary schools, with an age-range of 4 to 10/11
- middle schools with an age-range of 8 to 12 or 9 to 13
- secondary schools for 11 to 16/18 or 13 to 18
- sixth-form colleges – age-range of 16 to 18-plus
- tertiary colleges, incorporating sixth-form work and further education courses, age-range 16 and over
- independent schools, which can be primary (5 to 9/11), preparatory schools (7 to 13), and secondary (13 to 18-plus)
- special schools for handicapped children of all ages
- colleges of further education for students of 16-plus
- polytechnics, colleges and institutes of higher education, colleges of art and design, music, physical education, and universities.

Within these groups there are single-sex schools, boarding schools, local authority residential schools and special schools for children with handicaps, such as schools for the blind, deaf, partially sighted, physically and mentally handicapped.

Prospects

In the 1980s there was a considerable fall-off in the number of applicants for teaching, particularly graduates. However, the recession of 1990-1 led to a growth in applications for the teacher training courses. Nationally, there is a substantial demand for teachers of maths, physics, craft subjects, languages, design and technology. Indeed, physics teachers are desperately needed to remedy severe shortages. Opportunities exist for teaching jobs in all the categories of schools and colleges listed above. Some teachers go on to become educational advisers, inspectors, examiners or officers within the education departments of local authorities; others are promoted to senior teachers, deputies and headteachers.

Training

There are several ways to enter the teaching profession. One is for the student to take a degree in the subject he or she wants to teach and then, having completed this course, to take a one-year Postgraduate Certificate of Education (PGCE) course. An alternative to this route is to take a BEd course at a polytechnic or college. Similarly, it is possible to take a degree in art and design, music, physical education, or indeed any subject, and in the same way follow this up with a PGCE course, thus equipping the potential teacher with the skills needed for the classroom or lectureroom. A PGCE course can be taken immediately after a degree course, or after some years spent in a completely different job. A BEd graduate is more committed to teaching or educational work from the start.

Applications for a BEd course are made through the PCAS application procedure, with the exception of some BEd courses available at university, where applications are made via UCCA. There are special training courses for teachers wishing to work with handicapped children, although it is generally recommended that training for special schools is taken after a period teaching in a school for normal children. Some BEd and PGCE courses are specially designed with options or special courses to prepare teachers to work with handicapped children. Most (but not all) BEd courses are geared towards primary-school teaching, although it is possible to enter primary teaching by the degree-plus-PGCE route.

The minimum entry requirements for training are passes in five GCSE or O-grade subjects, including English language and mathematics, with two of these subjects also at A-level or three at H-grade. Most applicants have passes in excess of the minimum. Applicants for a degree course in physics, history, geography, economics or any other subject have to meet exactly the same entry requirements as anyone else for these degree courses. Entry to PGCE courses after taking a degree is more competitive than it used to be, although suitably qualified potential teachers of physics, maths and technology are welcomed. A degree in a school subject is obviously a help in getting a place on a PGCE course, and graduates in non-school subjects must expect not only to find it more difficult to get on to a PGCE course but also to have to teach other subjects once they are on the staff of a school. Scotland has its own entry qualifications: see below for details of where to write for information.

To obtain a post in a sixth-form college or college of tertiary or further education requires, first of all, a relevant subject qualification. This need not necessarily be at degree level: for craft teaching, other qualifications such as City and Guilds and BTEC may be acceptable. In further education it is not absolutely necessary to have a teaching diploma or certificate before taking up a post, but a teacher/lecturer will be required to take a part-time or a full-time course leading to a teaching qualification once some experience has been gained.

For lecturing posts in universities, polytechnics, colleges and institutes of higher education and other institutions, a degree and/or diploma is the first stage. For posts where it is difficult to recruit high-calibre teaching staff, such as computing, a first degree may be enough to secure a teaching post. But in most subjects a higher degree will be looked for, plus experience of industrial, commercial, research or teaching responsibilities. There is also a postgraduate teaching certificate course especially for lecturers in further education.

Information

The Department of Education and Science (DES), Elizabeth House, York Road, London SE1 7PH

The Advisory Service on Entry to Teaching, 5 Royal Terrace, Edinburgh EH7 5AF

The Graduate Teacher Training Registry, 3 Crawford Place, London W1H 2BN

The DES (address above) has several careers leaflets on teaching. Among them are: *A Career in Teaching; My Teacher – Teaching in Primary Schools; Teaching Handicapped Children; Teaching Craft, Design and Technology; Teaching Mathematics and Science; Teaching Business Studies*

Working in Teaching, COIC

Telecommunications

Telecommunications is one of the new industries with immense potential for industrial developments and therefore for careers. But what is it? It has been defined as 'the science of communication by radio and electronic means, through television, radio, telephone, cable and telegraph, in coded or pictorial forms'. Telecommunications thus includes virtually all forms of verbal, written and graphic communication, using all kinds of technical processes. In order to describe this industry thoroughly, it would be necessary to go into detail about **radio, television**, and so on. These have their own entries, although they include performers as well as engineers. 'Telecommunications' in terms of careers is normally used to describe the engineering applications, and this is the aspect of the industry dealt with here.

Prospects

Job prospects are excellent, so much so that graduates in physics and other branches of engineering are crossing into telecommunications. The Engineering Industry Training Board, the Department of Transport and other professional organisations sponsor or arrange courses to help train newcomers. At the technician and craft levels, employment prospects with British Telecom, the radio and television authorities, computer and electronic suppliers are just as exciting, and to support training for jobs colleges of further education offer all kinds of City and Guilds and BTEC courses.

Training

The engineer who works for British Telecom or for one of the large manufacturing companies that make, supply and sell equipment (Plessey, Racal, GEC, Thorn-EMI and so on) could be specially trained in telecommunications or have transferred from another discipline or subject, such as physics or electronic and electrical engineering. An honours degree course leading to BEng in communication engineering would be an excellent preparation, as would a more general degree course in electronics, electronic engineering, microelectronic systems, or physics. (For details of all these courses, and the institutions that offer them, see below.) It is also strongly advised that a course that appears on the Institution of Electrical Engineers (IEE) Bulletin list is chosen.

At a different level there are BTEC National Certificate and National Diploma telecommunications courses at numerous colleges throughout the UK, plus HNC and HND courses in electronic and communications engineering. The entry levels are: for a degree course, at least two A-levels in science subjects, of which physics and/or maths are often required; for HNC/HND courses, one A-level in a science subject, plus four GCSEs or O-grades which must include maths. For the BTEC and SCOTVEC Diploma Certificate level courses, the entry requirements range from two to four GCSEs/O-grades, again with passes in sciences.

The relevant school subjects are physics and maths, either at GCSE/O-grade or A-level/H-grade. Other very useful subjects are electronics, computing, engineering science and physical science, all of which can be taken at A-level. Grades required for the BEng courses vary greatly between academic establishments. Some universities require grades of A or B at A-level, but some polytechnics will take students with lower grades in two A-levels rather than three.

Information

British Telecom, Room 8078, 2–12 Gresham Street, London EC2V 7AG
Institution of Electrical Engineers, 2 Savoy Place, London WC2R 0BL
Institution of Electrical and Electronics Incorporated Engineers, Savoy Hill House, 2 Savoy Hill, London WC2R 0BS

Technology, Degree Course Guide, Hobsons
Directory of Further Education, Hobsons
Working in Radio and Telecommunications, COIC

Television

The broad picture of opportunities in **broadcasting** is given in that entry. This one describes in general the entry levels and training schemes for television, and stresses how difficult it is to get any kind of job unless it is in engineering. A glance at *TV Times* or *Radio Times* gives the impression that jobs are terribly glamorous. But the men and women who appear on the screen are not employees of the television companies. They are freelance actors, and they are often directed by other freelance staff working on contract. The employees are off-screen.

At one level are the producers and their assistants, the people who think up, plan, commission the script, engage the actors and make the programme. The producers, journalists and editors are the top-of-the-tree professionals on the staff of the companies. They are generally recruited from the universities and represent a mere handful of the thousands who apply each year. The BBC has several kinds of training scheme for people who are expected to rise to become producers or managers, and most young people on these schemes are very high-calibre graduates picked because they seem to have special talents or promise. The ITV companies run their own training schemes for journalists and managers, while producers, directors and production staff are usually appointed internally, promoted from other jobs.

Below this level are many other experts, all just as essential in the making of programmes. Among them are camera crews, film editors, floor managers, costume and wardrobe staff, music and dance directors and performers, designers, dressmakers, make-up and hairdressing staff, production secretaries and many other kinds of secretaries, scene artists/designers/shifters, projectionists, researchers, sound recordists, sound and vision mixers, stage managers, and a host of supporting engineers concerned with the technical work of recording, editing and broadcasting.

This list shows the wide range of skills and specialists required by the television industry. There are career opportunities for all these people – out of the camera's eye but still absolutely essential.

Another group of people, and so jobs, are those who *are* in public view – the announcers, presenters of programmes, experts and 'pundits'. Announcers often start in the theatre. The television newsreader is selected and trained for television from among many other colleagues. Presenters do not apply to be presenters: the producers look around and often choose actors or experienced broadcasters.

So, for the top posts, the producers and editors, a university degree is useful although not essential; the ambitious hopeful certainly needs talent, probably demonstrated in amateur theatricals or radio or broadcasting at college or in a job, perhaps in the theatre or in radio. For other skilled personnel – such as film editors, secretaries and hairdressers – training comes first. Again, good qualifications are necessary, but they must be in a certain skill rather than in academic promise. Once in, the job is very demanding: thinking up ideas is testing enough, but producers and their staff have then to translate the idea into a programme within a budget, and with the impending broadcasting date just ahead. To get in and to get on requires self-confidence and a willingness to work unsocial hours – weekends and evenings, depending on the availability of the studio. Support staff must accept the same conditions as producers.

School subjects, therefore, depend on the job – office and business studies for the administrative applicants; drama, English and communication studies for presenters and production; science and engineering subjects for people who are thinking of careers in telecommunications and television engineering; and art, for candidates for design, costume, make-up and hairdressing jobs. GCSEs, A-levels, City and Guilds and BTEC qualifications or equivalents all help in the hunt for these jobs. Many colleges and polytechnics run full-time courses in various aspects of film and television, but real experience counts more than any paper qualifications. In general, the broadcasting authorities look for keen interest and knowledge of the television output related to the jobs for which people apply.

Information

Appointments Department, BBC, Broadcasting House, Portland Place, London W1A 1AA (for information about all jobs except those in engineering or technical work)

The Engineering Recruitment Officer, BBC, Broadcasting House, London W1A 1AA (for all technical and engineering jobs)

Independent Television Companies Association, Knighton House, 56 Mortimer Street, London W1N 8AN

Film and Television Training, British Film Institute
Directory of Further Education, Hobsons
Working in Television and Video, COIC

Theatre

Live theatre is struggling to survive commercially. On the other hand, local amateur theatre is flourishing. So unless a fierce commitment burns in someone to write, direct, act or in some other way to perform or work in West End theatres, the best advice is to train for another job and to join a local dramatic society or theatre club and become an amateur instead of an out-of-work professional. Television has become the main employer, of actors, producers and directors. But few actors prefer film or television: once an actor has performed in a live theatre, the mysterious empathy between audience and actor is a powerful feeling.

For careers, training and employment as actors, the entry on **acting** describes the qualities and training needed. The entries on **radio** and **television** describe employment possibilities. There are jobs to be had in the theatre but not as spotlight performers. The jobs are those essential for the smooth running of a theatre and its commercial success.

One area for a career is in theatrical design. Costume designers, theatre designers, stage designers – they are all people who work in the theatre and specialise in clothes, sets, lighting, furniture, and so on. However, there are far more people who wish to make their career in theatrical design than there are vacancies, but there is scope for the exceptionally talented.

Theatres cannot operate without electricians, technicians, cashiers, accountants, managers, booking clerks, decorators, cleaners and other support staff. There are occasional opportunities, usually advertised in local newspapers (for provincial theatres) and London daily or evening newspapers for West End jobs. Again, the openings are few, because the supporting staff as well as the actors are usually bitten by the theatre's attraction, and staff remain loyal, rarely moving on.

For these jobs, from actor to cleaner, virtually any subject in the school curriculum could be appropriate. Obviously for acting, an interest in literature, drama, languages and English literature is essential, but academic qualifications do not have to be startlingly good. The main qualification is experience and talent, and this can only be gauged by taking part in school, college, local repertory or other theatrical productions, to gain knowledge and experience. For the non-acting support staff, skills such as secretary, cashier, handyman, painter and joiner are very important, and it is best to take a specialist course in these subjects and then look for a job in a theatre.

551

Information
Royal Academy of Dramatic Art, 62 Gower Street, London WC1E 6ED

Careers in the Theatre, Kogan Page
Working in the Performing Arts, COIC

Textiles

The textile industry (including the clothing industry and a very substantial coloration section) is still one of the largest industries in the UK, although it has declined in the face of stiff overseas competition, particularly from the developing countries with low labour costs. This decline is now slowing, and there is a new spirit of optimism for the industry's future. The industry is becoming more efficient, more automated and more competitive. There are many small firms, but this has advantages in making the industry more flexible and more innovative in its response to competition. The demand for skills is therefore not as machine operators but as designers, technologists, scientists, technicians and sales and marketing staff. To produce the high-quality, sophisticated textile products that will sell in the UK and overseas against foreign competition requires good training in textile production, allied to knowledge of what is going on in the wider commercial world.

Most people within and without the textile industry agree that there are too few well-qualified people of the right calibre. It has been estimated that in order to maintain the revival of the UK textile industry, over 500 young people are needed each year, either graduates or A-level school-leavers. Most of these require a technology training in textiles. There is no lack of designers: that is not an area of shortage, as UK textile, fashion and clothing design is thought to be very good. What is needed are skilled textile technologists responsive to design, backed by young executives, knowledgeable about business methods.

Training
There are degree-level textile courses that give this kind of training. Most of the institutions are in areas once famous for their textile manufacturing industries but now suffering from economic difficulties. For instance, at Leeds University and UMIST (Manchester) there are undergraduate courses in textile coloration, design, manufacturing,

management and economics; at Bradford, Manchester, Salford, Nottingham, Huddersfield, Leeds and Leicester polytechnics are similar courses at a slightly lower level; and at the Scottish College of Textiles, Galashiels, is a unique undergraduate course in applied chemistry with a specialisation in coloration or polymers. For the design courses, an A-level in art is needed in some cases (but not all). Maths and science subjects at A-level are required for all the degree-level technical courses. Certainly maths at GCSE level is needed for all technical degrees, and some institutions ask for A-level maths for some management marketing or technology courses. The A-level grades for entry do not need to be high: passes at C or D grade in two or three A-levels or H-grades is often sufficient to obtain a place on technology courses.

It is also possible to take other courses leading to the Associateship of the Textile Institute, or the Society of Dyers and Colourists, or a BTEC National Certificate or National Diploma in textiles and textile coloration, for which GCSE passes are needed. Three GCSEs or equivalents are required for BTEC National Diploma courses, but for City and Guilds and BTEC National Certificate courses entry qualifications are lower. (For a full list of all these courses, consult the *Directory of Further Education*.) These qualifications lead to jobs such as textile technician, dyeing technician, craftworker and operative.

Information

Textile Institute, 10 Blackfriars Street, Manchester M3 5DR
Society of Dyers and Colourists, Perkin House, PO Box 244, 82 Grattan Road, Bradford, West Yorkshire BD1 2JB
Clothing and Allied Products Industry Training Board, Tower House, Merrion Way, Leeds LS2 8NY

Occupations, COIC, has informative sections on craft and technician jobs, such as textile operative and technicians for production, dyeing and sales
Directory of Further Education, Hobsons

Town and country planning

Town and country planners

These planners are involved in the planning and implementation of policies for the development of rural and urban areas. They collect and study data on industrial needs, transport, roads, housing, education and social facilities, and then draw up development plans for an area based on this information. The planners need to know about government policies and should have considerable knowledge of local needs both for the community and for industry. An amazing number of different subjects comes into the portfolio of a planner. Among them are history, geography, geology, architecture, engineering, surveying, economics and social studies. Of course a planner cannot expect to be an expert in all these subjects, but they may all have to be understood for the purposes of the 'master plan' for the area.

Prospects

Most planners work in **local government**, although some are in central government, large companies, nationalised industries and private consultancies. Their work could be anything from agreeing to an extension to a local resident's garage to laying out a new town. Because local government finance is severely curtailed, fewer planners are being recruited now than in the 1960s, so jobs are not too easy to obtain.

Training

There are degree courses in town and country planning at several universities and polytechnics. Similar courses also come under titles such as 'urban studies', 'planning studies' and 'environmental studies'. The entry requirements for a degree course are two or three A-levels in any subject, although some are more highly regarded than others. The favoured subjects are maths, physics, economics, business studies, geography, environmental studies, surveying, sociology and geology. A pass in maths at GCSE or equivalent is required. A-level grades of BBC to CCD can generally secure a place at a university, and D and E grades are acceptable for polytechnic courses.

Planners are essentially managers with specialist knowledge of such subjects as population trends, economics, social science and architecture, and these subjects are contained within the degree course. Today, a major part of a planner's work may be to persuade firms to move into his or her area in an effort to improve employment prospects for local people. Having taken the four-year degree course, a planner who is employed by a local authority or government department would work on a series of projects: this gives practical experience needed for membership of the Royal Town Planning Institute. Graduates in other subjects can take a two-year full-time postgraduate course.

Planning technician

The job of a planning technician is to collect, interpret, collate and analyse planning information into a form that is suitable for work in a planning office. Technicians work alongside professional planners on all kinds of projects. Their duties extend to working in a team, and they need the knowledge and skills for cartographical draughtsmanship, design graphics, survey work, the preparation of plans, and using information and computer systems. There is a two-year part-time course which leads to a BTEC certificate in town and country planning or a SCOTVEC certificate in planning. The minimum entry require ments are four passes at GCSE or equivalent, including maths and a subject requiring written English. A further two-year part-time course leads to a BTEC HNC.

Information

The Royal Town Planning Institute, 26 Portland Place, London W1N 4BE
The Society of Town Planning Technicians, 17 Peacock Walk, Bewbush, Crawley, West Sussex RH11 8DR

A Career as a Town Planning Technician, Society of Town Planning Technicians
Architecture, with Town and Country Planning, Degree Course Guide, Hobsons
Directory of Further Education, Hobsons

Transport and distribution

Everyone relies on the road transport industry, whether as a regular bus passenger to school or to work, or travelling occasionally on a long-distance coach, or as a taxi passenger. But in addition to these road passenger services, there are the road, transport, haulage and delivery services which affect us all in many ways. The road haulage business alone is one of the most important service industries in the country, for over 80 per cent of Britain's goods are carried by fleets which together total over 430,000 heavy goods vehicles. Not surprisingly there are jobs at all levels in this big industry.

Transport manager

First, a transport manager's job is to plan and control the schedules of vehicles, drivers and loads. This can be a most complicated business, for it is uneconomic to have lorries travelling empty or drivers standing around without a vehicle. Route planning, manpower planning, costing, invoicing and other documentation are important, so a manager has to be able to cope with paperwork and to handle the details of moving goods or people. In their work transport managers deal with customers, mechanics, drivers, police, trade union officials and Department of Transport staff, so they need to be practical and sociable people, but also to be prepared to be tough in dealing with crises involving staff, customers and vehicles. A passenger transport manager who organises coach and bus services needs these qualities, too.

Training

In the past most managers started their careers as drivers, clerks or assistants, and worked their way up. No special qualifications were required, but to make it to manager several GCSE or O-grade passes were necessary. EC laws and rules now require all transport managers to hold a Certificate of Professional Competence (CPC) which is awarded by the Royal Society of Arts (RSA). To obtain it, apart from practical experience, a written examination has to be taken. However, corporate membership of a professional organisation such as the Institute of Transport Administration or the Chartered Institute of Transport gives exemption from the examination. To get to this level means that a manager needs a good standard of education, certainly to GCSE and better still to A-level.

Drivers

Another area for jobs is as a driver. Bus, coach and lorry drivers work either for local bus companies or local authority services, for long-distance and excursion-service companies, or as heavy goods vehicle drivers or as car, taxi or van drivers. Whoever the employer, in private or public sectors of the transport industry, the skills are much the same.

These are obviously driving skills, supported by PSV (public service vehicle) or HGV (heavy goods vehicle) licences. It is usual for an applicant to be selected for training by a Regional Transport Executive, National Bus Company or a private company.

Training

The training takes a minimum of three weeks and involves tuition and practice on a variety of routes. In practice only people over 21 are accepted for training for a PSV licence. An HGV driver can start training at 17. This will lead to a Royal Society of Arts 'associated knowledge' course, run by group training associations or at colleges of further education. Formal academic qualifications are not normally required. Some employers set practical, arithmetic or English language tests. Certainly a clean driving licence is essential, plus some indication of practical aptitude.

There are many other jobs in road transport. Taxi drivers hold a special licence; they are self-employed working alone or in association with garages, car hire firms or local taxi companies. Van and car drivers work for all kinds of companies and organisations. Their work comes into the area of distribution, which can mean the delivery of goods from a manufacturer to a warehouse, shop or wholesaler, or it can mean deliveries from shops to customers in their own homes or to business addresses. Either way, these drivers form a substantial sector of the distribution industry, directed by managers. Another type of job is that of a **driving instructor** both for the private sector and for industry. The specialised training scheme is described in the entry for driving instructor.

Finally, supporting the road transport and distribution industry is another group of experts – the **motor mechanics**. This is a special branch of engineering and technology and, as for the transport industry as a whole, employment prospects are good. The prospects and training for **automobile engineering** are described in that entry.

There are many school subjects that could be useful. For the practical driving jobs an understanding of mechanics is obviously very useful, and therefore passes in physics, engineering science, mechanics and subjects such as these to GCSE or beyond are very handy. The practical nature of an applicant's character may be revealed in other subject or courses, such as metalwork, technology or design.

For managers, useful courses are City and Guilds and BTEC/

SCOTVEC courses in road transport studies or engineering: for details of the courses and the colleges that offer them, see the *Directory of Further Education* Training and education in business studies, administration and/or distribution could be very useful.

Information

Road Transport Industry Training Board, Capital House, Empire Way, Wembley HA9 0NG

Institute of Transport Administration, 32 Palmerston Road, Southampton SO1 1LL

The Chartered Institute of Transport, 80 Portland Place, London W1N 4DT

Careers in Road Transport, Kogan Page
Directory of Further Education, Hobsons

Travel and tourism

After North Sea oil, tourism is Britain's second largest foreign currency earner, and has the potential to become the country's biggest industry by the year 2000.

More significantly, tourism, as a labour-intensive industry, is an area of considerable employment growth, currently employing in the region of 1.6 million people, and creating new jobs at the rate of 50,000 each year.

The figure of 1.6 million workers in tourism may appear high to those accustomed to thinking that anyone employed in tourism must be either a holiday rep, an air hostess, or a travel agent; but, although these jobs have an important part to play in the industry, they are all concerned with *travel* (most often overseas) which is only one component in an industry made up of a wide range of different sectors, all providing facilities and services for tourists and travellers. These sectors include accommodation and catering and transport, as well as travel trade organisations, such as tour operators and travel agents, and the national, regional and area tourist organisations or boards, which may be described as the 'official' face of tourism.

The tourist industry also includes those services that cater for tourists' (as well as residents') leisure activities and interests, in the form of recreation and entertainment, such as sports centres, country parks, theatres and cinemas, and tourist attractions such as museums, historic properties, zoos and theme parks.

Prospects

All places with a strong leisure or recreational element are likely to benefit from the current growth of tourism in this country, and provide excellent employment prospects for young people choosing to enter this industry. As domestic tourism flourishes, these jobs are to be found in all parts of the country not only in traditional 'tourist' areas. Some jobs are in small companies, run by one or two people; some are in very large organisations, with thousands of employees, providing the opportunity to make a career by moving around the organisation. Some jobs are in the public sector, as in the case of those employed in local authority leisure facilities, for example; and some have been created by the private sector activity in the industry. Furthermore, self-employment is extremely common in this industry, and owner/managers are found in this industry much more often than in many of the manufacturing industries, as people set up their own successful businesses in wine bars, small hotels, or as specialist tour operators, for example.

Training

Some school-leavers enter the industry directly and acquire their skills and expertise through post-entry training, or through some Youth Training schemes such as those run by the Hotel and Catering Industry Training Company (HCITC) or the Association of British Travel Agents (ABTA) National Training Board. Others take advantage of the vast range of education and training courses available throughout the education system, ranging from craft level to postgraduate courses in tourism-related subjects.

A large range of education and training courses is available for people involved in these industries. Details are given in the directories below. Some of the courses lead to City and Guilds certificates. For instance, there are courses in catering, cooking, hotel reception and leisure work, but particularly relevant courses are in subjects such as tourist information centre work, travel agency competence, travel agency management and accommodation services. The City and Guilds does not require any particular examination passes but many of the colleges that run these courses look for up to three good GCSE passes.

Furthermore, BTEC courses are available for all sectors of tourism and travel. There are business studies courses at National Certificate and National Diploma levels, with specialist options in tourist studies, in hotel and catering, and in horticulture, all of which could be appropriate. For these, good GCSE passes are required. At an advanced stage there are HNC and HND courses for students with at least one A-level and four GCSEs. The Scottish colleges offer modular programmes leading to SCOTVEC awards.

In addition, there are degree courses of particular interest to the tourist industry. Over 500 students a year graduate from degree and HND courses in hotel and catering administration, and some institutions have developed specialist courses in tourism. For postgraduates, there is an MSc course in tourism at the University of Strathclyde and postgraduate diploma courses at Manchester Polytechnic and the University of Surrey.

Relevant school subjects could be anything from cookery (for catering careers) to gardening (for horticulture). Tourist and travel companies, however, look for GCSE and A-level passes in subjects such as English, business studies, maths or arithmetic, social studies subjects and sciences. A pass in GCSE French, for instance, gives no guarantee that an employee can talk sensibly to a French tourist, but it helps. For overseas jobs, where real knowledge of a language is needed, companies recruit graduates.

Applicants with A-levels are taken on, but they have to catch up with the 16-year-old or Youth Training entrant, rather than leapfrogging ahead of them. The Thomson organisation has a graduate recruitment scheme: other companies recruit when they need to rather than in any planned programme.

Information

English Tourist Board, Thames Tower, Blacks Road, Hammersmith, London W6 9EL

ABTA National Training Board, 11–17 Chertsey Road, Woking, Surrey GU21 5AL

The Institute of Travel and Tourism, 113 Victoria Street, St Albans, Hertfordshire AL1 3TJ

The Directory of Courses in Tourism and Leisure, The Handbook of Careers in Tourism and Leisure, and *Finding Out About Tourism and the British Economy,* Hobsons

Working in Travel and Tourism, COIC

Valuer

A valuer examines property, assessing its value in terms of its location, condition, age, character, site and building costs. In assessing the value of a building, notice has to be taken of comparable transactions, e.g. sales and lettings of similar properties, the location of the property and of any local authority plans for road alterations or other developments. Similarly, if a valuer is looking at goods, the same sort of careful attention to age, condition and other factors has to be made. A valuer may also be an **auctioneer** (see entry for details).

Valuers often work for estate agents, or are **estate agents** (see entry). Most posts are in private practice, although there are posts, too, in local and central government. In the Civil Service valuations are needed for tax purposes, for the purchase or sale of public property and for accounting purposes. In local authorities valuers are generally employed as valuation officers who assess the rateable value of property on which rents and rates are levied. In addition, there are jobs in banks, building societies and industrial companies. Career prospects are quite good in the private sector because valuers often become partners in estate agent or auctioneering businesses. Promotion is normally slower in local or central government service.

Training

There are several ways to train as a valuer. For initial entry to membership of the Royal Institution of Chartered Surveyors (RICS), the educational qualifications must include two A-levels (for detailed information see **surveying**). For membership of the ISVA – the Incorporated Society of Valuers and Auctioneers – at least five GCSEs or equivalents including maths and English language are needed. For membership of the Rating and Valuation Association (RVA), four GCSEs or equivalents, including English language and maths, are demanded, together with at least one A-level or H-grade pass. Cadet valuers in the Civil Service (Inland Revenue) need two A-levels and at least three other GCSEs. Scottish candidates need three H-grades plus three O-grades, or four H-grade passes.

The most usual method of entry nowadays is to take a degree *before* employment: this should be a surveying degree or diploma recognised by the RICS which gives full exemption from RICS exams. The other route is to work full time in an approved office and to study part time for the exams of the RICS, the ISVA, or for a degree giving exemption from those examinations. Among the topics studied are law, land use, economics, building construction, taxation, valuation and business management.

Similarly, for membership of other professional bodies, such as the RVA, part-time courses are offered at various colleges throughout the UK: for details of the colleges that offer them consult the *Directory of Further Education*. As well as courses for RICS, ISVA and RVA, there are BTEC and SCOTVEC National Certificate and National Diploma courses in estate management and valuation, town and country planning, valuation and property management: for these, four GCSEs or equivalents are needed for the diploma course. For students with at least one A-level there are HNC and HND courses in similar subjects.

Information

The Royal Institution of Chartered Surveyors (RICS), 12 Great George Street, Parliament Square, London SW1P 3AD, and 7 Manor Place, Edinburgh EH3 7DN

The Incorporated Society of Valuers and Auctioneers (ISVA), 3 Cadogan Place, London SW1X 0AS

Rating and Valuation Association (RVA), 115 Ebury Street, London SW1W 9QT

Leaflets and booklets are available from the RICS, ISVA and RVA
Careers in Surveying, Kogan Page
Directory of Further Education, Hobsons

Veterinary nursing

Veterinary nurses usually assist veterinary surgeons in general practice who provide professional medical services for farm, racehorse, companion or pet animals but they are also employed in university veterinary schools, animal welfare societies (such as the PDSA and RSPCA), zoos and other establishments.

The law does not allow veterinary nurses to decide on treatment for animals – that is the province of the veterinary surgeon. However, the veterinary nurse can take part in the radiography of injured animals, assist in the operating theatre by helping the surgeon or anaesthetist, and carry out a number of procedures such as bandaging and the administration of medicines, as instructed. Some of the other tasks may involve holding, calming and controlling animals during examination, carrying out simple laboratory tests, and doing the various tasks allotted to the nurse by the veterinary surgeon. It is a caring profession, but it can involve long hours, some unpleasant duties and the pay is not high. Since there is no equivalent to the nursing service within human hospitals, there is no formal career structure and promotion prospects are limited.

Training

This matter-of-fact account of veterinary nursing is, nevertheless, unlikely to deter young girls who want to work with animals – and it *is* a girl's job. Out of about 2,000 veterinary nurses, only about a dozen are males. Anyone wishing to train as a veterinary nurse must be 17 years or over and have four GCSEs (or equivalents) including English language and a science or maths subject. This will enable enrolment to take place with the Royal College of Veterinary Surgeons provided the applicant has obtained full-time employment with a veterinary practice or veterinary hospital, approved by the RCVS as a training centre. Then follows a two-year period of on-the-job training, which may include part-time or block-release courses at technical or agricultural colleges. During the training period a preliminary and final examination (set by the RCVS) are taken. As a result of the 1991 Amendment to the Surgeons Act 1966, qualified veterinary nurses whose names are on the List held by the RCVS may now undertake, at the direction of a veterinary surgeon, medical treatment and minor surgery not involving entry into a body cavity, in respect of companion animals.

Veterinary science

Veterinary surgeons treat animals both medically and surgically. They have to diagnose problems and then deal with them, and at the same time cope with anxious and sometimes emotional owners. As well as treating sick animals, veterinary surgeons also advise on animal health care and breeding. Some veterinary surgeons are involved in research work, and others work for manufacturing companies in the development of preventive and curative medicines.

Most veterinary surgeons work in veterinary practice, usually with several colleagues within a practice. They may be assisted by **veterinary nurses** who feed, nurse and care for the animals when hospitalised. Most practices also employ a receptionist and a secretary. The veterinary surgeon's hours of work may be long and unsocial, with evening, night to deal with emergency cases. Outdoor work is not uncommon in those practices that deal with farm animals. A certain degree of physical fitness is also helpful, but sheer strength is not always necessary and many women veterinary surgeons will tell you that certain tasks are a matter of 'knack' rather than strength.

Of the 13,000 veterinary surgeons who are on the Royal College of Veterinary Surgeons (RCVS) Register, about 70 per cent work in private practice. Other opportunities are in research work, drugs firms, feed merchants, government departments, teaching in the university veterinary schools, the RAVC, local government, animal breeding centres, zoos and overseas. It is essential to have a veterinary degree in order to be entered on the RCVS register and practise as a veterinary surgeon.

Training

Competition for entry to the veterinary degree courses is high. There are six universities in the UK with veterinary schools, and there are only about 300 places a year. There are roughly five applicants for every place, and all applicants are likely to be offering good A-levels in the requisite subjects. At A-level the required subjects are usually chemistry, biology and physics or mathematics. Because of the demand for places, veterinary schools ask for A-level grades of AAA to ABB but lower grades are sometimes accepted. (Detailed information on the entrance requirements is given in the Degree Course Guide.)

Candidates are recommended to spend a period of time with a veterinary surgeon in practice before applying for a place at a veterinary school, as this will enable them to get an idea of what the work involves. The Royal Veterinary College (one of the six UK veterinary schools) makes the pre-entry period with a veterinary surgeon a formal requirement.

Applicants who are not totally single-minded about becoming veterinary surgeons, or who feel that they are unlikely to reach the required A-level grades, should also think of applying for other degree courses, for example agriculture, biochemistry or animal physiology. These degree courses usually require the same science A-level subjects as veterinary degree courses.

Information

Royal College of Veterinary Surgeons (RCVS), 32 Belgrave Square, London SW1X 8QP

A Career as a Veterinary Surgeon, RCVS
Careers Working with Animals, Kogan Page
Veterinary Science, Degree Course Guide, Hobsons

Waiter and waitress

In a good hotel or restaurant a team of people looks after the needs of customers in the restaurant, preparing and serving food and wine. Behind the scenes in the kitchen are the chefs, cooks and their assistants. In the restaurant itself are the smartly dressed staff: manager, *chefs de rang,* waiters, wine waiter, *commis* waiters and others. (In this entry, the term 'waiter' or 'manager' means female as well as male staff.)

The restaurant manager is in charge: deciding who sits where, which staff serve the tables, dealing with the hundreds of queries that arise on menus, bills and the many other details. *A chef de rang* is a senior post, a person who looks after a group of tables. A head waiter may be in charge of the day-to-day service – taking bookings, greeting customers and taking orders. The wine waiter needs to know all about wines, how to serve them, which wines go with which food, and so on. *Commis* waiters are trainees. Like the regular waiters, they serve customers, lay the tables, carry food to the table and clear up afterwards.

The work is tiring, and unsocial hours have to be worked, for the restaurant may be open until late in the evening. However, split shifts ensure that everyone gets a fair share of time off, although weekends and bank holidays are busy times when everyone is on duty.

Prospects

Prospects within the **catering industry**, of which hotel and restaurant catering is a part, are very good, for the influx of tourists to Britain and the growth in the number of restaurants ensure that there is a steady demand for waiters, cooks and chefs. Experienced waiters expect to become head waiters by the age of 25 to 30, and they could become restaurant managers in their 30s.

No formal entry requirements are required. However, a good educational standard is looked for, particularly in English and communication skills, because waiters must conduct themselves properly, speak clearly and understand the food and catering business. Among the school subjects that are useful are home economics, cooking, business studies and languages, for a knowledge of French is very useful for people who want to make their way in the catering business.

Training
In-service training is mostly on the job. Some of the big hotels have their own training schemes. Many colleges of further education offer full-time or part-time courses during the day and the evenings, and some of these courses lead to City and Guilds qualifications such as a food and beverage service certificate, an alcoholic beverages certificate (for wine waiters), and special skills courses in food service and counter service. For details of the colleges that offer these courses, consult the *Directory of Further Education*.

Information
Hotel and Catering Industry Training Company, International House, High Street, London W5 5DB. The HCITC produces leaflets on various jobs in the food industry

Careers in Catering and Hotel Management, Kogan Page
Working in Hotels, Hobsons
Working in the Hospitality Industry, COIC
Directory of Further Education, Hobsons

Warehousing

Warehouses are of many types but all perform the same basic function – they are places where goods are stored until needed. Thus they are a vital part of the distribution chain which employs approximately 10 per cent of the working population. The nature of the goods stored can vary enormously from raw materials to finished goods, be held at ambient or frozen temperatures and in quantities from one to many thousands. The size of warehouses varies from a small unit of perhaps a few hundred square feet serving a small local area to massive units of many thousands of square feet perhaps serving the entire UK.

To carry out this work requires a team of people. Leading it is likely to be a warehouse manager. There are four main tasks for warehouse managers and workers:

- to check goods in and out
- to 'order pick' (select goods ordered by the customer) and to assemble them

- packing and posting
- storekeeping – keeping the records of goods held in the ware-house, customer orders, deliveries and stock control.

There are plenty of jobs, probably because this is seen as an unglamor-ous occupation. On the other hand, warehousing requires good plan-ning skills, careful attention to detail and safety, and an understanding of business. Warehouses are found throughout Britain, storing food, books and hundreds of other items, so there are jobs in every part of the country. Employers include supermarkets, hospitals, engineering and every kind of manufacturing company, garages and educational in-stitutions. As well as managers there are jobs for warehouse workers, who do the checking, picking, packing and storekeeping, fork-lift truck drivers, supervisors and bookkeepers. Promotion from these jobs to manager depends on experience and training.

Warehouse work is becoming increasingly computerised, so there are jobs for stock records staff, computer operators and for trainees who are ready to learn the skills required of computer staff.

To become a warehouse worker, men and women need first to be fit. They should be able to communicate easily and understand arithmetic, so a good education, particularly in maths and English language, is needed, but no formal educational requirements are asked for. For the storekeeping duties, and for bookkeeping, some experience, backed up by City and Guilds or other qualifications, is needed. Training is normally on the job, given by experienced staff. Many firms take on youngsters on Youth Training schemes and offer them a combination of work experience and training.

The useful school subjects are business studies, English language, maths or arithmetic and communication studies – in fact any subject linked to business, and this includes economics, accounting, electronics and computing.

Some companies take on trainees destined for management posts. They need three or four GCSEs or one or two A-levels, or may be graduates. Women are increasingly occupying senior management positions, and women graduates are being deliberately sought by companies within the physical distribution industry. Any degree could be useful, but business studies courses are particularly appropriate.

Information

Institute of Physical Distribution Management, Management House, Cottingham Road, Corby, Northamptonshire NN17 1TT

Water industry

We all expect uninterrupted supplies of clear and healthy water – at home, school, work and in public places – and everyone takes the supply of good water for granted. The privatisation of the water indutry in 1989 underlined the importance – and the cost – of domestic and industrial water supplies.

For these reasons, a job with a regional water authority is not the most obvious career choice. Most people who work for a water authority have taken various preliminary routes and not usually by a deliberate choice. On the other hand, the water boards offer good career opportunities. Most of the jobs are for **civil engineers** who specialise in water services, but there are openings for **chemical engineers** and **chemists.** Water is a heavily used commodity and it has to be stored, cleaned and distributed by a complex system of engineering, and this requires considerable knowledge and experience.

Training

This is gained by taking a civil engineering degree at university or polytechnic and then specialising in water supply services. For students who do not go to university, there are BTEC and SCOTVEC HND courses in civil engineering studies at polytechnics and colleges throughout the UK, and for the craftworker and technician grades there are City and Guilds certificate courses in water supply, public health engineering and the water industry. Details of books on courses at colleges and polytechnics are given below.

As well as the engineering jobs, secretarial and administrative staff are employed to send out bills and correspondence, and there are openings for technicians and other supporting services.

Relevant school subjects are sciences for the engineering courses. For a civil engineering degree or an HND course, A-levels in maths and science subjects are needed, and the most suitable are physics or physical science, maths, chemistry and biology. For chemists who specialise in water supply services, a degree in chemistry is the starting point, and A-levels or H-grades in sciences, including chemistry, are required.

For BTEC, SCOTVEC and City and Guilds technician and craft-based courses, the requirements are wider, and other GCSEs and A-levels are acceptable.

Information
For information about careers, write to the appropriate regional water board

Technology, Degree Course Guide, Hobsons
Directory of Further Education. Hobsons

Wine trade

In recent years the wine trade has become an increasingly important commercial success story. Most of the trade is importing wine to the UK and this has come about because of the dramatic increase in wine-drinking over the past 20 years.

Unlike the beer and spirit trades, which have substantial production plants in the UK, nearly all wine is imported from Europe, although there is now a noticeable import of wine from the USA, South America, South Africa, Australia and New Zealand. Wine is made in England and Wales, but accounts for little more than two per cent of consumption.

Training
Most job opportunities are in London and the south-east of England, working for wholesalers and retailers, although there are openings in many other parts of the UK. Many of these jobs are likely to be in management, sales, marketing and advertising.

To prepare for these, the best method is often to take a business studies course, preferably one linked to a second language – most usually French or German, but possibly Spanish or Italian – and including economics or a similar business management course at degree, HND or National Diploma levels. Once qualified, those wishing to enter the wine trade should approach suitable companies either directly or through the national or trade press.

An alternative route would be to get a job in the trade as a GCSE or A-level-leaver (English language, history, language(s) and maths) and to obtain wine qualifications by part-time study through the Wine and Spirit Education Trust (WSET). These courses are run through the regional offices of the Wine and Spirit Association of Great Britain and Northern Ireland, or by some catering colleges. They are only open to those either already in, or intending to join the wine trade; the minimum age-limit is 18.

Another possibility might be for a school-leaver to join a retail company selling wines and spirits, many of which are owned by brewers or large drinks companies. But these, too, are likely to insist on a minimum age-limit of 18.

Retail groups include the large supermarkets, where basic product knowledge may be required in beer, wine and spirit departments and not the highly specialised advice that consumers look for from smaller retailers. Specialised wine shops, many of which are privately owned, are expected to employ sales staff with a detailed knowledge of wine, and accordingly arc likely to provide interesting job opportunities for those genuinely interested in wines and spirits.

A further job opportunity might be that of a wine waiter; further details are given in the entry on **waiter/waitress.**

Career opportunities are therefore at all levels from junior sales staff with basic wine knowledge, through the shipping and warehousing of wine, and the administration that these involve, to buying, not forgetting the need for managers and directors of wine businesses.

Information
The Wine and Spirit Education Trust (WSET), Five Kings House, Kennet Wharf Lane, Upper Thames Street, London EC4V 3AJ

Wool industry

Wool textiles, Britain's first manufacturing industry, are still important to the economy as a major supplier of the nation's textile requirements and an exporter of international reputation. Earnings of foreign exchange from wool textile exports run at more than £600 million a year. During the recent recession radical changes have occurred in the textile industry, but a more stable position has now been reached.

Three-quarters of the industry's productive capacity is based in West Yorkshire and east Lancashire, while about 20 per cent is in Scotland, and another important centre is in the West Country. The industry employs about 38,000 people. Although, for convenience, still using the 'wool textile' title, the industry operates nowadays on a broad multifibre basis. While it has for generations processed speciality natural fibres, notably mohair, cashmere, camelhair and alpaca, it also makes extensive use of man–made fibres, usually in blends with natural fibres.

Craft skills

For school-leavers of 16 who would prefer a job where the training is mostly practical, there are many opportunities as operatives, machine minders, or skilled workers, such as cloth menders. Supervisory technicians are responsible for the efficient operation of a section of processing machines and the control of departmental personnel in aspects of quality control, machine maintenance, training, discipline and safety.

Training

Trainees enter at 16 or 18 years and normally have gained or will be expected to gain good GCSE passes in at least maths, English language or a science subject. Trainees must also be able to demonstrate a practical aptitude in dealing with mechanical systems and concepts, and must not be colour-blind.

Trainees follow a training and education programme normally of four years' duration both on the job and at a college of further education on a part-time day-release basis following a BTEC National Certificate and HNC course. Opportunities exist for supervisory technicians to move into middle management, either in production or services, and further studies leading to a degree or professional qualifications are available.

Graduates

For students who stay on after 16 to take A-levels, there are openings at 18 for most of the jobs already described. Alternatively, there are degree, BTEC or SCOTVEC HNC or HND courses in textile technology. These courses concentrate on technology augmented by marketing and industrial design units, or modules, as part of the degree or HNC/HND courses run by polytechnics and colleges close to the traditional centres of the wool textile industry, namely Huddersfield, Leicester, Leeds, Galashiels, Nottingham, Manchester, London and Bolton. Other courses offered at these centres lead to the Associateship of the Textile Institute and the Society of Dyers and Colourists. Alternatively, there are BTEC and SCOTVEC HNC or HND courses, and National Diploma/Certificate courses in textiles, plus City and Guilds certificate courses in textile techniques. All these courses have specialist options in wool technology.

To prepare for the industry, the range of school subjects should include physics, chemistry and biology. The level depends on the course that attracts the candidate. Maths and science A-levels or H-grades are very useful for the technology courses, and GCSEs or equivalents in maths and at least one science subject are required. For the textile design courses the most suitable preparation is in art and design qualifications at any level, which includes art, fashion and home economics to GCSE and A-level.

Information
British Wool Marketing Board, Oak Mills, Station Road, Clayton, Bradford, West Yorkshire BD4 6JD
The Confederation of British Wool Textiles Limited, 60 Toller Lane, Bradford, West Yorkshire BD8 9BZ

Jobs in the Textile Industry, Kogan Page
Directory of Further Education, Hobsons

Youth and community work

The youth service is the responsibility of Local Education Authorities and voluntary organisations. The word 'community' is used for two reasons: because young people are part of the wider community, and because youth workers generally work with other groups from the community as well as with young people. The service is therefore very wide in its responsibilities. It is first and foremost an educational service and is not part of the social services.

Local authority spending on the youth service differs widely from one authority to another. London and the other city authorities spend most, the rural counties spend least. What they all do is to provide youth clubs, play centres and craft workshops. Many go further in arranging youth theatres, camping holidays, football teams, play schemes, discos and skill centres. Youth workers therefore have to be very adaptable. Apart from running the services already mentioned, they might be asked to teach all kinds of skills, from football to flower-arranging, or find staff who can teach these activities. Among the tougher problems that youth workers deal with are drug abuse, alcoholism, homelessness and unemployment. Now that their work includes the community too, some youth and community workers are drawn into adult work to improve literacy, social and work skills and to aid all kinds of people who are in trouble. In Scotland this integration is contained within the service, for the 'community education' professional takes on all aspects of adult education, from youth work to work with older adults.

About a third of the people employed full time in youth work are with local or national voluntary organisations, such as the YMCA and YWCA, Community Service Volunteers, Scouts and Guides, Outward Bound, church youth departments, youth clubs, boys' clubs, young farmers, and so on. They depend on voluntary support, plus some government financial help. Therefore, to the 5,000 full-time youth workers should be added another 500,000, who give their own time to help young people or who are employed on a part-time basis. There are broadly two groups of people: youth and community workers, who are closely involved with one or more group, centre or activity and spend all their time on this work, and officers, who have managerial tasks: planning, developing, staffing and supervising the service or part of it. Since the activities offered by clubs, voluntary groups and local authorities vary enormously, the range of responsibilities is equally wide. Therefore, people who want to enter this kind of work have to be very adaptable, sympathetic and yet firm. Above all, they must be prepared to spend their working lives in face-to-face situations with all kinds of problems, and be expected to solve, treat or in other ways deal with them. In career terms youth work is not an easy option; it is a tough and responsible job.

Training

To qualify as a youth and community worker or officer it is necessary to complete a recognised diploma or certificate course of initial training, or to qualify by taking a BEd degree which specialises in youth and community studies, or to take a degree course in another subject and then to take a postgraduate course in youth work.

There are flexible arrangements for training to allow mature people, whatever their age or educational qualifications, to have a chance of qualifying. Although applicants for courses are normally expected to have at least five GCSEs or their equivalents, applicants with lower qualifications may be accepted as long as they have experience of voluntary or paid work with young people. The minimum age varies, too, depending on the individual's experience and maturity of outlook. The main types of training are:

- a two-year full-time course at selected colleges leading to youth and community worker status. The minimum age for qualification is 23, so no applicant under 20 is generally accepted. These courses are endorsed by the Council for Education and Training in Youth and Community Work, and probably give the best preparation because they are specialised training courses. Five GCSEs or the equivalents are needed, but exemptions are made for experience and for other qualifications.
- a one-year full-time course leading to qualified youth and community worker status for graduates of any discipline or subject, backed up by evidence of practical, relevant work or experience with a voluntary organisation or local authority.
- four BEd courses include youth and community work options. At least two A-levels or three H-grades in any subject are required for entry to a BEd course, including English language and maths.
- in Scotland there is a three-year full-time course, and entrants must have at least two H-grade passes, plus three more subjects at O-grade.

The course syllabuses give clues to the appropriate school subjects. The content of a youth work course includes social history, law, welfare rights, administration and management, counselling and community studies. GCSEs and A-levels/H-grades that would be useful are the social studies and sociology subjects, plus communication studies, psychology, law, business studies, history, social biology and human biology. However, virtually any subject is acceptable because youth workers and officers may be called on to demonstrate knowledge and skills of anything from computing to fashion, photography to engineering, so any subject or combination could be useful later on.

Information
National Youth Bureau, Wellington House, 29 Albion Street, Leicester
LE1 6GD

Directory of Further Education, Hobsons
Careers in Social Work, Kogan Page

Training in Youth and Community Work, National Youth Bureau (address, see above)

Zoology
Zoologist

Zoology is a subject that is usually studied to A-level as part of biology, which includes the study of all living things – plants as well as animals. Zoology itself is the study of animals. As a degree subject it can lead to careers in **teaching**, research, **conservation**, and in industries concerned with animals, pest-control and similar areas. In the foreseeable future the supply of zoology graduates is likely to exceed the number of jobs for which a zoology degree is essential, and only those with excellent qualifications, perhaps including higher degrees, can be confident of success in this field. Inevitably some zoology graduates must be content with other careers for which a degree is desirable. In this respect a degree in zoology is similar to English or geography degrees – none of them is necessarily a specific vocational qualification.

Training
Degree courses in zoology or biological science including zoology are offered at most universities. Consult the Degree Course Guide for *Biological Sciences* for the differences between the courses. The special subject requirements are two or three A-levels (three or four H-grades) in sciences and maths. The subjects are not specified, but biology at A-level is generally looked for.

Zookeeping

Jobs with animals, including zookeeping, are keenly sought because of the undoubted job satisfaction, despite the material disadvantages of rather poor pay, limited opportunities for progression because of the relatively small numbers involved, long hours and often dirty and heavy manual work. Entry qualifications vary, but one can expect three good GCSEs (English language, maths and biology would be a good combination) or equivalents to be the minimum. More graduates are choosing to work in this field for the job interest.

Training

Training is mainly on the job, with day release in some cases to study at local colleges (e.g. for animal technician). There is a correspondence course leading to a City and Guilds qualification for zookeepers. Working with animals often involves working with people – as a **veterinary nurse**, for instance, with the owners of animals brought for treatment to a veterinary surgery or PDSA or as a zookeeper with the public visiting the zoo.

Information

Zoological Society of London, Regent's Park, London NW1 4RY
Institute of Animal Technicians, 5 South Parade, Summertown, Oxford OX2 7UL
Institute of Biology, 20 Queensberry Place, London SW7 2DZ
Nature Conservancy, 19 Belgrave Square, London SW1X 8PY

Working with Animals, COIC
Careers with Animals, Stanley Paul
Earning Your Living with Animals, David and Charles
Biological Sciences, Degree Course Guide, Hobsons